SHAKESPEARE

AND RENAISS

EUROPE

D1617419

THE ARDEN SHAKESPEARE

THE ARDEN CRITICAL COMPANIONS

GENERAL EDITORS

Andrew Hadfield and Paul Hammond

ADVISORY BOARD

MacDonald P. Jackson   Katherine Duncan-Jones   David Scott Kastan
Patricia Parker   Lois Potter   Phyllis Rackin   Bruce R. Smith
Brian Vickers   Blair Worden

Shakespeare and Renaissance Europe
ed. Andrew Hadfield and Paul Hammond
Shakespeare and Renaissance Politics   *Andrew Hadfield*
Shakespeare and the Victorians   *Adrian Poole*

Forthcoming

Shakespeare and Comedy   *Robert Maslen*
Shakespeare and Elizabethan Popular Culture
ed. Stuart Gillespie and Neil Rhodes
Shakespeare and Language   *Jonathan Hope*
Shakespeare and the Law   *Andrew Zurcher*
Shakespeare and Music   *David Lindley*
Shakespeare and Religion   *Alison Shell*

Further titles are in preparation

SHAKESPEARE
AND RENAISSANCE
EUROPE

Edited by
ANDREW HADFIELD and PAUL HAMMOND

The Arden website is at
http://www.ardenshakespeare.com

This edition of *Shakespeare and Renaissance Europe*
first published 2004 by the Arden Shakespeare

© 2005 Thomson Learning
Arden Shakespeare is an imprint of Thomson Learning

Thomson Learning
High Holborn House
50–51 Bedford Row
London WC1R 4LR

Typeset by LaserScript, Mitcham, Surrey

Printed in Croatia by Zrinski d.d.

British Library Cataloguing in Publication Data
A catalogue record for this book is available from the British Library

Library of Congress Cataloguing in Publication Data
A catalogue record has been requested

ISBN 1-90427-146-4 (paperback)
ISBN 1-90427-164-2 (hardcover)

NPN 9 8 7 6 5 4 3 2 1

CONTENTS

Chapter Seven
Europe's Mediterranean Frontier: The Moor   220
Nabil Matar and Rudolph Stoeckel

NOTES ON CONTRIBUTORS

Richard Andrews is Emeritus Professor of Italian at the University of Leeds. He is the author of *Scripts and Scenarios: The Performance of Comedy in Renaissance Italy* (1993), and essays on early modern French and Italian theatre.

Michael G. Brennan is Reader in Renaissance Studies in the School of English, University of Leeds. He is the editor of *The Travel Diary (1611–1612) of an English Catholic, Sir Charles Somerset* (1993), *The Travel Diary of Robert Bargrave, Levant Merchant 1647–1656* (1999) and *The Origins of the Grand Tour: The Travels of Robert Montagu, Lord Mandeville (1649–1651), William Hammond (1656–1658), and Banaster Maynard (1660–1663)* (forthcoming).

Susan Doran is Lecturer in Early Modern History at Christ Church, Oxford. She is the author of *Monarchy and Matrimony: The Courtships of Elizabeth I* (1996) and *Elizabeth I and Foreign Policy* (2000), and co-editor of *The Myth of Elizabeth I* (2003).

Stuart Gillespie is Reader in English Literature at the University of Glasgow. He is the author of *Shakespeare's Books: A Dictionary of Shakespeare Sources* (2001), and co-editor of *Shakespeare and Elizabethan Popular Culture* (forthcoming in the present series).

Andrew Hadfield is Professor of English at the University of Sussex. His books include *Literature, Travel, and Colonialism in the English Renaissance 1540–1625* (1998), *Amazons, Savages, and Machiavels: An Anthology of Travel and Colonial Writing 1550–1650* (2001), *Shakespeare, Spenser, and the Matter of Britain* (2003) and *Shakespeare and Renaissance Politics* (2004) in the present series.

Paul Hammond is Professor of Seventeenth-Century English Literature at the University of Leeds, and a Fellow of the British Academy. His books include *Dryden and the Traces of Classical Rome* (1999), *Figuring Sex between Men from Shakespeare to Rochester* (2002) and, as co-editor, the Longman Annotated English Poets edition of *The Poems of John Dryden* (1995– in progress).

Paulina Kewes is Fellow and Tutor in English at Jesus College, Oxford. She is the author of *Authorship and Appropriation: Writing for the Stage in England 1660–1710* (1998) and editor of *Plagiarism in Early Modern England* (2003).

François Laroque is Professor of Renaissance Studies and English Literature at the Université de la Sorbonne Nouvelle–Paris III. He is the author of *Shakespeare's Festive World* (1991) and *Shakespeare: Crowd, Court and Playhouse* (1993).

Nabil Matar is Professor of English at the Florida Institute of Technology. He is the author of *Islam in Britain 1558–1685* (1998), *Turks, Moors, and Englishmen in the Age of Discovery* (1999), *In the Lands of the Christians: Arabic Travel Writing in the Seventeenth Century* (2003) and *Britain and Barbary: From Peele to Dryden* (forthcoming).

Rudolph Stoeckel is Professor of English at the Florida Institute of Technology, and has written on Elizabethan emblems.

LIST OF ABBREVIATIONS

SHAKESPEARE

References to Shakespeare plays are to the most recent Arden editions unless otherwise specified.

Works by and partly by Shakespeare

The following abbreviations are used for individual works:

AC	*Antony and Cleopatra*
AW	*All's Well That Ends Well*
AYL	*As You Like It*
CE	*Comedy of Errors*
Cor	*Coriolanus*
Cym	*Cymbeline*
DF	*Double Falsehood*
E3	*King Edward III*
Ham	*Hamlet*
1H4	*King Henry the IV, Part 1*
2H4	*King Henry the IV, Part 2*
H5	*King Henry V*
1H6	*King Henry the VI, Part 1*
2H6	*King Henry the VI, Part 2*
3H6	*King Henry the VI, Part 3*
H8	*King Henry VIII*
JC	*Julius Caesar*
KJ	*King John*
KL	*King Lear*
LC	*A Lover's Complaint*
LLL	*Love's Labour's Lost*

Luc   *The Rape of Lucrece*
MA   *Much Ado about Nothing*
Mac   *Macbeth*
MM   *Measure for Measure*
MND   *A Midsummer Night's Dream*
MV   *The Merchant of Venice*
MW   *The Merry Wives of Windsor*
Oth   *Othello*
Per   *Pericles*
PP   *The Passionate Pilgrim*
PT   *The Phoenix and the Turtle*
R2   *King Richard II*
R3   *King Richard III*
RJ   *Romeo and Juliet*
Son   *Sonnets*
STM   *Sir Thomas More*
TC   *Troilus and Cressida*
Tem   *Tempest*
TGV   *The Two Gentlemen of Verona*
Tim   *Timon of Athens*
Tit   *Titus Andronicus*
TN   *Twelfth Night*
TNK   *The Two Noble Kinsmen*
TS   *The Taming of the Shrew*
VA   *Venus and Adonis*
WT   *The Winter's Tale*

OTHER WORKS CITED

CSP   *Calendar of State Papers*
STC   *A Short-Title Catalogue of Books Printed in England, Scotland and Ireland, and of English Books Printed Abroad, 1475–1640,* compiled by A.W. Pollard and G.R. Redgrave, 2nd edn, 3 vols (London, Bibliographical Society, 1976–91)

LIST OF ILLUSTRATIONS

A NOTE ON DATES

During the period covered by this book, England and continental Europe used different calendars. A considerable discrepancy had accumulated between the Julian calendar (established by Julius Caesar in 46 BC) and the actual movements of the sun and moon, so in 1582 Pope Gregory XIII decreed that 4 October that year would be followed by 15 October. The decree was implemented in most Roman Catholic countries, but many Protestant states rejected the new-style Gregorian calendar; eventually most adopted it in 1700. England, however, adhered to the old-style Julian calendar until 1752. Consequently there is often a discrepancy of around ten days between English and continental dates. In the present volume, old-style dating is followed, though the year is treated as beginning on 1 January, not on 25 March, which was commonly regarded as the start of the new year in the period.

CHRONOLOGY

Dates of Shakespeare's plays refer to their first performance, and are often conjectural, especially for his early career. Dates of other literary works, including plays, refer to their first printing, unless otherwise stated. For more detailed chronologies the reader is referred to Neville Williams, *Chronology of the Expanding World 1492 to 1762* (Oxford, 1994), though its accuracy is imperfect; Rosemary O'Day, *The Longman Companion to the Tudor Age* (London, 1995); Alfred Harbage, *The Annals of English Drama 975–1700*, rev. S. Schoenbaum (London, 1964); Michael Cox, *The Oxford Chronology of English Literature*, 2 vols (Oxford, 2002); and *The Riverside Shakespeare*, ed. G. Blakemore Evans (Boston, Mass., 1974), appendix C. The selection of English literary works stresses those with a continental European connection.

Paul Hammond

Date Shakespeare	English literature	European literature	English politics	European politics
1558	Virgil, *Aeneid* 1–7 trans. Phaer. Thomas Lodge and George Peele b. (?)	Du Bellay, *Les Antiquités de Rome*. Marguerite de Navarre, *Heptameron*. Fiorentino, *Il Pecorone*.	Death of Mary I. Accession of Elizabeth I. Protestant exiles begin to return from Zurich and Geneva.	Capture of Calais by France from England. Ferdinand I becomes Holy Roman Emperor. Mary Queen of Scots marries the Dauphin.
1559	*A Mirror for Magistrates* [written early 1550s]. George Chapman b. (?)	Amyot's French translation of Plutarch. Montemayor, *Diana*. Belleforest, *Histoires tragiques* (to 1582).	Acts of Supremacy and Uniformity establish queen's control over the church, and authorize first Elizabethan Prayer Book.	Pope Paul IV issues bull advocating deposition of rulers who support heresy. Peace treaty of Cateau-Cambrésis between England and France and Spain. Henri II of France d.: François II succeeds. Paul IV d.; Pius IV elected.
1560	Robert Greene b. (?)	First collected edition of Ronsard.	Treaty of Edinburgh annuls claim to English throne by Mary Queen of Scots. Geneva Bible.	Turkish galleys defeat Spanish fleet off Tripoli. François II d.: accession of Charles IX. Calvinistic church established in Scotland.
1561	Castiglione, *The Courtier*, trans. Hoby. Cortes, *Art of Navigation*, trans. Eden. *Gorboduc* perf. Sir John Harington and Francis Bacon b.	J.C. Scaliger, *Poetices Libri Septem*.	Mary returns to Scotland.	

Date Shakespeare	English literature	European literature	English politics	European politics
1562	Sternhold and Hopkins's metrical translation of the Psalms added to Prayer Book. Brooke, *Romeus and Juliet* (from Bandello via Boistuau). Machiavelli, *The Art of War*, trans. Whitehorne. Samuel Daniel b.	Ronsard, *Discours des misères de ce temps*. Tasso, *Rinaldo*. Rabelais, *Pantagruel*, bk 5. Lope de Vega b.	Elizabeth promises military assistance to Huguenots and invades France.	Third session of Council of Trent opens (to 1563). Duc de Guise forms league to prevent toleration of Huguenots. Attacks on Huguenots start French wars of religion. Emperor Ferdinand I signs truce with Suleiman I, Sultan of Turkey.
1563	Foxe, *Acts and Monuments* (in English; Latin edn 1559). Googe, *Eclogues, Epitaphs and Sonnets*. Michael Drayton b.	*Index Librorum Prohibitorum*.	Thirty-Nine Articles published.	Duc de Guise assassinated.
1564 Shakespeare b.	Christopher Marlowe b.	Galileo b. Calvin d.	Charter granted to Merchant Adventurers' Company. Elizabeth attempts to impose conformity on Protestant ministers.	War between England and France ends; English claim to Calais renounced. Emperor Ferdinand d.
1565	Bks 1–4 of Golding's translation of Ovid's *Metamorphoses* (completed 1567). Stow's *Chronicles*. Norton and Sackville, *Gorboduc*.	Cinthio, *Hecatommithi*. Ronsard, *Elegies*.		Mary Queen of Scots marries Lord Darnley. Turks abandon siege of Malta on arrival of Spanish troops. Pope Pius IV d.

Date Shakespeare	English literature	European literature	English politics	European politics
1566	Gascoigne's *The Supposes* (trans. from Ariosto) perf. Painter, *Palace of Pleasure* (inc. translations from Boccaccio, Bandello and Cinthio); vol. 2 1567.		James VI of Scotland (future James I of England) b.	Pope Pius V elected. Murder of David Rizzio on Darnley's orders. Political unrest in Netherlands. Renewal of Turko-Hungarian war. Suleiman I ('The Magnificent') d.
1567	Bandello, *Tragical Discourses*, trans. Fenton. Turberville, *Epitaphs, Epigrams, Songs and Sonnets*. Thomas Nashe and Thomas Campion b.	Guicciardini, *L'Historia d'Italia* (complete posthumous edn).	Shane O'Neill (leader of rebellion in Ireland) assassinated.	Darnley murdered on orders of Earl of Bothwell. Mary Queen of Scots marries Bothwell, then abdicates; accession of James VI. Spanish general the Duke of Alva starts reign of terror in Netherlands.
1568			Commercial relations with Spain severed. English College at Douai founded by Jesuits to train men for the ministry. Bishops' Bible. Mary Queen of Scots flees to England.	Peace between Turks and Holy Roman Empire. William the Silent continues revolt of the Netherlands against Spanish rule. Moors in Spain revolt against oppression and are massacred.
1569			Northern Rebellion by Catholic nobles. Rebellion in Ireland continues until 1574.	Union of Lithuania and Poland.

Date Shakespeare	English literature	European literature	English politics	European politics
1570	Ascham, *Schoolmaster*. Robert Henryson, *Fables*. De Serres, *Discourse of the Civil Wars in France*, trans. Fenton. Thomas Dekker and (?) Thomas Middleton b.	Castelvetro, *Poetica d'Aristotele*. Palladio, *I Quattro Libri dell'Architettura*.	Pius V issues bull excommunicating Elizabeth and absolving her subjects from their allegiance.	Turks declare war on Venice for refusing to surrender Cyprus.
1571	*Amadis de Gaul*, trans. Paynell.		Negotiations for marriage between Elizabeth and Duc d'Anjou. Ridolfi Plot exposed.	Turks capture last bastion in Cyprus. Turkish fleet defeated at Battle of Lepanto by Don John of Austria.
1572	John Donne b.	Camões, *Os Lusiadas*. Ronsard, *La Franciade*.	Negotiations for marriage between Elizabeth and Duc d'Alençon. Execution of Catholic Duke of Norfolk.	Dutch Revolt escalates with capture of Brill by the rebels. Pope Pius V d.; Gregory XIII elected. Huguenots killed in St Bartholomew's Day Massacre in Paris and provinces.
1573	*Aeneid*, trans. Phaer and Twyne. Gascoigne, *A Hundred Sundry Flowers*. Ben Jonson b.	Tasso, *Aminta*. Bandello, *Novelle*, vol. 4.		
1574		Justus Lipsius's edn of Tacitus.	First Catholic priests arrive from Douai.	Charles IX of France d.; accession of Henri III.

Date Shakespeare	English literature	European literature	English politics	European politics
1575	John Marston, Cyril Tourneur and Samuel Purchas b. (?)			
1576	Della Casa, *Galateo*, trans. Peterson. Erection of The Theatre (first London playhouse).	Bodin, *Les Six Livres de la République*. Gentillet, *Discours . . . contre Nicolas Machiavel* (Eng. trans. 1602).		Accession of Rudolph II as Holy Roman Emperor. Spanish troops sack Antwerp.
1577	Holinshed, *Chronicles*. The Curtain Theatre opens. Robert Burton and (?) Thomas Coryate b.		Francis Drake begins his circumnavigation of the globe (returns 1580).	
1578	Lyly, *Euphues*. George Sandys b. *A Mirror for Magistrates*.	Ronsard. *Sonnets pour Hélène*. Du Bartas, *La Semaine*. Mercator, *Tabulae Geographicae*.		King Sebastian of Portugal invades Morocco and is killed at battle of Alcazar.
1579	Guicciardini's *History of the Wars of Italy*, trans. Fenton. Amyot's Plutarch, trans. North. Spenser, *Shepheardes Calender*. Gosson, *School of Abuse*. John Fletcher b.		Duc d'Anjou visits Elizabeth to court her. Desmond rebellion in Ireland.	Foundation of Dutch Republic by Union of Utrecht; southern provinces of Netherlands reconciled to Spain by Peace of Arras.

Date Shakespeare	English literature	European literature	English politics	European politics
1580	Stow, *Chronicles*. John Webster b. (?)	Montaigne, *Essais* (2 bks; bk 3, 1588). Camões d.	Robert Parsons and Edmund Campion begin Jesuit mission in England. England signs commercial treaty with Turkey.	Spanish conquest of Portugal.
1581	*Iliad* 1-10 trans. Hall (via French). Seneca, *Ten Tragedies*, trans. Newton. Guazzo, *Civil Conversation*, trans. Pettie (completed 1586).	Tasso, *Gerusalemme Liberata*.	Marriage treaty negotiations with Anjou. English Levant Company founded.	Peace between Spain and Turkey.
1582 Shakespeare marries Anne Hathaway.	Hakluyt, *Voyages*. *Aeneid* 1-4 trans. Stanyhurst.	Buchanan, *Rerum Scoticarum Historiae*.	Anjou marriage negotiation fails (Elizabeth's last serious attempt to marry).	Gregorian calendar widely adopted in continental Europe. Catholic English translation of New Testament publ. in Rheims. Anjou's expedition to the Netherlands.
1583	Philip Massinger b. Queen's Company of players formed.	Grotius b.	Throckmorton plot exposed.	
1584	Scot, *Discovery of Witchcraft*. Francis Beaumont b.	Bruno, *Spaccio della Bestia Trionffante* (ded. to Sidney) and *Le Cena de le Ceneri*.	Revelation of plan for Catholic invasion of England: Bond of Association signed to defend Elizabeth.	Ivan the Terrible d. Duc d'Anjou d. William the Silent assassinated.

Date Shakespeare	English literature	European literature	English politics	European politics
1585		Bruno, *De gli Heroici Furori* (ded. to Sidney). Ronsard d.	Elizabeth pledges military aid to Dutch. Establishment of Ralegh's colony at Roanoke, Virginia.	Pope Gregory XIII d.: Sixtus V elected. Sack of Antwerp by Spanish.
1586	Sidney d. Camden, *Britannia*. De la Primaudaye, *The French Academy*, trans. Bowes. *Lazarillo de Tormes*, trans. Rowland. John Ford b.		Earl of Leicester leads English forces in Netherlands. Mary Queen of Scots found guilty of treason and sentenced to death (executed 1587). Star Chamber institutes licensing of publications.	Battle of Zutphen in the Netherlands, at which Sir Philip Sidney is killed.
1587	First English actors visit Germany. Turberville, *Tragical Tales* (trans. from Roseo and Boccaccio).		Elizabeth attempts to sign alliance with Turkey against Spain. Leicester recalled from Netherlands.	Drake sacks Cadiz. Pope proclaims crusade against England.
1588	Robert Greene, *Pandosto*. Thomas Hobbes b.		Defeat of Spanish Armada. *Martin Marprelate* tracts.	Duc de Guise, leading Catholic League, captures Paris, then assassinated.

Date Shakespeare	English literature	European literature	English politics	European politics
1589 1 Henry VI	Hakluyt, Principal Navigations. Puttenham, Art of English Poesy.	Guarini, Il Pastor Fido.	Elizabeth sends troops to aid Henri IV. Delegation from Morocco visits London.	Sir Francis Drake attacks Corunna, but fails to place Don Antonio on the Portuguese throne. Henri III of France assassinated; Henri IV (Henri de Navarre) succeeds, and campaigns against the Catholic League.
1590	Amadis de Gaul, trans. Munday. Marlowe, Tamburlaine the Great (acted 1587–8). Sidney, Arcadia. Spenser, The Faerie Queene (bks 1–3).			Pope Sixtus V d.; Urban VII elected, then d.; Gregory XIV elected. Spanish army relieves siege of Paris. Maurice of Nassau's military campaign in northern Netherlands.
1591 2 and 3 Henry VI	Spenser, Complaints (inc. 'Visions of Bellay', 'Visions of Petrarch'). Ariosto's Orlando Furioso, trans. Harington. Tacitus' Histories, trans. Savile. Lodge, Robert Duke of Normandy. Sidney, Astrophel and Stella.		Elizabeth sends forces to Brittany and Normandy. Revenge captured off the Azores.	Pope Gregory XIV d.; Innocent IX elected and d. Philip II suppresses revolt in Aragon.
1592 Richard III Titus Andronicus	Rose theatre opens. Kyd, The Spanish Tragedy Anon. prose translation of Faustbuch. Robert Greene d.	Montaigne d.		Pope Clement VIII elected. Discovery of Pompeii. Siege of Rouen.

Date Shakespeare	English literature	European literature	English politics	European politics
1593 *Comedy of Errors* *Taming of the Shrew* *Venus and Adonis*	Plague closes theatres for two years. Hooker, *Laws of Ecclesiastical Polity*. Christopher Marlowe d. George Herbert b.			Henri IV becomes a Catholic.
1594 *Lucrece* *Two Gentlemen of Verona* *Love's Labour's Lost*	Tasso's *Gerusalemme Liberata*, 1–5, trans. Carew. Peele, *Battle of Alcazar* (perf. 1588–9). Greene, *Orlando Furioso*. Marlowe, *Massacre at Paris*. Nashe, *Unfortunate Traveller*.	Mercator, *Atlas*. Tasso, *Discorsi del Poema Eroico*.	English campaign in Brittany. Earl of Tyrone rebels in Ulster, asking Philip II for aid. Elizabeth sends an organ to the Sultan of Turkey.	Henri IV enters Paris. Lisbon spice market closed to English and Dutch merchants, prompting voyages to the Far East.
1595 *Romeo and Juliet* *Richard II* *Midsummer Night's Dream*	Machiavelli, *Florentine History*, trans. Beddingfield. Thomas Kyd d. (?)	Tasso d. Final form of Montaigne's *Essais*.	Robert Southwell SJ hanged. Tyrone's rebellion in Ireland. Delegation from Morocco visits London. Ralegh's voyage to Guiana.	France declares war on Spain.
1596 *King John* *Merchant of Venice*	Spenser, *Faerie Queene*, bks 4–6. Munday, *Palmerin of England* (trans. from Portuguese). Blackfriars theatre opened.	Descartes b.	English expedition sacks Cadiz.	Turks defeat imperial army in Hungary.

Date Shakespeare	English literature	European literature	English politics	European politics
1597 1 and 2 Henry IV	Bacon, Essays.		Essex and Ralegh's failed voyage to the Azores.	Nassau's military campaign in Brabant and Flanders.
1598 Much Ado about Nothing Henry V Merry Wives of Windsor	Iliad 1–7 trans. Chapman. Florio's Italian dictionary. Montemayor, Diana, trans. Young. Boiardo, Orlando Innamorato, trans. Tofte.	Voiture b.		Edict of Nantes grants limited toleration to Huguenots, ending Wars of Religion. Philip II of Spain d.; Philip III succeeds. Treaty of Vervins ends Franco-Spanish war.
1599 Julius Caesar	Globe theatre built. Bishops' ban on satire. Spenser d.		Essex made Lord Lieutenant of Ireland, signs truce with Tyrone, returns, and is arrested.	
1600 As You Like It Twelfth Night	Dekker, Shoemaker's Holiday. Tasso's Gerusalemme Liberata, trans. Fairfax. Livy, trans. Holland.	Bruno burnt. Calderón b.	Delegation from Morocco visits London.	Gowrie conspiracy against James VI.
1601 Hamlet	Pliny, Natural History, trans. Holland. Thomas Nashe d.	Charron, De la sagesse.	Essex's revolt and execution. First East India Company voyage. Spanish landing at Kinsale in Ireland.	

Date Shakespeare	English literature	European literature	English politics	European politics
1602 *Troilus and Cressida*	Marston, *Antonio and Mellida* and *Antonio's Revenge*. Guarini, *Il pastor fido*. trans. Dymock.			Dutch East India Company founded.
1603 *All's Well that Ends Well Othello*	Montaigne, *Essays*. trans. Florio. Knolles, *General History of the Turks*.		Elizabeth I d.; James I succeeds. 'Main' and 'Bye' Plots against James. Tyrone surrenders.	
1604 *Measure for Measure*	Marlowe, *Dr Faustus* Marston, *The Malcontent*.		Hampton Court conference to discuss religion.	Peace treaty between England and Spain.
1605 *King Lear Timon of Athens*	Bacon, *Advancement of Learning*. Du Bartas, *Divine Weekes and Workes*, trans. Sylvester. Heywood, *If You Know Not Me, You Know Nobody*, 2 pts (perf. 1603–5; pub. 1605–6). Chapman *et al.*, *Eastward Ho* (its authors then imprisoned). Dallington, *View of France and Survey of Tuscany*.	Cervantes, *Don Quixote*, pt 1.	Gunpowder Plot.	Pope Clement VIII d.; Leo XI elected and d.; Paul V elected. Time of troubles in Muscovy (to 1613).
1606 *Macbeth*	Suetonius trans. Holland. John Lyly d.	Pierre Corneille b.	Oath of Allegiance imposed on Catholics. Virginia companies granted charters.	Peace treaty between Turkey and Austria.

Date Shakespeare	English literature	European literature	English politics	European politics
1607 *Antony and Cleopatra*	Jonson, *Volpone*. Barnes, *The Devil's Charter*. Chapman, *Bussy D'Ambois* (perf. 1604). Dekker and Webster, *Westward Ho* (perf. 1604).	Malherbe, *Odes*.	Jamestown colony in Virginia founded. Irish earls flee to Spain.	
1608 *Coriolanus*	Chapman, *The Conspiracy of Byron*. Ariosto, *Satires*, trans. Tofte. John Milton b.			
1609 *Pericles* *Sonnets*	Heywood and Rowley, *Fortune by Land and Sea* perf. (publ. 1655).	Grotius, *Mare Liberum*.		Twelve-year truce between Spain and United Provinces of the Netherlands. 500,000 Moors and Moriscos expelled from Spain. Catholic English translation of Old Testament publ. in Douai. Julich–Cleves dispute.
1610 *Cymbeline* *The Winter's Tale*	Heywood, *1 Fair Maid of the West* perf. (publ. 1631).	Galileo, *Siderius Nuncius*.		Henri IV assassinated; Louis XIII succeeds with Marie de' Medici as regent.
1611 *The Tempest*	*Iliad* trans. Chapman completed. Coryat, *Crudities*. Cotgrave's French–English dictionary.		Authorized Version of the Bible.	Charles IX of Sweden d.: Gustavus Adolphus succeeds. Start of Dano-Swedish war.

Date Shakespeare	English literature	European literature	English politics	European politics
1612 *Henry VIII*	Cervantes, *Don Quixote*, pt 1, trans. Shelton. Webster, *The White Devil*. Sir John Harington d.		Prince Henry d.	Holy Roman Emperor Rudolph II d.: Matthias succeeds.
1613 *Two Noble Kinsmen*	Globe theatre burns down. Purchas, *Purchas his Pilgrimage*. Chapman, *Revenge of Bussy D'Ambois*.	Cervantes, *Novelas Ejemplares*. Lope de Vega, *Fuenteovejuna*.	James's daughter Elizabeth marries Frederick V of the Palatinate. Gondomar becomes Spanish ambassador in England.	
1614	*Odyssey*, 1–12 trans. Chapman. Lucan, *Pharsalia*, trans. Gorges. Webster, *The Duchess of Malfi* perf. (publ. 1623). Ralegh, *History of the World*.			Reopening of Jülich–Cleves dispute.
1615		Cervantes, *Don Quixote*, pt 2.		
1616 Shakespeare d.	Chapman's Homer completed. Jonson's folio *Works*. King James I, *Works*. Francis Beaumont d.	D'Aubigné, *Les Tragiques*. Cervantes d.	Villiers becomes James's new favourite. Trial of Earl and Countess of Somerset for the Overbury murder.	Rise to power of Richelieu.

Date Shakespeare	English literature	European literature	English politics	European politics
1617	Moryson, *An Itinerary*. Hall, *Just Censure for Travel*. Thomas Coryat d.		Ralegh's expedition to Guiana.	End of regency in France.
1618			Ralegh executed.	Start of Thirty Years War. Synod of Dort (to 1619).
1619	Samuel Daniel d.	Sarpi, *Istoria del Concilio Tridentino*.		Olden Barnevelt executed in The Hague.
1620	*Don Quixote*, pt 2, trans. Shelton. Boccaccio, *Decameron*, trans. anon. Thomas Campion d.		Anglo-Spanish treaty for Prince Charles to marry the infanta. Pilgrim Fathers leave for America.	Frederick of Bohemia defeated by the Catholic League at battle of White Mountain.
1621	*Courante, or Newes from Italy and Germany* (periodical). Burton, *Anatomy of Melancholy*, 1–5. Ovid, *Metamorphoses*, trans. Sandys. Andrew Marvell b.	La Fontaine b.	Bacon impeached.	Pope Paul V d.; Gregory XV elected. Philip III of Spain d.; Philip IV succeeds.
1622	Middleton and Rowley, *The Changeling* perf. (publ. 1653).	Tassoni, *Secchia Rapita*. Molière b.		Olivares becomes chief minister in Spain. Richelieu created cardinal.

Date Shakespeare	English literature	European literature	English politics	European politics
1623 *Mr William Shakespeare's Comedies, Histories, and Tragedies* (the First Folio)	Massinger, *The Duke of Milan.* Alemán. *The Rogue*, trans. Mabbe. Daniel. *The Whole Works.*	Campanella. *La Città de Sole.* Pascal b.	Journey of Charles and Buckingham to Madrid. Spanish match broken off.	Pope Gregory XV d.: Urban VIII elected. Dutch massacre English colonists at Amboyna.
1624	Middleton, *A Game at Chess* perf.		England declares war on Spain.	
1625	John Fletcher and (?) John Webster d.		James I d.: Charles I succeeds, and marries Henrietta Maria.	

Introduction

SHAKESPEARE AND RENAISSANCE EUROPE

Andrew Hadfield

About two-thirds of the way through Thomas Nashe's picaresque novella, *The Unfortunate Traveller*, the roguish hero, Jack Wilton, encounters a banished English earl living in Italy, who has come to watch his execution (which is fortunately not carried out). Jack has travelled through Europe, following the route through France, Germany and Italy that was fast to become a key part of many young English aristocrats' education in the subsequent century and a half, and known as 'The Grand Tour'.[1] But he is given a long lecture by the anonymous earl explaining why travel is an evil pastime that serves no educational purpose, being at best pointless, at worst corrupting. The opening words of his speech express the essence of the case against travel:

> Countryman, tell me, what is the occasion of thy straying so far out of England to visit this strange nation? If it be languages, thou may'st learn them at home; nought but lasciviousness is to be learned here. Perhaps, to be better accounted of than other of thy condition, thou ambitiously undertakest this voyage: these insolent fancies are but Icarus' feathers, whose wanton wax, melted against the sun, will betray thee into a sea of confusion.[2]

Travel abroad, according to this worldly-wise aristocrat, teaches the traveller nothing useful that he could not have learned at home, substituting false pleasure for true knowledge. Those who were trying to learn foreign languages in order to serve their country will only harm it, as they will return with increased – and more perverse – appetites.[3] Those who travel out of a combination of pride and curiosity, like Icarus, who died when he flew too close to the sun and his wax wings melted, will also suffer. The earl concludes that much more can be learned from books than from travel: 'What is here but we may read in books, and a great deal more too, without stirring our feet out of a warm study?'[4] Jack, after witnessing two executions described in graphic detail, loses his wanderlust, marries his sweetheart and flees back to the English camp in France, the place where his story began.

Shakespeare would probably have read Nashe's novella. It was published in 1594, near the start of Shakespeare's career; there are numerous echoes of other works by Nashe in Shakespeare's plays (some believe that the character of Moth in *Love's Labour's Lost* (*c.* 1594) is based on Nashe); and Nashe was a well-known figure among the writers who lived in London in the 1580s and 1590s, collaborating with Christopher Marlowe to produce *Dido, Queen of Carthage* (published 1594, probably written and performed in the late 1580s).[5] Although some have made the case that Shakespeare travelled abroad during the 'lost years' (1589–92), or visited Italy with the Earl of Southampton in 1593, it seems unlikely that he did travel abroad, unlike many of his contemporaries, Ben Jonson and Marlowe among them.[6] It is clear from Nashe's story that a writer did not need to visit other countries in order to acquire an intimate knowledge of their geography, people, and cultural and political affairs. The great editors and collectors of travel literature in the late sixteenth and early seventeenth centuries – most notably Richard Hakluyt the younger and Samuel Purchas – were not themselves travellers. Shakespeare shows a keen interest in a large range of European countries, giving many of his non-specifically English or British historical plays distinct European settings, including a wide variety of national identities: Denmark (*Hamlet*), France (*All's Well That Ends Well, As You Like It*), Spain (*Love's Labour's Lost*), northern Italy (*Romeo and Juliet, The Two Gentlemen of Verona, The Taming of the Shrew, Much Ado About Nothing*), an unnamed island in the Mediterranean (*The Tempest*), Venice (*The Merchant of Venice, Othello*), southern Italy (*The Comedy of Errors, The Winter's Tale*),

Athens (*A Midsummer Night's Dream*, *The Two Noble Kinsmen*), Vienna (*Measure for Measure*), Illyria (the Balkans) (*Twelfth Night*). But Shakespeare is less concerned with careful geographical accuracy or reproducing the lands and peoples of Europe as they could be found catalogued in a readily available work such as Abraham Ortelius's *Theatrum Orbis Terrarum*, published in Latin in 1570, or Gerardus Mercator's *Atlas*, published in 1595, also in Latin. The famous 'slip', whereby Bohemia is given a coastline in *The Winter's Tale* (following Robert Greene, who makes the same error in *Pandosto*), or the fact that the forest in *As You Like It* seems to owe more to the Forest of Arden that Shakespeare knew in his youth than the more carefully represented Forest of Bordeaux in his source, Thomas Lodge's *Rosalynd*, indicates that knowledge was always placed in the service of dramatic action.[7] Rather, Shakespeare was concerned to employ what John Gillies has called a 'poetic geography', a mode of perception that envisaged the world existing in terms of ideas, not areas.[8]

English Renaissance representation of the world could be clear and straightforward at some points – notably in the distinction between the civil and the savage – and somewhat less well defined at others, as the above examples indicate. The Venice of the first act of *Othello*, for example, is meticulously represented, as the plot depends on our seeing the institutions in Venice functioning successfully.[9] Cyprus, where the main action of the plot develops, appears to have no real dramatic substance and functions as a contrast to the ordered city-state, an outpost where civilized order is always under threat. Shakespeare's play represents Venice as a complex and ambiguous location. On the one hand it is central to European identity, the major entrepôt, secure enough because of its vast wealth and power to include strangers such as Othello, acting as the gateway to the wider world. On the other hand, Venice could be regarded as an isolated and vulnerable anomaly whose power would decline once the Ottoman Empire managed to dominate the Mediterranean.[10] *Othello* reveals the acute anxieties that haunt Venetian life. The Turkish fleet is destroyed in a storm, but, as Othello himself often fears, the Europeans and their allies are in danger of 'turning Turk' and doing their enemies' work for them. Earlier in his career Shakespeare, in *The Merchant of Venice*, had represented Venice as a bigoted and intolerant society unable to accept strangers in its midst.[11]

Othello, for all its differences from the earlier play, also shows a society tearing itself apart. The true villain of *Othello* remains invisible to the characters on stage, who think that Iago is an honest man, while the audience know the full extent of his evil behaviour, a dramatic irony that is probably meant to show how Europeans miss what is disguised amongst them. Racist abuse against foreigners exists in Venice, as Brabantio's tirade against his son-in-law demonstrates, but it can be controlled because the problem is recognized by the authorities.[12] Iago and Roderigo's actions escape detection, as they exhibit no easily observed marks of difference, yet their names are Spanish. This might well have suggested a comparison with Jesuits for a contemporary audience. Jesuits, although they were not exclusively Spanish, of course, were easily associated with England's major Catholic enemy of the 1580s and 1590s and were notorious for their duplicity or 'equivocation', as well as their subversive and underhand tactics.[13] *Othello* perhaps suggests that divisions within Europe are as significant as those between Europe and the rest of the world, and that they are probably more dangerous and insidious because harder to detect, since they were based on religious allegiance (Spain being Catholic, and England Protestant) rather than pigmentation. A Spanish king had ruled England in the middle years of the sixteenth century when Mary had married Philip II of Spain, a union that had proved problematic and had helped to foster an English fear of foreign monarchs and government from overseas.[14] Anglo-Spanish relations had started to deteriorate seriously in the early 1580s when the Spanish gave aid to the Catholic conspiracies, the Throckmorton Plot (1583) and the Babington Plot (1586), which had planned to assassinate Elizabeth and replace her with Mary Stuart (Mary Queen of Scots).[15] War had broken out in 1584 and England had been seriously threatened in 1588 by the Armada, which, like the Turkish fleet that sailed towards Cyprus in *Othello*, had been dispersed by the elements and providence as much as careful military preparation and strategy. The war had continued unabated throughout the 1590s, and Jesuits who had come to England to further the Counter-Reformation were often captured and executed as traitors.[16] Moreover, when Shakespeare was writing *Othello*, it was possible that the Spanish infanta could succeed Elizabeth as queen, showing how topical was a story of devious, malicious and disguised Spaniards.[17] This may be far too much to read into the play, and it does need to be noted that no one actually registers that Iago and Roderigo are Spanish names. Nevertheless, Shakespeare does seem to be drawing our attention to the fact that enemies within the realm can be more dangerous than those outside.

It could be argued that the religious division within Europe is the key to understanding how Elizabethan and Jacobean writers made sense of who they were and how they understood the rest of the world. Thomas Kyd's *The Spanish Tragedy* (written *c.* 1589, published 1592) represented its Spanish protagonists trapped within a destructive cycle of revenge that was controlled by pagan gods, showing that the Spanish were pagan rather than Christian, and so were damned.[18] Arguments for colonialism in the Americas by Richard Hakluyt and others made the case that if Protestant England did not start to establish colonies in the New World then the Spanish, who had a significant head start, would become too powerful to resist and so would dominate the world.[19] Propagandists of the 'Black Legend', who sought to highlight Spanish atrocities in the Americas in contrast to the virtuous behaviour of Protestants, often made a close link between Spanish behaviour in the Netherlands (which were trying to resist Spanish rule) and colonial America.[20] Debates over Shakespeare's *The Tempest* have seen critics try to establish whether the play should be read as European (the action takes place on an unnamed island in the Mediterranean, the characters are Italian, and the action refers back to events in Milan and Naples) or belonging to the colonial New World (Shakespeare seems to have read William Strachey's pamphlets telling the story of his shipwreck on Bermuda, and Caliban is a near-anagram of 'cannibal').[21] The point is undoubtedly that the play situates itself within both continents; or, rather, that Renaissance English writers were reluctant to divide the world of their imagination up so neatly.

What were the boundaries of Europe then? Where did Europe stop? Today this is still a complex question and different answers can be given, different maps drawn up, even if now we have a clearer sense of the boundaries of nations fixed by international treaties. The basic shape of the continent is easy to visualize, but its extent is more problematic to define. The westward edge of Europe is established by the Atlantic ocean; the south-western boundary by the Mediterranean; and the northern boundaries by the northern seas above Britain and Scandinavia. But how far does Europe stretch south-eastwards? How European is Russia? One answer used to be to define it as both Asiatic and European, but this feat is less easy to imagine since the break-up of the USSR in 1991. Is Turkey European? There has been vigorous debate as to whether it should join the European Union, which has concentrated on its human rights record, not its geographical location, even though it is situated on the far side of the Mediterranean. The same is true of Israel. At times, people appeal to gradations of 'Europeanness'. Hence it is common to hear northern Italians argue that the south of Italy is really 'African' in character, a division most famously articulated in Carlo Levi's *Christ Stopped at Eboli* (1945). Greece is sometimes represented in the same way, seen as less European, because it is less centralized and more 'primitive'. And, as tragic events in the last decade have emphasized, the former Yugoslavia contains a substantial Muslim population who were once part of the furthest reaches of the Ottoman Empire that stretched into the Balkan states and parts of present-day Romania and Bulgaria.

The Ottoman Empire was generally regarded as the antithesis of Christian Europe from the Crusades onwards, a dangerous, aggressive culture keen to expand its territories into those of its major rival. English literary texts contain numerous examples of hostile representations of the 'turban'd Turk', including the Saracen knights, Sansfoy, Sansjoy and Sansloy, who threaten Una and the Red-Cross Knight in Edmund Spenser's *The Faerie Queene* (1590) – another work that Shakespeare certainly read – and more recent examples such as the Saracen plays that are performed in Thomas Hardy's *The Return of the Native* (1878).[22] King James VI of Scotland, later to succeed Elizabeth as James I of

England, wrote a long poem celebrating the Venetians' victory over the Turks in the Battle of Lepanto (1571), seeing it as a triumph of Christian virtue over paganism.[23] Yet, as many were all too aware, the boundary between the Ottoman Empire and Europe was permeable and confusing.

The great European geographer, Gerardus Mercator, who produced the cartographic masterpieces, the world map (1569) and the map of Europe (1572), recognized this problem in his *Historia Mundi, or, Mercator's Atlas* (translated into English in 1635, but known and used in England much earlier).[24] The frontispiece to the English edition shows all the four known continents – Europe, Asia, Africa and America – represented as female figures. Europa, the legendary founder of Europe, is shown holding an open 'Biblia Sacra', a cross and a cornucopia (a horn of plenty), full of ripe fruit.[25] Next to her is an ass, a symbol of humble spirituality, and in the background a church (Figure 1a). Facing her, Asia wears a substantial oriental crown and brandishes a spear. Behind her are the buildings of a powerful, grand city (Figure 1b). Asia's proud expression and trappings of worldly vanity are a pointed contrast to the submissive and modest demeanour of Europe and would seem to mark her out as a type of the whore of Babylon, the evil creature of the Revelation whose appearance signified the beginning of the last days of the world before Christ's return.[26]

However, Mercator's text acknowledges that this clear distinction between the continents is effectively problematic, 'For ancient Writers doe not agree concerning the Easterne boundes of Europe.'[27] Mercator chooses to place the boundaries at the Caspian Sea (the Majestic Lake) and the Bosphorus, but admits that other authorities draw different boundaries. The map shows Europe as a peninsula jutting out of Asia: self-contained and distinct in one sense but also a promontory of a larger landmass struggling to retain its identity. Abraham Ortelius's *Theatrum Orbis Terrarum (The Theatre of the Whole World)* also defines Europe as a peninsula and acknowledges the problems of fixing its eastern boundaries. Europe borders Barbaria in North Africa and Tartaria, the kingdom of the Tartars, in Asia.[28] The threat to Europe is made even clearer in the map of Turkey, which shows how little Europeans could take for granted (Figure 2).

FIGURE 1 Gerardus Mercator, *Historia Mundi, or Mercator's Atlas* (1635), detail of the frontispiece, showing (a) Europa and (b) Asia.

FIGURE 2 Map of the Turkish Empire from Abraham Ortelius, *Theatrum Orbis Terrarum* (1608), fol. 110.

Nevertheless, Mercator's Atlas is unashamedly Eurocentric in content – Ortelius's somewhat less so – devoting 813 of its 930 pages to European countries and regions. Europe

> not onely farre excell[s] the other parts of the World in the wonderfull temperatenesse of the climate, temper, pleasantnesse, and great company of the inhabitants; but also in the abundance of Fruits, Trees, and Plants, all kinde of living Creatures, Mettals; and in the plentie of all other thinges which are necessarie to sustaine mans life.[29]

In addition, the cities of Europe are said to rival – if not excel – those built in the other parts of the world. And both works claim that more than twenty-eight European countries officially adhere to the Christian faith.

Mercator's Atlas performs another function that many early modern English books provided for their readers: a handy list of the characteristics of peoples for ease of reference, but which could often lapse into easy prejudice masquerading as knowledge. Mercator concludes his account with the following description which is worth citing at length because it is typical of so much early travel writing:

> It would be too much to reckon up the vertues of the Inhabitants, but as for the vices (as who is without some?) they are noted in some short sayings, which I will here adde: The people of *Franconia* are foolish, rude, and vehement. The *Bavarians* are prodigal, gluttons and railers. The *Grisons* are light, talkative, and braggers. The *Turingi* are distrustfull and contentious. The *Saxons* dissemblers, craftie, selfe-willed. The *Low-countrey men* are horsemen, delicate, and tender. The *Italians* proud, desirous of revenge, and wittie. The *Spaniards* hautie, wise, covetous. The *French* eloquent, intemperate, and rash. The people of *Denmarke* and *Holsteine*, are great of stature, seditious, and dreadfull. The *Sarmatians* great eaters, proud, and stealers. The *Bohemians* inhumane, new-fangled, and robbers. The *Illyrians* unconstant, envious, seditious. The *Pannonians* cruell, and superstitious. The *Greeks* miserable. And there is another saying no lesse pleasant.

A bridge in *Poland*, a Monke in *Bohemia*, a Knight of the *South*, a Nunne of *Servia*, the Devotion of *Italie*, the Religion of *Prutenicks*, the Fasts of *Germans*, and the Constancie of *Frenchmen* are worth nothing.[30]

Such lists supplied convenient means of characterizing the peoples and nations of Europe for those who did not have the time to explore the areas in greater depth, whether as a traveller (a privilege granted to a very few) or as a reader. Books full of maxims, sententiae and proverbial wisdom were ubiquitous in the Renaissance and probably formed the key ingredient of many readers' reading experiences. Books were produced which tabulated vital pieces of information and summarized complex arguments and dense passages of discursive prose for those who were too busy to spend their time in scholarly activity. Individuals noted down key sentences and phrases in their own commonplace books for future reference.[31] It is hardly a matter of surprise that out of such an intellectual culture handy brief descriptions of foreigners and foreign lands should develop and define how English men and women encountered other regions.

Shakespeare's plays show obvious signs of being influenced by this mode of thought. The Germans and the Dutch are typically referred to as corpulent, as when Iago boasts that the English are able to out-drink 'your swag-bellied Hollander' in the 'brawl scene' in *Othello* (2.3.73). The Italians are seen as crafty, cunning, treacherous and lustful. Gremio, the aged rich suitor of Bianca, refers to himself as 'An old Italian fox' (*The Taming of the Shrew*, 2.1.397) when presented with an opportunity to press his suit in an underhand manner; in *Cymbeline*, Pisanio, Posthumus's servant, describes Iachimo, who he believes has stolen Imogen from his master, as a 'false Italian / (As poisonous tongu'd as handed)' (3.2.4–5), alluding to the belief that poisoning was a common means of settling disputes in Italy.[32] The French are said to be 'confident and over-lusty' in *Henry V* (4.0.18), and 'perfidious' in *Henry VIII* (1.2.156). The Welsh are seen as mystical, addicted to song (*Henry IV, Part 1*, 3.1; *The Merry Wives of Windsor*, 2.1; 5.3.11–12) and cheese (*Merry Wives*, 5.5.82). The Spanish are noted for their hot breath, indicating their unstable and violent temperament (*The Comedy of Errors*, 3.2), and the Jews, an important European people, for their business acumen, miserliness and thirst for revenge, especially against Christians (*The Merchant of Venice*).[33]

The most spectacular rhetorical set-piece depicting the nations of the world – but predominantly those in Europe – occurs in *The Comedy of Errors* when Dromio of Syracuse describes the object of his affection, Nell the kitchen wench, to his master, Antipholus. Nell's rotundity makes her resemble the world, and it is likely that Shakespeare had Mercator's globe in mind for this extended description:

ANTIPHOLUS S.   Then she bears some breadth?

DROMIO S.   No longer from head to foot than from hip to hip; she is spherical, like a globe; I could find out countries in her.

ANTIPHOLUS S.   In what part of her body stands Ireland?

DROMIO S.   Marry, sir, in her buttocks; I found it out by the bogs.[34]

ANTIPHOLUS S.   Where Scotland?

DROMIO S.   I found it by the barrenness, hard in the palm of her hand.

ANTIPHOLUS S.   Where France?

DROMIO S.   In her forehead, armed and reverted, making war against her heir.

ANTIPHOLUS S.   Where England?

DROMIO S.   I looked for the chalky cliffs, but I could find no whiteness in them. But I guess it stood in her chin, by the salt rheum that ran between France and it.

ANTIPHOLUS S.   Where Spain?

DROMIO S.   Faith, I saw it not; but I felt it hot in her breath.

ANTIPHOLUS S.   Where America, the Indies?

DROMIO S.   O, sir, upon her nose, all o'er-embellished with rubies, carbuncles, sapphires, declining their rich aspects to the hot breath of Spain, who sent whole armadoes of carracks to be ballast at her nose.

ANTIPHOLUS S.   Where stood Belgia, the Netherlands?

DROMIO S.   O, sir, I did not look so low.

(3.2.112–38)

Such literary pyrotechnics are not likely to rank among the most profound lines that Shakespeare wrote. But they may make a serious point about representation of others rather like that made by Thomas Nashe. Nell does not appear in the play and Dromio's witty use of xenophobic cliché needs to be set against the lack of detail we are given representing his homeland, Syracuse, a region once centrally important to the economic, cultural and political life of the known Mediterranean world, but marginal in terms of late sixteenth-century Europe.[35] Geography could often be an elusive and misleading subject.

Shakespeare was undoubtedly far better informed about places and events in Europe than such light-hearted and frivolous passages suggest, even though he chose not to write directly about contemporary European events as many of his contemporaries did. Yet, even here, there are clear references to European politics. When Dromio says that France resides in Nell's forehead, 'making war against her heir', the pun reminds readers that the French crown was disputed and that France had suffered serious civil wars as a result (see chapter 1 for details).[36] Nevertheless, there is nothing in Shakespeare's dramatic output that deals as directly with recent events in France as Christopher Marlowe's *The Massacre at Paris* (c. 1589), which told the horrifying story of the Massacre of St Bartholomew's Day (24 August 1572), when French Catholics slaughtered Protestants in the capital city as a means of establishing their sectarian hegemony, an event that was to cast a shadow over European politics until well into the seventeenth century.[37] But other dramatists did write plays which were set in France of that time, most notably George Chapman's *Bussy D'Ambois* (performed 1604, published 1607) and its sequel, *The Revenge of Bussy D'Ambois* (performed c. 1610, published 1613) (Chapman also wrote a play based on even more recent events in French history, *The Conspiracy and Tragedy of Charles, Duke of Byron, Marshal of France* (1608)). Later, Thomas Middleton sailed even closer to the wind in his explicitly allegorical *A Game at Chess* (performed 1624), which satirized the projected match between Prince Charles and the Spanish infanta in a manner that was simple to decode. It played to packed houses in the Globe theatre until it was closed down after nine performances.[38]

Shakespeare might have avoided such direct representation of European politics because he was more naturally cautious than his contemporaries and as much an astute businessman as an intellectual; it may be that he had to write for more popular audiences than writers such as Chapman and so chose to concentrate on more accessible subjects; he might have chosen to represent English rather than European history in the 1590s as a means of tackling contemporary domestic political issues.[39] The reasons are hard to determine.

Many of Shakespeare's plays demonstrate an informed awareness of events taking place in contemporary Europe. *Hamlet*, for example, contains a sophisticated discussion of revenge that goes beyond the staple fare of the genre of the revenge tragedy, and suggests that Shakespeare was well versed in the 'monarchomach' literature produced in Europe – notably France and Scotland – which debated if and when a monarch could be violently overthrown.[40] *Hamlet's* choice of university, Wittenberg, was the place where Martin Luther nailed his Ninety-Five Theses to the Cathedral door in October 1517, a detail that probably has little direct bearing on the play itself, but shows that events represented on stage can be related to the fundamental split in existence in post-Reformation Europe. Shakespeare's religion – like his politics – is a matter of ongoing controversy; but, whatever his own personal leanings may have been, his plays often show a clear awareness of religion as a divisive phenomenon.[41] *Measure for Measure*, set in Vienna, a city which may or may not have had a specific reference for the audience, balances representations of Catholics and Puritans, most explicitly when the repressed and hypocritical Angelo confronts the virtuous Isabella in secret.[42] *Macbeth* contains the famous porter scene which has a series of references to Jesuit 'equivocation' at the trial of the Gunpowder Plot conspirators, a passage that can be compared to Shakespeare's representation of Iago in *Othello*.[43] Certain plays have plots that deal more directly with divisions within Europe. *Henry V* shows the king leading a British army into France and so uniting them – at least for the time being – against a common enemy. It is hard not to read the play in terms of the struggle between Protestants and Catholics in Europe, especially given the threat to England from

Ireland, where the rebellion of Hugh O'Neill, Earl of Tyrone, had developed into a full-scale war (the Nine Years War, 1594–1603), with the Spanish intervening on his side to try to expel the English and establish a Catholic ally.[44] In a later play, *Cymbeline* (*c.* 1610), loosely based on the few surviving details about an ancient British king, the British are seen surrendering to the Romans – perhaps a suggestion that a *rapprochement* with Europe was possible now that the hostility with Spain had passed and a more ecumenical age begun.[45]

Shakespeare would have been able to obtain a significant knowledge of European events in London, even if he had not had connections with important government figures, either through reading books himself, or through talking to those who had read them. The news book had not developed yet as it did in the middle years of the seventeenth century, but many short, quickly produced tracts did appear chronicling recent stories, especially sensational incidents, marvels and the numerous atrocities that took place throughout the continent.[46] There were pamphlets – as well as more discursive and analytical works – dealing with every major European country and area, more and more being published as the sixteenth century drew to a close. These would all have been on sale in printers' shops which were situated mainly near St Paul's cathedral, not far from the playhouses, among the other commercial outlets in the city. Shakespeare could have either read some of these printed works himself, or learnt of them from other Londoners, given their ready availability and topical nature.[47] Works published on contemporary Germany, to take just one example, include a gory murder story detailed in *Newes out of Germanie* (1584); another pamphlet of the same title (1611) chronicling the siege of Prague by Archduke Leopold; *The Picture of a Puritane* (1605), which tries to show that English Puritans are just like the notorious Anabaptists of Münster, who rebelled against their prince and set up a republic where everyone was equal, before they were brutally suppressed, an episode recounted in Nashe's *Unfortunate Traveller*;[48] *A Strange Report of Sixe most Notorious Witches* (1607); and, for those wishing to examine German society and customs at length, there was William Phiston's *The Estate of the Germaine Empire* (1595). Those keen for information on the Low

Countries would have been able to find *A Briefe Report of the Militarie Service done in the Low Countries, by the Erle of Leicester* (1587) by Thomas Digges; *The Description of the Low Countreys and of the Provinces thereof* (1593); and Edward Grimestone's translation of Jean-François Le Petit's *The Low-Country Commonwealth* (1609). It was also easy enough to find descriptions of other European countries with which England had diplomatic and trade links, such as George North's *The Description of Swedland, Gotland and Finland* (1561), a translation extracted from Sebastian Münster's influential *Cosmography.* The major European countries that dominated English foreign policy and travel – France, Germany and Italy – also dominated the publishing trade. Shakespeare's work may often demonstrate a lack of interest in geographical accuracy: attempts to relate the setting and plot of *Love's Labour's Lost* to events at the French court have been less than convincing, despite its use of topical names and allusions.[49] However, we do know that Shakespeare would make use of the material available to him when it suited his purposes. As is well known, he cited Montaigne's essay, 'Of the Canniballes', when writing the first act of *The Tempest*. More significantly, he made extensive use of Gasparo Contarini's celebratory *The Commonwealth and Government of Venice*, translated by Sir Lewis Lewkenor in 1599, when representing the institutions of Venice in *Othello*.[50]

But the major European influence on Shakespeare's writing was, of course, literary and he clearly read and consulted a large number of various works: prose fiction (often Italian, sometimes via a French translation); plays (again, often Italian, as well as Roman models); discursive works of fine style such as Montaigne's *Essais*; and poetry, especially French and Italian lyric poetry for the *Sonnets*. Only a few of Shakespeare's plays – *Love's Labour's Lost* and *The Tempest* being the obvious examples – do not have directly attributable sources. As the above list indicates, his imagination was largely inspired by French and Italian models. For instance, the Italian novellas of Giovanni Baptista Cinthio provided the source material for *Othello* and, probably, *Measure for Measure*. Giovanni Battista Guarini's play, *Il Pastor Fido*, was in Shakespeare's mind when he wrote *Measure for Measure* and, probably,

All's Well That Ends Well. Although there are no direct verbal parallels, it is likely that Shakespeare knew of the French dramatist Robert Garnier's *Marc-Antoine*, rendered into English by Mary Sidney in 1585, before he wrote *Antony and Cleopatra.* Boccaccio's *The Decameron*, a fourteenth-century collection of miscellaneous tales which was well known in England in its original Italian and in translation, provided material for *All's Well* and *Cymbeline*; and the French translator and novella writer, François Belleforest, produced a version of the story of Hamlet that Shakespeare probably knew.[51]

The essays in this collection attempt to illuminate our understanding of the impact of Europe on Shakespeare's life as a writer. They examine his imaginative engagement with Europe's culture and literature, as well as his understanding of the importance of the continent in which he lived, and his understanding of its political life and geographical features. In the opening chapter Susan Doran surveys the political events that took place in Shakespeare's Europe and what exactly would have been known about them by ordinary citizens. Although foreign policy and diplomacy were fiercely guarded as the prerogative of the monarch alone, details of major European events were clearly circulating via a number of printed sources, eyewitness accounts and general gossip. Attempts to control and censor information failed to prevent the natural force of people's curiosity. Susan Doran shows how France often dominated English perceptions of Europe, being the closest continental neighbour, and also a land torn apart by sectarian strife which many felt could engulf England too. Spain was just as significant, especially from the 1580s onwards when a protracted 'cold', occasionally 'hot', war broke out. Both relationships demonstrate that religion was the most important factor that determined both the course of political histories and the ways in which one nation perceived another.

Michael Brennan shows in chapter 2 that even though relatively few Englishmen travelled abroad in Tudor and Stuart England their experience had a significant impact on their contemporaries, either through the publication of their observations and impressions, or through reporting the knowledge they had acquired to the masters they served. Something that would have struck contemporary readers and confidants of travellers was how vociferously Protestant they often were, denigrating European Catholics, partly out of distaste and a sense of innate superiority to such superstitious creatures from the dark ages, and partly out of fear. The three major travel accounts published in the early seventeenth century – Thomas Coryat's *Coryat's Crudities* (1611); Fynes Moryson's *An Itinerary Containing his Ten Yeeres Travell through the Twelve Dominions of Germany, Bohmerland, Sweitzerland, Netherland, Denmarke, Poland, Italy, Turky, France, England, Scotland & Ireland* (published 1617, but based on journeys undertaken mainly in the 1590s); and William Lithgow's *The Totall Discourse of the Rare Adventures & Painfull Peregrinations of long Nineteene Yeares Travayles from Scotland to the most famous Kingdomes in Europe, Asia and Affrica* (1632, but earlier versions had appeared in 1614 and 1615) – are all notable for their acute xenophobia and Protestant bias.[52]

In chapter 3 Stuart Gillespie provides an analysis of Shakespeare's reading of European literature, attempting to reconstruct the intellectual context from which Shakespeare's work developed. He points out that literature was, in effect, European by definition, since no other forms of literature were known to Elizabethan and Jacobean readers. We are also restricted by our use of the term 'literature', which we use in a post-romantic manner to mean 'imaginative, fictional writing'.[53] For Renaissance readers, literature constituted a much wider category, covering all areas of 'humane learning': poetry, history, science, geography, philosophy, theology, oratory, and so on. Stuart Gillespie shows that we cannot always prove exactly what Shakespeare read, unless there is a reference to a specific work. However, it does not follow that Shakespeare did not read widely in the vast array of European letters available to him, or that the diversity of European culture did not determine what he wrote. Rather, we have to infer what he may have known from the available evidence, establishing what ideas are central to his work, and examining the reading of his contemporaries.

Richard Andrews explores the relationship between Shakespeare's plays and Italian comedy. As he points out in chapter 4, verbal echoes of Italian plays have been spotted by numerous scholars. What has been missing is an understanding of how Italian dramatic practice was central to Shakespeare's development as a playwright. Shakespeare was clearly influenced by the style of *commedia dell'arte*, as well as individual works, in the plots of comedies such as *A Midsummer Night's Dream* and *The Merry Wives of Windsor*, and its dramatic theory in *The Tempest* – perhaps a sign of where his career would have gone had it continued. Shakespeare's dramatic confidence and inventiveness were such that he was able to transform standard Italian comic plots into tragedies in *Romeo and Juliet* and *Othello*.

Paulina Kewes's chapter neatly complements that of Stuart Gillespie. She examines the representation and significance of European themes in the drama of other playwrights also working in London at the same time as Shakespeare. Chapter 5 demonstrates that English readers read classical, native and European history in similar ways, as repositories of examples that would instruct them how to live, rule and obey.[54] Many examples of behaviour were, of course, negative as well as positive, as in Walter Ralegh's depiction of foreign monarchs (see below, p. 155), who usually showed Englishmen how not to govern and be governed. Even though successive governments censored plays dealing with foreign subjects, they were popular with audiences and continued to be written and performed.

In chapter 6 François Laroque shows how the concept of Europe as a continent appeared in Shakespeare's imagination. Geography was as much a means of exploring imaginary worlds and fictional lands as it was a way of establishing accurate details and knowledge of the real world. There was a romance of geography, as well as a science, which is demonstrated in plays such as *Othello* and *The Tempest*. Furthermore, geography did not have to exist solely in the present but could be employed to conjure up past worlds, as in *King Lear*, which opens with the division of the kingdom of Britain when the old king produces a map. In *The Merchant of Venice*, the cynical world of new comedy exists side by side with the old romance of travel (see below, p. 197). Shakespeare's geography is indeed imprecise, but it is never vague or lacking in purpose.

In the final chapter, Nabil Matar and Rudolph Stoeckel establish what the boundaries of Europe would have been for Shakespeare and his contemporaries. Europe was considered to be the civilized world, inheriting a Christian and a classical legacy, which it needed to promote and defend. The continent was surrounded by various groups of hostile, pagan and savage peoples: Turks, Tartars and North Africans. To complicate matters still further, England's relationship with Europe and its own neighbours in the British Isles was also problematic, and the general fear that Protestant England could be overwhelmed by Catholicism increased a sense of isolation of a people who felt themselves to be simultaneously at the very edge of the world, and its centre. Shakespeare was deeply aware of these cultural and geographical divisions. A number of his plays have African characters or associations, most importantly *Titus Andronicus*, *The Merchant of Venice*, *Othello* and *The Tempest*. Africa was both dangerous and seductive for Europeans, making the Moor, an ambiguous and ubiquitous figure, Europe's 'other'. Europe had three frontiers during Shakespeare's lifetime, two across the Mediterranean, the other being the Ottoman–Habsburg Empire in central Europe (see below, p. 222). Moors, most especially Turks, were seen as the most potent threat to European life, always about to invade the continent.

Nevertheless Europe, however Europeans might have seen themselves, could not isolate itself from the rest of the world. Trade between European countries and the Ottoman Empire flourished and formed a key component of English economic life, acknowledged via the establishment of the Barbary Company in 1585 (see below, p. 224). Although it was asserted often enough that Turks and Moors would eventually be converted into Christians, the reality was that cultural traffic was more often the other way. Some Englishmen acknowledged that their culture could not exist in isolation. Throughout his career in the theatre Shakespeare was always aware that he belonged not only to Europe but also to a wider world beyond its boundaries – a realization that this volume explores.

Chapter One

THE POLITICS OF
RENAISSANCE EUROPE

Susan Doran

During Shakespeare's lifetime, England's political relations with the European powers were thought to be solely the concern of the monarch. As part of the *arcana imperii* – the Tacitean phrase meaning the mysteries of state – foreign policy was one of several political issues which came under the royal prerogative and could not be discussed publicly without the sanction of the ruler. Furthermore, English monarchs had no responsibility to explain their dealings with other states to their subjects; as Elizabeth I declared in 1585: 'kinges and princes soveraignes, owing their homage and service onely unto the Almightie God the king of al kings, are in that respect not bounde to yeelde account or render the reasons of their actions to any others but to God their only soveraigne lorde.'[1] For the same reason, ordinary subjects were not expected to offer counsel on foreign policy, and Elizabeth's Parliaments consequently stayed clear of initiating debates on European affairs. When in 1621 James I's Parliament did turn its attention to foreign matters and urged the king to 'take the sword into your hand' against Spain, James forbade its members 'to meddle with anything concerning our government or deep matters of state'.

Given this royal hostility to independent discussion on matters relating to European politics and English foreign policy, how could ordinary men and women outside the circle of the court obtain knowledge and form views about European politics? Well, despite their elevated view of the royal prerogative, both Elizabeth and James were prepared to allow their subjects some access to information about events taking place in Europe, and indeed resorted to the press to influence public opinion. After 1559 all printed works had to be approved by a group of Privy Counsellors and receive a licence from the Stationers' Company, while new regulations in 1586 confirmed the licensing system and prohibited the publication of any book which had not been authorized by the Archbishop of Canterbury and Bishop of London.[2] It was therefore with official approval that many documents, pamphlets and books as well as a fair number of poems and ballads dealing with foreign matters came into print for sale in London bookshops. Unsurprisingly, some of this printed material was straightforward governmental propaganda, designed to justify the English monarch's political or military actions – as when, for example, Christopher Barker printed a declaration from the queen which explained her reasons for giving aid to the rebels in the Low Countries who were fighting against their ruler Philip II, or when in 1596 Barker printed a short pamphlet justifying Elizabeth's decision to send a navy against Spain.[3]

Other publications also expressed the monarch's line on foreign affairs, although they were less obviously governmental propaganda. In the immediate run-up to the Elizabethan war against Spain, a significant number of pamphlets were produced to warn readers of that country's treacherous and ungodly activities.[4] Thomas Stocker's translation, *A Tragicall Historie of the Troubles and Civile Warres of the Lowe Countries* (1583), was but one of many accounts describing the 'barbarous crueltie and tyrannie of the Spaniard'.[5] Once the Anglo-Spanish war broke out, still more was disseminated about Spanish cruelty and treachery, fairly typical being the 1596 ballad, *The Miraculous Preservation of a Child of Seaven Yeeres old from the Bloody Spanyardes that soiled Narden a Towne in North Holland.*[6] Similarly in the 1580s and early 1590s propaganda against the Catholic League and the Guise family painted a vivid picture of the religious division, aristocratic unrest and disputes over the succession, which were then taking place in France and might well be transplanted to England if 'correct' policies were not undertaken.[7] Few historians doubt that Lord Burghley, in co-operation with Sir Francis Walsingham (until the latter's death in 1590), was responsible for many of these publications. After peace with Spain was signed in 1604, however, the tone and content of licensed printed material began to change and early Jacobean foreign news and opinion were not usually slanted quite so obviously in an anti-Spanish or anti-Catholic direction.

There was evidently a ready market in London for news about continental politics and warfare. Many men and women were interested in learning about the state of affairs in Europe, because of their commercial concerns, religious commitments or intellectual curiosity. England's participation in the continental wars undoubtedly fuelled this interest, and a ready market for news from abroad expanded between 1585 and 1604 when English troops were based on the continent. To meet this demand, printers frequently published pamphlets or newsletters that provided up-to-date information about the wars and other political events. The London printer John Wolfe was particularly enterprising in this respect, for he seems to have operated his own private news-reporting service between England and the continent, and his press regularly turned out pamphlets and newsletters from abroad. Indeed, Wolfe has been credited with introducing the 'corantos' into England (small booklets including news from abroad from a variety of informants in different countries which were a precursor of the newspaper).[8] Other London printers were also active in this field and produced materials on foreign affairs at the behest of booksellers operating in the City. Although many of these writings purported to be 'true' accounts, they were frequently inaccurate because of the haste in which they were produced as well as sensationalist in their authors' desire to boost sales. In addition to this reportage, English translations of official documents from abroad were printed often without editorial comment, so that readers might have what seemed to be firsthand knowledge of political events. In 1595, for example, Peter Short printed Henri IV's declaration of war against Spain; in 1599 Richard Field published the Edict of Nantes; and in 1609 John Windet printed the articles of the truce between Spain and the States General of the Low Countries.[9] Maybe one-third of the publications on France between 1561 and 1600 were translations of official documents.[10] For those readers who wanted to know about the political background to contemporary events, booksellers provided recent histories of France and the Low Countries, such as translations of Jean de Serres, *The Commentaries of the Civill Warres in Fraunce and the Low Countrie of Flanders* (1573–6), and Antony Colynet's *The True History of the Ciuill Warres of France, betweene the French King Henry the 4. and the Leaguers from 1585 untill October 1591* (1591).[11]

Three-quarters at least of the translations of newsletters and pamphlets from Wolfe's presses were reports about France and the Low Countries; some of these were polemical tracts, some concerned diplomatic matters, while a significant proportion carried news of military engagements. During the years when England was at war against Spain, the battles taking place in France and the Low Countries dominated newsletters. Most common were those in which the Protestants had won the day or an English contingent had participated; bad news in fact was often left unreported. Henri IV's triumphs over the Catholic League received particular attention. Similarly Maurice of Nassau's victories in the Low Countries were given considerable publicity, and the campaigns at Rhineberg (1597), Turnhout (1597), Nieupoort (1600), Bercke and Grave (1602) were recounted mainly in translations of foreign newsletters. Regular news was also provided of the progress of the long, and ultimately successful, Spanish siege of Ostend (1601–4), which Sir Francis Vere and his company of English soldiers were helping to defend.[12] On a different theme, Felix Kingston printed in 1602 a translation of a Dutch account of the recent destruction of six Spanish galleys.[13]

After the accession of James I and the peace with Spain, far fewer pamphlets dedicated to foreign news were licensed. The news that was authorized tended to concentrate on dramatic events like the assassination of Henri IV in 1610, the murder of the Russian tsar Demetrius in 1606 and the expulsion of the Moriscos in 1611.[14] Also forthcoming was information about foreign royals: the wedding of Louis XIII to the infanta of Spain in 1612, for example, and the election of Matthias as Holy Roman Emperor in 1612.[15] The appetite for news, however, probably did not desist with the arrival of peace, for the

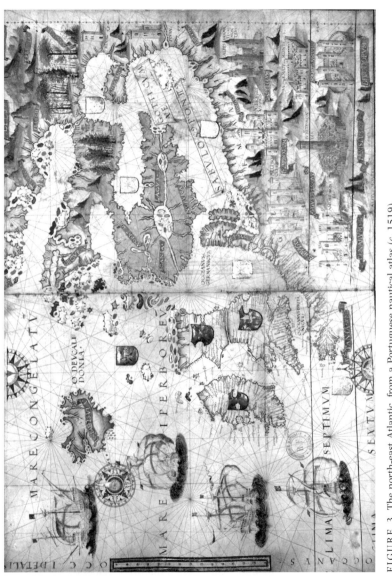

FIGURE 3 The north-east Atlantic, from a Portuguese nautical atlas (c. 1519).

import of unlicensed foreign newsbooks and 'corantos' seems to have increased as merchants and officials sent them into England, often in exchange for bulletins from home. Their printing in England was prohibited and so entrepreneurs in London copied them in manuscript and sold them unofficially. The government apparently tried to clamp down on these unofficial and unlicensed sources of news but, it seems, with limited success.[16]

Londoners interested in European affairs were not dependent on print for information, for news also circulated by word of mouth. The pulpit was probably one method of dissemination. Certainly it was said that preachers who served the French congregation in London delivered intelligence about France in their sermons, and, according to the minister Henry Smith, other preachers would mention current events to attract people to attend their lectures: 'if the Preacher say any thing of our Armies beyond sea, or counsell at home, or matters at Court, that is his lure'.[17] Although most extant printed texts of sermons have in fact little or nothing to say about affairs in Europe, we do know that preachers asked their listeners to pray for England's security against a specific foreign threat, urged aid for co-religionists abroad, and justified the war against Spain. In February 1591, for example, Roger Hacket, a fellow of New College, Oxford, exhorted his listeners at Paul's Cross to spare no effort, whatever the financial cost, to aid Henri IV against the Catholic League and Philip II.[18] Preachers also delivered sermons which gave thanks for English victories against Spain; among the many sermons which were delivered to offer thanks for the defeat of the Spanish Armada was one held at Paul's Cross on 8 September 1588 at which eleven ensigns captured from the Armada were displayed 'before the preacher and the audience (which was great)'. The Earl of Essex's victory at Cadiz was commended in a sermon by William Barlow.[19]

Other means of conveying and receiving information included gossip, rumour and private letters. There can be no question that the oral transmission of news was rife in late Elizabethan London, some of it true, much of it false or questionable. To take a few examples: in May 1589 there was 'a great bruit' in London that the Duke of Parma was dead, but the truth was that he was merely ill. On 9 August 1599 the

Londoner John Chamberlain informed his friend Dudley Carleton by letter that the previous Monday 'came newes (yet false) that the Spaniardes were landed in the yle of Wight, which bred such a feare and consternation in this towne as I wold litle have looked for, with such a crie of women, chaining of streets and shutting of the gates as though the enemy had ben at Blackewall'. Towards the end of the month Chamberlain also heard 'the alarme at hottest that the Spaniards were at Brest, which was as likely and fell out as true as the rest'. On the other hand, one accurate piece of news heard by Londoners was the start of the siege of Geneva by the Duke of Savoy which John Manningham jotted down in his diary.[20]

News of this kind circulated around the Royal Exchange, along Cheapside to St Paul's churchyard and walk, in the inns along Fleet Street, and in the Strand. It was well known that at the Royal Exchange 'from all countreys there was dayly newes to be heard by one means or other'.[21] Information about campaigns abroad often had their origin in the tales told by soldiers or sailors who had been present; other news was passed on by merchants or by gentlemen associated with the court. From London news was taken back to the provinces either by word of mouth or in letters from men in London to friends and employers in the country.[22] Sometimes the government tried to suppress rumours: a proclamation of 1580 condemned 'murmerers and spreaders' of rumours of an invasion attempt by Catholic rulers abroad, and warned that they would be brought before the justices and public officers as 'sowers of sedition'.[23] Occasionally pamphlets were written to dispel false rumours or slanders: Fabian Johnson's newsletter of 1591 was intended to counter 'uniust rumors secretlie dispersed' about the state of English forces in France.[24] In 1602 Sir Robert Mansell (the Admiral in the Narrow Seas) wrote a 'true report' of his service against six galleys to set right a 'report very vulgar in many men's mouthes in the City, and by this time perhaps sped over the Realme'.[25] In 1605 a pamphlet was licensed for printing which claimed to be a true report of the Earl of Nottingham's embassy and entertainment in Spain, because 'it came to our knowledge how many false and ill-contrived reports had been bruited abroad' about the mission.[26]

With both official and unofficial information at their disposal, not to mention works printed on underground presses or circulating as manuscripts, interested literate and semi-literate Londoners had plenty of opportunities to be at least partially informed about the political situation in Europe, especially events in France and the Low Countries. Historians have little idea of the type and extent of the readership of newsletters and pamphlets,[27] but there are hints that they were popular with a fairly wide group of people. A pamphlet describing the battle of Nieupoort went into a second edition, presumably because the first had sold out; no doubt for the same reason, several editions of Walter Bigges's description of Sir Francis Drake's voyage to the West Indies were printed.[28] Direct references to newsletters, moreover, can be found in contemporary diaries, letters and even a couple of plays. Manningham, for example, mentioned in his diary 'a booke of newes' describing an incident during the siege of Ostend in which Sir Francis Vere offered to parley with the Archduke Albrecht.[29] Christopher Marlowe's play *The Massacre at Paris* (produced 1593) seems to have relied heavily on contemporary pamphlet literature for its characterization of the Duc de Guise and Catherine de' Medici, as well as for its description of the assassination of Henri III.[30] The victory at Turnhout was celebrated in a play, which is not extant but probably received its information from pamphlets describing the battle.[31] Playwrights like Shakespeare could, if they wished, make direct or oblique references to the politics of Europe and be fairly confident that their audiences would understand their allusions.

What were the main political and religious developments taking place in Europe between 1560 and 1620? On the international front, Italy ceased to be the battlefield of Europe and the focus of rivalry between France and Spain after the signing of the 1559 Treaty of Cateau-Cambrésis, which recognized the Spanish monarch's sovereignty over Milan and Naples. Under the *pax hispanica* which followed, the peninsula was to benefit from some fifty years of peace and political stability. International conflicts centred instead on the north-east and the Mediterranean. In the Baltic area, Sweden, Denmark and Muscovy began the wars for control over Livonia and Estonia which were to last until 1621. In the Mediterranean, the Ottoman Empire continued under Suleiman the Magnificent (1520–66) and Selim II (1566–74) to challenge the maritime strength of the Venetians and Spaniards. Although the Turks were defeated in October 1571 at Lepanto by the naval force of the Holy League (Venice, Spain and the Papacy) in the biggest battle of the sixteenth century, they soon recovered, took Tunis in 1574 and extended Ottoman control over the North African coast.

The main religious developments of the period were first the dynamic spread of Calvinism directed from Geneva and second the resurgence of Catholicism under the leadership of the Pope. As will shortly be seen, Calvinism had a major impact on France and the Low Countries, but Reformed churches were also established in Poland, Hungary, Bohemia and Germany. The Catholic Church, meanwhile, gained in strength and confidence during the 1570s and 1580s; in many areas of central and eastern Europe, the Jesuits spearheaded a conversion programme while Catholic princes began to impose religious uniformity in their territories. In the Holy Roman Empire, the Catholic princes also tried to prevent further territorial losses to Protestantism by the use of force – successfully in the cases of the archbishopric of Cologne (1593–8) and the imperial free city of Donauworth (1607). Consequently the Religious Peace of Augsburg, which in 1555 had put an end to open confessional warfare in the empire, began to look temporary and fragile. But a major war was held off until 1618 when the Bohemian revolt against the emperor plunged the empire into crisis.

Significant as these developments are to historians, it was events in France and the Low Countries which were thought most important and received the most attention in Elizabethan London – certainly judging by the publication of news in these years. Consequently this chapter will concentrate on developments in these areas as seen through the eyes of contemporaries.

FRANCE

From 1562 until 1598 France was beset by a series of civil wars which brought the country close to anarchy. Although few Londoners outside the court could have had more than a hazy knowledge of the complex political narrative of those years, reports of the most momentous events were circulated in print both at the time and soon afterwards in chronicles or recent histories. From these writings, it seemed obvious that the wars were caused by a collapse of monarchical power, a factious nobility, and confessional conflict.

The unexpected death of Henri II in July 1559 began the course of events that led to war as it left his realm without effective leadership and the Crown at the mercy of a divided nobility. Henri's immediate heir was the sickly fifteen-year-old François II, who allowed royal authority to be exercised by his wife's maternal uncles, François Duc de Guise and the Cardinal of Lorraine, to the intense annoyance of the Bourbon princes of the blood, Louis Prince de Condé and Antoine King of Navarre. François II died, however, in December 1560 to be succeeded by his brother Charles IX, who at ten years old was too young to rule. Without a strong monarch at the helm, the rival noble houses of Guise, Bourbon and Montmorency vied for position at the French court, seeking to control the king's person and direct policy, but the official position of regent was taken up by the Dowager Queen Catherine de' Medici. At stake in these power struggles was not just the political prospects of the nobility but the future of religion in France, for the heads of the Guise family were deeply committed Catholics, whereas members of the Bourbon family had converted to Protestantism, and the Montmorency family was divided in its religious allegiances. Victory for one family would have determined whether or not Protestantism would be tolerated within France. Although no pamphlets relating to France were licensed during the years 1559–61, several publications appeared in English in 1562 which explained the factional conflicts under François II and the regency from the perspective of Condé and the Huguenots.[32]

Protestantism had begun to make inroads into France during the late 1550s thanks to a well-targeted missionary effort directed by John Calvin in Geneva. Many members of the nobility were soon attracted to Calvinism, and through their influence the Reformed faith percolated downwards to their clients. Artisans and merchants also became early converts to Calvinism, especially in towns south of the River Loire, where fledgling Reformed churches began to be established in the early 1560s. Historians have estimated that by 1562 perhaps some 1,200 Reformed churches were operating in France, and calculated that about 10 per cent of the population were Protestant. Elizabethans, of course, would not have known these details, but Calvinists abroad corresponded with sympathizers in England, and English residents in France observed and reported back on this reconfiguration of religion.

Under Henri II and François II, Protestantism was effectively outlawed in France, but in 1561 Catherine de' Medici allowed some concessions for the Huguenots (as the French Calvinists were somewhat mysteriously known), and in January 1562 she introduced an edict which permitted them for the first time to worship in public under certain conditions. Catherine's aims were to effect reconciliation amongst the nobility and bring an end to religious conflict by relaxing persecution. Most Catholics, however, were outraged by the compromise, and communal violence against the Huguenots erupted in many towns throughout 1561 and 1562. The most famous incident of violence occurred on 1 March 1562 when the Duc de Guise came across a congregation worshipping in a barn within the walled town of Vassy, close to his estates. Contemporary French reports of what happened next vary, but the final outcome of the encounter was the murder of the worshippers. According to one Huguenot account, translated for an English readership, Guise and his men put to the sword at least fourteen men, women and children and another eighty or a hundred were wounded 'whereof a great parte were out of all hope of life'.[33] Another contemporary pamphlet, however, put the immediate death toll considerably higher: 'such and so cruel a buchery and slaughter of poore people' left no fewer than eighty dead and as many or more hurt 'amonges whom there were women and little children'.[34] From narratives such as these, the image of the ruthless and cruel Guise family was born in England.

This massacre of Vassy sparked off the first in the long series of destructive civil wars in France.[35] During their course the kingdom ceased to operate as an effective force within Europe. As the English schoolmaster, Edward Grant, wrote:

> Oh France thou famous realme before, and eke moste populous
>   place;
> Thou arte dispeopled, wasted, torne, thy owne doe thee deface.
> Thy cities crackte, thy townes berefte, thy men and nobles rackt,
> Thy people pollai [sic], thy subiectes slayne, thy wealth and
>   strength is sackt:
> Ah pitie pitie to beare how altered is thy state.[36]

For most English people, this change in the fortunes of their traditional enemy was no cause for celebration. Rather they saw it as a terrible warning of the disasters that could befall any nation if it lost the favour of God and succumbed to religious division and political unrest. Besides, English Protestants could not afford to sit back and gloat. They sided with the Huguenots, believing that the Guise family were allies of the Pope and Spain in a Catholic conspiracy to suppress true religion throughout Europe.[37] A Guise victory, English Protestants feared, would undoubtedly result in the supply of French military aid for Mary Queen of Scots (the widow of François II and niece of the Guise brothers), who was the Catholic claimant to the English throne. English Protestants, moreover, strongly disliked the policy of religious persecution which they associated with the Guises, and hoped for 'the advance of true doctrine in France'.[38] Consequently, Elizabeth's government gave open armed assistance to Condé in the first civil war, while during the wars of the 1570s it allowed help to go secretly to the Protestants at La Rochelle. A number of Englishmen joined the Huguenots as volunteers, while others raised funds to assist their co-religionists during moments of crisis.

The 'crueltie' of Vassy and the other massacres of Protestants that disfigured France in the 1560s were nothing compared to the wave of violence known as the Massacre of St Bartholomew in 1572. This event was truly shocking because of both the scale and the timing of the slaughter. The numbers murdered are disputed but a conservative estimate is that some 3,000 were killed in Paris on 24 August, and another 3,000 in the provinces during September, although some historians put the total figure as high as 10,000. Initiated by Charles IX and the members of his council, the killings in the capital took place barely a week after the wedding of the king's sister, Margaret, to the young nominal leader of the Huguenots, Henri King of Navarre, a wedding which was understood at the time to be a symbol of reconciliation and religious peace.

The massacre was widely reported in England during 1572; indeed Philip Sidney and Sir Francis Walsingham had been in Paris at the time and felt relieved to have escaped death as they and others huddled for safety in Walsingham's house. Some sixty pastors and countless lay refugees fled from France to London and towns in the south where they were available to provide eyewitness accounts of the horrors they had seen. Their plight inspired a wave of generosity from English Protestants; the Archbishop of York raised £50 from his diocese for the French Reformed Church in London, while collections were organized in Gray's Inn and the Company of Merchant Taylors in London. Individual donors included churchmen (ministers as well as bishops), London merchants and members of the court and Privy Council.[39] Details of the massacre were also disseminated through the medium of print. Henry Bynneman published *A True and Plaine Report of the Furious Outrages in France*, while Thomas Vautrollier, himself an earlier Huguenot refugee, printed a translation of Jean de Serres's Latin life of Admiral Coligny, who had been a victim of the massacre.[40] Although historians now debate whether or not St Bartholomew was premeditated and where responsibility for it lies, few at the time doubted that the king and Catherine de' Medici were the main 'inventors of this monstrous bloodshedding'. According to one contemporary English report, the 'King is now become so bloody that it is impossible to stay his thirst to quench the same in innocent blood.' But it was Catherine who 'with her loving and motherly persuasions' had convinced him that all the Huguenot leaders should die. Henri Duc de Guise had merely been 'used as a butcher for the slaughter' and not been party to the decision-making.[41] In 1579 Philip Sidney still blamed the French royal family for the carnage; when he wrote his famous letter against

Elizabeth I's project to marry François Duc d'Anjou, he called Catherine de' Medici 'the Jezebel of our age' and condemned Charles IX for making 'oblation of his own sister's marriage, the easier to make massacres of all sexes'.[42]

The nightmare of the St Bartholomew Massacre was not easily erased from the English mind. Twelve years afterwards, the physician Thomas Bright, who had been in Paris in August 1572, recalled 'those days of terror in France, when the blood of the godly was everywhere being shed by fiendish killers'.[43] Memory of the massacres was also kept alive in printed works: John Foxe's 1583 edition of the *Acts and Monuments* devoted five pages to the event; Anne Dowriche's poem on murderous events in France included a long section on the 'bloodie plot to have the godlie slaine' and the carnage that followed; while translated versions of French histories of the civil wars which were published throughout the late sixteenth century invoked St Bartholomew as an event of 'marvailous carnage and butcherie'.[44]

St Bartholomew undoubtedly changed the nature of the civil wars in France. First of all, those Huguenots who survived it no longer claimed they were fighting merely against the king's enemies and not the king himself. Huguenots now attacked Charles IX as a tyrant, some even calling for his deposition; their polemicists, moreover, developed theories of resistance in works such as the *Francogallia* (1573) of François Hotman and the *Vindiciae contra Tyrannos* (1579), published under the pseudonym Stephanus Junius Brutus but generally thought to be the composition of Philippe du Plessis-Mornay. This extremist stance of the Huguenots, however, did not last long and began to be revised in the mid-1580s when their leader, Henri de Navarre, emerged as the heir to the French throne. Mornay then started to write treatises with a royalist bent, while Hotman agreed to dilute his theories in a new edition of the *Francogallia*. In fact Huguenot resistance theories had a very restricted circulation in Elizabethan England. Hotman's original treatise was never translated into English, while only the selected fourth part of the *Vindiciae* was printed in an English translation in 1588 and then under a different title.[45] None the less, some educated Englishmen did have access to the early works in their original language. They were certainly read within Philip Sidney's circle during the 1570s and early 1580s, and a little later on writers such as Richard Hooker and Richard Bancroft discussed the political and constitutional ideas raised in Huguenot resistance literature.[46]

Politically, the Huguenots were severely weakened by the St Bartholomew Massacre. Many of them had been forced to abjure their faith to save their lives, while others returned to the Catholic Church in response to the harsh anti-Protestant measures introduced in the massacre's wake. Among the defectors were Henri de Navarre and the young Prince Henri de Condé, who were kept virtual prisoners at Charles IX's court. Yet, even without their leadership and despite the many desertions from their ranks, the Huguenots were not defeated. La Rochelle on the Atlantic coast and Sancerre in Berry succeeded in withstanding sieges by the royal army, while the fortress towns of Montauban and Nîmes in the Languedoc became centres of resistance. Again Protestants in England proved sympathetic to their co-religionists in France; merchants, for example, with the collusion of Privy Counsellors, found ways of supplying loans and munitions to La Rochelle.

The death of Charles IX in May 1574 brought his brother Henri III to the throne but not an end to the civil wars. The new king's quarrels with his younger sibling, François, aristocratic discontent with the royal government, local feuds, not to mention religious conflict, kept France in a state of anarchy for most of Henri III's reign. Even when France was officially at peace, independent noblemen waged war against each other with their own private armies. During this period news from France was intermittent in England, but it was clear to observers that the peace was fragile and monarchical power weak. Between 1579 and 1582, however, English people were generally more exercised by the prospect of a marriage between their queen and the Duc d'Anjou. The match was highly unpopular and condemned in sermons, pasquins, and the unlicensed pamphlet *The Discovery of a Gaping Gulf* written by John Stubbs.[47]

Political unrest in France took a dramatic new turn after 30 May 1584 when Anjou, the last of the Valois brothers, died, leaving Henri de

Navarre as next in line for the throne by right of the Salic law and primogeniture. Predictably, European Catholics found the prospect of Navarre's accession entirely unacceptable, since he had reassumed his Protestant faith as soon as he could after St Bartholomew. They rallied instead behind an alternative candidate, the elderly Cardinal of Bourbon (Navarre's uncle).[48] Anjou's death therefore sparked off a long succession crisis which provoked the most serious challenge to royal authority in France before 1789.

Even before Henri III's death, Catholic leaders began to organize their resources against a Protestant succession. In September 1584 Henri Duc de Guise and his brothers, the Duc de Mayenne and Cardinal of Guise, formed an association, known as the Catholic League, to prevent Navarre's succession. At the end of December 1584 they met with representatives of Spain and signed the Treaty of Joinville, whereby Philip II offered the League monthly subsidies to levy an army to fight against Navarre. Many Catholic nobles joined the Guises, and Henri III proved impotent in the face of the challenge to his authority from the League. Indeed in late June 1585 the king was compelled to capitulate to the League and sign the Treaty of Nemours, which stipulated that Catholicism was to be the only religion practised in France. The treaty did not explicitly recognize the Cardinal of Bourbon as Henri's successor, but a few months afterwards Pope Sixtus V nullified Navarre's right to the throne by declaring him a relapsed Catholic. Although Navarre's supporters tried to make light of this act, which was described as a 'paper shot' or 'feeble fier-flash' in Christopher Fetherstone's English translation of Hotman's *Brutum Fulmen*, the Huguenots and Navarre were in reality very much on the defensive, forced to fight for their survival.[49]

News of these events struck fear into Elizabeth I and her ministers.[50] A Guise victory with the support of Spain would be not only a terrible setback for international Protestantism but also a major security threat for Elizabethan England. None the less, already committed to military action in the Low Countries and hearing rumours of an impending invasion from Spain, the queen felt unable to send troops to France. All the same, she could hardly leave Navarre and the Huguenots to the fate spelled out in the Nemours treaty or permit the League as an ally of the Spanish king to win control of France. Consequently, she agreed to contribute to the pay of German mercenaries who would fight for Navarre. She also fruitlessly tried to persuade Henri III to declare Guise a traitor and take up forces against the Catholic League himself. Instead the king raised an army under his favourite the Duc de Joyeuse, which took to the field against Navarre in the west.

With the help of the German mercenaries Navarre invaded Lorraine and Champagne, and in 1587 a series of campaigns took place which became known as the 'War of the Three Henris' (Henri de Guise, Henri de Navarre and Henri III). The most significant engagement of the war was the pitched battle of Coutras, made known to Londoners in a John Wolfe publication. Here Navarre scored a notable and unexpected victory over the royal army, leaving more than 3,000 of the enemy killed including Joyeuse.[51] Although the war left no side the overall winner, Henri III came out of it the weakest and soon afterwards was put under intense pressure from the League. In January 1588 its leaders presented him with a number of tough demands, and in May 1588 the Duc de Guise mounted a direct challenge to the king when he entered Paris with a small retinue in defiance of royal orders and to the delight of the crowd. When Henri III reacted by sending a detachment of Swiss troops into the capital, the Parisians erected barricades and attacked the king's soldiers. Ignominiously Henri escaped to Chartres, where he published a declaration (translated into English and printed in London), claiming unconvincingly that his departure was merely to prevent further damage and danger to the city.[52] Soon afterwards Henri capitulated to the League, agreeing to almost all their demands of the previous January. He also recognized the Cardinal of Bourbon as his closest male relative, and appointed the Duc de Guise as lieutenant-general of the realm.

Henri III, however, took his revenge on the Guises at the end of the year. On Christmas Eve 1588 the duke was assassinated by the king's personal guards in the royal château at Blois. Other members of the Guise family and prominent Leaguers were arrested at the same time, and the following day the Cardinal of Guise was murdered in his cell.

These proceedings were presented in one Huguenot account printed in London as 'extraordinarie, but necessarie, and not at all to be condemned considering the circumstances'. Indeed, in the writer's view, the murders could be considered an act of 'God's justice upon carnell men destitute of the right knowledge of God', an opinion no doubt shared by Protestants in England.[53] But Paris and other cities loyal to the League were horrified by the murders and rejected Henri III's explanation that he had acted in self-defence.[54] The Sorbonne pronounced the king's deposition, Parisian preachers defended regicide, and the League re-formed itself around the Duc de Mayenne, the younger brother of the Duc de Guise. Politically isolated, militarily weak and desperately short of money, Henri III had little choice but to come to terms with Henri de Navarre, who had managed to hold on to his position in southern France. In late March 1589, the two Henris signed a truce, described by Elizabeth's Lord Treasurer as 'the work of God for our good', and they then combined their forces to march on Paris.[55] Not surprisingly, the king's behaviour intensified the hatred of many Catholics, who urged his death. On the morning of 22 July 1589 a fanatical friar, who had listened to inflammatory sermons of this kind, was received into the royal camp at Saint-Cloud and then fatally stabbed the king in the abdomen, an act condemned in a discourse 'Englished out of the French copie' as 'verily utterlie unworthy a christian', since regicide was proscribed in the Scriptures. Before dying the following night, Henri III named Navarre his heir, but, despite this endorsement, some of his captains refused to accept the Huguenot leader as their legitimate ruler and abandoned the royal army.[56] Weakened by their desertions, Navarre lifted the siege on Paris.

Elizabeth's government was kept well informed of all these events by agents of Navarre and the English ambassador attending upon Henri III, while Londoners could read of them in newsletters and other publications. The number of works printed about France during the period of conflict over the succession is staggering: between 1585 and 1595 nearly 150 translations of French pamphlets and books concerning the religious wars are known to have been published in London. A peak was reached between 1588 and 1590 when between fifty and seventy translations appeared. During 1590 alone, thirty-eight news items (including pamphlets, ditties, ballads and letters) dealing with events in France were licensed by the Stationers' Company.[57]

After Henri III's assassination and with Navarre in desperate straits, Elizabeth could no longer hold back from more direct intervention. In 1589, therefore, she offered the new and as yet uncrowned French king £40,000 in loans and reluctantly agreed to send English troops to fight in Normandy. Before they were dispatched, however, Henri IV had won another unexpected victory, this time over the Duc de Mayenne's superior forces at Arques (near Dieppe) in September 1589; according to a contemporary newsletter, Henri had set forth with 9,000 men against an army of 25,000 'knowing that God could as well vanquish with a small as a great number'.[58] His 'happy' victory briefly led Elizabeth to reconsider the necessity of sending English reinforcements, but, despite her misgivings, an English army of about 4,000 men under Lord Willoughby joined Henri IV and participated in an attack on Paris. The royal army, however, could not take the strongly defended city and so resumed its campaign in Normandy and Maine, where in March 1590 Henri IV won his memorable victory over Mayenne at Ivry. Although no Englishmen fought in the battle, Ivry was celebrated in England in at least one 'excellent Ditty', a large woodcut ballad and four newsletters as 'the most notable victorie that of late was heard of' and one that came from God.[59]

Henri followed up his success at Ivry with another siege of Paris. This one lasted from April until the end of August 1590 and inflicted terrible suffering on the city's inhabitants. Historians have estimated that some 13,000 people died from hunger in the siege, and one of the newsletters published by Wolfe described the famine in graphic terms for its readers:

> They [the citizens] are enforced to eate Horses, Asses, Dogges, Cattes, Rattes, Mice and other filthie and unaccustomed things for their sustenance, yea that which is more odious in respect of their necessitie, it is sayd that they are enforced to feede one upon

an other: and that through feeblenesse and want of victuals they fall downe dead in the streetes and in their houses.

This human tragedy was not viewed by Wolfe's reporter with much sympathy but rather as a divine punishment; 'the extreame famine', he pronounced, God had sent as a 'sharpe messenger of revenge' for the Massacre of St Bartholomew and the Parisians' rebellion against their sovereign.[60] Despite their great hardship, the Parisians did not capitulate and were eventually rescued when Philip II of Spain ordered Alexander Farnese, Duke of Parma (his commander in the Low Countries), to invade France and relieve the capital. Parma seized a town on the river Marne which allowed supplies to enter Paris, and then took the town of Corbeil, where, it was reported, 'all the Inhabitants [were] wofully put to the sword' before he withdrew to the Low Countries.[61] Spanish involvement in the succession crisis in France was further stepped up when Philip II put forward his daughter, the infanta Isabella Clara Eugenia, as a candidate for the French throne on the death of Charles de Bourbon in May 1590. Although some leaders of the League would not accept her claim, the danger grew that France might become a satellite of Spain if Henri IV failed to impose his rule on his rebellious subjects.

Spanish intervention induced Elizabeth to send more help to Henri IV. During 1591 armies under Sir Roger Williams and the Earl of Essex arrived in Normandy to participate in a siege to take Rouen. In May the same year, Sir John Norris arrived in Paimpol in Brittany at the head of some 3,000 men with instructions to join up with the Prince de Dombes, Henri IV's governor of the province. Historians have tended to be highly critical about both these operations, as Norris's men achieved little in Brittany and the siege of Rouen was an expensive failure, wasting thousands of soldiers' lives and over £35,000 of the queen's money. Londoners, however, were soon receiving news of military success. Thanks to 'the wonderful paines and continuall travel of Sir John Norreys', the town of Guingamp 'is rendered to the Prince D'ombes [sic]', reported one of John Wolfe's correspondents.[62] Skirmishes during the summer in which English soldiers performed 'with valour and reputation' were likewise described, and Williams in some accounts was the hero of the hour; 'like a true Christian knight' he threw himself and his men against the superior forces of the enemy and obtained a 'wonderfull victorie' against the governor of Dieppe. Praise was given to God and psalms sung in the English camp.[63]

By September 1591, though, the news from France was less encouraging. Pamphlets were reporting disagreements between the English and French commanders in Brittany and disaffection among the English soldiers who 'have borne the entire burden of this Sommer's service'.[64] In April 1592 Elizabeth heard of serious setbacks in Brittany, but no reports of these reverses appeared in the press. The siege of Rouen also progressed badly. Despite reports of Anglo-French bravery and the distress experienced by Rouen's inhabitants, the town could not be taken, and Essex was recalled to England leaving Williams in charge of a dwindling English force. At last in April 1592 the siege was lifted when Parma arrived with 12,000 infantry and 4,000 horsemen. No battle took place between the two armies, merely skirmishes in which it was reported that only six Englishmen were slain and twenty wounded.[65] Parma too suffered a wound and soon afterwards retired to the Low Countries, where he died towards the end of the year.

The military campaigns proved no more decisive elsewhere during 1592, and Henri IV came to recognize that he could win outright victory and secure his throne only by turning Catholic.[66] Informal talks with Mayenne and other League leaders took place throughout 1592, but it was only in May 1593 that Henri revealed his decision to receive Catholic instruction. Rumours that he had abjured reached London in June 1593, and Elizabeth, it was reported, 'stormed at first but it is believed that nought would come of the matter'.[67] The general disbelief was understandable, for Henri's declaration before the city of Paris in July 1590 had been widely recounted: 'neyther this Crowne, nor the Empire of all the whole earth were able to make me change the Religion wherein I have bene brought uppe and instructed from my mothers pappes, and the which I uphold to be true'.[68] Elizabeth, however, needed to be certain and therefore sent an envoy to France to discover the truth. When the news was confirmed, she was publicly furious and threatened to recall her troops from Normandy and Brittany.

Henri IV's abjuration was not announced in any newsletter from France, although the truce that followed between Henri and the League was printed, as was a detailed description of the anointing and crowning of the king in a Catholic ceremony at Chartres in February 1594. Although some later histories wrote of Henri's conversion (with approval or contempt, depending on the author's religion), one short biography written by an Englishman ignored it totally.[69] The abjuration was undoubtedly a grievous blow for many in England. Throughout the recent wars, the king had emerged as a Protestant hero; in printed works he had been portrayed as God's champion – as David from the Old Testament and St George against the dragon – and his war against the League was presented as a struggle 'for the recovery of his right and advancement of God's glory'.[70]

Although some Catholics doubted his sincerity, Henri's abjuration won him the loyalty of most of his kingdom. In March 1594 he entered Paris and in the autumn he reached an agreement with the Pope. Philip II of Spain, however, still refused to recognize his legitimacy and continued to supply aid to the areas of League resistance in France. In January 1595, therefore, Henri declared war on Spain in the hope that it would unite France against a foreign enemy. Londoners kept abreast of these developments through the usual channel of newsletters and gossip.[71] Henri tried to persuade Elizabeth to remain his ally and keep her troops in France, but she refused on the grounds that they were needed to suppress rebellion in Ireland. Furthermore, England was beginning to suffer from war-weariness, and the City of London was having difficulty in levying its quotas of men, while desertions were common.

Despite Elizabeth's intention to disengage totally from the war in France, she briefly intervened during emergencies when English interests were at stake. She ordered some 3,000 men to Brittany in July 1594, when news was confirmed that the Spaniards had finished fortifications within the port of Crozon and were intending to send a fleet there. Sir John Norris arrived at the beginning of September, and during a three-month operation both Morlaix and Crozon were captured. But the victory in Brittany was marred by the deaths of Sir Anthony Wingfield, the Sergeant-Major General (shot through the bowels), and Sir Martin Frobisher (from a slight wound which turned gangrenous). None the less, on the queen's accession day in November 1594, three flags captured from the Spaniards in the campaign were presented to her, while Norris was hailed as a hero.[72]

Elizabeth had also intended English troops to participate in the defence of Calais when the town was suddenly attacked by an army from Flanders in April 1596. Some 6,000 soldiers were levied in England to protect the French town, and on Easter Sunday 1,000 armed men were levied in the City of London. But, before they arrived in Dover, news arrived that the citadel had fallen; one report said that the French soldiers defending it had easily surrendered to the Spaniards, declaring, 'If the Spaniards win it, yet there is good hope by mediation of the Church to regain it; but if the English repossess it, they will never restore it.'[73] Soon after this loss, England joined with France and the Low Countries in a formal Triple Alliance against Spain.

The Franco-Spanish war came to an end in May 1598. Henri IV made a separate peace with Philip III of Spain at Vervins, shortly after the last of the League's commanders had capitulated. Although Elizabeth's government was dismayed at Henri's unilateral withdrawal from the Triple Alliance, a translation of French verses celebrating the peace was printed in London, in which Henri IV was extravagantly lauded as France's saviour.[74] The Edict of Nantes, which provided the Huguenots with a degree of toleration and ended for a time the religious conflict, was also printed with approval. From then onwards, printers and booksellers showed little interest in France. It was only Henri IV's assassination that attracted wide coverage. Reports of Henri's 'deplorable' murder, descriptions of his funeral and the coronation of his young son Louis XIII, together with histories and poetical panegyrics praising the late king as a 'thundring Jove' and 'all-conquering Mars', all hit the presses in 1610 and 1611.[75] Readers with a taste for the gruesome could also peruse a sensationalist account of the assassin's 'strange execution' and the tortures that had led to his death, a report which was justified on the grounds that it provided 'an example of terror made knowne to the world to convert all bloody minded traitors from the like enterprise'.[76]

During the regency of Marie de' Medici a small number of newsletters filtered through to England. A few were published that dealt with events likely to cause anxiety among English Protestants: the 1612 alliance with Spain and Louis's marriage to the infanta of Spain.[77] On the other hand fears that France might succumb to another bout of internal unrest during a period of monarchical weakness were probably allayed by the publication of Louis's confirmation of the Edict of Nantes in 1613 and the peace terms agreed in 1616 between the regent and the Prince de Condé, who was threatening an armed rising.[78]

SPAIN AND THE LOW COUNTRIES

By the late 1580s, the Low Countries had been in revolt against their ruler Philip II of Spain for some twenty years. The revolt began in 1566 when the minor nobility presented Philip's regent, Margaret of Savoy, with a petition demanding religious toleration, the grandees refused to carry out orders to suppress heresy in their regions, and Calvinist preachers in the summer months incited disaffected crowds in towns throughout the Low Countries to pillage churches and destroy images. Clearly religious unrest was a crucial factor in creating discontent and encouraging violence, but political conflicts between the nobility and their absentee ruler as well as the economic grievances of the general populace, stimulated by a trade recession and bad harvests, also lay at the heart of the troubles.[79]

The initial noble opposition and popular violence were in fact quickly suppressed by the regent. None the less, Philip II decided on strong-arm tactics to crush all opposition and punish disobedience, and in 1567 he sent the Duke of Alva to Brussels with a force of 10,000 men to take control and execute reprisals. Under Alva's command, some 12,000 people implicated in the rebellion were put on trial, almost 9,000 were condemned to lose part or all of their goods, and over 1,000 were executed, including the main noble opposition leaders. At the same time Alva's government attempted to stamp out all heresy, with the result that some 60,000 Protestants fled abroad, to England, France and Germany.[80] Despite Alva's repression and military strength, a new revolt broke out in 1572 within the towns of Holland and Zeeland, which spread to the south in the mid-1570s after Spanish troops mutinied for lack of pay and went on the rampage in several towns, most notably Antwerp in 1574 and 1576.

The Protestants who arrived in London as well as English merchants who were working in Antwerp (England's main trading partner) did much to publicize the horrors of the Duke of Alva's regime. Londoners were also given the viewpoint of the rebels in a small number of printed books and translated documents. They could, for example, read an English translation of the declaration of William of Orange, the acknowledged leader of the noble opposition by 1568, which explained 'the cause of his necessary defence against the Duke of Alba', and could learn that his actions were not intended as rebellion against his sovereign but to protect his country against the 'unspeakable iniuryes and villanies that are daily committed by the soldiers of the sayd Duke of Alba'.[81] Yet relatively few polemical works supporting the rebel cause were licensed in the early years of the revolt, and no reports appeared in English describing the Spanish massacres at Mechelen, Zutphen and Naarden in 1572 or Haarlem in 1573. No doubt this restraint was deliberate governmental policy, for, despite pressure from some of her councillors to send aid to the rebels, Elizabeth tried to maintain cordial relations with Spain and pose as neutral in the dispute between Philip and his subjects, even though in practice she permitted some covert help to be provided for Orange and his followers.

The sack of Antwerp in 1576 was by contrast well reported in England. With some 8,000 deaths and 1,000 houses destroyed, this major incident could hardly be ignored. Throughout Europe paintings, engravings, books and ballads were produced memorializing the occasion. In England, horrified English merchants and soldiers then present in Antwerp first passed on the news to friends and contacts in London; soon afterwards a spate of ballads and pamphlets were written telling of the terrible destruction, looting and murders.[82] The writer and poet George Gascoigne, who was in the city at the time, wrote a pamphlet (printed anonymously soon afterwards) which described in moving terms the 'outrageous crueltie' of the Spanish soldiers who murdered the town's inhabitants not only 'when the chase was hot' but also in cold blood when they were 'victors without resystaunce', sparing 'neither friende nor foe'. Gascoigne also wrote a play *A Larum for London, or The Siedge of Antwerpe* (printed in 1602 but performed earlier), which similarly described the cold-blooded butchery. In both works Gascoigne fell back on conspiracy theories and presented the sack as a premeditated affair designed by the Spaniards 'to strip her [the city] of her pouches'.[83]

Writers used the sack of Antwerp as an opportunity not only to berate Catholic Spain but also to pronounce a word of warning for complacent Londoners. One ballad of 1577 dwelt little on Spanish cruelties but preferred to draw from Antwerp's fate a cautionary lesson for cities like London which were falling into sin:

> Be vigilant, sleepe not in sin:
> Lest that thy foe doo enter in.[84]

The figure Time, at the end of Gascoigne's play, came up with a similar moral, intoning that Antwerp's miseries

> May be a meane all Cities to affrighte,
> How they in sinne and pleasure take delight.

Another English writer took from the experience a more specific message. That such a powerful and rich a city as Antwerp could suffer such a fate should teach London the futility of relying on its wealth for security. Instead its citizens needed to build up a body of professional soldiers and encourage martial arts:

> But Antwerpe thou thy woful wracke, thy spoyle hath proved plain
> Where martiall minded do want, no state in safety may remaine.[85]

After the sack of Antwerp and the escalation of the revolt to the southern provinces of the Low Countries, Elizabeth came under great pressure to give aid to the rebels. By this time the northern provinces had withdrawn from the allegiance of Philip II, and William of Orange offered sovereignty to Elizabeth in 1576. The queen turned down the invitation promptly, but over the next few years she toyed with, and then rejected, the idea of sending the rebels a contingent of English troops. Instead she assisted their cause by sponsoring expeditions by John Casimir of the Palatinate and François Duc d'Anjou against the Spanish army. By late 1584, however, Elizabeth was persuaded that there was no alternative but to dispatch an English army to the Low Countries in order to prevent their conquest by Spain. Earlier in the year William of Orange had been assassinated (an event strangely ignored in works printed in England), which left the rebels leaderless. Furthermore, the refusal of Henri III to enter a league against Spain and send a force to Flanders meant the rebels could no longer count on any assistance from France. Yet aid to the rebels was urgently needed because the politically astute and militarily gifted Duke of Parma had recently taken the towns of Bruges, Ghent and Brussels, and was beginning the siege of Antwerp. For all these reasons Elizabeth opened up negotiations with representatives of the Low Countries, and in August and September 1585 she signed the treaties of Nonsuch, which promised them some 6,400 infantry, 1,000 cavalry and loans of £126,000 per annum. These treaties were in effect a declaration of war against Spain, and by the end of the year an English army under the Earl of Leicester was stationed at Flushing and Sir Francis Drake had attacked the Cape Verde islands and was on his way to wreak destruction on the Spanish Indies.

The war was presented to Elizabeth's subjects as both a fight against Spanish tyranny and a godly struggle against the enemies of Christ. In a declaration published at home and abroad explaining her decision, Elizabeth focused on the former, but prayers composed for the safety of Leicester's army stressed the religious dimension, petitioning God to 'take the wicked by the heele' and provide help against 'thy enemies, which disturb thy peace and afflicte our poore neighbours of the Lowe countries', just as He had enabled Joshua to defeat the five kings and Abraham to punish the sinners of Sodom and Gomorrah.[86]

Leicester's campaign of duty, however, was hardly a great success. The treaties of Nonsuch were signed too late to prevent the fall of Antwerp, while the arrival of English troops failed to save the port of Sluis from capture. The death of Sir Philip Sidney from a musket wound incurred at the battle of Zutphen in September 1586 was a demoralizing blow for the English, although supporters of the war stage-managed the state funeral which took place at St Paul's the following February to make the procession resemble a military triumph. At the same time, Sidney's life and death were memorialized in panegyric verse which compared the young soldier to Alexander and Hector, and praised his chivalry and fame.[87] Another blow for the English army was the treachery of Sir William Stanley and Rowland Yorke, who handed over the towns of Deventer and Zutphen respectively to Parma in early 1587.[88] Leicester meanwhile quarrelled with the Dutch and angered Elizabeth by accepting sovereignty of the Low Countries against her orders; in the autumn of 1587 the earl finally retired from duty, leaving Lord Willoughby as general of the English troops.

By contrast the sea campaign against Spain was a resounding success. In 1586 Drake burned and looted Spanish settlements in the West Indies, and in 1587 he attacked the Spanish and Portuguese coast, sinking or capturing twenty to thirty ships in the raid on Cadiz. These exploits were widely publicized in England, and Drake was praised for several years afterwards in verse and prose reports, where he was compared to classical and Old Testament heroes, while the Spanish king took on the guise of God's enemies – Pharoah, Amalek and Nimrod. [89]

Outraged by the intervention of Leicester and the incursions of Drake, Philip II immediately put into operation a project to invade England and overthrow the Elizabethan regime. His plans inevitably could not be kept secret and news of the construction of a Spanish Armada was circulating around Europe years before it was launched in the summer of 1588.[90] The Armada's defeat was greeted in England with great relief, jubilation and thanks for God's blessing, some of the reactions being spontaneous, some orchestrated by the government. The queen attended a grand service of thanksgiving at St Paul's in

November; ballads and woodcuts were disseminated to celebrate England's triumph and God's providence; pamphlets were written spreading the news to foreign courts; and artefacts (fireguards and cushions, for example) were produced to mark the English victory. Forty years afterwards, the Armada remained part of patriotic and anti-Catholic discourse; sermons continued to thank God for England's delivery from the Spanish invasion, while images of the Armada were still incorporated in engravings, paintings and 'monuments' to be placed in private homes or parish churches.[91]

The English war against Spain did not end with the Armada; indeed two new military fronts opened up in 1589 when Sir John Norris led an expedition to Portugal (which ended disastrously) and Lord Willoughby was sent to fight alongside Henri IV in France. The war also continued in the Low Countries, where Orange's second son Count Maurice of Nassau took charge of the Dutch field army and proved a very able commander. Between 1590 and 1594 he began a successful campaign to drive the Spanish army out of the inland provinces of the north. In 1591 with the crucial help of a small English contingent under the command of Willoughby's replacement, Sir Francis Vere, Nassau recaptured Zutphen and Deventer.[92] From there they went on to take a number of Friesland towns until at last in July 1594 Groningen fell and the Spanish army was pushed out of the northern provinces.

Although historically more significant, Nassau's victories before 1594 did not seem to engender the same degree of popular excitement in England as did his campaigns in Brabant and Flanders after 1597. By the late 1590s the prince had no rival for public attention and his successful battles were recounted in newsletters, ballads and at least one play. There was also a 1613 translation of a French history of his campaigns, which was reprinted in 1620.[93] Many Englishmen not only were gripped by the thrilling tales of battle but also cared about his cause, especially since English troops were fighting alongside him. As John Chamberlain explained in June 1602,

> I begin to have an extraordinarie care of them [the United
> Provinces] and me thinckes beare a great venture with them,

now we are so far ingaged in honor and have eight thousand
English in theyre camp, which is the greatest number of
disciplined men of our nation that hath ben seen together in
our age.[94]

Although historians today play down the importance of Nassau's later
campaigns and victories, contemporaries were deeply impressed by
them, particularly his two most famous battles, Turnhout in Brabant
and Nieupoort in Flanders. One hyperbolic newsletter written by an
Englishman described Turnhout (January 1597) as 'the greatest and
most notable victorie' in the civil wars against Spain, and highly
praised the English role in the military encounter, patriotically
attributing 'the greatest part of the honor of that daie's victory' to
Sir Robert Sidney, the lord governor of Flushing, and also commending
Sir Francis Vere. What made an impression on this writer was that so
few men were slain on Nassau's side while 2,300 of the enemy lay dead
on the field and all the Spanish ensigns were taken.[95] Historians,
however, point out that the victory did not result in any long-term
strategic gain, since there was no follow-up.

Similarly the role of Vere and his 1,600 English troops at Nieupoort
(June 1600) was embellished in many of the triumphalist written and
spoken accounts of the famous victory. According to Chamberlain, one
semi-official oral report of the battle was 'so partiall, as yf no man had
stroke strike but the English, and among the English no man almost but
Sir Fra: Vere'. Vere's role, which was certainly distinguished, was also
given undue prominence in a godly ballad and a newsletter purporting
to be composed by an Englishman. Contemporaries tended to inflate the
significance of the battle as well: 'But suere', wrote Chamberlain, 'yt is
the greatest battayle, and best fought that hath ben betwixt two
disciplined armies in our time in christendome.' It seemed to many that
for the first time the Spaniards had been beaten in the open field, since
they had reportedly lost at least 6,000 men and over 100 ensigns,
while their commander Archduke Albert, the governor of the Spanish
Netherlands, had allegedly been wounded and fled the battle scene.[96]
The victory, claimed a ballad, rescued England's friends from the

servitude of Spain and would banish idolatry from Flanders.[97] Again, historians are more sceptical about the extent of the victory, pointing out that the allies suffered heavy losses, that Albert was soon able to reinforce his depleted army, and that Nassau made no strategic gain in Flanders, not even the town and castle of Nieupoort.

Over the next few years, Nassau repeatedly failed to follow up individual victories and take control of the south. As a result, some Londoners began to question his strategy and think less well of his abilities, although he continued to be lauded in print. In October 1602 Chamberlain for one criticized the previous summer's campaign as 'a perambulation to no purpose'.[98] Chamberlain was also concerned at the length of the Spanish siege of Ostend, which started in late June 1601 and did not end until 1604. News dribbled through to London of the state of the English garrison in Ostend and the bombardments of the Spanish, but Londoners were perhaps most aware of the siege because of the 'violent' impressment of men for service there and the call for volunteers 'with sound of drumme'.[99]

There can be little doubt that England was suffering from acute war-weariness by the end of Elizabeth's reign. On both land and sea, spectacular victories had been few and far between; the sack of Cadiz in August 1596 was treated as a greater victory than it really was when a 'great triumph was made at London' but there had been little cause for celebration thereafter.[100] The toll on manpower and the economy, meanwhile, was causing discontent in many parts of England. Peace discussions had been held at various times, but it was only after James I's accession that terms could be agreed. The Treaty of London, signed in August 1604, ended the Anglo-Spanish war on terms which were on the whole favourable to England, although disliked by many London merchants. The Dutch chose not to join the discussions that led up to the peace but, thanks to French mediation, they signed a Twelve Year Truce with Spain in 1609.

With this truce it seemed as if a new phase of international peace was about to begin, but perspicacious readers of newsletters and other printed works would have been able to detect ominous signs of future religious and political conflicts. The formation of the Protestant Union partly in response to a disputed succession in the duchies of Cleves-Jülich, and the fighting which broke out in 1614 over the same issue, exposed religious tensions in the Holy Roman Empire as well as the continuing distrust between Spain and the Dutch.[101] Similarly, the 1609 'troubles' in Prague between Protestants and Catholics who were 'ready to go together by the eares, the one against the other' and the emperor's promulgation of the Letter of Majesty granting freedom of worship in an attempt to bring religious peace were also warnings that confessional disputes were not a thing of the past.[102]

CONCLUSION

During the lifetime of William Shakespeare, Europe's wars of religion dominated accounts of the political affairs of Europe, bringing in their wake regicide, political assassinations, judicial murders, sectarian massacres and civic violence. For many English men and women these horrific events were both a warning of the workings of divine providence and an object lesson in what might lie ahead, should a Spanish invasion or disputed succession destroy the Elizabethan peace. Unlike other playwrights, Shakespeare did not draw on European current affairs for the plots of his plays, but his Roman and history plays did confront many of the issues that arose from them: the nature of tyranny, the consequences of regicide, and the terrible destruction caused by civil and international wars. Given the level of printed material and gossip about contemporary European events in London, Shakespeare's audiences would surely have found in these themes much of political relevance.

Chapter Two

ENGLISH CONTACT WITH EUROPE

Michael G. Brennan

SHAKESPEARE'S NON-SPECIFIC CONTINENTAL GEOGRAPHIES

And I shall lose my life for want of language.
If there be here German, or Dane, Low Dutch,
Italian, or French, let him speak to me.

(AW 4.1.70–2)

These panic-stricken words are spoken by the cowardly Frenchman Parolles outside the military camp at Florence during the Tuscan wars as he is seized and blindfolded by some of his fellow nationals. But they serve only to prompt his captors into a mischievous teasing of his real ignorance of foreign tongues. Their flurry of guttural gobbledegook – '*Throca movousus ... Boskos thromuldo boskos ... Oscotbidulchos volivorco*' – underlines Parolles's comic unsuitability for military action on the continental stage. As a parochial parasite of Bertram, Count of Roussillon, Parolles's irritating posturing as a wordly-wise soldier and traveller, who has 'a smack of all neighbouring languages', is cruelly exposed by his fellow officers. In an earlier play, *The Two Gentlemen of Verona*, Shakespeare had specifically addressed this kind of problematic innocence among young men who had no firsthand experience of other countries. 'Home-keeping youth have ever homely wits,' Valentine advises Proteus, as he dreams of seeing 'the wonders of the world abroad' rather than staying 'dully sluggardis'd at home' (*TGV* 1.1.2–7).

A well-planned programme of time spent overseas was seen to offer a means of broadening the mind and tempering prejudices and super-stitions, as the worldly Panthino explains to Proteus's father, Antonio, in an eloquent endorsement of educational travel:

> He [Antonio's brother] wonder'd that your lordship
> Would suffer him [Proteus] to spend his youth at home,
> While other men, of slender reputation,
> Put forth their sons to seek preferment out:
> Some to the wars, to try their fortune there;
> Some, to discover islands far away;
> Some, to the studious universities.
> For any, or for all these exercises,
> He said that Proteus, your son, was meet,
> And did request me to importune you
> To let him spend his time no more at home;
> Which would be great impeachment to his age,
> In having known no travel in his youth.
>
> (*TGV* 1.3.4–16)[1]

Shakespeare, it might be assumed from these lines, well understood the growing importance attached by his contemporaries to a firsthand knowledge of the geographies and customs of continental countries. But, pointedly, the opening scene of *Two Gentlemen* offers no physical description of Verona (we only know from the title that it is located there); and Milan exists simply as the place from where Valentine will hopefully send letters about his love-affairs. The situation is rendered even more confusing by the earliest surviving text of the play (in the 1623 folio) in which the Duke of Milan appears to think that he rules over Verona (3.1.81); and, when clearly in Milan, Speed heartily welcomes Launce to Padua (2.5.1). But, on another level, geographical exactitude perhaps has little to do with the play's memorably cosmopolitan appeal. This lies far more in Shakespeare's dramatic reworking in *Two Gentlemen* of the prose romance story of 'Felix and Felismena' from Montemayor's *Diana* – a pan-European bestseller written in Spanish by a native of Portugal who had worked in Spain, visited England and resided in the Italian Piedmont. In this case Shakespeare's purpose on stage, it seems, was not to create a tangible Verona and Milan but rather to utilize their nominal allure to position his play within the current orbit of continental literary fashion.

In political terms, as Shakespeare perhaps knew (since, as *All's Well* demonstrates, he was aware of the Tuscan wars), Verona's early modern history had been marked by the violent dynastic struggles of the papal Guelfs and the imperial Ghibellines, followed by the more peaceful rule of the della Scala family (one of whom, Cangrande I, had protected Dante Alighieri after he became a political exile in 1302 from his native Florence). But when Shakespeare was drafting another Italianate romance of the mid-1590s the grand historical clashes of Verona's civic past were largely ignored in favour of the more localized and domestic hostilities between the families of two of its young citizens, Romeo Montague and Juliet Capulet: 'Two households both alike in dignity, / (In fair Verona, where we lay our scene)' (*RJ* Prologue), who were reputed to have lived during the reign of Cangrande I's elder brother, Bartolomeo della Scala.[2]

While geographical and historical exactitude may be of only secondary importance to a writer of dramatized fictions, the fact remains that Shakespeare's Italianate settings habitually skate lightly over continental locations which would have been viewed with considerable suspicion by at least some members of his audiences. From the time of Roger Ascham's condemnation of 'filthiness of living' at Venice in *The Schoolmaster* (1570) until Joseph Hall's denunciation of the corrupting allure of Rome for young Englishmen in *Quo vadis? A Just Censure of Travel* (1617), the cities of Italy could be depicted, simultaneously, as picturesque havens for lyrical lovers or as hotbeds of spiritual and sexual decadence. A venial English youth sent 'to serve Circe in Italy', Ascham proposed, could return home utterly corrupted by 'vanity and vice': 'And so, being mules and horses before they went, returned very swine and asses home again; yet everywhere very foxes with subtle and busy heads and, where they may, very wolves with cruel malicious hearts.'[3] At the heart of this deeply paradoxical perspective lay the duality of England's own post-Reformation unease over positioning itself in relation to the rest of continental Europe. At one extreme, Protestant England became during the 1540s more defensive and proudly separatist: stances which could easily be transmuted by skilful propagandists into outright xenophobia. In contrast, eager observation by scholars, diplomats and civil servants of the flourishing royal and civic courts of France, Germany and Italy fostered a growing nationalistic desire for the emulation of continental cultural achievements.

In sharp contrast to these elevated academic ideals, like many of his contemporaries Shakespeare was not immune to the socially pervasive racial stereotyping of his continental neighbours. His plays are populated by farcical examples of the 'subtle-witted French' (*1H6* 1.1.25); the boastful and fantastic Spaniard (Don Armado, *LLL*); the 'old Italian fox' (*TS* 2.1.396) and 'poisonous-tongu'd' Italian (*Cym* 3.2.5); 'drunken Germans' (*MV* 1.2.82–7), 'hasty Germans and blunt Hollanders' (*3H6* 4.8.2) and the 'swag-bellied Hollander' (*Oth* 2.3.73). *The Comedy of Errors* memorably draws together many of these national stereotypes in Dromio's 'grand tour' of the anatomy of his kitchen-wench, who is 'spherical, like a globe … I could find out countries in her.' His stooge, Antipholus of Syracuse, mischievously asks:

ANTIPHOLUS S.   In what part of her body stands Ireland?

DROMIO S.   Marry, sir, in her buttocks; I found it out by the bogs.

ANTIPHOLUS S.   Where Scotland?

DROMIO S.   I found it by the barrenness, hard in the palm of the hand.

ANTIPHOLUS S.   Where France?

DROMIO S.   In her forehead, armed and reverted, making war against her heir.

ANTIPHOLUS S.   Where England?

DROMIO S.   I look'd for the chalky cliffs, but I could find no whiteness in them. But I guess it stood in her chin, by the salt rheum that ran between France and it.

ANTIPHOLUS S.   Where Spain?

DROMIO S.   Faith, I saw it not, but I felt it hot in her breath …

ANTIPHOLUS S.   Where stood Belgia, the Netherlands?
DROMIO S.   O, sir, I did not look so low.

(3.2.114–38)

Shakespeare was also very much intrigued by long-established superstitions about racial difference, which taught that each regional grouping had its own identifiable characteristics. Most notably the notion known as 'climate theory' proposed that western Europe could be broadly categorized into three geographical areas of 'northern' (cold), 'southern' (hot and passionate) and 'temperate' (balanced and controlled) peoples. It had been keenly debated by ancient writers (Aristotle, Hippocrates and Galen) and more recently reinvigorated through the publication of *Methodus ... ad facilem historiarum cognitionem* (1579) by the French political philosopher Jean Bodin. Certainly, one experienced continental traveller from the period, Stephen Powle, seems to have been earnestly studying his Bodin while abroad. In a long letter written in June 1581 from Strasbourg he excitedly explained to his father:

> By dividing the world into three parts, cold, temperate, and fervently hot, philosophers have noted that as air is affected with divers qualities so the minds of inhabitants be disposed by divers affections. The Northern people be strong of body, and apt to be cruel, yet very faithful and secret, of wit dull and lumpish, therefore they must be governed by force. Temperate persons be apt to speak and therefore by laws and pleadings polished. The Meridianal persons be melancholic, *propter adustam choleram*, therefore to be governed by religion and ceremonies. And it hath been observed that the Northern people have prevailed in conquest over the Southern, that the Meridian people have filled the world with arts, sciences, and ceremonies, that the Temperate climates first invented laws and pleadings.[4]

More practically minded English travellers on the hard post-roads of western Europe may have been somewhat sceptical of such neatly schematic theories, as they daily mingled with other nationalities in the acquisition of horses, coaches, food and accommodation. Firsthand observations of the mundane character foibles of the French, Germans, Dutch and Italians would have suggested more rational conclusions. Certainly Thomas Wright pointedly advised the readers of his *The Passions of the Mind* (1601) that Englishmen were in many respects little different from their continental counterparts:

> I would not have any man to thinke that I am of opinion, that all Italians and Spaniards go beyond all Englishmen in subtiltie and warinesse, for I have found divers of our nation, whom I beleeve, neyther Italian, nor Spanyard could over-reach, in what negotiations soever.[5]

SHAKESPEARE ABROAD?

Determining how much Shakespeare himself may have known about the geography and natives of western Europe is seriously hampered by the paucity of surviving biographical evidence. Interestingly (but also inconclusively), Shakespeare was residing in about 1604 with an émigré French Huguenot family called Mountjoy, near St Olave's church, Cripplegate.[6] Many readers have also been tempted to wonder whether the young Shakespeare ever ventured across the English Channel during his so-called 'lost years'?[7] There has been periodic speculation that he may have served as a soldier, perhaps in the Low Countries. Certainly, several of his plays reveal a particular sensitivity to the ravaged landscapes of continental battlefields:

> Look on thy country, look on fertile France,
> And see the cities and the towns defac'd
> By wasting ruin of the cruel foe.
>
> (*1H6* 3.3.44)

However, it should also be remembered that the enduring popularity of the idea that Shakespeare could have travelled more widely in Europe ('with long travel I am stiff and weary', *CE* 1.2.15) was in no small measure an early nineteenth-century construct, aimed at drawing the national dramatist into a growing English love-affair with all things Italian. Keats's friend, Charles Armitage Brown, claimed in *Shakespeare's Autobiographical Poems* (1838) to have deduced from the plays that Shakespeare may have traversed Italy, taking in Venice, Padua, Bologna, Florence, Pisa, Rome and Verona; and his speculations were enthusiastically endorsed by Charles Knight in his influential *William Shakespere: A Biography* (1842–3). Almost a century later, John Dover Wilson's *The Essential Shakespeare* (1932) gave these views a new spin by proposing that Shakespeare had entered the service of the Earl of Southampton during the early 1590s and met another of his employees, the Italianate John Florio (to whom Ben Jonson personally dedicated a copy of the 1606 quarto of *Volpone*). Wilson fondly imagined Shakespeare and Florio heading off to Italy together, thereby providing the dramatist with firsthand knowledge of Venetian topography.[8] But the essential letters, reports and other contemporary references to support such alluring theories are entirely missing. As Park Honan sensibly concludes, Shakespeare 'may have known the ache of a traveller's bones overseas, and peered "in maps for ports, and piers and roads" (*MV* 1.1.19) in Denmark, the Lowlands, or Italy – but we lack evidence of this'.[9]

Despite this hazy biographical context, the fact remains that Shakespeare's post-classical dramas regularly traverse the (albeit often indistinct) geographies of western Europe, especially France and Italy. In *1 Henry VI* Shakespeare's theatrical career opens within the environs of Orleans, Rouen, Paris, Bordeaux and Angiers. It moves on to Navarre for *Love's Labour's Lost* and to Roussillon, Paris, Marseille and (briefly) Florence for *All's Well*. *King John* visits Angiers and embraces a strikingly cosmopolitan cast, including a French king and his dauphin (Philip Auguste and Louis VIII); the Archduke of Austria (Limoges); a papal legate (Cardinal Pandulph); and a Castilian princess (Blanche). *Henry V*'s triumphal English nationalism is defined against the backdrop of Harfleur, Rouen, Picardy and Agincourt. Shakespeare's fictional *giro* or tour of Italy also encompasses several of the key locations popular with real travellers. An evening at the playhouse could transport a ticket-holder from Deptford or Blackfriars to Verona, Milan and a forest near Mantua (*TGV*), Verona and Mantua (*RJ*), a country house near Verona (*TS*) – did James Burbage's 'Theatre' in Shoreditch, where most of these early dramas were probably staged, possess stage props especially suited to a Veronese location? – Venice (*MV* and *Oth*) and Sicily (*MA* and *WT*). While the exotic settings of these plays in no way attempted to delineate the realities of Italian city life, they at least enabled their audiences for a few magical hours to imagine places which they were never likely to see themselves.

DIPLOMATS, EXILES AND CULTURAL EXPLORERS IN ITALY 1547–1553

The disparate assembly of aristocratic and republican city-states of Italy in the mid-sixteenth century in no sense formed a unified country; but this constitutional diversity rendered it all the more intriguing and malleable for English observers. With the dissemination of humanism during the early Tudor period, knowledge of Italy (seen both as the motherland of new learning and the enduring focus of ancient imperial civilization) was keenly sought after by the English court intelligentsia. The linguist and historian William Thomas perhaps did more than any other mid-sixteenth-century traveller to make readily accessible the history, language and civic constitutions of the Italian states. His credentials for such a role were, to say the least, unlikely. He had first made his way to Venice in 1545 as a bankrupt Protestant gambler fleeing a charge of embezzlement. After incarceration there at the behest of the English ambassador until his debts were repaid, Thomas made his way to Padua, before heading south to Bologna and Florence. There he attended the newly established Florentine academy, where his fascination with Italian language and culture flourished, sparking a parallel concern for the enhancement of his own vernacular tongue as an educational tool. The sustained dominance of these two cities as international centres of academic excellence is eloquently recalled by Shakespeare's Lucentio, who was 'brought up in Florence' before heading off to 'fair Padua, nursery of the arts ... The pleasant garden of great Italy', where he hopes to 'institute / A course of learning and ingenious studies (*TS* 1.1.2–9).[10] Lavish theatricals were also a staple part of Duke Cosimo I's Florence during the late 1540s and Thomas could have witnessed there the first performance of Nicolo Secchi's *Gli Inganni* (printed 1562), a source for *Twelfth Night*.[11]

While in Italy, Thomas put together the first Italian grammar and dictionary to be compiled by an English speaker, specifically aimed at the 'better understanding of Boccace, Petrarcha and Dante'.[12] At Florence he also probably began to draft *The History of Italy* (1549). Thomas's *History* offered its English readers a comparative consideration of Italy's great city-states, including Venice, Naples, Florence, Genoa and Milan, thereby demonstrating 'what profit they may gather by traveling therein' (dedication to John Dudley, Earl of Warwick). Venice, depicted as a cosmopolitan and commercial utopia, synthesized for Thomas the very best that Italy could offer in terms of political and mercantile models. Venice's constitution (with its elections, ballots and the interdependent relationship of the doge with his elected councils) offered a working model of democratic government which clearly intrigued him. Above all, its upholding of the absolute liberty of the individual in both spiritual and personal matters was a subject of unambiguous wonder for this itinerant Englishman:

> he that dwelleth in Venice may reckon himself exempt from subjection. For no man there marketh another's doings, or that meddleth with another man's living. If thou be a papist, there shalt thou want no kind of superstition to feed upon. If thou be a gospeler, no man shall ask why thou comest not to church. If thou be a Jew, a Turk, or believest in the devil (so thou spread not thine opinions abroad), thou art free from all controlment. To live married or unmarried, no man shall ask them why.[13]

Envisaged as an educational guide to continental statecraft, Thomas's *History* also traced, in contrast to Venice, the more problematic tensions between liberty and tyranny in the histories of Florence, Genoa and Milan. There was an unmistakably Machiavellian flavour to Thomas's interpretations, in that Florence (formerly destabilized by the factious Guelfs and Ghibellines – 'The Tuscan service ... may serve / A nursery to our gentry, who are sick / For breathing and exploit', *AW* 1.2.13–17) had been peaceably unified by the ruthlessness of the Medici. The unwavering justice and sexual morality of Cosimo I is firmly praised alongside his benign omnipotence:

> He hath divers fair children by his wife and loveth her so well that in manner he never goeth abroad (unless it be to church) without her and is reputed to be a very chaste man. He is learned and wise; he useth few words and is nevertheless in his own tongue eloquent. In the administration of justice he is so sincere that since the time of his reign, which is now above ten years, I have not heard that he hath pardoned any person condemned to die. He hath restrained the vice of sodomy (which heretofore reigned more in Florence than elsewhere in Italy) with pain of death and hath brought his state to such quietness as it hath not been this 300 year past; so that Florence may well say that in him she hath found her long-desired liberty.

In contrast, the great military and trading port of Genoa, with its enduring antagonisms between its populace and aristocracy, had enjoyed a period of stability under the firm rule of Andria Doria, only for the self-destructive insurrections of the Fieschi and Cibo to break out while Thomas was still in Italy. Acutely sensitive to these social instabilities, Thomas immediately homed in on the relative libertinism of its citizens, in a way which inevitably brings to mind the touching Shakespearean scene with Juliet 'above at a window' and Romeo below in the Capulet orchard (*RJ* 2.1):

> I saw in no place where women have so much liberty. For it is lawful there openly to talk of love with what wife soever she be, insomuch that I have seen young men of reputation, standing in the street, talk of love with young mistresses, being in their windows above, and openly rehearse verses that they had made one to the other.[14]

It is noticeable that Thomas's description of the apparently innocent lovemaking of the Genoese during the late 1540s, like that of the fictionalized Romeo and Juliet at Verona, takes place against (and is perhaps symptomatic of) a background of factional unrest and murderous violence. By blending his careful historical and constitutional expositions with this kind of telling sociological detail, Thomas offered his readers – and it is tempting to wonder if Shakespeare ever browsed through this elegantly written and imaginative volume – a compelling insight into the achievements of Italian civic humanism, ducal absolutism and democratic republicanism.[15]

Back in England, Thomas was appointed through the influence of his patron, John Dudley, to the prestigious position of Clerk to the Privy Council. In this capacity, he also drafted a series of heavily Machiavellian discourses (paraphrasing key passages from the *Discorsi* and *Il Principe*) for the young king, thereby casting himself in the potent role of an Italianate educator of the English monarch. Italy, however, was not the only focus of Thomas's attention. In 1551 he joined the Marquis of Northampton's embassy to France to present Henri II with the Order of the Garter, as part of an ambitious plan (largely formulated by Dudley) to win his daughter's hand for Edward VI. If this remarkable (but now largely forgotten) act of marital diplomacy had succeeded, the dynastic and cultural implications of a harmonious Anglo-French unification could well have changed the course of England's relationship with western Europe for the rest of the century. As Queen Isabel points out in *Henry V* at the marriage of Henry and Katherine (perhaps echoing both this diplomatic venture and the 1579/80 marriage proposals for Elizabeth and François, Duc d'Anjou; see p. 72), such a match would have ensured henceforth 'That English may as French, French Englishmen, / Receive each other' (5.2.359–60).

ENGLISH VIEWS OF FRANCE AND ITALY DURING THE EARLY 1550s

'This best garden of the world, / Our fertile France' (*H5* 5.2.36–7), for an Englishman of the 1550s, was not necessarily to be regarded as an entirely alien country, since the landscapes of its northern regions were woven into the very fabric of English history: 'By east and west let France and England mount / Their battering cannon charged to the mouths' (*KJ* 2.1.381–2). The military conflicts of Shakespeare's *Henry IV–VI* plays had transported generations of noble warrior-knights and peasant infantrymen to the battlefields of France during the Hundred Years War; and these dramas respectfully commemorated those countless Englishmen who had left 'their valiant bones in France' (*H5* 4.3.98). Shakespeare, it seems, was very much preoccupied with the national identity of France (making over 450 individual references to France and the French throughout his plays). Moreover, where England ended and France began was still a fraught constitutional and geographical issue. The first part of Edmund Spenser's *The Faerie Queene* was pointedly and unusually dedicated in 1590 to 'Elizabeth by the Grace of God Queen of England, Fraunce and Ireland and of Virginia', a defiant echo of England's former authority over northern France. Spenser's dedicatory words, however, also seem to prefigure Shakespeare's nostalgic insistence upon the royal unification of England and France in *Henry V* (performed 1599), when King Henry proudly promises Katherine: 'England is thine, Ireland is thine, France is thine' (*H5* 5.2.236–7).[16]

During the lifetimes of Shakespeare's grandparents the influence of the Roman Catholic Church had also ensured a sustained level of contact between the devout of England and France. Generations of English pilgrims had followed one of three major routes through France: down the Rhône valley to Marseille and then by sea to Italy; from Paris to Lyon and then across the Alps; or, most commonly, from the Seine to Etaples, then via a great chain of monastic abbeys and hospices (some specifically founded for English pilgrims, such as St Josse at Ponthieu) as far as Besançon and then on through Switzerland. Helena's disguised progress as a 'holy pilgrim' from France to Florence in *All's Well* would have poignantly recalled for some members of Shakespeare's audiences the pre-Reformation devotional progresses across western Europe of their forebears. (See p. 77 for Sir Robert Throckmorton's pilgrimage in 1519.)

The cultural vitality of the long reign of François I (1515–47) had fostered an alluring landscape of French architectural and artistic riches which Thomas was keen to explore. He was accompanied on

Northampton's embassy by Thomas Hoby, the translator of Castiglione's *The Courtier*, whose importance to the development of an English awareness of Italy ranks second only to that of Thomas himself. From late 1547 Hoby had studied at Strasbourg under Martin Bucer and the Florentine exile, Peter Martyr Vermigli. He then moved on to Italy and from July 1548 attended lectures at the University of Padua, where he met Sir Thomas Wyatt (the Marian conspirator and son of the poet), before moving on to Venice, Florence and Siena.[17] By November 1549 he had reached Rome to observe a papal election (and, incidentally, made the first known reference by an Englishman to Michelangelo). Designated as 'the prototypical Grand Tourist' by Edward Chaney, Hoby then travelled to Naples, reaching as far south as Sicily in early 1550. On a second brief tour, Hoby and some English friends were entertained by the duchess and her son at Amalfi, in the very castle where almost forty years earlier John Webster's Duchess of Malfi and her children had reputedly been murdered. These experiences were carefully written up in about 1564 in his manuscript memoir, 'Book of the Travel and Life of Me Thomas Hoby'.[18]

This slim journal of firsthand observations (blended with passages lifted silently from Leandro Alberti's renowned guidebook, *Descrittione di tutta Italia*) confirms Hoby's fascination with the landscapes, architecture and antiquities of Italy; and, like Thomas's *History*, it champions the acquisition of modern vernacular languages as a means of balancing the scholastic dominance of Latin and Greek. Hoby's network of personal contacts provides an equally eloquent insight into the extent of his continental interests. He was the half-brother of Sir Philip Hoby, the friend of Holbein, Titian and Aretino, whose diplomatic duties included an embassy for Edward VI to Emperor Charles V and acting as an intermediary between Queen Mary and Philip II of Spain. As a young man Thomas Hoby had studied at Cambridge with the renowned Greek scholar John Cheke, who later served his own exile at Padua and contributed the prefatory letter to Hoby's *The Courtier* which again reiterated the importance of the English vernacular. One of Hoby's travelling companions during his 1550 Italian trip was Peter Whitethorne, whose own interests culminated in his translation of

Machiavelli's *Art of War* (1560). Hoby was also an intimate of the Italianate Henry Fitzalan, Earl of Arundel (who accompanied Henry VIII to France in 1532, served as Lord Deputy of Calais in the early 1540s and toured Italy in 1566–7). The trajectory of Hoby's education for a diplomatic career (he was appointed in 1566 as ambassador to France but died in the same year) illustrates how, for an élite group of Englishmen during Edward VI's reign, a detailed knowledge of continental courts was both highly desirable and readily accessible.

The career of Queen Elizabeth's Protestant Secretary of State, Thomas Wilson, exemplifies a similar range of interests. Leaving England during the Marian persecutions, Wilson travelled as a religious exile on the continent between 1555 and 1560, years which encompassed for him the extremes of a period of study at Padua with John Cheke, torture and imprisonment at Rome by the Inquisition as a 'heretic', and receiving an LL.D degree from the University of Ferrara. During Elizabeth's reign he also undertook diplomatic assignments in Portugal and two postings to the Low Countries to mediate between the Protestant Dutch and their Spanish rulers. Wilson was one of the earliest English writers to formulate a clear pedagogic statement on the benefits of continental travel. In his *Art of Rhetoric* (1553) he offered 'An Oration Deliberative' on 'travel beyond the seas for the knowledge of the tongues and experience in foreign countries', systematically enumerating (like Panthino to Antonio in *Two Gentlemen* and, some fifty years later, Francis Bacon in his famous essay 'Of Travel') its numerous advantages to the 'body', 'the increase of wit' and 'the getting of experience', along with a pithy summary (which Thomas or Hoby could well have written) of the major pleasures of travel:

> first, the sweetness of the tongue, the wholesomeness of the air in other countries; the goodly wits of the gentlemen; the strange and ancient buildings; the wonderful monuments; the great learned clerks in all faculties; with divers other like and almost infinite pleasures.

Wilson, it is also useful to note from a dramatic perspective, was not averse to playing upon the kind of simplistic national stereotypes which were to become so popular on the late Elizabethan stage. His *Rhetoric* is populated by such gently comic figures as an 'abbot in Italy, being gross of his body and unwieldly to behold', and a 'hermit of Italy' who turns out to be 'a very lewd man'. He also pokes fun at those Sir-Politic-like Englishmen who gain nothing but affectation from their experiences abroad:

> Some far-journeyed gentlemen at their return home, like as they love to go in foreign apparel so they will powder their talk with overseas language. He that cometh lately out of France will talk French English and never blush at the matter. Another chops in with English Italianated and applieth the Italian phrase to our English speaking.

Sir Thomas Lovell echoes these sentiments in Shakespeare's *Henry VIII* when he mocks 'our travelled gallants / That fill the court with quarrels, talk and tailors', bringing home nothing but 'remnants / Of fool and feather that they got in France' (1.3.19–27). Similarly, in *The Merchant of Venice* Portia ridicules the provincial Falconbridge's posturing affectation of continental sophistication:

> he understands not me, nor I him: he hath neither Latin, French, nor Italian ... How oddly he is suited! I think he bought his doublet in Italy, his round hose in France, his bonnet in Germany, and his behaviour everywhere.

> (1.2.65–73)

But for Thomas Wilson the rhetorical appeal of such stereotypical representations went hand-in-hand with a firsthand knowledge of the truth of their countries. Rather than being merely contradictory or incompatible, reality and caricature were for the humanist rhetorician (as for the dramatist) simply two very different literary modes available for the depiction of national and ethnic difference.[19] Nor was continental travel in itself, unless sensibly directed, always to be viewed as intrinsically beneficial to the individual. As Sir Thomas Lovell pithily puts it: 'an English courtier may be wise / And never see the Louvre' (*H8* 1.3.22–3).

THE REIGN OF QUEEN MARY AND
SHAKESPEARE'S POLITICAL EXILES

The accession of a Catholic queen in July 1553 realigned English perspectives on the continent in two major ways. First, it necessitated a sectarian redefinition of the burgeoning English interest of the early 1550s in all things Italian. Now, instead of the Protestant outward gaze of the likes of Thomas, Hoby and Wilson upon Italian cities, a fresh vision of Italy was supplied by the returning English Catholic émigrés led by Cardinal Pole, who during the 1520s had studied at Padua, visited Rome and resided at Paris, and then voluntarily returned to Padua in January 1532 when he refused to accept royal supremacy over the English church. Second, Mary's marriage to Philip of Spain, with its resulting interaction of English and Spanish courtiers, led to a heightened awareness of (and covert hostility towards) the imperial might of Spain. But it is debatable whether this marriage rendered the geographical mainland of Spain itself of much more relevance to culturally curious Englishmen. Rather, the return of Pole and his associates brought to the English court a richly informed knowledge of Italian humanism and civic statecraft. For these returning Catholic Englishmen, the views of Thomas and Hoby would have struck many familiar chords, not least their fascination with the constitutional workings of the Italian city-states and the Republic of Venice. Mary's accession also created yet another new generation of English exiles to Italy. The Protestant Francis Walsingham, for example, fled England and was elected on 29 December 1555 as chancellor of the *Anglica natio* at the University of Padua – a period of exile which stood him in good stead for his later role as, effectively, the director of the Elizabethan foreign intelligence-gathering service.[20]

   This influx and exodus of returning Catholics and fleeing Protestants serves as a useful reminder of Shakespeare's own insistent preoccupation with concepts of political exile as an enforced motivation for continental travel. Cardinal Pole's return home prefigures how in *Macbeth* Malcolm can only offer new hope for the future by 'calling home our exil'd friends abroad' (5.9.32). These returning exiles in

Shakespeare's play offer to a dislocated Scottish state both a fresh start and a sense of constitutional continuity, just as Pole's entourage offered to the Marian regime both a new vision of England's political role in western Europe and a strong personal link back to the pre-Reformation days of Henry VIII's Catholic court. Numerous other characters in Shakespeare's plays, including Romeo (*RJ* 3.2.131), Suffolk (*2H6* 3.2.382), Coriolanus (*Cor* 4.6.133) and Posthumus (*Cym* 3.5.36), suffer involuntary exile. The political message of several other plays rests upon the motif of unjust political exile. In *Richard III*, we recall the sad figure of Dorset, 'that with a fearful soul / Leads discontented steps in foreign soil' (4.4.311–12); and in *Richard II* the sheer injustice of Bolingbroke's tactical withdrawal to the continent seriously damages the king's authority: 'Must I not serve a long apprenticehood / To foreign passages' (1.3.271–2); 'And sigh'd my English breath in foreign clouds, / Eating the bitter bread of banishment' (3.1.20–1).

While Shakespeare's history plays might well be expected to engage with the concept of political exile, it is noticeable that several of the comedies are also strongly permeated with similiar ideas. Most famously, at the opening of *As You Like It*, the Chorus informs us that 'the old Duke is banished … three or four loving lords have put themselves into voluntary exile with him' (1.1.99–102); and the audience is invited to revel in the rural exile of the duke and his 'co-mates and brothers in exile' (2.1.1). As might be expected, the archly continental perspectives of *Two Gentlemen* also prompt a powerful consideration of the insidiously divisive social effects of political exile. One of the most curious but telling scenes in the play, *TGV* 4.1, is when Valentine and Speed are ambushed by three notorious outlaws, 'the villains / That all the travellers do fear so much' (4.1.5–6), only for the incident to end amicably because all of its protagonists – the bandits and their intended victims alike – discover that they are to a man bound in a secret brotherhood of exile from their home towns of Verona and Mantua.

The final and irrevocable loss of Calais to the French in January 1558 not only blighted the last months of Mary's reign but would also very probably have lingered long in the minds of Shakespeare's late Elizabethan audiences. Certainly, in *Henry V* for example, there is an

insistent nostalgia for the lost dream of a unified England and France:
'France being ours, we'll bend it to our awe' and 'No king of England, if
not king of France' (1.2.224 and 2.2.193). But the play's concluding
Chorus sombrely traces what happened to the Anglo-French dominion
after Henry V's glorious victory:

> And of it left his son imperial lord.
> Henry the Sixth, in infant bands crowned King
> Of France and England, did this king succeed,
> Whose state so many had the managing
> That they lost France and made his England bleed.
>
> (*Epilogue* 8–12)

Although Shakespeare tactfully refers here only to the reign of Henry
VI, informed viewers attending its staging in 1599 could have readily
made the connection between the destructive factional power struggles
of the reigns of Edward VI and Mary and the pointed condemnation
inherent in the phrase 'so many had the managing'. But as Mary died,
reputedly claiming that 'Calais' would be found graven on her heart,
the political landscapes of France and Italy, from an English perspective,
were already undergoing radical reshaping. In 1559 the Peace of
Cateau-Cambrésis concluded the French wars with Italy, facilitating far
easier access for travellers between the two countries during the reigns
of François II and Charles IX (1559–74).

ENGLISH TRAVELLERS AND PROTESTANT
POLEMICISTS 1558–1575

The early years of Queen Elizabeth's reign seemed a more promising
time for continental travel. One Englishman who in 1563 reached as far
as Rome (via Antwerp, Cologne, Augsburg, Innsbruck, Venice, Padua
and Florence) in the diplomatic entourage of Sir Edward Unton was an
unassuming servingman called Richard Smith. Although he was a
literal observer of classical antiquities and modern buildings (he was
especially impressed by Pope Pius IV's ambitious building programmes
at Rome), Smith's diary remains a fascinating record of how an ordinary

visitor to Italy, armed with a copy of *The History of Italy*, set about exploring his new surroundings.[21] But the publication in 1567 of Pope Pius V's bull *In coena domini* (excluding heretics from Italian states) engendered, in overt retaliation, a powerful Protestant reaction against Italy as a dangerous and forbidden territory for Englishmen. This sense of alienation was compounded by the Catholic-inspired Northern Rebellion (1569), the papal excommunication of Queen Elizabeth (1570), various 'Italianate' conspiracies such as the Ridolfi Plot (1571), and the execution of England's leading Catholic peer, the Duke of Norfolk (1572).

Roger Ascham's virulent condemnation of Italian degeneracy, which unexpectedly concludes the first book of the otherwise pedagogically outward-looking *Schoolmaster*, exemplifies this defiantly polemical level of Protestant response to papal Italy's hostility towards the English monarchy.

> Virtue once made that country mistress over all the world. Vice now maketh that country slave to them that before were glad to serve it ... For since, by lust and vanity, hath and doth breed up every where common contempt of God's word, private contention in many families, open factions in every city, and so, making themselves bond to vanity and vice at home, they are content to bear the yoke of serving strangers abroad. Italy now is not that Italy that it was wont to be and therefore now not so fit a place as some do count it for young men to fetch either wisdom or honesty from thence.

Ascham's only firsthand experience of Italy had been nine days spent at Venice in the summer of 1552 during a busy continental itinerary – incorporating Bruges, Antwerp, Brussels, Louvain, Cologne, Augsburg, Munich, Innsbruck and Strasbourg before a return to Brussels (where he met Philip and Thomas Hoby) – as secretary from 1550 until 1553 to Sir Richard Moryson, English ambassador to Emperor Charles V. Despite his anti-Venetian comments in *The Schoolmaster*, Ascham had long been an enthusiastic Italianophile. The dedication to his treatise on archery, *Toxophilus* (1545), had openly solicited Henry VIII's support for his ambition to study 'for some years in Italy and other transmarine lands'; and, even in *The Schoolmaster*, his devotion to 'the Italian tongue, which next the Greek and Latin tongue I like and love above all other', was obvious.[22]

Whether Ascham himself intended his educational treatise to be put to this crude anti-Italian propagandist use is unknown, since it was posthumously published from his private papers. But the jarringly polemical tone of these few lines should not deflect attention away from Ascham's true identity as an advocate for a greater English awareness of western European statecraft and culture. Although now rarely read, Ascham's incomplete *A Report and Discourse of the State of Germany* (also printed posthumously in 1570) stands as a pioneering example of early English responses to the new methods of continental historiography and as an enlightened precursor for the English histories of Bacon and Camden. It has far more of lasting substance to say on Germany than *The Schoolmaster* has about Italy. Similarly, his impressively diverse personal contacts and correspondence with the logician Peter Ramus (based at Paris), the medical pioneer Vesalius (Paris, Louvain, Augsburg and Venice), the educationist Johann Sturm and the theologian Martin Bucer (both at Strasbourg), and the Portuguese Ciceronian, Jeronimo Osorio, demonstrate Ascham's earnest commitment to pan-European humanist learning.[23]

Despite such superficial (but potent) Italian xenophobia, the signing of the Treaty of Blois in the spring of 1572 began to open up possibilities for young Englishmen to travel on the continent for educational purposes. In the early summer of 1572 Philip Sidney (later the author of *Arcadia* and *Astrophel and Stella*), along with a family servant of Italian extraction called Lodowick Bryskett, set off to join the diplomatic entourage of Edward Fiennes de Clinton, Earl of Lincoln, the leader of the English delegation for the signing of the Treaty of Blois ('A noble troop of strangers ... as great ambassadors from foreign princes', *H8* 1.4.53–6). This was a crucial mission in terms of Anglo-French relations, since Lincoln had also been ordered to pursue tacit negotiations for a match between Queen Elizabeth (then aged thirty-nine) and the Duc d'Alençon (then eighteen). According to his travel licence, Philip Sidney was allowed abroad specifically 'for his attaining to the knowledge of foreign languages' but he was also ordered not to 'haunt nor repair into the territories or countries of any prince or potentate not being with us in amity or league' (i.e. Spain and Italy).

After a formal welcoming of Lincoln's party at Saint-Denis and the staging of an Italian comedy for their entertainment on 17 June at Paris, Philip Sidney took up residence in the Faubourg Saint-Germain with Sir Francis Walsingham (whom we last encountered at Padua in 1555), the resident English ambassador.[24] Following the ratification of the Treaty of Blois, hopes for a more accessible western Europe were further raised in mid-July when the Spanish commander, the Duke of Alva, defeated the combined French, Dutch and English forces at Mons, effectively ending direct French military intervention in the Low Countries. But the unexpected slaughter of thousands of Huguenots during the St Bartholomew's Day Massacre of 23–24 August 1572 (poignantly commemorated in Marlowe's *The Massacre at Paris*, 'Surcharg'd with guilt of thousand massacres', 21.93) turned France overnight from a welcoming territory into a highly dangerous one for English visitors. The Privy Council and the Earl of Leicester immediately sent anxious orders to Walsingham to ensure Philip Sidney's safe return. But, before these instructions arrived, he had already fled France for Germany, passing through Strasbourg and Heidelberg on his way to Frankfurt, where he took refuge for the winter.

Through the survival of much of his correspondence from this period, the impressive extent of Sidney's travels and contacts with leading European statesmen and scholars can be mapped in detail. By midsummer 1573 he had reached the imperial court at Vienna, from where he took a brief excursion into Hungary during early September. The allure of Italy, however, was simply too strong, despite the clear prohibition of his licence, and by early November he had taken up residence in Venice. Sidney's impressions of Italian society and constitutions were distinctly mixed, as this advice from a letter written in May 1578 to his younger brother Robert makes clear:

> As for Italy I knowe not what wee have, or can have to doe with them, but to buye their scilkes and wynes, and for other

provinces (excepting Venice) whose good lawes, & customes wee can hardly proporcion to our selves, because they are quite of a contrarie government, there is little there but tyranous oppression, & servile yeilding to them, that have little or noe rule over them ... they are all given to soe counterfeit lerning, as a man shall learne of them more false groundes of thinges; then in any place ells.[25]

Philip Sidney remained in Italy, based alternately at Venice and Padua ('for the great desire I had / To see fair Padua', *TS* 1.1.1–2) until about August 1574 before heading north to Verona and crossing the Brenner Pass into Austria. Pausing again at Vienna, he made a short visit to Poland in late autumn 1574 ('here in Vienna, / And he supposes me travell'd to Poland', *MM* 1.3.13–14) before travelling to the imperial court at Prague in Czechoslovakia in February 1575. His return journey home took him back in a broad sweep through Germany and the Low Countries, and he sailed from Antwerp for England in early March 1575. This continental education soon bore fruit when in February 1577 Sidney (still only twenty-two) was selected to lead an embassy to the court of Emperor Rudolph II and his mother to offer Elizabeth's condolences on the death of the late emperor. Passing through Ostend, Brussels, Louvain and Heidelberg, he headed to Prague, where the funeral was to be held in April. There he encountered a former family servant, Edmund Campion, then Professor of Rhetoric at the Jesuit college. He returned home to England, now a fully fledged diplomatic servant of the queen, via Heidelberg, Frankfurt, Antwerp, Bruges and Ghent.[26]

Sadly, Sidney himself left no diary of his day-to-day travels and his routes; nor, for that matter, did any of the other known English travellers on the continent during the 1570s. For example, Edward de Vere, later 17th Earl of Oxford, withdrew to Flanders in 1572 soon after his marriage to Lord Burghley's daughter, Anne (who had previously been courted as a possible spouse for Philip Sidney). He probably returned to England in 1574 but then set out again to tour Italy in 1575–6, although little is known about his activities there. If such

FIGURE 4 The departure of a traveller.

documentation had survived, it would have been fascinating to compare the travels of this young aristocratic poet with those of Philip Sidney, since their paths crossed on several occasions in later life.[27]

ENGLISH TOURISTS, CATHOLIC EXILES AND SHAKESPEARE 1575–1585

> A traveller ought to have
> The back of an ass,
> The belly of a sow,
> The eares stopped,
> The eyes shut up
> His purse open,
> The ears of a merchant.[28]

As a young man, the soldier and scholar Sir John North – who later fought with Philip Sidney in the Low Countries campaign of 1585–6 –

travelled through Flanders, Germany and Switzerland during the mid-1570s and lived from 1575 to 1577 in Italy. Keen to nurture the linguistic benefits of his travels after his return home, for two years he continued to record in Italian his daily accounts and details of various English journeys.[29] Numerous less socially visible individuals continued to travel throughout western Europe but their experiences went largely unrecorded. One such person who did pen some fascinating and detailed reminiscences was Stephen Powle, who travelled to Geneva, Basle and Strasbourg between 1579 and 1581, and was sent as an intelligence gatherer to Venice by Sir Francis Walsingham in 1587 to report on rumours of Spanish preparations for an invasion of England. Here, for example, is Powle's racy account of his accommodation at Venice among the famous ladies and courtesans:

> If to be well neighboured be no small part of happiness, I may repute myself highly fortunate, for I am lodged amongst a great number of Signoras. Isabella Bellochia in the next house on my right hand and Virginia Padoana, that honoreth all our nation for my Lord of Oxford's sake, is my neighbour on the left side. Over my head hath Lodovica Gonzaga, the French King's mistress, her house ... Pesarmia with her sweet entertainment and brave discourse is not two canals off. Ancilla (Master Hatton's handmaid) is in the next Campo; Paulina Gonzaga is not far off; Prudencia Romana with her courtly train of French gentlemen every night goeth *a spasso* (unemployed) by my pergola. As for Imperia Romana, her date is out which flourished in your time.[30]

But English travellers in France (and onwards into Germany and Italy) became less common during the tumultuous reign of Charles IX's brother, Henri III (1574–89), who was behind the murder at Blois of the ultra-Catholic Henri, Duc de Guise (which, in turn, led to his own assassination at Saint-Cloud in 1589).

In 1580 the situation for English Catholics worsened dramatically when in June the government tightened procedures against recusants, with repressive new anti-Catholic legislation receiving the royal assent in March 1581. One Englishman who was sent abroad at this period for travel through the Low Countries, Germany, Czechoslovakia, Italy and France was Arthur Throckmorton, whose family's allegiances had frequently wavered between Catholicism and Protestantism. Uniquely for the period, a detailed (sometimes daily) manuscript record of his travels has survived. Throckmorton came from a background in which firsthand knowledge of continental Europe was highly prized. His grandfather Sir Robert had died in Italy in 1519 while on pilgrimage to the Holy Land (recalling Norfolk in *Richard II* who 'retir'd himself / To Italy; and there at Venice gave / His body to that pleasant country's earth', 4.1.96–8); and his uncle Michael had shared Cardinal Pole's long exile at Padua as his secretary. His father Sir Nicholas, who had fled to France in 1555 in the wake of the Wyatt Rebellion and participated in the victory at Saint-Quentin, had been appointed in May 1559 as Queen Elizabeth's resident ambassador at Paris.

Like the Sidneys, European travel for the Throckmortons was viewed as an integral part of the linguistic, cultural and political education of their sons. Arthur began his continental travels by accompanying the French embassy of Sir Amyas Paulet in September 1576. With the outbreak of renewed hostilities with Spain, he then headed to the Low Countries in the summer of 1578 to join Sir John Norris's regiment under the overall command of Prince Casimir. He returned to England in late 1578 but in July 1580 he crossed the Channel once again. Passing rapidly through Holland, he visited Cologne, Frankfurt and Nuremberg, before wintering at Prague, then newly invigorated by the first year of the reign of Emperor Rudolph II, an accomplished linguist, patron of the arts, and amateur scientist, who was to invite Dr John Dee to his court in 1584. From Prague, Throckmorton then headed to Vienna and in April 1581 he crossed the Alps into Italy, where he resided (like Philip Sidney before him) mainly at Padua and Venice.

Filling his time with learning Italian, music lessons and sightseeing, Throckmorton met a surprising number of Englishmen there, including some Jesuits and youthful members of the Leigh, Ratcliffe, Sentry, Crichton, Carew, Savile and Spencer families. By September he moved

on to Florence, where his diary records the purchase of numerous
historical and genealogical volumes. He began studying the lute again
and engaged a singing tutor, Vincenzo Galileo (the scientist's father).
He also fraternized with the small resident English community at
Florence, including one Anthony Standen, a Catholic exile who secretly
provided Walsingham with intelligence about the Duke of Florence and
the activities of his co-religionists. At about this time Throckmorton
heard that John Pickering (from a Northamptonshire family whom he
knew back home) had been imprisoned as a spy at Rome. Somehow
extricated, Pickering fled to Florence and took refuge with Throckmorton
in a house owned by a priest called Monsignor Stephano. Such
involvements were turning rather too perilous for Throckmorton and
he rapidly left Florence (with Pickering in tow), making a hasty trip
back to England through Italy and France during the Christmas and
New Year season of 1581–2. Despite such dangers, the educational
experiences of Arthur Throckmorton's travels seem to have been well
enough regarded by his family for them to send his younger brother,
Nicholas, on a similar tour during the late 1580s.[31]

During early 1579 it was the turn of Philip Sidney's younger
brother, Robert, to undertake this kind of extended continental
itinerary. By November 1580, after a period spent travelling in the
company of Stephen Powle, Robert had reached Prague and written a
letter to his father, Sir Henry Sidney, informing him that he was hopeful
of making a trip to Italy some time in the New Year, followed by a
journey through France. He also mentioned that his elder brother,
Philip, had recently advised him to keep an eye out for 'any good wars',
a timely reminder (along with Throckmorton's 1578 excursion to the
Low Countries' battlefields) that such travels were not merely intended
for cultural purposes alone. Henry Sidney's inconclusive reply to Robert
well illustrates the geographical and political difficulties inherent in
gaining firsthand knowledge of western European countries during the
early 1580s. He firmly approved of Robert's sojourn at Prague and
commended his decision to visit Vienna. But he could offer no useful
advice on exploring Italy, nor did he recommend such a journey in view
of the virtually perpetual state of hostilities between Protestant Europe

and the Pope. He also observed that Englishmen were then under a prohibition against travelling in Spain; France seemed to have endless civil troubles of its own, and the Low Countries were in a state of irrecoverable misery. Ultimately, he left the final decision to Robert as to whether he should return to Prague after seeing Vienna, or if it might even prove of more use to base himself at Vienna for the coming summer. Henry Sidney's final, speculative thought was that Robert could perhaps usefully employ himself by visiting Moravia, Silesia and Cracovia; and from thence head off through Saxony, Holst and Pomerland to Denmark and Sweden.[32]

The possibility of Shakespeare's own youthful contacts – specifically within the context of Catholic recusancy – with English families who had relatives residing on the continent at this period might also be raised here. His parents, John and Mary, were almost certainly Catholics who, like thousands of others, opted for quiet public conformity (although Shakespeare's elder daughter, Susanna, was cited in a 1606 recusancy list). Attending the King's New School at Stratford during the early 1570s, he would have been taught by Simon Hunt, who was reputed to have left England in 1575 to attend the Catholic seminary at Douai. The father of another of his teachers, Thomas Jenkins, was a servant of the staunchly Catholic founder of St John's College, Oxford, Sir Thomas White. A third teacher at the school was a Lancashire man called John Cottom, whose brother, Thomas, entered the Jesuit novitiate of St Andrew at Rome in April 1579. He returned as a missionary priest to England, where he was captured in June 1580, arraigned in November 1581 (along with Campion) and executed as a traitor in May 1582. It is difficult to imagine how Shakespeare could not have been aware of the fates of the likes of Cottom and Campion – and yet the silence in his plays on such matters is resounding.[33]

If, as E.A.J. Honigmann argues, the young Shakespeare served the Hoghton family of Lancashire, then his personal contacts with English Catholic exiles on the continent seem even more likely. Thomas Hoghton, an unwavering recusant, departed from England in 1569 and never returned, dying at Liège in 1580. His son Thomas was ordained as a priest, leaving his brother Alexander – who mentioned a 'William Shakeshafte' in his will – to inherit the family estates. A batch of letters, beginning in September 1576 and written from abroad by Thomas to his brother, Richard Hoghton, make several references to family servants, led by one Brian Jackson, travelling to and from the continent with money and messages for him. Richard had assumed the guardianship of his brother's personal and business affairs (following his 1569 exile); and in 1576 he received a royal licence to travel to Antwerp: 'to the intent to advise, persuade and consel Thomas Hoghton, late of Hoghton ... to return unto this our realm'. After Campion's capture in 1581, rumours circulated that he had been harboured by various Catholic families in Lancashire and the Privy Council ordered searches, 'especially the house of Richard Hoghton', where Campion was thought to have left his books.[34]

It is certainly tempting to speculate that Shakespeare knew something of this world of religious exile and intrigue. If he did, he may even have come across some of the rarest (in terms of their surviving records) of English travellers at this period – resolute Catholic women who left for the continent rather than denying their faith. One such individual (an exact contemporary of Shakespeare's twins, Hamnet and Judith) was Mary Ward (b. 1585), founder of the Institute of the Blessed Virgin Mary. Raised in Yorkshire, she first left England in 1606 to enter the Poor Clare convent at Saint-Omer. During the next thirty-three years, the epic mileage of her journeys ranks her as one of the most prolific English travellers of her generation. Spreading the faith and seeking personal enlightenment, she went on foot from Liège to Rome, and from there to Naples and Perugia. She walked twice from Rome to Munich and back, and also visited Vienna and Bohemia. She made at least ten crossings of the English Channel; six winter crossings of the Alps; and traversed numerous battlefields of the Thirty Years War. Her last journey between 1637 and 1639 took her across the breadth of western Europe from Rome to Yorkshire.[35] And yet, probably because of her religion and her sex, the literature of English western European travel has remained strangely silent about her remarkable achievements.

ENGLISH DIPLOMATS, POLITICAL THEORISTS
AND GUIDEBOOKS 1585–1603

There are so few detailed accounts available of English travels in western Europe after the mid-1580s that conclusions about their scope or cultural significance are elusive. A rare survival is the voluminous diary of the Irishman, Henry Piers, a Catholic convert and exile, recording his explorations of the Low Countries, Germany and Italy between 1595 and 1598.[36] But of the numerous other Englishmen known to have been travelling abroad during the 1590s (Sir Thomas Chaloner complained that 'Such a rabble of English roam now in Italy') little documentation survives.[37] Fortunately, one of those whose youthful travels visibly impacted on his later career did write retrospectively about his experiences. In June 1592 Henry Wotton, who served three times as James I's ambassador to Venice (his presence there merited two references in Jonson's *Volpone*), was based at Florence, learning the pure Tuscan dialect. He wryly recalled the city's lurid reputation as the home of 'the murderous Machiavel' (*3H6* 3.2.193) and 'a paradise inhabited by devils'. Wotton once even found himself, disguised as an Italian called Octavio Baldi, serving the Grand Duke in his attempts to foil a Spanish-inspired plot to displace James VI of Scotland in favour of the infanta in the English line of succession. Such stratagems recall Lucentio's cunning ploys: 'I will some other be, some Florentine, / Some Neapolitan, or meaner man of Pisa' (*TS* 1.1.204–5).[38]

    In 1595 Wotton entered the employment of Robert Devereux, Earl of Essex, as a collector of foreign intelligence. Frustrated by an ageing and increasingly autocratic queen, Essex became a keen student of alternative continental models of government. Within his closest circle of allies, which included Robert Sidney, the writings of Livy and Tacitus in particular became a publicly acceptable route into considering the problems of tyranny and, by implication, the more dangerous attractions of democratic republicanism. Robert Sidney's heavily annotated copy of Justus Lipsius's 1585 edition of Tacitus still survives; and when Tacitus is aligned with Machiavelli (also avidly read by the

Sidneys), it is apparent that the Essex circle was immersing itself in a telling combination of ancient and modern Italianate perspectives on the nature of absolute authority. Much of this Tacitean interest may be directly attributed to the influence of the Sidneys. In 1585 Giovanni Maria Manelli had dedicated to Robert Sidney his edition of Tacitus' eulogy of his father-in-law as the ideal ruler, *La vita di Guilio Agricola*; and the brutal Low Countries campaign of 1585–6 had taught the Sidney brothers the modern relevance of Tacitus' urbane analysis of absolute power. The leader of the English forces, Robert Dudley, Earl of Leicester (Philip and Robert Sidney's uncle, and the son of John Dudley to whom William Thomas's *The History of Italy* had been dedicated), even took time out from his pressing military duties in early March 1586 to hear Lipsius lecture on Tacitus' *Agricola* at Leiden. Most pointedly, when Philip Sidney was delegated to negotiate the specific terms of Leicester's governorship of the Netherlands in January 1586, he made an impassioned speech to the Dutch States-General which oozed the combined political philosophies of Tacitus and Machiavelli:

> he had learnt from history that when the state of the Republic of Rome had been in utter peril or danger, as the Netherlands nowadays are ... it had been necessary to create a dictatorship, with absolute power and disposition over everything concerning the prosperity of the country, without any instruction, limitation or restriction.[39]

Another influential member of Essex's circle, Sir Robert Dallington, accompanied Roger Manners, Earl of Rutland (the future husband of Philip Sidney's only daughter Elizabeth), through France, Italy and Germany from 1598 until 1600; and he later travelled with Roger's younger brother Francis on a similar tour. From these experiences he compiled two renowned guides, *The View of France* (1605), examining culture and society under Henri IV, and *A Survey of the Great Dukes State of Tuscany* (1605), detailing the treasures of Medicean Florence. But Dallington's guides were also sharply focused on the importance of civil liberties and the dangers of an over-concentration of power in the hands of the few. Once again we find that the republican constitution of

Venice is seen as the ultimate ideal, with France (most resembling England in its royal and aristocratic hierarchies) receiving heavy criticism for its suppression of individual freedom.[40]

Dallington's two volumes stand as landmarks in the compilation of self-consciously nationalistic guidebooks, specifically aimed at both informed domestic readers and politically aware English travellers in western Europe. Several earlier volumes had been readily available but these were often translations from foreign sources, lacking a specifically English perspective on continental Europe. For those embarking by ship, there were translations from Latin of Hieronymus Turler's *The Traveller* and from the Dutch of Cornelius Antonisz by Robert Norman of *The Safeguard of Sailors*, detailing the depths, tides and distances by sea. For those on land, there was *The Post of the World* by Richard Rowlands (Verstegen); Sir John Stradlings's translation of Lipsius's *Direction for Travellers*; John Browne's *The Marchant's Aviso*; and Giovanni Botero's renowned *The Traveller's Breviat*, translated from Italian by Robert Johnson, with valuable information not only on Europe but also on Spanish and Portuguese commercial activities in Persia, East Africa, India and China.

WRITERS, SPIES, ACTORS AND IMMIGRANTS 1585–1603

Frequently, all too little is known about the familiarity of other English writers with continental Europe. According to Izaak Walton, after participating in the 1596–7 Azores expeditions John Donne travelled in both France and Spain. But modern research has cast doubt on this claim, and, if he did travel abroad, it must have been between 1589 and 1591. If so, he could have visited his exiled Jesuit uncle, Jasper Heywood, at Naples, where he died in 1598.[41] Disliking his stepfather's trade of bricklaying, Ben Jonson claimed to have joined the English army in the Low Countries in about 1591 and 'in the face of both camps killed an enemy and taken *optima spolia* from him'.[42] And what exactly was Christopher Marlowe doing in the Low Countries – intelligence-gathering by posing as a Catholic in order to infiltrate

Spanish groups seems most likely – when he was arrested at Flushing in January 1592 at the order of Robert Sidney (the town's governor) on suspicion of counterfeiting coinage?[43] In October 1595 the translator and prose writer, Anthony Munday, received a passport from the Spanish authorities, permitting him to travel through the Low Countries – but for what purpose?[44] The apparently harmless devotional poet and author of *Ecclesiastes* (1597), Henry Lok (a nephew of the renowned traveller, Michael Lok), was also skilled in cipher and dabbled in the dangerous world of spying. In 1599 he was in Bayonne, assiduously collecting political intelligence for Sir Robert Cecil. Unfortunately, he soon aroused the suspicions of the locals, who doubted his claim that he was merely an English traveller en route for Spain with the entourage of the French ambassador. With his cover blown and back in London by April 1600, Cecil rapidly dispensed with his services.[45]

Two of the most intriguing intelligencers of the late Elizabethan period were the Standen brothers, both called Anthony. (Arthur Throckmorton, as already noted, met one of them at Florence in 1581.) The elder was knighted in 1566 and the younger was known as Mr Anthony Standen, Gent. Sir Anthony first served Margaret Countess of Lennox, mother of Lord Darnley, who was the second husband of Mary Queen of Scots. Then both brothers entered Darnley's service. Sir Anthony saved Mary's life (and that of her unborn son, the future James I of England) when her secretary, David Rizzio, was murdered, and he assisted her escape from Holyrood. With Prince James safely delivered, Standen was sent to France to inform King Charles IX. His licence to travel was for two years but he seems to have spent most of the next thirty years abroad, including work as an informer and news-gatherer in Italy and among English refugee Catholics in the Netherlands. The younger Anthony spent long periods in Spain as an agent of Walsingham, under the pseudonym Pompeo Pellegrini; and one of the brothers received a pension in Brussels in 1574 as a refugee Catholic. In 1603 Sir Anthony was sent by James I to Italy to announce his accession to the throne of England. He also secured a private audience with Pope Clement VIII, who presented him with various devotional items for King James and Queen Anne. Sir Anthony wrote a letter concerning these tokens to Father Parsons which was intercepted; and, suspected of being a papal agent, he was incarcerated in the Tower on his return to England in January 1604. His release was secured by November and he was recorded as heading to France on unspecified business in July 1605. After this date, nothing is known about either brother.[46]

Other writers, who could well have come into personal contact with Shakespeare, may not have left any systematic record of their travels but still provide in their own compositions a clear sense of the formative influences of their activities abroad. One of Samuel Daniel's earliest published works was a translation of Paolo Giovio's *Dialogo dell'Imprese* (1585). This volume, the first continental emblem book to be printed in English, was dedicated to Sir Edward Dymoke (officially the 'Queen's Champion' at the annual Accession Day tilts), who had himself travelled extensively abroad, especially in Italy. Daniel had probably learned his Italian while studying at Oxford from John Florio (who reputedly married Daniel's sister Rose). By 1586 Daniel was writing from Paris to Sir Francis Walsingham, since he was then apparently in the service of the English ambassador, Sir Edward Stafford. In about 1590–1 he made a more prolonged continental journey, which took him and Dymoke to Italy, where they met the pastoral dramatist Giovanni Battista Guarini, at either the University of Padua or his private residence between Padua and Venice.[47]

It has been surmised, largely because of his vivid references to Italian affairs in *The Unfortunate Traveller* (1594) ('Italy, the paradise of the earth and the epicure's heaven ... From thence he brings the art of atheism, the art of epicurising, the art of whoring, the art of poisoning, the art of sodomitry'), that Thomas Nashe may have made a hasty tour through western Europe between 1588 and 1592. This is an attractive idea, not least because the volume was dedicated by Nashe to Shakespeare's patron, Henry Wriothesley, Earl of Southampton, who is known to have encouraged the Italian interests of John Florio. Unfortunately, there is not a scrap of external evidence to suggest that Nashe ever set foot on continental soil, although he usefully reminds us how most English writers probably gained their knowledge of continental Europe. In his *Lenten Stuff*, Nashe readily admits: 'I have not travail'd far', but in defence of his use of foreign locations in his fictions he simply asserts: 'though conferred with farthest travailers, from our own Realm'.[48]

One predictable source of such information for London dramatists about western Europe would have been through casual conversations with fellow actors and other entertainers who had travelled there. The lutenist John Dowland, for example, made several journeys to Italy and Germany during the 1590s and played a major role in the transmission of continental influences into English court music. Like Marlowe and Lok, he also seems to have undertaken covert intelligence-gathering, secretly forwarding to England the names of compatriots whom he had met abroad.[49] Turning once more to the Sidneys, in the autumn of 1585 the Earl of Leicester was appointed to command the English militia in the Low Countries, with Philip as his deputy and Robert as an officer. His arrival was celebrated at Utrecht, Leiden and The Hague with pageants of dramatics, dancing and tumbling, including performances by a troupe of English actors who had accompanied the English forces to the continent. The actor Richard Wilson was among their number; as was the extemporizing comedian Will Kempe (probably the first Falstaff), since he was recorded at Dunkirk in November 1585. Philip Sidney refers to him as 'my lord of Leicester's jesting player' in a letter to Walsingham of March 1586, as the carrier of earlier missives (which, unsurprisingly, 'the knave' had failed to deliver properly). Another of Leicester's players, the clown Richard Tarleton, even persuaded Philip Sidney to stand as godfather to his son. Kempe, along with several other English actors, moved on during the summer. In June 1586 Kempe, George Bryan, Thomas Pope, Daniel Jones, Thomas Stevens, Thomas King and Robert Percy performed for the Danish royalty at Elsinore. Kempe then returned to England in September but Bryan and Pope headed eastwards and performed for Christian I, Elector of Saxony, at his court in Dresden and other German provincial locations until July 1587.

At least two of these actors, Bryan and Pope, later joined Lord Strange's and then the Lord Chamberlain's Men, where they would have certainly known Shakespeare. There are also records of Kempe abroad once more in Italy and Germany during 1601. Some English acrobats reached as far south as Madrid in January 1583; an English troupe of actors leased the theatre of the Confrères de la Passion at Paris in the summer of 1598; and another English performance was held on 18 September 1604 in the Great Hall at Fontainebleau for the French royal court. One actor, Robert Browne, spent a considerable amount of time in Germany with various troupes of actors, tumblers and dancers between 1590 and 1620. As regards incoming foreign entertainers, troupes of Italian players made sporadic visits to England during the 1570s; three generations of the Ferrabosco family contributed to English court entertainments; and Petruccio Urbaldino, an illuminator, translator and contributor to dramatic diversions, resided in England from 1562 until 1586. Predictably, while abroad some theatre-going English travellers were keen observers of French and Italian drama. Here, for example, is Thomas Coryat at Venice (and see Figure 5):

> I was at one of their Play-houses where I saw a Comedie acted. The house is very beggarly and base in comparison of our stately Play-houses in England: neyther can their Actors compare with us for apparell, shewes and musicke. Here I observed certaine things that I never saw before. For I saw women acte, a thing that I never saw before, though I have heard that it hath beene sometimes used in London, and they performed it with as good a grace, action, gesture, and whatsoever convenient for a Player, as ever I saw any masculine Actor.[50]

Another oral source of dramatically useable information about European locations, cultures and societies would have been available to dramatists from conversations with natives of the Low Countries, France, Germany, Scandinavia and, even on a lesser scale, Italy and Spain (depending upon the fluctuating nature of Anglo-Italian and Anglo-Spanish relations). Such individuals might have been merely passing through England on official business; and their numbers would have included international merchants, sailors, couriers, scholars, clerics and foreign diplomats with their enormous entourages not only

FIGURE 5 Thomas Coryat meets a Venetian courtesan, from *Coryat's Crudities* (1611), facing p. 261.

of aristocrats and civil servants but also of personal servants, cooks and stableboys. Others, usually through economic or religious pressures in their native lands, were in England on a more permanent basis. Shakespeare would certainly have known of 'Petty France' in Bishopsgate ward, and 'Petty Almaine' and 'Petty Flanders' in Thames Street.

The census of 1567 lists 2,030 Dutch in London – 'Dutch' at this period usually denoted German-speakers rather than just natives of Holland – out of a total of 2,730 aliens. The other main linguistic–ethnic grouping from the Low Countries, the 'Flemings', were also commonly resident in England, especially throughout the southern counties and East Anglia. Some 4,000 were estimated to be living in 1567 at Norwich alone, with perhaps about 60,000 scattered throughout England.[51] Shakespeare, of course, could have familiarized himself with the history and geography of the Low Countries through such popular volumes (those sold as octavos and quartos rather than as expensive folios) as Ludovico Guicciardini's *Low Countries* (1593) and Edward Grimeston's translation of Jean Le Petit's *The Low-Country Common-Weath* (1609). But they do not offer the kind of character types found in English drama of the period. Instead, the 'Hollanders', as delineated by the London dramatists, are clearly drawn from the oral culture of racial caricature, often prompted by the resentments of local tradesmen against an influx of alien workers with comparable, or higher, levels of skills.

DREAMS OF ANGLO-EUROPEAN INTEGRATION AT THE JACOBEAN COURT 1603–1612

The early Jacobean period experienced a significant growth in western European travel, due to greater accessibility engendered by peacetime conditions. The Edict of Nantes (1598) allowed freedom of conscience to the Huguenots in France and effectively ended the Wars of Religion of the Catholic League. From the early 1600s, Maximilien de Béthune, Duc de Sully, greatly improved the road system and instigated the Briare Canal (completed under Louis XIII), linking the Seine and the

Loire. Younger members of the aristocracy, both Catholic and Protestant, began more commonly to undertake the *giro* or cultural itinerary, usually following the long-familiar travellers' routes through France, Spain, Italy, Germany and the Low Countries. James I's chief minister, Robert Cecil, Earl of Salisbury, and the powerful Howard family, were firm believers in the benefits of this form of education. In 1603 Theophilus Lord Howard de Walden, later Earl of Suffolk, travelled to France; and two youthful Cecils, William Lord Cranborne, later Earl of Salisbury (who recorded in schoolboy French his travels from 1608 to 1610 through France, Italy and Germany), and William Lord Roos (who explored Spain in 1610) left juvenile but engaging accounts of their travels. In 1607 Robert Devereux, later Earl of Essex, married Frances Howard, elder daughter of the Earl of Suffolk, and went abroad in the following year. It became customary for young noblemen to disappear abroad soon after their wedding, as was the case with Lord Cranborne who married Suffolk's younger daughter just before his departure. These inexperienced travellers were invariably accompanied by a more mature guide. Henry Lord Clifford, who had recently married the Earl of Salisbury's daughter Frances, had his studies abroad directed by William Bercher, who later became a diplomat; and in 1610 Thomas Lorkin acted as tutor to Sir Thomas Puckering.[52]

Italy was now well within the reach of young Englishmen, although not all travelled there for educational reasons. One Angelo de Angelis, who regularly supplied intelligence about English visitors to Italy, wrote to Sir Henry Neville in May 1607 about the naval engineer Sir Robert Dudley, the illegitimate son of the Earl of Leicester and Lady Douglas Sheffield. Dudley had left England (deserting his wife and seven children) with a mistress, Elizabeth Southwell, disguised, in true Shakespearean fashion ('Maids as we are, to travel forth so far', *AYL* 1.3.105), as his page. He turned Catholic, married by papal dispensation and fathered another thirteen children. As a skilled engineer, Dudley entered the service of the grand dukes of Tuscany and was responsible for draining the marshes near Pisa. Robert Sidney, who regarded himself as the legitimate heir to his uncles, the earls of Leicester and Warwick, entered into protracted legal proceedings with Dudley, who was also laying claim to these estates. Angelis's letter details his attempts to raise Sidney's case personally with Dudley's employer, the Grand Duke Ferdinand I. As might be expected from an experienced news-gatherer, Angelis's letter also passes on other interesting snippets of information. At Genoa he had recently met Sir Edmund Withipole (knighted January 1600 and married to Frances, daughter of Sir William Cornwallis); a Charles Clement (unidentified); and Sir Oliver Manners (the younger brother of Roger, Earl of Rutland, the future husband of Philip Sidney's daughter, Elizabeth), who was knighted in 1603. Manners had gone abroad in 1605, and had his licence to remain overseas renewed in 1608 and 1611. But then, reported as a 'pervert', he chose to remain abroad permanently, dying in Italy in September 1613.[53]

The assassination of Henri IV in May 1610 by a Catholic fanatic escalated anti-papist hysteria at the English court and prompted the departure abroad of several members of the English Catholic hierarchy, including Sir Thomas and Sir Charles Somerset, the sons of the staunchly Catholic Earl of Worcester. Sir Charles, who had also recently married, left a sophisticated narrative of his travels in 1611–12 through France, Italy, Germany, the Low Countries and Flanders which was probably intended as a reference manual on travel and statecraft for his family and court circle. Like Thomas Coryat, he was keenly interested in theatricals, as is evident from his description of the Huguenot temple at Dieppe:

> it is even built just as one of the play-houses in London, not anie thing to choose, with sundrie doores to come in, in so much that if I had not bene tolde what it had bene, I should have sooner tooke it for such a kinde of house, that the towne had built for to sporte themselves then an other.

Somerset may even have had Friar Laurence's 'distilling liquor' or sleeping potion in mind from *Romeo and Juliet* ('A cold and drowsy humour, for no pulse / Shall keep his nature progress but surcease', 4.1.96–7) when he described the renowned 'fundarie' or 'stilling-house' of the Duke of Florence, which produced

the rarest abstractions and quintiscences of things extracted that
can be thought of; for when he would present anie king or prince
with a present, it is of these rare abstractions & waters, which
will keepe a man alive for some little space without a pulse; such
is the excellencie of them.[54]

Somerset's experiences of European travel and diplomacy closely
linked him with the circle of King James's eldest son, Prince Henry. The
prince consciously revived the Earl of Essex's continental interests and
encouraged members of his own court entourage to avail themselves of
any opportunities to acquire firsthand knowledge of European affairs
and diplomacy. Thomas Coryat confidently assumed Henry's personal
interest when dedicating to the prince his *Crudities* (1611), recounting
his own peregrinations through western Europe.

it may perhaps yield some little encouragement to many noble
and generous young gallants that follow your Highness's court,
and give attendance upon your peerless person, to travel into
foreign countries, and enrich themselves partly with the
observations, and partly with the languages of outlandish
regions, the principal means (in my poor opinion) to grace and
adorn those courtly gentlemen, whose noble parentage, ingenious education, and virtuous conversation have made worthy to
be admitted into your Highness's court.[55]

Such interests were entirely predictable, since King James had
surrounded his eldest son with courtiers and advisers who had
extensive experience of western European courts. Sir Thomas Chaloner,
one of Henry's childhood mentors and his Lord Chamberlain from
1610, had travelled to Italy during the 1580s and lived at Florence
from 1596 to 1598 as Essex's agent. Similarly, Henry's secretary, Adam
Newton, had taught in France during the 1580s; and his comptroller,
John Holles, later First Earl of Clare, had travelled extensively in France
and Italy.[56]

The European interests of Prince Henry's court mark the culmination during Shakespeare's lifetime of England's intellectual openness to

continental influences and mark a distinct shift from the isolationism of the mid-1590s, as typified in the image of England projected in *King John*:

> England, hedg'd in with the main,
> That water-walled bulwark, still secure
> And confident from foreign purposes.

(2.1.26–8)

From the mid-1600s until Henry's death in 1612, firsthand knowledge of continental affairs became both fashionable and politically essential for ambitious English courtiers. Henry was kept especially well informed of continental military, diplomatic and religious affairs. Sir Charles Cornwallis, later treasurer of the prince's household, was appointed resident ambassador in Spain in 1605 and became one of his earliest foreign correspondents. In 1606 the prince also began a correspondence with his great hero (and friend of Robert Sidney), Henri IV of France; and by 1610 Prince Henry was receiving regular reports on French politics from Sir Thomas Edmondes, the English ambassador at Paris. Even his childhood companions participated in this kind of intelligence-gathering, as exemplified by Sir Charles Somerset's travel diary. Similiarly, in 1608 the sixteen-year-old John Harington toured the Low Countries, Germany, Switzerland, Italy and France, sending home to Henry formal letters in both Italian and Latin, detailing his observations of architecture, fortifications and military engineering.[57]

Prince Henry also aspired to a reputation as a connoisseur of the arts – a model later followed with passionate commitment by his younger brother, King Charles I. Sir Dudley Carleton was instructed to acquire paintings for the prince's collections when he became ambassador at Venice in 1610; and Sir Edward Conway (then governor of Brill), performed a similar task in the Low Countries. Foreign states responded to these interests with alacrity. From Venice came paintings, and from the Grand Duke of Tuscany a set of twelve bronzes from the studio of Giambologna (recalling Shakespeare's 'rare Italian master, Julio Romano' (d. 1546), *WT* 5.2.98). Henry also sought to recruit artists, architects and designers from abroad; and his circle even took a keen interest in continental fashions of dress. In March 1611 the Venetian ambassador drily reported that his boyish household had recently adopted an Italianate style, in preference to their previously favoured French garb.[58] Such youthful vacillations in fashion were by now a staple of dramatic comedy, as recalled in Don Pedro's description of Benedick:

> There is no appearance of fancy in him, unless it be a fancy that he hath to strange disguises – as to be a Dutchman today, a Frenchman tomorrow, or in the shape of two countries at once, as a German from the waist downward, all slops, and a Spaniard from the hip upward, no doublet.

> (MA 3.2.29–34)

THE VALUE OF WESTERN EUROPEAN TRAVEL

The interests of Prince Henry's circle mark the culmination of sixty years of English acquisition of informed knowledge of continental affairs; and they paved the way for the renowned cultural explorations of Inigo Jones and Thomas Howard, Earl of Arundel, in Italy between 1613 and 1615. Arundel (along with Robert Sidney) had been appointed as one of four royal commissioners to accompany Prince Henry's sister, Elizabeth, back to Heidelberg after her marriage to Frederick, Elector Palatine. The passage of this enormous entourage across France and Germany (with some of its members then heading off into Italy) effectively marked the beginning of a new political and cultural phase in Anglo-continental relations. Henceforth, the trials and tribulations of Elizabeth of Bohemia and her family (including her son, the royalist general Prince Rupert), along with those of her French sister-in-law, Queen Henrietta Maria, formed an unwavering European focus of interest for the English royal family and their supporters during the next half-century.[59]

How, then, might a London dramatist have gained access to these rarefied court circles? One possible connection is through the likes of Dudley Carleton, who, as revealed in his correspondence, was a keen observer of dramatic entertainments. He attended Daniel's *The Vision of the Twelve Godesses* (1604) and *The Masque of Blackness* (1605) by Ben Jonson and Inigo Jones; and he probably knew personally some of those who contributed to court entertainments. Carleton was typical of the new breed of highly educated, continentally aware civil servant at the Jacobean court. After Christ Church, Oxford, he went to France twice in 1596–7, seeking employment in the service of Sir Anthony Mildmay, the English ambassador at Paris. By spring 1598 he was at Ostend as secretary to the governor, Sir Edward Norris; and in April 1602 he was appointed secretary to the newly appointed ambassador in France, Sir Thomas Parry. In March 1605 Carleton joined the embassy of Charles Howard, Earl of Nottingham, to deliver James's ratification of the recently signed Anglo-Spanish peace treaty to Madrid. Appointed ambassador to Venice in early 1611 in succession to Sir Henry Wotton, he remained there until October 1615 when he took up his new post as ambassador to The Hague in March 1616 (a month prior to Shakespeare's death). Here he came across yet another member of the Sidney family, Robert's sister, Mary Sidney Herbert, now Dowager Countess of Pembroke, who was travelling on the continent for her health.[60]

Printed accounts of continental journeys were now also beginning to circulate with two major volumes, Coryat's *Crudities* and Fynes Moryson's *Itinerary*, providing a wealth of firsthand descriptions of western Europe during Shakespeare's own lifetime. *Crudities* adopted an eccentric narrative style to record a rich blend of personal observation and, probably, a pinch of fictional reconstruction. Ben Jonson, along with numerous others, contributed a commendatory acrostic poem to the *Crudities*; and in the spring of 1612 he himself travelled to Paris as tutor to Sir Walter Ralegh's wild son, Wat, staying on the continent to visit Brussels, Antwerp and Leiden before returning to London by June 1613. In contrast to Coryat's volume (which was probably self-financed), Moryson's *Itinerary* (1617) was conceived essentially as a scholarly volume; and it remains the most authoritative work of travel writing printed during the Jacobean period (even though it described Moryson's experiences abroad in 1591–7). Its methodologies were essentially objective and forward-looking in their reliance upon empirical observation and the best available secondary works. Moryson's writings firmly distanced themselves from an older world of suspicion about other European nations. He argued that travellers should not seek to denigrate other nations or jingoistically assert the innate superiority of the Englishman. Dismissing 'climate theory' as mere superstition, Moryson proposed that virtues and vices are not determined by local and regional conditions but by the individual's observation of philosophical precepts and the tenets of his religious faith:

> Therefore not the North, nor the South, but Phylosophicall precepts, godly lawes, and the knowledge of Gods word, or otherwise the wants thereof, make men good or ill, and where knowledge, religion, and good lawes flourish, there vertues are practised, but among barbarous and superstitious people, living in Cimerian darkenesse, all vices have ever, and will for ever flourish ... knowledge and religion are the causes of all vertues, as ignorance and atheisme or superstition, are the causes of all vices, neither are these causes hereditary to any clime or nation, but are dispersed through the world by supernal distribution diversly at divers times.[61]

The cautious perspectives of *An Itinerary* remind us that geographical and sociological exactitude are not necessarily the stuff of good drama. While, for example, Jonson painstakingly documents the topography of a real Venice in *Volpone* – he certainly seeks to show that he *knows* this landscape – the reality of this world is illusory, since its characters are larger than life and the game of 'legacy hunting' belongs more properly to the Roman Empire rather than the Venetian republic.[62] His traveller, Sir Politic Would-be, is the naïve innocent who believes himself to be knowledgeable – he claims (4.1.40) to have read Lewkenor's 1599 translation of Contarini's *The Commonwealth and Government of Venice* – even though he misunderstands everything he sees.[63] He only perceives the superficialities of his geographical location and thereby confirms that travel remains valueless without judgement. Through the likes of

Jonson's Sir Politic and Shakespeare's 'brave Master Shoe-tie the great traveller' (*MM* 4.3.17), or his vaingloriously comic Armado, 'a man of travel, that hath seen the world', who is simply 'too peregrinate' (*LLL* 5.1.100, 14), we are reminded that travel can actually accentuate an individual's predisposition to folly. The wise old lord Lafeu shrewdly dismisses Parolles with the words 'You are a vagabond and no true traveller' (*AW* 2.3.255–6); and Rosalind derides how a foolish traveller demeans his own nationality:

> Farewell, Monsieur Traveller. Look you lisp and wear strange suits: disable all the benefits of your own country; be out of love with your nativity, and almost chide God for making you that countenance you are; or I will scarce think you have swam in a gondola.

> (*AYL* 4.1.31–6)

Shakespeare's plays demonstrate that the mere specifics of location should always be filtered through the more potent lenses of imagination and judgement. Does it, then, really matter that Proteus and Valentine in *Two Gentlemen* (2.3.33) undergo a sea-journey from Verona to Milan (while the disguised Julia plans to make the same journey by land); or that in *All's Well* (3.4.4 and 3.5.34) Helena seeks a route from Roussillon in France to Compostella in Spain via Florence; or, most famously, in *The Winter's Tale* (1611), that Perdita is shipwrecked on the sea-coast of land-bound Bohemia? One answer, it seems, lies in simply recognizing that an unavoidable (but sometimes highly creative) tension will always exist between the factual demands of travel writing and the imaginative aspirations of theatrical representations of foreign lands.

Chapter Three

SHAKESPEARE'S READING OF MODERN EUROPEAN LITERATURE

Stuart Gillespie

Neither the word 'literature', nor the words 'modern' or 'European' used in literary contexts, carried the same meaning for Shakespeare and his contemporaries as they do today. 'Modern' is the least vexed of them, and in this chapter denotes 'the near-contemporary' rather than the larger categories of 'post-classical' or 'not ancient' that Shakespeare's era often used it to cover (as in the contrasting of 'ancients and moderns').[1] 'European' was not a *category* of the literary: it *was* the literary. English-language writing was separable only in linguistic terms from the broader European tradition, and with the exception of the Scriptures, no other bodies of writing (such as Middle Eastern) were generally known to English readers. Hence 'European literature' is neither discussed nor available as a subject for discussion in the Renaissance. As for 'literature', it existed mainly in the guise of 'letters', one (but only one) of the origins of the concept as it is used – increasingly tendentiously – today. 'Letters' were, of course, associated with reading, and so tended not to include, for instance, oral works (such as legends, or most popular songs) or the more improvisatory kinds of dramatic material (such as mystery plays). And they were associated with durable, serious reading matter, so pamphlets, or tracts, for example, would not usually have counted. But letters embraced some types of writing that would usually not be considered 'literary' today, in particular works of history and scholarship. These early modern boundary-lines have been kept in mind in determining the scope of the present discussion.[2]

Would Shakespeare have tended instead to think in terms of 'Spanish writing' or 'Flemish letters'? Not nearly as much as we might be disposed so to do today. For one thing, the pace of exchange at both the physical and the intellectual level between the states of later sixteenth-century Europe ensured that, in many cultural fields, national traditions did not develop discretely. The Portuguese writer (and Shakespeare source) Jorge de Montemayor (*c.* 1521–61), for example, took up court appointments in Spain in his twenties, but acquired the ideas for his principal work, a pastoral romance, from the Italian *Arcadia* of Jacopo Sannazaro (perhaps during an extended visit to Italy), as well as more episodic material from Italian *novellieri* such as Bandello and Boccaccio. He also travelled in Flanders, and may have accompanied Philip of Spain to England on the journey which ended in the king's marriage to Queen Mary; but he employed the Spanish tongue for his masterpiece, *La Diana Enamorada* (1559). Montemayor's artistic cosmopolitanism was by no means unusual, and his physical rovings hardly unique. The still widespread use of Latin throughout Europe for literary as well as scientific and technical texts adds another dimension: Spanish writers need not write in Spanish, nor French ones in French. The Scottish poet and playwright George Buchanan (1506–82) studied at the Sorbonne, taught in Bordeaux, composed psalm translations in Portugal, translated classical Greek tragedies, wrote Latin poems and plays redolent of the French Renaissance (and admired by Sidney in the *Apology for Poetry*), and after his return to his native country in *c.* 1561 wrote a treatise on kingship and a history of Scotland which may have directly influenced *Macbeth*.[3] Almost all Buchanan's work was composed and printed in Latin, and his writings were published during or immediately after his lifetime in the Netherlands, Germany, Switzerland, England, Scotland, France and Bohemia.

Shakespeare and his contemporaries were in many ways likelier to connect writers through generic links than nationality, and in some respects these links supersede chronological considerations too – the concept of separate literary periods, so prevalent in literary study today, was of less account for Renaissance readers. The novelistic storytellers whose work contributed to a veritable ocean of tales (in prose or in verse, in printed or oral forms) that lapped around the shores of Europe, and of which playwrights eagerly availed themselves, exemplify this. They included immediate predecessors of Shakespeare such as Matteo Bandello (1485–1561; *Novelle* in three volumes, 1554), François Belleforest (1530–83; *Histoires Tragiques extraictes des Oeuvres Italiens de Bandel* in seven volumes, 1559–82) and Giovanni Cinthio (1504–73; *Gli Hecatommithi*, 1565), all well-known sources of Shakespearean plot material. But their collections were not really separate entities, since each writer felt free to retell stories from previous compilations. Hence the Frenchman Belleforest, for example, began by 'extracting' tales from Bandello, subsequently adding into his collection stories from a range of other classical and medieval sources. Most of Bandello's tales had by the end of the sixteenth century been translated, retold and adapted in English, by writers including Arthur Brooke, William Painter and Geoffrey Fenton (all of them read by Shakespeare), sometimes via Belleforest, sometimes within collections which, once again, mixed in a further range of sources. Lying behind the work of all these sixteenth-century figures, sometimes as formal models but often in the very direct sense that their tales are recycled in a later collection, are earlier writers of the European Renaissance, notably the Italian *novellieri* Giovanni Boccaccio (1313–75; *Decamerone, c.* 1348–51), Masuccio of Salerno (*c.* 1415–*c.* 1477; *Cinquante Novelle*, 1476) and Giovanni Fiorentino (fourteenth century; *Il Pecorone*, printed 1558). Particularly once a unified style is imposed on these writers' stories in a contemporary English translation, their own and their period's characteristics tend to disappear amid the impression of a homogeneous mass of material.[4] Painter's very popular *Palace of Pleasure* (1566–75) is a good example, a generally faithful and accurate rendering of 101 'pleasant histories and excellent novels' selected 'out of divers good and commendable authors', including all of the French and Italian ones mentioned in this paragraph, additionally incorporating extracts from writers a thousand years apart from them in time – Livy, Apuleius, Plutarch, Xenophon.

In the cases of many Shakespeare plays it is established that a tale from one or more of these sources is adapted, but, where several alternative versions were available to him, it can be hard to say exactly which he used. For some specialized purposes it will sometimes be important to determine the particular original; the point here, however, is that for Renaissance English readers, and probably even more so for writers, the European novelistic tradition largely transcended national and period boundaries. It had largely ceased to matter what country or language a tale initially belonged to, since its constituents had been naturalized in many; or to what century, since it had been repeatedly retold, adapted, updated. For such reasons, the remainder of this discussion will be divided along loosely generic lines, and the principal categories it will examine are romances; novels; and texts of ideas. But it is worth raising first the question of how Shakespeare would have been able to approach foreign-language texts, and in what forms they were available to him.

SHAKESPEARE'S READING

A long-running scholarly discussion of Shakespeare's knowledge of the classical languages has tended to conclude in acknowledgement that he must have possessed what by today's standards is a high degree of competence in Latin. This was nothing unusual for grammar school products of his time.[5] It can be shown that he also had passable French – again, like many English people, especially Londoners, of the Elizabethan age. As displayed in the plays (primarily *Henry V*), Shakespeare's French is not quite of impeccable standard, perhaps because he did not draw on a native speaker's help; there has also been some speculation that he used a popular 'teach yourself' manual, John Eliot's *Ortho-Epica Gallica*.[6] It now seems possible to add that he also had Italian. Though there are perhaps no decisive cases in which his reading of a known source could *only* have been done in that language, there are a number of occasions on which he seems to follow details found solely in the Italian versions, not in French or English adaptations and translations.[7] Several such cases cumulatively constitute strong evidence.[8] As with Eliot's French manuals, there has been speculation that Shakespeare used John Florio's Italian primers, *Firste Fruits* and *Second Frutes*. The most important point here may be that Shakespeare's knowledge of both French and Italian seems more a practical skill or 'working knowledge', than a matter of scholarly training or social 'accomplishment' (something which might help to account for his apparently limited firsthand knowledge of French and Italian poetry).[9] There are very few suggestions that he knew any other modern language.

Shakespeare is not likely to have read large chunks of foreign-language material. There is repeated evidence for his use of English translations of more extensive works, in preference to the non-English originals that would usually have been readily obtainable. Shakespeare availed himself of the quite suddenly rising tide of English translations of his day. For this reason it is important to bear in mind what kind of thing an Elizabethan literary translation was.[10] Apart from special cases such as the Bible, 'Englishing' often meant something more like what we might today call 'rewriting', as the translator-adventurer conquered and colonized foreign territory and brought home its spoils (such metaphors are common in the period). Not untypical is Sir John Harington's version of Ariosto's *Orlando Furioso* (1591). Harington added material of his own, and imposed cuts; he omitted allusions to Italian life; and he aimed 'to provide a self-consciously rational and moral perspective on the marvelous world of the *Furioso*',[11] in particular by spelling out in added discursive material his own understanding of the 'morals' of the stories. Harington's work is in some respects conservative: other Renaissance English translators simply change names and places at will, and some translations are in fact what we would call synopses, sometimes under the label 'epitome'. In a word, when dealing with Shakespeare's use of a translated work it is often essential to consult the version he would have known, since it cannot be automatically assumed that this will reflect its original in any particular respect.

Beyond this lies a range of still less direct forms of contact which Shakespeare can hardly have avoided making with the work of

European writers by way of adaptations and recyclings, transmissions by intermediaries, or other kinds of indirect influences. Rabelais's larger-than-life characters, for instance, might legitimately be felt to lie somewhere behind Falstaff even if Shakespeare had never heard his name, because other English artists whose work Shakespeare did know had responded to the Frenchman.[12] The importance of this wider European context for Shakespeare's work will be raised again in the final section of this discussion. For the present we shall stay with direct traces of Shakespeare's activity as a reader, and consider the principal kinds of writers involved, and what sort of effects they had on his work.

ROMANCIERS: MONTEMAYOR AND ARIOSTO

That the name of Jorge de Montemayor is unfamiliar to students of English literature is a reminder of the standard assumption about Shakespeare that his creativity characteristically takes the form of transforming the material he found in minor, provincial works into the stuff of timeless masterpieces. For Montemayor's *Diana* is very far from being the transiently fashionable text retrieved from a far corner of the continent that this unfamiliarity would seem to suggest. The fame of this intricately plotted romance throughout western Europe over a period of some 200 years – it was first published about 1559, and a new abridgement appeared as late as 1737 – is reflected in Shakespeare's time in admiration on both sides of the English Channel, from such figures as Calderón, Cervantes, Sidney, Drummond of Hawthornden, Donne, Beaumont and Fletcher, and, it seems, Spenser. There were at least four attempts at an English translation, culminating in the 1598 publication of Bartholomew Yong's rendering, which it is likely Shakespeare read either before or after its public appearance, perhaps in conjunction with other English versions.[13] On another level, the case of Montemayor is a reminder that Shakespeare not only transformed the European literature he knew but was transformed by it; even that his European sources may sometimes be of greater stature than the works deriving from them. The effect of comparing Montemayor's romance to the earliest Shakespeare play it affected,

The Two Gentlemen of Verona, is to show that the *Diana* is a mature masterpiece, whereas the *Two Gentlemen* is not.

The *Diana* is a pastoral romance – a romance, that is, of a kind it is less than easy to find our way back to in the English-speaking world, where the epic kind became the norm. Pastoral comedy is less alien, mainly owing to Shakespeare himself. Montemayor's heroine Felismena, who rescues her lover from several knights while disguised as a shepherdess, may appear to the English reader a peculiar mixture of Shakespeare's Rosalind and Spenser's Britomart. And, though plot material and/or particular incidents in *Two Gentlemen*, *As You Like It*, *Twelfth Night* and, more tenuously, *A Midsummer Night's Dream* can be traced back to Montemayor,[14] of much more significance is the generic correspondence – in a word, the ethos of pastoral romance. Judith Kennedy, the twentieth-century editor of Montemayor's translator Bartholomew Yong, has described these affinities quite precisely:

> In both [Shakespeare and Montemayor] we find a compelling vision of the attraction of the pastoral idea. In both love and lovers are supreme. In both (and this is by no means generally true of the pastoral convention) we are considerably more interested in the heroines than in the heroes. In both we confidently expect a happy outcome to the trials of love. In both a major virtue of love, which brings the reward of happiness, is constancy. So great is the power of this virtue, that a lover's constancy may redeem the inconstancy or lack of faith of the beloved.[15]

Strikingly, although this description refers to *Two Gentlemen*, it would pass muster as an account of the characteristics of Shakespeare's comedy in general. Given that we know the playwright read Montemayor very early, and had his work in mind over a long period, the possibility exists that the *Diana* should be thought of as foundational for Shakespearean comedy.[16]

We shall now return to Ariosto. Although it is a different kind of relationship I want to focus on here, a case has been made on a principle similar to Kennedy's for the *Orlando Furioso* as the inspiration behind *A Midsummer Night's Dream*. Shakespeare seems to have known the poem, and used it elsewhere; why then may not the affinities between their moods suggest a deeper relationship here? This is the line of thought pursued by Mario Praz, who argues:

> Ariosto's world was, in its very essence, alien to Spenser, but Shakespeare, the same Shakespeare who in his Italian plays represented the Italians like men, and not like the frantic puppets who formed the stock-in-trade of the Elizabethan blood and thunder tragedies, Shakespeare could seize the spirit of Ariosto's poem.[17]

What is this spirit? *Orlando Furioso* is one of the great European narrative poems, with an immense cast of characters kept in constantly shifting play, a sparklingly diverse epic of 'splendour and plenitude', 'regaling the mind and senses with vivid awareness of the multi-fariousness of life'.[18] As such it could and did sponsor the work of a wide range of imitators and followers, but Praz has in mind particular affinities in theme and tone with the *Dream*, in particular 'capricious and despotic love, which changes allegiance, maddens the heroes and the heroines, making them dote on a base object'. For present purposes we may note the suggestion without adjudicating the case. As well as the possibility of a direct filiation, with Harington's 1591 translation published at the right moment for Shakespeare to have encountered and used it, Ariosto's followers, such as the Italian pastoral playwrights Della Valle, Pasqualigo, Guazzoni and others, wafted the spirit to which Praz refers widely around Europe. My business, however, is with the part played by *Orlando Furioso* in *Much Ado about Nothing*, and another kind of effect this case allows us to witness.

Ariosto's Canto 5 (see Figure 6) tells a version of the story, widespread in Europe by the sixteenth century, of a lover tricked by an enemy into believing his beloved is false – the Hero–Claudio plot of Shakespeare's play. In *Orlando*, Genevra has the Hero role: she is a Scottish princess in love with, and loved by, the noble Ariodante. Her maid Dalinda has been secretly visiting Polynesso, Duke of Albany, in Genevra's room, by the use of a rope ladder. The treacherous Polynesso has aspired to the hand of Genevra herself, and, his love turning to jealous hatred, he has resolved to undo the noble lovers by having

FIGURE 6 Plate illustrating Canto 5 (a source for *Much Ado about Nothing*) from Ariosto's *Orlando Furioso in English Heroical Verse*, trans. Sir John Harington (1634), p. 31; first published 1591.

Dalinda pose at the window as Genevra in order to deceive Ariodante. All this is reported to the brave Renaldo by Dalinda, whom he rescues on his arrival in Scotland from assailants commissioned by Polynesso after Dalinda has outlived her usefulness to him. Renaldo then undertakes to rescue the accused Genevra from her captors, and succeeds.

But Ariosto, though an accepted source for Shakespeare's plot, is not the only one. Shakespeare resisted the exaggerated romance figures the Italian epic offered, developing his narrative away from them partly by helping himself to ingredients from another version of the tale, Matteo Bandello's in his *Novelle* of 1554 (no. 22). This combining of two sources from a single European tradition is the key to the remarkable adroitness of the play's main plot.[19] Bandello's version, closer to Shakespeare's overall, offered a far less romantic story: there is, for example, the realistic explanation of the Hero figure's withdrawal from society after the failed wedding ceremony, that her father sends her to the country in the hope of marrying her off later under another name. It also offered a number of striking episodes to any playwright: the scenes of public rejection of the bride by her lover, her swoon and apparent death, the obsequies and epitaph, and the whole episode of the 'substitute' bride who turns out to be the original one. Clearly, many effects, too diverse to explore here, flow from these dramatic choices and combinations, but two things perhaps stand out as indicating Shakespearean habits of composition: the tonal departure from the Ariostan starting-point, and his deliberate use of two sources of the same narrative. In Ariosto, the sense of tragic danger and murderous violence issues at the close in the villain Polynesso's destruction and death, while Dalinda enters a nunnery: the extreme romantic level on which *Orlando* operates was not what the dramatist wanted. *Much Ado* is situated, rather, in a tragicomic realm, which Bandello's conclusion takes Shakespeare some way towards. As the Arden (series 2) editor of the play, A.R. Humphreys, writes: 'Interweaving Bandello's materials with Ariosto's, Shakespeare shows a mind ranging over elements loosely similar but so markedly variant in tone and incidents that only the shrewdest of judgements could co-ordinate them into a theme of such tragi-comic force.'[20] The playwright's dual debt, far from merely making him doubly derivative, funds *Much Ado*'s originality.

STORYTELLERS: BANDELLO, CINTHIO, BELLEFOREST, MASUCCIO, BOCCACCIO, FIORENTINO

This discussion has already had to make room for one of the 'storytellers' or *novellieri* of the Italian Renaissance,[21] and suggested one or two reasons for their importance to Shakespeare: their realism, their provision of a vantage point firmly fixed in the everyday world. They claimed, in fact, to be depicting the everyday Italian life of their time. The type of narrative for which they are best known today, involving the cuckolding of a jealous husband, say, or a randy monk, might suggest their effects on Shakespeare would be felt predominantly in the comedies. This is arguable, but certain of the tragedies and 'problem plays' are very much part of the picture here. This is compatible with the novel's realistic modality, and compatible too with its less widely understood tonal and stylistic variety. Bandello translated Euripides, and both he and Cinthio courted the contemporary taste for Senecan tragedy in their tales. Such *novellieri* cultivated the moment of extreme passion, 'the quick gush of blood, the sound of chattering teeth, the odour of carrion and sudden attack of nausea'.[22] The flexibility of the form they developed was comparable to that of theatrical tragicomedy, something Shakespeare recognized in drawing upon it in, particularly, *All's Well* and *Measure for Measure*. Moreover, as one or two examples will indicate, a common feature of the novelists' work is an ethical ambiguity or ambivalence, from straightforward mockery of what is respectable and reputable, to the creation of an unbridgeable gap between a tale pointing one way and a framing narrative which implies a quite different interpretation.

The following summary sets out the approximate picture for debts of a more than incidental kind ('approximate' most often because of uncertainties about which version of a tale the playwright used), and notes in parentheses doubtful cases and indirect use:

Boccaccio: *All's Well*, (?)*Cymbeline* (*Troilus and Cressida* via Chaucer, but not a novel)

Bandello: *Othello*, *Much Ado* (*Romeo and Juliet* via Arthur Brooke, *Twelfth Night* via Belleforest and Barnaby Riche, (?)*Two Gentlemen of Verona* (?)via Montemayor)

Belleforest: *Hamlet*

Masuccio: (?)*Merchant of Venice*

Fiorentino: (?)*Merchant of Venice*, (?)*Merry Wives of Windsor*

Cinthio: *Othello*, *Measure for Measure*

My focus within this mass of material will be on the 'problem plays', a key part of Shakespeare's work in the present context because here 'theatrical experimentation [is] combined with a close reading of Italian sources and analytical attention to issues of central importance in the culture of the Renaissance'.[23] Shakespeare's handling of the sources for *Troilus and Cressida*, *Measure for Measure* and *All's Well* can readily be seen in these terms.

In the first two cases the parts played by the novelists are less direct than in the last. As noted above, Boccaccio lies behind *Troilus and Cressida*, but the story he tells is mediated to Shakespeare through Chaucer, and independently through a much larger group of writers who throughout the Renaissance had used it to explore issues both of heroism and of literary aspiration. Shakespeare's handling of these subjects in this play, relating them to such things as hierarchy, Machiavellian policy and rhetoric, is set within a narrative context which allows him to invoke the very beginnings of European cultural history as he understood it; to reflect on the classics, and even, as far as he ever did, to think his way back towards Homer.[24] One could in fact argue that *Troilus and Cressida* is his most 'European' play. Cinthio's *Measure for Measure* narrative (*Hecatommithi*, 8.5), the story of Promos and Cassandra, comes to Shakespeare primarily through George Whetstone's two versions, one dramatic and the other novelistic. These are adaptations rather than translations of Cinthio, so that, for example, Whetstone's prose version, in the *Heptameron of Civil Discourses*, introduces low-life scenes (and the name 'Isabella'). Still, Whetstone's work could not have come into existence were it not for that of the Italian. Whetstone takes an interest in the theme of civic government and the control of corruption, as well as the hierarchy of secular power. His dramatic version, probably Shakespeare's dominant source, is in some ways a limited achievement. It is not disputed, however, that Shakespeare, in a recent editor's formulation, 'deliberately used' the 'main components' and 'basic structural pattern' of Whetstone's Cinthio, an act which (for example in the acceptance of the low-life dimension) implies the importation of some of its concerns as well as its story and incidents.[25]

But it is *All's Well* that deserves centre-stage in this discussion, as one of Shakespeare's most direct and important approaches to the European novelists. Boccaccio's version[26] of the traditional 'clever wench' tale forms the ninth story of the third day of the *Decameron*. Giletta de Nerbone, like Shakespeare's Helena, is the daughter of a physician who uses her inherited talents well. Boccaccio's tale belongs to a group illustrating how personal goals can be accomplished through *industria* (application and enterprise), the sexual form Giletta's 'industry' takes creating another and partly ironic dimension. Giletta effects the cure of the king, who rewards her with the hand of Beltrano, the Count of Roussillon. The count refuses to consummate the marriage, requiring that she bear him a child (though a virgin) and produce a ring from his finger. Giletta undertakes a pilgrimage to Florence, returning to find the count attempting to bed another woman. With her connivance, this is turned to account as Giletta's opportunity to acquire the ring and become pregnant; Beltrano accepts her hand when he sees the valuable commodity her wits represent.

In Shakespeare, several early departures from Boccaccio (and Painter) are significant. Helena's social position is humbler than Giletta's: the latter, as the daughter of a very wealthy individual, now deceased, is at much less of a remove from the man she loves, and hence her advancement is less improbable. Shakespeare's king, and what we hear of the old count, establishes a contrast that does not exist in Boccaccio between a noble old order and a corrupt new age. Both features move Shakespeare's plot away from Boccaccio and towards the different literary tradition of tales illustrating the exemplary worth of a humble individual who regenerates a stricken kingdom through a mysterious inherited skill, to be rewarded by marriage to an aristocrat of the realm. In other words, Shakespeare has imposed a chivalric quest pattern on to Boccaccio's tale.

This redirecting of the plot is not, of course, without its problems and tensions (the addition of the figure of Parolles bringing in another set). But it is sufficiently clear that Shakespeare has turned a relatively slight narrative into something more ambitious and multi-layered. He generates questions about gender roles, and provides much more intimate insights into the emotions of his central characters. Nevertheless, it should not be assumed that this is a simple case of a sophisticated Shakespeare transforming an undemanding original, for Boccaccio's starting-points may have been crucial. All traditional versions of the chivalric quest employ a male hero and take place within a male arena; Shakespeare's does neither, and the clear reason for this is his plot source. As suggested above, there is in Boccaccio's Giletta a hint of sexual impropriety; she is described as more closely attached to the young count than would have been proper in a maiden of her years. This looks like the origin of Shakespeare's interest in the gender roles the story develops, as Leah Scragg has explained: 'Rather than being written from the perspective of a male protagonist, the play ... encourages audience alignment with the female point of view, the implication of impropriety in Boccaccio's narrative functioning as a springboard for an exploration of the assumptions governing gender behaviour encoded within the traditional story.'[27] Giletta has done what is normally considered laudable, in using her talents to gain her ends: 'Nature hath given us wit to flout at Fortune' (*AYL* 1.2.41) is Boccaccio's main theme (and one which several other Shakespearean heroines embody too – Portia, Rosalind and Celia as well as Helena). But below this most obvious level there runs another current in the novella: is Giletta immodest or forward in her attachment, or dishonest in duping and bedding Beltrano? Such suggestions, it would seem, rather than the plot itself of the Italian story, sowed the seeds of Shakespeare's exploration of romantic and sexual conventions in this play.

TEXTS OF IDEAS:
ERASMUS, MACHIAVELLI, MONTAIGNE

In the past, it has often been assumed that the most noteworthy ways in which Shakespeare is affected by his fellow writers' work are in matters of plot and storyline. Geoffrey Bullough's *Narrative and Dramatic Sources of Shakespeare* assembles eight volumes of materials which show mainly these kinds of patterns. But there are other, arguably more important, ways in which one writer's work can impact on another's. Some of these have already been suggested. This section focuses more squarely on these matters, in relation to what I am calling 'texts of ideas'.

Within this category fall, first, several European writers whose tracks in the Shakespeare corpus are probably confined to a single play, or in many cases a single passage. Such seems to have been the effect, for example, of Palingenius's *Zodiacus Vitae* (1530s), a Latin verse compendium of astronomical, moral and philosophical thought which Shakespeare may well have encountered at school, on Jacques's 'All the world's a stage' speech.[28] A little higher up the scale in terms of its effects on Shakespeare is the Flemish writer Alexandre Sylvain's work called (in the English translation of 1596 by 'L.P.') *The Orator*. Sylvain's book consists of a series of rhetorical debates on moral-cum-legal issues, one of which concerns 'a Jew, who would for his debt have a pound of the flesh of a Christian', and another three of which offer parallels to the situations of *Measure for Measure*. The work is not a narrative text but a debating vehicle, and its importance for Shakespeare probably lies here rather than in its exiguous stories: the two opposing sides of the dilemmas it develops generate the kind of structured dialectic on moral and judicial matters that he seems to have aimed at in the 'problem plays'.[29]

In such a case we begin to see how the European tradition was able to offer Shakespeare a range of works which, though not possessing imaginative or dramatic appeal, could stimulate on other levels, structural or conceptual. But Sylvain was not a figure of any great intellectual stature, and if Shakespeare did use his book it probably came in his way largely by accident. Far more important for Shakespeare among 'texts of ideas' is the mainstream European humanist tradition of such writers as Petrarch, Erasmus and Montaigne, a tradition whose impact is felt over the length and breadth of Shakespeare's work. Yet its importance for that work is far from universally recognized, one reason being the difficulty of proving direct influence. There are no plots for Shakespeare to draw on in the work of these non-narrative, non-dramatic writers, and few standard translations where one might look for verbal parallels – assuming we expected their influence to be apparent in Shakespeare's lexical choices. Moreover, since the humanists characteristically dealt in arguments and ideas adopted from the classics (such as Seneca, Cicero or Plutarch), it is often possible to show in a given case where Shakespeare's train of thought seems to resemble Montaigne's or Erasmus's that he could have arrived at the material independently.[30] In the cases of Petrarch and Erasmus, the extremely wide diffusion of their work often makes it impossible to trace a direct connection, and it is often likely that one or several intermediary texts lie between their work and the dramatist's.

But none of this should prevent us from accepting that the spirit of these humanists echoes through Shakespeare's writing. It almost goes without saying, for example, that Erasmus's hugely influential *Institutio Principis Christiani* lies somewhere in the background of *Henry V*, though no verbal resemblances are known.[31] Or take the very plausible connection between the *Moriae Encomium* (*Praise of Folly*, 1511) and Shakespeare's interest in the figure of the wise, critical fool. While it would be rash to propose the *Praise of Folly* as the *fons et origo* of *King Lear*'s obsession with folly, or of Hamlet's habitual way of thinking, and while unambiguous verbal echoes of the Erasmian text cannot be produced from either the Latin or the available English translation (Thomas Chaloner's of 1549), one can go further than the merely neutral term 'analogue'.[32] We are not dealing here with a unique parallel existing in a vacuum: Erasmus's work was part of the mental furniture of the later sixteenth century, and can hardly have failed to contribute to making available some of Shakespeare's modes of thought.[33] This would be so even if Shakespeare had never read a word of this seminal work. The stress Erasmian humanism generated on Christ as a fool – Erasmus's presentation of Christ's 'folly' – is biblically based, but cannot reasonably be imagined to have no connection with Shakespearean episodes such as Cordelia's 'foolish' conduct.[34]

I have already suggested that it is impossible to separate out the influence of the Greek and Latin classics from that of the humanists, and nor should we wish to. For the high European culture of which England was partaking, somewhat belatedly but none the less enthusiastically, was unified above all by the Greek and Latin heritage. Indeed, the writers we are considering here spent their lives promoting that heritage. European artistic and intellectual priorities took their rise from the classics, with European artists and thinkers symbiotically selecting and promoting those which seemed to serve their purposes best. Erasmus and his followers are the inaugurators of the classical phase of English and European literature, and mediate the classics to the moderns. Emrys Jones has written, 'Shakespeare ... must be seen as a writer who unavoidably breathed the neo-classical atmosphere', adding: 'without humanism there could have been no Elizabethan literature: without Erasmus, no Shakespeare.'[35]

I shall take just one of Erasmus's works for more detailed illustration. An Erasmian text of some significance here is the *Adagia* or *Adages* (*Collectanea Adagiorum Veterum*, 1500), his collection of proverbs and *sententiae* from Greek and Latin authors which developed over many years of revised and expanded editions. This achieved a particularly wide audience, mainly because of its status as a school text, and its percolation down through further compilations such as elementary dictionaries which drew on it. The nature of the *Adages* is such that its influence can easily function fleetingly, in a resonant word or image, rather than in a conceptual way. One plausible example of Shakespeare's use of it, often noted by editors and others, is in Lucrece's lament:

> 'O opportunity, thy guilt is great!
> 'Tis thou that execut'st the traitor's treason;
> Thou sets the wolf where he the lamb may get;
> Whoever plots the sin, thou poinst the season.

'Tis thou that spurn'st at right, at law, at reason;
   And in thy shady cell where none may spy him,
   Sits sin to seize the souls that wander by him.

'Thou mak'st the vestal violate her oath;
Thou blow'st the fire when temperance is thaw'd;
Thou smother'st honesty, thou murder'st troth,
Thou foul abettor, thou notorious bawd!
Thou plantest scandal, and displacest laud:
   Thou ravisher, thou traitor, thou false thief!
   Thy honey turns to gall, thy joy to grief . . .'

                                (*Luc* 876–89)

As has been noticed before, this seems to draw on Erasmus's exposition of the proverb *Nosce tempus*, quoted here from Richard Taverner's translation of the *Adages* (first published 1552):

> Know time. Oportunitie is of such force, that of honest it maketh unhonest, of dammage avauntage, of pleasure, grevaunce, of a good turne a shrewed turne, and contrariwise of unhonest honest, of avauntage dammage, and brieflie to conclude it cleane chaungeth the nature of thinges. This oportunitie or occasion (for so also ye maye call it in aventuringe and finishinge a busines) doubtles beareth the chiefe stroke, so that not without good skill the painims of old time counted it a divine thinge.[36]

But, given that Shakespeare's use of Erasmian 'concepts' is so hard to demonstrate, how can such examples of local echoes be said to signify more than an opportunistic appropriation of a word or image? It is a question of the habits of thought they suggest. A few lines earlier in the poem Lucrece has been reflecting thus:

The aged man that coffers up his gold
Is plagu'd with cramps and gouts and painful fits,
And scarce hath eyes his treasure to behold;
But like still-pining Tantalus he sits,
And useless barns the harvest of his wits,

> Having no other pleasure of his gain
> But torment that it cannot cure his pain.
>
> *(Luc* 855–61)

Erasmus's *Adages* incorporate the most plausible literary source connecting Tantalus with miserliness: it was Horace who, in his *Sermones*, had cast Tantalus in this role for the Renaissance, and Erasmus had quoted the passage.[37] Even so comparatively incidental an echo within Shakespeare's work suggests how a reading of Erasmus is, in effect, a reading of the classical heritage behind him, and reminds us of Erasmus's role as one of the great European mediators of the classics. Further ramifications of Shakespeare's lines into the parable of the covetous man in Luke 12 (explained by T.W. Baldwin and Kenneth Muir) hint, beyond this, at the compatibility between the work of this great Christian humanist and the biblical material of which Shakespeare makes so much imaginative use.

Machiavelli was a humanist too – or at least a classicist. In a celebrated letter of 10 December 1513 he writes of 'entering the venerable courts of the ancients' and 'nourishing myself on the food which *alone* is mine, and for which I was made'.[38] Machiavelli's two most prominent works in Shakespeare's time, *Il Principe* (written 1513; published 1532) and the commentary on republican principles known as the *Discorsi sopra ... Tito Livio* (published 1531), both attracted and repelled many readers and, more interestingly, often had both effects on the same reader – one case in point perhaps being Shakespeare. John Roe, in the most recent study of the phenomenon, remarks:

> In some places Shakespeare seems to take his lead from Machiavelli (or from what is recognizably Machiavellian) and proves to be as skilful a negotiator of morally dubious action as the Florentine. In other places, he seems more inclined to resist Machiavelli's challenge.[39]

Once again, the question arises of how Shakespeare approached his reading: the issue here is complicated by the intervention of Innocent Gentillet's *Discours contre Machiavel* in 1576, a comprehensive, if long-winded, refutation of Machiavelli's arguments so widely used that for some readers it was the nearest they came to Machiavelli's work itself (which went unlicensed – but was not unobtainable – in England until later in the seventeenth century).[40] Gentillet's polemic may also have been the nearest Shakespeare came to reading Machiavelli, in which case his 'resistance' is the less surprising. At all events, *The Prince* is at the least an exhilarating study in leadership, and Shakespeare's leader figures owe something to it whether directly or indirectly.

Many English playwrights used 'Machiavel' types, and, as is often pointed out, their frequency can be seen as a reflection of the shock the English felt at Machiavelli.[41] On this side of the equation, Shakespeare's response was perhaps not so unusual, his sense of the assumptions that are questioned and the codes that are violated if Machiavelli's idea of political *virtù* is put into practice emerging in a figure like Iago. But to place such figures in the context of realistic plays on English history, as Shakespeare does, is to open up possibilities not always noticed by his fellow dramatists. For one thing, it encourages the presentation of plausibly articulate and (since history's villains often win) effective Machiavels. Shakespeare's Machiavels are not always entirely unattractive figures, their plain speaking and pragmatism cutting a swathe through other characters' more conventional postures (the modernity of *The Prince* is felt in such casual propositions as 'putting aside, then, all the imaginary things that are said about princes and getting down to the truth'[42]). The portrayals of Richard III and Bolingbroke exploit both positive and negative responses towards Machiavelli: Richard's tactical audacity is breathtaking, and fully Machiavellian in making the most of Fortune's opportunities (as in chapter 25 of *The Prince*), though audience revulsion is ensured when it is time for his career to end.[43] Edmund, too, scores a number of points off his chosen adversaries, especially early on in *King Lear*. And it has been argued that, by the time he writes *Macbeth*, Shakespeare is presenting a villain who dies because he fails to follow Machiavellian principles, and a successor (Malcolm) who survives because he adopts them.[44]

Montaigne's case used to be thought radically different, and entirely one-directional. This humane and bookish essayist so appealed to

Shakespeare scholars that, at the peak of the phenomenon in the early twentieth century, scores if not hundreds of passages in the playwright's work were being found to show cast-iron verbal evidence of indebtedness to Florio's translation of him.[45] Retrenchment has been radical, and only one considerable passage is now widely accepted as manifesting verbal echoes: Gonzalo's description of his imaginary commonwealth.[46] It now tends to be assumed that Montaigne's presence is to be found in more diffused and more subterranean ways, but nevertheless that Shakespeare's habits of mind are very much in tune with the Frenchman's.[47] The *Tempest* passage is the obvious test case for these claims.

The source is Montaigne's essay 'Of the Caniballes':

Al our endevours or wit, cannot so much as reach to represent the neast of the least birdlet, it's contexture, beautie, profit and use, no nor the webbe of a seelie spider. *All things* (saith *Plato*) *are produced, either by nature, by fortune, or by arte. The greatest and fairest by one or the other of the two first, the least and imperfect by the last.* Those nations seeme therefore so barbarous unto mee, because they have received very-little fashion from humane wit, and are yet neere their originall naturalitie. The lawes of nature do yet commaund them, which are but little bastardized by ours. And that with such puritie, as I am sometimes grieved the knowlege of it came no sooner to light, at what time ther were men, that better than we could have judged of-it. I am sorrie, *Lycurgus* and *Plato* had it not: for me seemeth that what in those nations wee see by experience, doth not onelie exceede all the pictures wherewith licentious Poesie hath prowdly imbellished the golden age, and al hir quaint inventions to faine a happy condition of man, but also the conception and desire of Philosophie. They could not imagine a genuitie so pure and simple, as we see it by experience; nor ever beleeve our societie might be maintained with so little arte and humane combination. It is a nation, would I answere *Plato*, that hath no kinde of traffike, no knowledge of Letters, no intelligence of numbers, no name of magistrate, nor of politicke superioritie; no use of service, of riches, or of poverty; no contracts, no successions, no dividences, no occupation but idle; no respect of kin[d]red, but common, no apparrell but naturall, no manuring of lands, no use of wine, corne, or mettle. The very words that import lying, falshood, treason, dissimulation, covetousnes, envie, detraction, and pardon, were never heard-of amongst-them. How dissonant would hee finde his imaginary common-wealth from this perfection?[48]

The verbal similarities in Gonzalo's speech – 'No occupation, all men idle' (*Tem* 2.1.155), and so on – cannot readily be explained as anything other than direct echoes. (It would still be worth asking the questions outlined earlier about the form Shakespeare's knowledge took, however – an unusually retentive verbal memory, and a copy of the passage open on his desk, are two different things.) But Shakespeare's passage is not a simple absorption of Montaigne's raw material:

GONZALO

    I'th' commonwealth I would by contraries
    Execute all things, for no kind of traffic
    Would I admit; no name of magistrate;
    Letters should not be known; riches, poverty
    And use of service, none; contract, succession,
    Bourn, bound of land, tilth, vineyard – none;
    No use of metal, corn, or wine or oil;
    No occupation, all men idle, all;
    And women, too, but innocent and pure;
    No sovereignty –

SEBASTIAN   Yet he would be king on't.

ANTONIO The latter end of his commonwealth forgets the beginning.

GONZALO

    All things in common nature should produce
    Without sweat or endeavour; treason, felony,
    Sword, pike, knife, gun, or need of any engine

> Would I not have; but nature should bring forth
> Of its own kind all foison, all abundance,
> To feed my innocent people.
> SEBASTIAN   No marrying 'mong his subjects?
> ANTONIO   None, man, all idle – whores and knaves.
>
> (*Tem* 2.1.148–67)

The drift of Montaigne's account is in fact contested in the Shakespearean episode.[49] First, read carefully, Gonzalo's 'all men idle ... And women, too, but innocent and pure' edits out Montaigne's more radical image of a freethinking, quasi-communist society ('no respect of kin[d]red, but common, no apparrell, but naturall'). Second, the objections of Sebastian and Antonio cannot simply be brushed aside: even the qualified version of Montaigne that Gonzalo offers is subjected to a critique of some force. While Antonio and Sebastian's cavils are mean in spirit, they are none the less recognizable in their general tendency as a not unreasonable corrective to Gonzalo's romanticism. In Montaigne's *Essays* we hear Montaigne's voice, but drama is inherently polyvocal, and in this passage in *The Tempest* we are presented with the interplay which is inevitable when several voices speak to each other. The effect is, as Fred Parker writes, that 'Montaigne's affirmation of a radical naturalness, of the sovereignty of our "puissant mother Nature", cannot be so vigorously affirmed in Shakespeare; it has to be hedged a little by Gonzalo, and provokes in reaction a destructive, cynical voice altogether foreign to Montaigne.'[50] And of course, in the wider context, Montaigne's cannibals become Caliban, who claims allegiance to the 'lawes of nature' and speaks of himself as corrupted by his education.

Parker sums up his sense of Shakespeare's relationship with Montaigne as one of engagement combined with recoil. While the ambition of much scholarly analysis used to lie in demonstrating Shakespeare's proximity to the essayist, it now seems more helpful to point to the latter element. Whereas Montaigne in the *Apology for Raimond de Sebond* insists on the limitations of human reason and recommends humility, Shakespeare (in *Lear*, say), while accepting its precariousness, stresses its preciousness. Whereas Montaigne accepts the equation of man with animals, Shakespeare patrols the boundary. 'Montaigne, whose vision is never tragic, sustains a double perspective which tolerates contradiction: licentiousness is written deeply into the nature of life, but no less necessarily part of our foolish, self-tormenting condition is the impulse to suppress or regulate such energies.'[51] But the energies of Shakespearean tragedy often derive precisely from the impulse to resist the threat of this division. Shakespeare 'engages' with the paradoxes Montaigne offers (whether or not this derives immediately from the essayist's work in particular instances) without adopting Montaigne's positions. After all, a writer does not use another writer most productively when there is a complete accordance between them, but rather in negotiating the space that separates them (when that space is perceptible, but not unmanageably large). The existential questioning of the 'problem plays', and their chronology that seemed to make a fit with the availability of Florio's translation, used to be invoked as indicating the arrival in Shakespeare's work of a modern, sceptical self-consciousness easily discerned in the *Essais*. To locate Montaigne's main effects elsewhere, from the tragedies onwards, allows us to stress that the effect of his work was not to overwhelm but to stimulate Shakespeare, and underlines the example of Machiavelli to show that, while confluences and congruities between Shakespeare and contemporary European thinkers are important, so too are divergences.

CODA: PLAYWRIGHTS

This discussion of Shakespeare's use of European literature has not deliberately avoided his fellow playwrights: there is good reason why the topic has been confined in the present volume to the treatment of the Italian comic dramatists in chapter 4. Giovanni Cinthio (1504–73) and Robert Garnier (1544/5–90) furnish some of the many examples of European dramatists whose lives overlapped with Shakespeare's but whose work has been found to touch only incidentally on his.

Cinthio's tragicomedy *Epitia* (published 1583) is a dramatized adaptation of the *Measure for Measure* source story which he had originally published as a novel in his *Hecatommithi*, a novel rehandled in George Whetstone's play *Promos and Cassandra* (published 1578), used by Shakespeare as well as others. But, although Shakespeare's acquaintance with the Italian stage version is suggested by some verbal and plot echoes,[52] there are very few signs of an affinity between Shakespeare and Cinthio as playwrights – *Measure for Measure* parallels are less likely to be found here than in Cinthio's prose tale, and less likely in either case than in Whetstone's play. The Frenchman Robert Garnier was celebrated in the French avant-garde theatre of the later sixteenth century, and translated by Mary Sidney and her circle in the 1590s – but, again, Shakespeare's interest in and/or knowledge of his work appears small, even in the one instance where some local debts look likely, his version of the Antony and Cleopatra story (*Marc-Antoine*, 1578; Englished 1592).[53] In the cases of both these playwrights, Shakespeare was attracted to other treatments of the material they handled, even though they provided dramatic rather than narrative models: there seem to have been few affinities between his artistic inclinations and theirs.

'Affinity' is an excellent term for the relation between Shakespeare and some of the Italian comic and pastoral playwrights. Even here, proofs of direct contact have proved extremely hard to come by; but a case can be mounted to support the sense that the Italian stage offered important patterns and potentialities. This is a subject for another chapter.

Chapter Four

SHAKESPEARE AND ITALIAN COMEDY

Richard Andrews

It is a commonplace that many of Shakespeare's plots are 'Italian stories on the stage'.[1] Some of those stories do appear in Italian dramatic works of the sixteenth or early seventeenth centuries; but the original or translated sources which were most available, and which Shakespeare is hypothesized as having used, are often texts for reading rather than for performing. It is also the case that, although Italian renderings of certain plots may have been the most accessible versions, the tales themselves often belong to much wider narrative traditions stemming from Europe, the Mediterranean or beyond. Moreover, some 'Italian' plot formulae had already been adopted and transmuted by other European writers before they reached Shakespeare, who no doubt was supremely indifferent in any case to exact definitions of their origin. (An example is Montemayor's *Diana*, the Spanish pastoral romance of 1559: its central intrigues may have contributed directly to *The Two Gentlemen of Verona* and to *Twelfth Night*, but Leo Salingar among others would trace them back in their turn to the anonymous Sienese play *Gli ingannati* of 1532.[2])

All researches and critical arguments on such questions are ultimately concerned with 'units of fiction', or narremes – the things which Shakespeare chooses to make happen in the stories which he dramatizes – and perhaps also with the motivation of his characters. On these subjects the analyses which we pursue, and the judgements which we make, do not often differ materially whether we are dealing with prose or verse narrative on the one hand, or with drama on the other. What tends then to be left out of the equation, in a pursuit of Shakespeare's 'Italian sources', is his relationship specifically to Italian *theatrical* practice. It is one thing to identify stories as fictional events; it is another thing to investigate those methods of presentation of stories and of characters which are peculiar to a text composed for the stage. In this volume, chapter 3 deals principally with the sources of Shakespeare's narrative material and of the attitudes or ideas which accompanied it. This chapter attempts instead to focus exclusively on the ways in which this supreme English dramatist reflects, or does not reflect, techniques belonging to the most important and seminal body of non-English dramaturgy which existed in his time. Questions of plot material and characterization cannot be entirely separated from such an inquiry; but the aim is to avoid dwelling here on any Italian texts or practices not intended for stage performance.

We are not going to argue that Shakespeare (or any other Elizabethan or Jacobean dramatist) looked exclusively to the Italian material and techniques which we shall now describe, or was a simple offshoot from them. There are too many other proven influences on English theatre, often originating from closer to home, to make such an argument tenable; and we cannot fail to acknowledge at every turn the extent to which Shakespeare's personal talent subverts, transforms and transcends any format derived from elsewhere. But an awareness of how Italian innovations had set new standards for European theatre must have existed in England as well as everywhere else. Printed editions of plays and of dramatic theory from Italy were easily available: some of the plays are known to have been translated or adapted, and knowledge of the theory is indisputable in writers such as Sir Philip Sidney and Ben Jonson. In addition we should take much more account than some scholars have been willing to do of an inevitable oral transmission of dramatic ideas within the theatre profession – even if, by definition, the details of such transactions are untraceable in surviving records. Actors in the early modern period were nomadic by nature, and copying or adapting one another's material, even across linguistic divides, was a way of life for them. The greatest amount of promiscuity in this regard occurred between Italy and France; but it is difficult to deny that for the English theatre too Italian drama was simply *there*, to be noted, half remembered, sometimes copied, sometimes deliberately resisted. Shakespeare made use of it when he chose – consciously or not, and more in some plays than in others. Its nature needs to be properly delineated and understood, placed alongside all the other influences, and then given neither more nor less than its due weight. However, because of some misconceptions which are still current, the delineation must first be done with some care.

Italian Renaissance drama was born in the court and the schoolroom, under the banner of what we now call 'humanism' or the 'classical revival'. Scholars and gentlemen in the various Italian states insisted dogmatically that, in the new cultural world which they were creating for society's élite, ancient Greek and Roman models should be followed and medieval ones obliterated. All the drama of the recent past was seen as totally lacking in cultural and (just as importantly) social prestige.

This Italian revolution had a fundamental effect on performed art in western culture and civilization, setting in motion a series of major transformations in terms of how theatre was conceived and managed. These affected not only the structure and content of plays; not only the social, physical and economic organization of theatres and theatre performances; but also (as is less often recognized) the whole cultural status of theatre and of playwriting. In the medieval period, the production of playtexts had been seen as an ephemeral and occasional activity: if scripts were preserved (as was the case with civic collections of mystery plays), then their authorship was both collective and unimportant and their value purely local. But the humanists had inherited from Greece and Rome texts of stage comedy and tragedy which had been preserved and studied for centuries, and which had been appreciated in antiquity on the same level as the greatest epic poetry. They wished now, as part of their campaign to re-acquire classical styles and values, to bestow Authorship, and hence Authority, on correctly composed dramatic compositions; and hence to grant them the new immortality of publication in printed form. Regular printing of new Italian plays in the classical style was established without controversy, as much as a century before Ben Jonson was derided in England for publishing his dramatic *Workes* in 1616.[3] Jonson was an open and enthusiastic proponent of Italian principles in drama, including the principle of authorial immortality. The evidence suggests that Shakespeare himself was less systematically interested in publication – or else his company was more concerned to keep commercial control of his texts, rather than release versions which could then be performed by others. But the existence of millions of critical words composed on Shakespeare over 400 years, including the present volume, shows that the Jonsonian, and hence the Italian, view has prevailed. We now accept without question that dramatic literature is an integral part of 'culture' in its highest sense, and that dramatists should be considered as Authors. Heminge and Condell presumably thought the same, when they put together the First Folio.

The humanist vision had a radical effect on the composition of Italian plays, which was transmitted in greater or less degree to the rest of Europe. It established (spuriously, as it happens) a five-act structure as canonical; and introduced sharply delineated genres of comedy and tragedy, which were defined as much in terms of the social class of their main characters as by tone and content. (According to allegedly classical precept, kings and shepherds were not supposed to appear in the same play: scholars' knowledge of Seneca was apparently more accurate than their knowledge of Sophocles.)

Comedy, dealing with the urban middle class and its servants or hangers-on, was decisively the first genre to be attempted. Ariosto's first two full-length comedies were performed in 1508 (*La cassaria*) and 1509 (*I suppositi*).[4] They were acted and then printed in prose, an unheard-of innovation in itself. Ariosto himself did not approve of dramas in prose, but had at this initial stage to accept the clear preference of his ducal patrons in Ferrara. Most (though not all) Italian dramatists continued to use prose for comedy; and George Gascoigne's *Supposes* of 1566, a translation of *I suppositi*, was then the first prose playtext in English. In other respects, the new Italian comedy was based initially on the models of Plautus and Terence, with early plot contributions from scurrilous medieval *novelle*, particularly from Boccaccio's *Decameron* (*c.* 1350). The introduction of romance motifs, and particularly of heroines with an extended presence on stage, is attributable almost entirely to comedies from Siena; and it took some time for other Italian dramatists to follow the same trend.

Non-comic drama continued to be written in verse. There is absolutely no equivalent in Italy of the history play (and therefore little to be said in this essay about Shakespeare's histories, apart from the plainly comic scenes involving Falstaff). The imitation of classical tragedy was approached cautiously, in print rather than on the stage, until the production of Giraldi's *Orbecche*, in Ferrara once again, in 1541. The introduction of 'regular' pastoral plays in five acts, which dates from 1545[5] and also began in Ferrara, was a more innovative step, because such compositions had no proper classical antecedents, and the genre soon became partially identified with 'tragicomedy', also a controversial concept.[6] From then on, although all theoretical discussions of dramaturgy had to claim dutifully to be following Aristotle and Horace, there was tension between the desire simply to resurrect an antique form of theatre and the need to create a modern one. In fact, from the 1540s on, theoretical debate was plentiful and energetic in Italy, alongside the writing and performing of plays. Eventually the Italians inflicted on dramatic theory the constraints of the 'three unities' – time, place and action – allegedly derived from Aristotle. These rules were then adopted rigorously in France, but taken with much greater pinches of salt in England and Spain, where there was more continuity with the imaginative and poetic insights of pre-Renaissance drama. (In particular, the convention which insisted on staging plays in the public street, so that scenes could never take place *inside* a domestic dwelling, was a crippling restriction on the development of Italian comedy.)

In the first half of the sixteenth century, all this innovative work which heralded and created modern European theatre was written by gentlemen amateur dramatists, and performed by amateur actors in princely courts, in private houses or on the premises of budding academies. The middle of the century then saw the rise of professional companies, which (although they accepted princely patronage whenever they could) had to tour round the various Italian centres, and rely for survival on commercial appeal to a paying public. One of their most important strategies was a method of constructing a dramatic spectacle which dispensed with the services of a dramatist. Actors trained themselves in specialist roles: they 'learned their part' over a whole career by accumulating and memorizing suitable speeches and by soaking themselves in a linguistic and stylistic idiom which was appropriate to their more or less fixed character. Their repertoire was then deployed within three-act scenarios, whose surviving texts summarize what had to happen in the play, scene by scene, but do not reproduce any of the words to be spoken. This technique was most easily applied to comic scripts, though pastoral, tragicomic and mixed genres were also acted by the new professionals – it is still believed, though not with total certainty, that the Compagnia dei Gelosi premiered Tasso's internationally celebrated pastoral *Aminta*, in Ferrara (yet again) in 1573. In that case, of course, they would have stuck to a carefully composed script. But the use of improvisation was striking, as was the growth of fixed roles, and the tendency for the more comic figures (*parti ridicole*) to wear facial masks as well as immediately recognizable stylized costumes. What was generally characterized just as 'Italian comedy' has now come to be known as *commedia dell'arte*, although there is no evidence for this term until Goldoni used it in 1750.

Considerable misunderstandings still linger regarding the nature of Italian improvised theatre, especially in its golden period from around 1570 to 1630, and consequently also regarding its possible influence on English dramatists.[7] It has often been assumed that there was an unbridgeable gap between professional improvised theatre and written 'literary' drama in the period; that the theatre of *commedia dell'arte* was more physical than verbal; and that the undoubted input of elements from folklore and carnival produced spectacles which were always populist, knockabout and farcical – 'a jocose pantomime', as Frank Kermode puts it in a thoughtful and lucid discussion which is nevertheless based as we shall see on some factual misconceptions.[8] More recent Italian scholarship has undermined these assumptions. The material which the *arte* actors collected in their commonplace books (*zibaldoni*) for recycling into improvised spectacle was heavily literary both in derivation and in character. The scenarios themselves were also recycled permutations of plot elements and scenes filched from written plays; and it was not long before there was a two-way traffic, often impossible for us now to unscramble, between the 'literary' amateurs and the 'theatrical' professionals. (Part of our difficulty in tracing these exchanges comes from the fact that they involved an overlap between oral and literate transmission of cultural ideas and artefacts.[9]) *Arte* practitioners such as Cecchini, Scala and the Andreini family published fully scripted plays, and tried in print to assess the relative merits and status of the two methods of constructing a dramatic spectacle. The preparation of a professional actor was concentrated most of all on learning *words*, and the comic roles were characterized principally by their verbal styles and dialects, however much contribution was also made by gesture, slapstick and music. And, although there was a statistical predominance of comic spectacle, Italian comedy itself had absorbed a greater mixture of tones during the second half of the sixteenth century, seeking greater moral solidity in what has been characterized as *commedia grave* and greater emotional penetration by merging comic elements with the pastoral genre.[10]

This broader tendency to present the rhetorical, the sentimental and even the tragic was reinforced by another revolutionary phenomenon which the Italians introduced to western performing art – the rise and the acceptance of the actress. It was the *arte* professionals who created the female stage star, in the teeth of formidable opposition from social and religious prejudice. Women were starring in, and even directing, touring companies by the year 1567. The great *dive* such as Isabella Andreini (d. 1604) gained their reputation from a wide range of improvisatory talents, which included the comic and the relatively scurrilous but also covered big emotional moments such as laments, mad scenes, and the ability to improvise verse and song. (Some of them, such as Isabella's daughter-in-law Virginia, also took roles, and sang passionate arias, in the emerging genre of opera.) English theatre, determinedly all-male, had an uneasy awareness of what was going on in Italy which scholars are only now beginning to revisit and explore.[11]

The implications of all this are that Italian drama, before and during Shakespeare's career, showed an unbroken continuum between composed 'literary' texts and the repertoire of improvisation; and also more overlap than has sometimes been supposed between different dramatic genres, most particularly between comedy and pastoral. (Louise George Clubb writes of 'a consanguinity of common aims and repertories of movable parts', embracing 'commercial companies everywhere with the learned and courtly drama'.[12]) Italian tragedy, which was most heavily based on imitation of classical texts, perhaps stood slightly apart. But all other genres, whether written or improvised, shared one identifiable dramaturgical tendency. Humanist playwrights as well as opportunistic actor-managers composed plays out of pre-existing units of plot and character, what Clubb has called 'theatergrams'.[13] That professional scenarios should be constructed in this way is obvious and understandable, granted that they were produced in considerable haste. But there is evidence that more thoughtful dramatists were inclined to adopt the same approach. In 1561 Alessandro Piccolomini – a Sienese aristocrat, churchman and academic dramatist with time on his hands – explained in a letter to a friend how he had a project for collecting together examples of social and psychological types who could be represented on stage, to attribute suitable speeches and paired-off dialogues to them, and thus to assemble what we would now call a data-bank of re-usable scenes for future dramatists: 'I had planned to create various scenes for each of these couples, having an eye always to verisimilitude ... so that they could be applied to many different stories, with just small additions and omissions.'[14] The gentleman scholar Piccolomini was attempting to identify irreducible units of dramatizable behaviour, based on a generalizing view of the permanent qualities of human nature. For the professional actor, and for the *capocomico* constructing a scenario at high speed, the same concepts became items of repertoire, to be memorized, adapted and recycled into any dramatic context which they would fit. Italian dramaturgy makes very frequent use of such movable units; and this was a characteristic shared equally by scripted and improvised theatre. The 'units' concerned could provide structures for individual scenes, but also for whole plots. Italian dramaturgy, scripted and improvised, tended towards a 'modular' structure. As a result, it would be possible now, in retrospect, to identify a limited number of 'typical' Italian plots, which were subject to endless variations of detail. Here are just three examples, which we might find relevant:

A A pair, or two pairs, of young lovers find their desire to marry impeded by one or both of their respective fathers. The young triumph, and the old are defeated, either by trickery or by the revelation of true identities and family relationships. Meanwhile, the unsuitable desires of older or more ridiculous characters (a soldier, a pedant, and/or one of the old fathers) are frustrated by tricks played on them, often by inducing them to adopt a humiliating disguise. Low-life servant characters figure, either effectively or ineffectively, in both levels of intrigue.

B In a vague or mythical Arcadia, various young shepherds are in love with one another in patterns which do not allow them to pair off comfortably. (Some of the young maidens may be rejecting the idea of love as a matter of principle.) The pairings are achieved by means and events which induce a change of heart in one or more of the characters: these may or may not involve intervention from a supernatural figure. Emotional attitudes are meticulously expressed, at all stages, in poetic and rhetorical speeches.

C An isolated island is ruled by a magician, whose power within his territory is limitless. A range of characters find themselves on the island, against their will – they include lovers and others from gentlemanly classes, and more ridiculous masked figures from improvised comedy. By the end of their encounters with each other and with the magician, reconciliations both sentimental and comic, and some form of self-discovery for some characters, have been achieved: these solutions may involve the magician himself, in relation to his past life.

The point about such formulae is that they belong specifically to no individual play, but generically to many: they are theatregrams *frequently and regularly repeated* in Italy, *both in scripts and in scenarios.* Their possible relevance to Shakespeare is immediately apparent. Scenario A contains the events most often recycled in Italian comedy; and it shows that *The Merry Wives of Windsor* (perhaps surprisingly) is in plot terms Shakespeare's most 'Italianate' play.[15] *A Midsummer Night's Dream* appears as a conflation of scenarios A and B; while the relevance of scenario C to *The Tempest* seems indisputable.

It is the case of *The Tempest* which points up most clearly some of the theoretical principles involved. Kermode's considerable reluctance to include *commedia dell'arte* as an influence on the play stems from a desire to identify single individually persuasive source texts; and from a habit of distinguishing firm 'sources' from mere 'analogues and pseudo-sources'.[16] He notes that the specific scenarios cited in evidence by Neri and Lea are of disputable date, and may have been drafted later than *The Tempest*.[17] He is also hampered by his inherited view of improvised theatre as being a totally separate genre concentrating on popular farce ('jocose pantomime'). What can now be argued is that the surviving evidence is cumulative, and stems from a large tradition of both scripted and improvised drama which offers many different levels of jocosity or seriousness. Whether certain specific surviving texts date from before or after 1612 is irrelevant – they are single representatives of a repeated tendency in the longer term. To put the matter another way, an accumulation of 'analogues' can arguably take on the character of a 'source', particularly in a theatrical culture where performance ideas were constantly being transmitted orally and by direct experience from one practitioner to another. The intertextuality of theatre culture, especially in this early modern period in Europe, cannot be traced only in relation to material which was set down on paper, and which happens to have survived. *The Tempest* resembles not just a couple of late scenarios but a repeated Italian 'repertoire plot', which coalesced out of a mingling of comedy, pastoral and romance.

The repertoire of Italian theatregrams operated also on a smaller scale, affecting both the content and the structure of individual scenes and dialogues. Stock roles (lovers, fathers, captains, servants, named masks such as Zani and Pantalone) possessed stock speeches, both monologues and diatribes directed at other characters. (An obvious example of the latter is a homily delivered by a father to a son – Polonius to Laertes.) For improvising actors working without a dramatist, these were essential equipment in their repertoire, but written scripts incorporate them too. Improvising technique also made much use of what have been described as 'elastic' or open-ended sequences, in which back-and-forth repetition could be prolonged or curtailed at will until a prearranged punchline, or interruption, brought it to an end.[18] This technique could apply to comic gags of suspense and frustration, in which the anticipated outcome or statement was held off for as long as possible (Zani deciding whether to open the door; the revelation that father and son are pursuing the same woman). But it could also be used for open-ended sequences such as the recital of lists, or the commented reading of documents; or for more sophisticated emotional material. Two lovers could compete with one another with affecting rhetorical tropes; or in offering mythical or literary parallels for their current state of mind – like Lorenzo and Jessica capping one another's examples of legendary lovers who sought each other 'on such a night as this'.[19] In an improvised scenario, probably a third character would need to interrupt them before they ran out of material; where there is a dramatist, he can make his own decision about how the sequence concludes. In this 'elastic' kind of structure, an element of mirror-imaging or echoing is common, because whoever speaks or acts second can take the tone, rhythm or style from the item which came first.

The fact that these modular blocks of material, and characteristic patterns of dialogue, may have originated in improvisation technique was no bar to their adoption by literary dramatists, who recognized their stage effectiveness and included them in written scripts. They appear plentifully in certain seventeenth-century Italian plays which aim to mimic the improvising professionals as closely as possible;[20] and they are central to the dramaturgy of Molière, who had Italian models before him throughout his career.[21] For Shakespeare, by comparison, this methodology and the material that went with it were no doubt a more distant resource, which he could choose to exploit or to ignore. An examination of his comic writing in particular shows that he did both, in different ways and on different occasions.

We have proposed not to linger over the 'stories' recounted by Shakespeare, accepting that in a great number of cases these were not taken directly from dramatic sources. Most exceptions to this statement are well recognized and can be quickly listed. The subplot of *The Taming of the Shrew* (Bianca, Lucentio and the pretended father) is taken from Ariosto's *I suppositi* via Gascoigne's *Supposes*. The tangle of misdirected lovers in *A Midsummer Night's Dream* is a generic idea inspired by numerous plots in Italian pastoral drama; and the 'chain' of Silvio–Phebe–Ganymede/Rosalind–Orlando in *As You Like It* is another version. As has been shown, the tricks of induced disguise and humiliation played on Falstaff in *The Merry Wives* are entirely Italianate: the *topos* first appears textually in Piccolomini's *Alessandro* of 1545, and is endlessly repeated in scenarios where the victim is usually Pantalone or a Capitano. In this context, it has been suggested more than once that the plot of *Othello* is a parody of an Italian comedy format, with Iago presenting himself for the audience's collusion as a Zani figure playing an aggressive trick on a kind of braggart soldier. *Romeo and Juliet*, with its clash between children and parents and its heroine's bawdy nurse, is easily seen as a standard Italian comic story which happens to end badly.[22]

Helena's disguise as a female pilgrim in *All's Well* might come directly from Bargagli's *La pellegrina*, composed in the 1560s and eventually performed at the Florentine grand-ducal wedding of 1589. Imogen in *Cymbeline* reflects tales about falsely accused virtuous wives forced to wander in male disguise: a theme which recurs frequently in non-dramatic narrative, but which also has an Italian stage tradition, in plays both humanist and pre-humanist from the city of Siena.[23] Then there are other women as yet unmarried who take on male identity while pursuing their lovers – Julia, Viola, Rosalind. They are repeating a device often used in Italian comedies and scenarios, partly as an excuse to get heroines out of their domestic purdah (which reflects Italian social realities) and on to the street which is the stage. Most frequently discussed have been the links between *Twelfth Night* and the important Sienese play *Gli ingannati*, composed collectively by the Accademia degli Intronati and performed in 1532.[24] The relationships between Orsino, Viola ('Cesario'), Sebastian and Olivia reproduce exactly the ones in that earlier play between Flamminio, Lelia ('Fabio'), Fabrizio and Isabella. In many other cases, Shakespeare uses Italian settings, Italian names for his characters, and sometimes (as in *Much Ado*) a pronounced Italian cultural atmosphere; but the stories actually told do not come straight from Italian stage plays.

A comparison between *Gli ingannati* and *Twelfth Night* can draw attention to some important ways in which Shakespeare sometimes diverges from Italian theatre formulae, whereas in other cases he follows them more closely. Both the heroines of *Gli ingannati* are natives of Modena, where the action takes place: they both face the demands of family honour and the authority of their respective fathers, who are major (largely comic) participants in the plot. Isabella lives at home; Lelia is running around disguised in a city where she might at any moment meet her father; and her twin brother Fabrizio, believed lost, returns home unexpectedly to seek his family. Only Flamminio is a totally free agent. In his version of the story, Shakespeare chooses to release all four lovers from any such constraints. Viola and Sebastian are far from home, Olivia is her own mistress, and Orsino is actually the Prince of Illyria. They have no one to think about but themselves, and one another. This complete liberation from parental pressure is an extremely un-Italian tendency; and Shakespeare seeks it in other ways in some other comedies. In *The Two Gentlemen of Verona* the parents of Julia are mentioned but effectively discarded by the dramatist, and her male disguise is negotiated merely with a servant. In *Love's Labour's Lost* the lovers are young independent aristocrats, though the death of a distant father unexpectedly curtails their self-regarding games. Bassanio and Portia in *The Merchant of Venice* have no parents living (though Portia is following her dead father's instructions); nor do any characters in *Measure for Measure*. In *A Midsummer Night's Dream* and

As You Like It the young fledglings are separated in different ways from the parental nest, and return to it with their destinies already settled. In terms of genre, both of these latter flights involve a move from the city, which in Italian terms is the setting for comedy, to the less socialized wilderness which is proper to pastoral. In Italy, in fact, only the pastoral genre normally permitted stage lovers to pursue their self-discoveries outside a parental framework. (It did not always happen even in Arcadia: the most influential pastoral text of all, Guarini's *Il pastor fido*, is dominated by the oppressive presence of patriarchs.) In this respect, the Italian tendency in comedy was more socially realistic: escape from the family, at that point in European history, was strictly a romantic fantasy. Since Shakespeare's comedies of unfettered lovers include some of his most popular ones, there is a temptation to regard them as thoroughly typical of his plotting; but one needs to remember that *The Shrew*, *Two Gentlemen* (as regards Silvia), *The Merchant* (as regards Jessica), *Much Ado*, *Cymbeline*, *Pericles* and *The Tempest* all involve relations between parents and children; as of course does *Romeo and Juliet*, emphasizing its links with comic plot formats. In *The Winter's Tale* the bucolic world inhabited by Perdita does not escape generational conflict. *Much Ado about Nothing*, in particular, has in the figure of Leonato an absolutely typical Italian stage father, trapped in the rules of Mediterranean family honour which entirely dictate his emotions. Like his Italian counterparts, he is obliged to be potentially violent when he is threatened with shame through his daughter, and equally obliged to be gracious and friendly when the misunderstanding is cleared up. This play also typifies the Italian, and Shakespearean, tendency for lovers to have one parent on stage rather than two (Hero's mother Innogen having been written out on second thoughts), and for that one usually to be a father (*pace* Bertram in *All's Well*). In this respect, the two full sets of parents in *The Merry Wives* are a remarkable exception for comedy.

The case of *Twelfth Night* also introduces observations about the treatment of heroines in comedy, and about female characters in general. In 1532 *Gli ingannati* broke the previous mould of Italian *commedia erudita* in giving its heroine Lelia considerable stage time in which to explain her emotions to the audience; and in constantly allowing women, including servants, to control the plot and get the better of men. Up to then, the new comic drama had followed Plautus and Terence in treating women as the prizes for which men contended, but either keeping them offstage altogether or treating them patronizingly when they were on stage; and the relative feminism introduced by the Sienese was not followed by other Italian dramatists for some time.[25] Lelia is allowed to take initiative in the intrigue, with her decision to adopt male disguise and actively to sabotage Flamminio's courtship of Isabella; though eventually she retreats in despair, and Flamminio is induced to love her once again by the astute persuasions of her nurse. In Shakespeare, Viola's version of Lelia's predicament – her entrapment between Orsino and Olivia – is not represented as a situation of her own choosing; and, rather than playing dishonourable tricks, she adopts the virtue of patience in adversity and leaves the untangling to Time.[26] This more 'feminine' passivity had been celebrated frequently in Italian *commedia grave*, in the second half of the sixteenth century, in a Counter-Reformation context which urged a faith in the workings of Providence.[27] Shakespeare in fact fluctuates enormously in the amount of scope and control he gives to his women characters in comedy, and in the amount of extra wisdom and emotional insight which they possess as opposed to the men. Portia and Rosalind are memorable models of female supremacy on both counts, and they are joined by the women of *Love's Labour's Lost* and of *Two Gentlemen*, by Helena in *All's Well*, and by the eponymous Merry Wives. Imogen in *Cymbeline* takes some initiative, but could still be seen as one of the patient suffering heroines of *commedia grave*. Women come off much worse, however, or are at least more subordinate, in many other plays – *The Taming of the Shrew* is not an isolated exception. In *The Comedy of Errors* wifely jealousy is castigated (though admittedly by an older female character). Titania in the *Dream* is soundly gulled by Oberon, and the female lovers are no more sensible or in control than the men. In *The Winter's Tale* and *The Tempest* daughters have to defer to fathers. Beatrice in *Much Ado* is full of wit, but cannot intervene in events except by begging Benedick to act for her, and she is the victim rather than the perpetrator of the main comic deception. The most complex examples of the treatment of 'female status' are *Measure for Measure*, where women are ambiguously balanced between initiative and subjection; and *Twelfth Night* itself, which contains deliberately contrasting speeches about the emotional fidelity of the male and female sexes. (Viola speaks of female 'frailty' in 2.2; Orsino of male 'fancies ... giddy and unfirm' two scenes later.)

The attention and imaginative care which Shakespeare devotes to his women removes him very far from what most Italian dramatists achieved in written comedy. If he was learning from anywhere other than from his own insights and genius, then his models could have been Italian pastoral and tragedy (both much more attentive to heroines and to female psychology), or native English precedents such as the plays of Lyly. The greater rhetorical and emotional range brought to Italian theatre by the rise of actresses may have had some indirect influence on the content of English dramatic texts. However, the clear opposition of English professional actors to accepting women on stage makes this an intricate question which probably needs exploring further. A wider issue, of which the question of female roles is only a part, is that of the sympathy demanded for comic characters in general. Italian classical comedy began, and continued for some time, with no apparent desire to steer its spectators into empathy for any of the figures on stage. Young lovers had to win the contest with their fathers, because that was the rule of comedy; but the young men are usually blinkered, amoral or at least confused (rather like Shakespeare's Valentine and Proteus); and the young women in early plays are hardly characterized at all. Victims of comic aggression and trickery are chosen precisely because no one wants to identify with them, or to have any consideration for their feelings, and their defeat is supposed to provoke nothing but glee. (One can identify even today, in popular Italian formats of comic performance, an almost mystical search for the perfect sucker, to whom everyone can feel derisively superior.) Regular persecution in scenarios of the half-dehumanized masks of Pantalone and the Dottore simply continues the treatment of their earlier equivalents in written drama. In this respect, Ben Jonson is clearly (perhaps consciously) more 'Italian' than Shakespeare, with *Volpone* in particular containing a level of pitiless contempt for practically everybody which goes even beyond Mediterranean models. Shakespeare, by contrast, is notoriously unwilling to deny that even his most unsympathetic victims 'have feelings too'. Shylock bleeds when he is pricked; the ragging of Malvolio is recognized in the end to have gone slightly too far; and even Parolles, who comes nearest to being totally dismissed, is taken grudgingly into the household of Lafeu as part of a general mood of reconciliation. The most striking example is Falstaff. No Italian dramatist shows anything like the subtlety which could allow a character so contemptible in objective terms, and so thumpingly humiliated in the drama, to creep back into forgiveness and sympathy. Yet we all know that Falstaff manages this, mainly by rueful wit directed against himself, both at the end of *The Merry Wives* and in episodes of *Henry IV*. Comparisons with the normal treatment of Italian braggart Capitani, in both scripts and scenarios, underline the distance which Shakespeare has travelled from such models, if he had them in mind – a journey achieved through a combination of human sensitivity and sheer power of writing. Of the latter, we shall have still more to say.

A final point worth making on the subject of plotting relates to the observation of sexual codes. Italian comic *novelle*, at least from Boccaccio's time, deal on a regular basis with illicit sexual liaisons. Many of them are about adultery, and lead to completely amoral 'happy endings'. Many others depict young lovers who force their parents to allow them to marry by consummating the relationship in advance and leaving their families no choice. (This resigned acceptance of a *fait accompli* is reflected in real legal and social practice in Italy, to judge by such studies as have been made of the matter.[28]) *Commedia erudita* in the sixteenth century made more limited use of adultery stories – though some very famous ones, such as Machiavelli's *Mandragola*, are in that category, and the theme lingers through into some of Flaminio Scala's scenarios published in 1611. Pre-marital sex leading then to marriage was, however, an utterly standard *topos* in comedy (though not in pastoral), even in comedies which sought a more romantic or sentimental tone. English drama, including Shakespeare, tended of course to observe the social decencies, as though this was essential in order to retain audience sympathy for the young lovers concerned. In *Gli ingannati*, both pairs of lovers have made love before the end of the play, and both events are subject to bawdy commentary by witnesses; in *Twelfth Night*, Olivia seizes Sebastian and rushes him to the priest, rather than directly to the bedroom. There are numerous other examples which need not be listed. Shakespeare as an individual dramatist was no doubt seriously interested in the subject of marriage; but he was writing in any case in a society which was unsympathetic to stage fornicators. His two examples of the 'bed-trick' (a very Italianate motif in itself), in *All's Well* and *Measure for Measure*, reinforce the insistence on wedlock. Of the two errant males who find themselves after all in bed with the 'right' woman, Bertram is already married and Angelo ought to be. By contrast, Italian dramatists and narrators were just as likely to use the device to bring about an adultery.

In the interests of complete coverage we must assess quickly the relationships, often already well known, which exist between Shakespeare's characters and stock figures or masks from the Italian stage. The most ubiquitous such category is that of young people in love, which has been addressed already. Where less sympathetic characters are concerned, Italian comedy, both scripted and improvised, provided a small traditional set of foolish figures to be mocked by the audience. In *Love's Labour's Lost* we have in Armado and Moth an apparent braggart Capitano with his traditionally derisive servant; and a possibly Italianate Pedante/Dottore[29] in Holofernes. Falstaff is a Capitano too, however subtly developed: he has a cruder version of the same mask alongside him in the form of Pistol. Parolles in *All's Well* has been described accurately as a merger between the Italian figures of the braggart and the parasite.[30] In *The Merry Wives* (where we have seen that the whole plot structure is very close to that of standard Italian comedy), Sir Hugh Evans has many of the verbal characteristics of a Pedante/Dottore, and Dr Caius is another version of the braggart, especially since he possesses the secondary trait of speaking in a heavy foreign accent. (Capitani on the Italian stage were usually Spanish.) For *The Taming of the Shrew*, there has been speculation on possible relationships between Petruchio (Italian 'Petruccio') and comic servants like Pedrolino. In fact the greatest similarity might be with the aggressive Scaramuccia or Scaramouche, who was a merger of servant and Capitano masks. Coincidence is more likely here, however, than direct influence: Scaramouche, in the person of Tiberio Fiorilli, really gained his reputation in France, and well after Shakespeare's time.

It is harder to find real equivalents in Shakespeare of the most central and standard figures of *commedia dell'arte*, or their immediate ancestors in *commedia erudita*: the miserly lustful father who became Pantalone, and the servant of peasant origins who became Zani.[31] Ludicrous caricatures of misguided old age do not seem to have interested our author, except for their one devastating tragic transformation in King Lear. Gremio in *The Shrew* is referred to as a 'pantaloon', but otherwise under-characterized. English audiences perhaps preferred to treat stage patriarchs with respect – as indeed was also recommended by the more moralistic Italian theorists of comedy. Prospero, as we have indicated, is an Italianate figure, but a sympathetic one. Subordinate or servant characters are not allowed to control the plot, as happens in so much Italian comedy – except again in tragically subverted mode, in *Othello*. In Shakespeare's clowns we shall be able to point below to some examples of 'elastic' improvisatory technique, but it is hard to see in their characters or verbal style anything which is other than firmly English, or original to their author. The most obvious trait of a Zani – his overwhelming carnivalesque preoccupation with food – is not to be found in any Shakespearean clown, and indiscriminate lust is not common either. Male and female servants are not regularly paired off at the end of comic plots, like Zani and Francheschina. Touchstone and Audrey are an almost parodic exception, like Dromio of Ephesus and his fantastically evoked Nell whom we never see; and Gratiano and Nerissa are dependants but not servants of the lowest class. (In this respect, Shakespeare diverges from Lyly as well as from Italian sources.) Bestial lust is found in the equally exceptional figure of Caliban, who in this respect and others derives from the satyr of Italian pastoral.[32]

In Italian drama, stock characters were associated with stock material. Some items of such material in Shakespeare have clear similarities to an Italian antecedent. The two voices in Launcelot Gobbo's head – 'conscience' and 'the fiend' (*MV* 2.2) – resemble a device found in a monologue by 'Ruzante' (Angelo Beolco) in the *Dialogo facetissimo* composed around 1529. Falstaff's excuses after Gadshill, where he steadily multiplies the number of men he claims attacked him (*1H4* 2.4), are a futile trick tried by the Ruzante character in the *Parlamento* of similar date.[33] A lover's speech in which he justifies his own indignity by comparing himself to prestigious legendary or mythological figures (Armado and Berowne in *Love's Labour's Lost*, Falstaff in *The Merry Wives*) was a standard *topos* for Italian Pantaloni, Dottori and Capitani. Where the material itself cannot be seen as derivative, the structure of a comic scene may nevertheless be reminiscent of patterns used by improvising actors, however firmly one may also feel that Shakespeare has stepped in as dramatist to take control of his material. This refers most of all to the open-ended 'elastic' structure, capable of functioning in either lengthened or shortened form, and therefore easy for improvising actors to vary and manipulate. A simple example of this is the scene in *1 Henry IV* (2.4), where the Prince and Poins have Francis chasing backwards and forwards with his 'Anon, anon, sir!': the joke really needs to be left in the hands of the actors, who should decide at each performance how long it should be kept (literally) running. And in *Part 2* (5.1) it is surely up to the actor playing Shallow to decide each night how many times he should say 'Sir John, you shall not be excused.' On a more complex level, Launcelot Gobbo and his father keep interrupting each other in *The Merchant of Venice* (2.2) when asking Bassanio to take Launcelot into his service: if the scene were improvised, it would be up to the actor playing Bassanio to decide when to call them to order and move the scene on. And it is easy to imagine the pseudo-foreign gibberish directed at the blindfolded Parolles (*AW* 4.1 and 4.3) as a gag which could be prolonged for much longer than the surviving script records. The most natural form of improvisable scripting is of course simply to leave a space in the text which allows comic actors to insert their own material. Shakespeare, perhaps sharing Hamlet's prejudice against clowns who speak more than is set down for them, very rarely does this. The 'Anon, anon' scene just referred to ends, uniquely, in a stage direction ('*Here they both call him* ...') which gives the actors their head. In *The Merchant of Venice*, Martin Banham has persuasively suggested that Launcelot Gobbo's entrance in 5.1 leaves the clown free to improvise a sequence of night-time confusion before he finds the people he wants to speak to.[34] Those two examples seem to stand alone.

However, elastic structures are not confined to scenes aimed at raising a laugh, as appears in the example of Lorenzo and Jessica already quoted: their formally echoing repetitions of 'On such a night ...' usually attract romantic sympathy, however playful they may also be. The list of suitors passed in review by Portia and Nerissa, in 1.2 of the same play, is also an open-ended pattern (we could have as many or as few suitors as somebody chooses) – and one not unknown in Italian plays which mimic *commedia dell'arte*. This reminds us, importantly, that dramaturgical patterns as such can be as significant as the content they convey. An attempt to assess possible derivations from the practices of Italian Renaissance theatre must take full account not only of individual pieces of material, but also of the larger compositional and structural tendencies described earlier in this essay. Shakespeare's plays can be read with an eye to identifying the extent to which they assemble 'repertoire' items – units or sections of text which can be seen as movable, re-usable in modular fashion in other plays and contexts. These may be autonomous set speeches, and they may be associated with a single stereotype character: the essence of Portia's speech on mercy could on the face of it come from any Renaissance commonplace book, and Falstaff's discourse on honour could be reassigned to any braggart soldier. But we can equally be dealing with dialogues or scenes, rather than speeches; and the 'recyclable' character of a sequence can sometimes be inherently apparent, whether or not it has yet been documented as being used in another dramatic text.

There are, of course, pitfalls involved in a reading of Shakespeare dedicated exclusively to identifying such movable units of modular dramaturgy. One can end up seeing things which (in other readers' eyes) are not there, or which have alternative explanations. The

Renaissance interest in *sententia* and generalization produced a tendency to fill plays with observations of universal moral interest, which might thus be transferred *from* the playtext *into* commonplace books, rather than vice versa. Such a preoccupation with aphorism, fixed categories and 'wisdom literature' (which had kept the plays of Terence in the schoolroom throughout the Middle Ages) perhaps helped to form the methods of Italian dramaturgy, as is shown by the project of the humanist Alessandro Piccolomini; but it could have entered English practice spontaneously and separately. It is no doubt absurd to assume that every single reflective or generalizing speech in a play by Shakespeare proves a dependence on Italian theatre. Moreover, where open-ended repetition is concerned, a pattern of reiteration and delay may simply be a mnemonic resource hit upon naturally by all human brains (especially, in the first instance, illiterate or semi-literate ones), and therefore again not culture-specific: there is a technique called 'unpacking the parcel' used by clowns in Chinese theatre, which is similar to what is found in Italian sources. Will Kempe may have used his own 'elastic gags' without reference to any foreign influence. Nevertheless, we would argue that this kind of analysis, the hunt for the repertoire number and for overall modular structure, can at the very least turn up observations which are of interest in their own right in characterizing Shakespeare's dramaturgy. In some cases, then, the parallels can be extremely striking to those familiar with the Italian material.

Also striking, however, is the degree of variation which appears from one play to another, when they are examined via this particular choice of tunnel vision. At one end of the scale, we could single out *As You Like It*, which presents itself in part as an assemblage of various kinds of set piece, many of which have something in common with Italian antecedents. There is a substantial list of speeches which aim at the status of generalizations or *sententiae*: Duke Senior in 2.1 on the contrast between court and rural life (a subject pursued further by Touchstone and Corin in 3.2); many speeches made by, or about, the character of Adam; Rosalind's discourse on the different speeds of Time in 3.2, and her reflections on love and lovers in 4.1; and, inevitably, most of the lines given to Jaques. We need not distinguish too sharply between unbroken harangues and those turned into dialogue: a memorized repertoire number in the Italian tradition can often be partially disguised by allowing room for other characters to interrupt it from time to time, but this makes little difference to the actor who memorized it in the first place. Sequences involving Silvius and Phebe are highly redolent of movable repertoire dialogues from Italian pastoral: they culminate in the repetitive echoing scene involving also Orlando and Rosalind/Ganymede ('And so am I for ...', 5.2). Here the format is played out to the point of parody, as Rosalind herself recognizes in exasperatedly bringing it to an end. Touchstone the jester has a whole series of autonomous routines, resembling just as often the traditional material of a *commedia dell'arte* Dottore as that of a Zani or clown. He overwhelms both Corin and William by deploying a torrent of repetitive synonyms, and by developing ridiculous arbitrary steps of logic to reach a desired conclusion (as in his 'proof' that Corin is damned, in 3.2). His essential difference from Dottor Graziano is that he knows exactly what he is doing, and uses his verbiage ironically as a weapon: Italian (and French) Doctors are merely silly without knowing it. His number about duelling procedures in 5.4 (inserted, in good modular fashion, to cover Rosalind's change of costume) is a mnemonic *tour de force*, in which he challenges himself to repeat all his allegedly improvised nonsense in the proper order – this too was a feature of the Dottore mask, if we are to judge by Molière's Docteur in the early farce *La Jalousie du Barbouillé* (scene 2). Altogether, *As You Like It* represents a distinctly modular approach to playwriting.

At the other end of the scale of comparison comes *Much Ado about Nothing*, which is difficult if not impossible to break down in the same way. This is all the more surprising because the play is so heavily Italianate in other respects: its setting, the derivation of its story-lines, and some of its stock characters (such as Leonato, already discussed). By comparison with *As You Like It*, *Much Ado* seems entirely void of rhetorical elaboration, and of pauses for generalized comment. The longer and more intense speeches which it does contain, whether monologues or outbursts to other characters, seem always to be pushed out of those who speak them by sheer pressure of emotion, comic or serious as that may be; so the words and concepts are specific to the character and the situation, difficult to extract and recycle elsewhere. The two eavesdropping scenes, when Benedick and Beatrice are successively deceived about each other, could have invited a set of echoes and mirror-images. No Italian dramatist could have resisted such a temptation, and for improvising actors it would have been a godsend; but Shakespeare seems to have worked quite hard to avoid it, so that although the situational parallel is unmistakable it is not reinforced by detailed verbal patterns. Dogberry could have been conceived as an Italian clown, but he is not: his malapropism is shared both with Zani and Dottori, but his scenes are mostly 'through-composed' rather than repetitive or elastic. The passages of wit between Benedick and Beatrice could be seen in some ways as set pieces, but do not have any of the autonomy or the repetitive features of similar Italian repertoire. In this case (as also in particular with *Love's Labour's Lost*), Shakespeare's long-recognized debt to John Lyly seems more important than any Italian derivation; and Lyly's structures are concentrated and individual, quite unlike the patterns thrown up by Italian modular improvisation.

On the strength of this kind of analysis, *The Merchant of Venice* also comes out as a comedy which assembles a notably high number of movable dramaturgical theatregrams, often with links to material in Italian plays and scenarios. We cannot pretend to mount a firm statistical comparison in relation to individual elements or units, each one of which could be subject to discussion; but on an impressionistic reading other comedies with a 'high modular quotient' would include *The Merry Wives*; *Twelfth Night* and *All's Well* specifically in their comic rather than romantic scenes; and *Measure for Measure* in the restricted sense that it contains a kind of internal debate which produces set speeches on either side. (Where editors of the text see a single speech by the Duke as having perhaps been awkwardly split between 3.2 and 4.1, one could see this as a 'modular' manipulation of preconceived material in an attempt to cover a practical stage lacuna.)[35] Comedies which present themselves less in terms of such pre-baked building blocks include *The Comedy of Errors* (perhaps showing that here Shakespeare was looking directly to Plautus rather than to Italian intermediaries); *Love's Labour's Lost* (where the dramaturgical structure confirms the influence of Lyly); and the later comedies (if that is what they are), *Pericles, Cymbeline* and *The Winter's Tale* (whereas *The Tempest*, as we shall see, is another matter). *The Shrew, Two Gentlemen* and *A Midsummer Night's Dream* are in different ways more complex cases, under this sort of heading, and would each need a separate detailed analysis; here we can only remark in passing on how much the *Dream* both depends on and diverges from the formats of Italian pastoral.

A more ambitious and risky type of analysis would move from considering 'elastic' dialogues and scenes to potentially 'elastic' plots. In *The Merchant of Venice* there is no limit in theory to the number of suitors who make wrong decisions about Portia's caskets, and who postpone the anticipated triumph of Bassanio. This example perhaps acts as a warning – a reminder that such open-ended delay is common in folk narrative as well as in theatre (and that there is a strong tendency in both cases to fall back on the 'rule of three'). *The Tempest* is a more complex case. We have already alluded to the strong similarities between its overall plot and an Italianate format which was very familiar in both written and improvised drama. On the level of scene structure, a number of sequences are capable of being analysed (if one chooses) in relation to improvisation practice: Prospero's long *protasis* narrative (1.2), which has to be rather pedestrianly interrupted by Miranda and by Ariel in order to make some dialogue out of it; Gonzalo's moralizing speeches (2.1), similarly broken up by the mockery of the other lords; Trinculo under Caliban's cloak (2.2), where Stephano's puzzlement could be prolonged, together with the number of times he feeds drink into various orifices; Ariel's invisible repetitions of 'Thou liest' (3.2), which lead to an undeserved beating for Trinculo, in *commedia dell'arte* style. Such items are not unique in Shakespeare, but in this case the analysis could be extended on to a larger scale. Discussions of the play's textual status have sometimes proposed that there are some scenes missing: that in an earlier version both Ferdinand's ordeal of carrying logs and the build-up of Caliban's plot against Prospero once lasted for longer and involved more episodes.[36] Whether or not this argument is textually tenable, it does highlight the fact that the plot has the potential in theory to be extended in such a manner; this could be taken as another reason for seeing Italianate influences on the structure, as well as the content, of Shakespeare's last play. Like some other features which we have indicated, however, this tendency may be an exception rather than a rule.

This chapter has confined itself primarily to considering Shakespeare's comic drama, simply for reasons of space. As has been briefly indicated, it is possible to see some of the tragedies too as containing (always alongside many other elements) some deliberate twists and subversions of theatregrams which began their life in Italy. *Romeo and Juliet*, *Othello* and *King Lear* can certainly be joined by *Hamlet* in this respect: Polonius and his family are a grimmer version of comedy stereotypes, and the hero himself adopts complex strategies to portray his 'antic disposition', some of which can allude to the personality and routines of the Italian clown.[37] We must conclude, however, by stressing once again how Italian precedents may underlie some of Shakespeare's dramaturgical choices, but can never explain them; and how our author regularly transcends the limitations which Italians tended to set (sometimes consciously and deliberately) to their theatrical offerings. Most Shakespeare criticism reveals a level of thematic and verbal complexity which Italian drama never approached. Part of the reason for this may lie precisely in the Italian tendency to build plays out of pre-existing blocks. In order to construct an integral play with a unique message, the modular method of dramaturgy needs to be overseen, perhaps overridden, by a dramatist who is both sufficiently eclectic and sufficiently single-minded to know exactly what he wants to achieve. When the Italians chose to improvise rather than compose what they came to call 'premeditated' scripts, their problem was even greater. Modern students of drama often love to acclaim and romanticize 'actors' theatre', but it usually takes 'dramatists' theatre' to transfer an original vision to the stage in a coherent manner. When we have argued that Shakespeare used modular dramaturgy, or that some of his scenes and speeches possess a transferable character, this was not intended to imply that any of them was in fact written by someone else. A large aspect of what we call his genius was his ability to take total possession of everything he borrowed, including a range of compositional methods which he perceived would work on stage in different chosen circumstances. In addition, of course, he was a poet in a vigorously developing language, which still possessed much more flexibility than Italian was prepared to allow itself. Where Italian dramatists chose a rhetoric which had already been recognized and approved by their audience, Shakespeare chose poetry, and constantly broke existing moulds.

Italian drama, especially its comedy, had its contrasting merits. Not even a Shakespeare can cover everything which can be done in theatre, and all positive choices involve rejecting some equally positive alternatives. In the end, though, those merits were never fully realized by any playwright or practitioner from Italy itself. That achievement had to wait for Molière, who imposed his own 'dramatist's theatre' on Italian formats but brought less change to their basic character. An interesting exchange is recorded by the actor Anthony Sher about the contrast between the English and French masters. He was conversing with Christopher Hampton, who was the translator of Molière's *Tartuffe*:

> The problem with Molière's writing is the deceptive thinness of it. There's no poetry, no sub-text, just a very basic situation, like sit-com. Chris says, 'All there is is what is there, but that happens to be brilliant.' He says the French find Shakespeare difficult for the opposite reason. Why is he so oblique, they cry in Gallic confusion, why doesn't he just say what he means?[38]

In Shakespeare's Italian sources, too, 'all there was was what was there', brilliant or not as it may have been. It was his insistence on meaning more than just what he said which made those sources, and all his others, into far more than the sum of their parts.

Chapter Five

CONTEMPORARY EUROPE IN ELIZABETHAN AND EARLY STUART DRAMA

Paulina Kewes

Elizabethan England saw itself at once as part of Europe and as a distinct world. Public drama sometimes emphasized common European identity and sometimes embodied insular notions of Englishness. It asserted the country's solidarity with European Christendom under siege from the Ottoman Turks. But it also proclaimed an emergent sense of nationhood, defined in cultural and religious terms, which distanced England from the continent. Theatrical representations of contemporary Europe, principally of France, Spain, Italy, the Low Countries and Germany, are a special case. For, in contrast to plays with settings remote in time or place, those set on the continent provided Renaissance spectators with an imaginative representation of nations and states whose politics, religion and commerce directly impinged on their own lives.

Modern scholarship of Renaissance historical drama has focused on the so-called English histories and Roman plays. It has for the most part overlooked dramatizations of contemporary Europe. In his study of *Images of Englishmen and Foreigners in the Drama of Shakespeare and His Contemporaries* (1992), A.J. Hoenselaars refers to *The Massacre at Paris* as 'the only play based on recent French history written before *Bussy D'Ambois*'.[1] Yet, as we shall see, there were several; for instance, a four-part sequence on the French civil wars had been commissioned for the Admiral's Men in 1598–9.[2] 'Only a handful of renaissance plays', maintains Ivo Kamps, 'based their plots on contemporary events.'[3] This assertion too is belied by evidence of surviving playtexts and others now lost. With the notable exception of Shakespeare, most major and minor Renaissance playwrights – Marlowe, Peele, Drayton, Jonson, Chapman, Dekker, Webster, Massinger, Fletcher, Glapthorne, Brome, Heywood, Day, Rowley, Wilkins, Henry Shirley, James Shirley – dealt, in one way or another, with the political and religious crises that engulfed contemporary Europe. 'The theatre of England since the mid seventeenth century', declares Ronnie Mulryne, 'has largely neglected the history of Europe', a view reiterated by Hoenselaars in his contribution to *The Cambridge Companion to Shakespeare's History Plays* (2002).[4] But a glance at the *Annals of English Drama* beyond the year 1642 yields dozens of dramatic pamphlets, closet pieces and theatrical scripts about the very recent and the more remote continental past, from R.B.'s *The Rebellion of Naples* (1649) to the French, Spanish, Portuguese, Italian and Dutch history plays by Dryden, Otway, Lee, D'Urfey, Settle and others.[5]

The contemporary European dimension in English Renaissance drama has been overshadowed by the towering presence of Shakespeare, who wrote a series of plays about ancient Rome and medieval and Tudor England but did not dramatize recent European history. Eschewing geographical and historical precision, the plays he set on the continent evoked imaginary places such as the coastal state of Bohemia. Shakespeare's fellow dramatists, by contrast, produced remarkably acute and accurate depictions of specific figures and events. Occasional distortions and misrepresentations are a clue to the playwright's aims, for tendentious reporting of European affairs could be a means of influencing public opinion. It could also suggest that the situation at home might be read through a foreign lens.

To what uses, then, did Elizabethan and Stuart dramatists put the recent European past? How did plays set in contemporary Europe address issues of religion, politics and England's colonial expansion? Does a sense of shared European identity emerge from them and, if so, what does it entail? We know very little about the reception of individual plays. Changing political circumstances at home and abroad altered government policy and, albeit more slowly, transformed popular sentiment. As part of a booming entertainment industry, public drama naturally exploited fears and anxieties and shaped opinions. But its main aim was to make money, not to teach political lessons. History plays set on the continent, especially those about prominent contemporaries – popes, kings, queens, military commanders, royal favourites, pirates – spoke directly to audiences' prejudices and sympathies, reproducing national stereotypes and modifying them in their turn.

HISTORY, NEWS AND THE DRAMA

Two daies agoe, the overthrow of *Turnholt*, was acted upon a Stage, and all your Names used that were at yt [*sic*]; especially *Sir Fra. Veres*, and he that plaid that Part gott a Beard resembling his, and a Watchet Sattin Doublett, with Hose trimd with Silver Lace. You was also introduced, Killing, Slaying and Over-throwing the *Spaniards*, and honorable Mention made of your Service, in seconding *Sir Francis Vere*, being engaged.[6]

By the time of Elizabeth's accession in 1558, England's foreign policy was in tatters. Mary Tudor's relentless drive to re-Catholicize the country, her marriage to Philip II of Spain, England's embroilment in Philip's wars, and the loss of Calais, England's last continental foothold, to the French – all this had severely damaged the country's international standing as well as feeding xenophobic sentiment. 'Hath not the wynninge and keeping of this [Calais] bred throughout Europe honorable opinion and reporte of the English nation?' asked the Lord Keeper at the opening of Elizabeth's first Parliament on 25 January 1559.[7] The coronation pageantry mounted for Elizabeth earlier in the month had been insular in its themes and iconography, invoking precedents of domestic peace and good government exclusively from native history ('The uniting of the two Howses of Lancastre and Yorke') and the Bible ('Debora the judge and restorer of the house of Israel, Judic. iv.'). Its sponsorship too was pointedly insular: 'the Citie ...

without any forreyne persone, of itselfe beawtifyed itselfe',[8] claimed the printed account, emphasizing that no pageant had been prepared by foreign merchants resident in London.

Less than half a century later, in 1604, the *Magnificent Entertainment* for Elizabeth's Stuart successor, James I, was advertised as having been put on 'As well by the English as by the Strangers'. The foreigners' 'sundry languages & habits', stressed the printed account, 'under Princes Roofes render excellent harmony'.[9] Among the pageants that greeted the new king on his passage to his first Parliament, we find triumphal arches by the Italians and the Dutch living in the capital. The aspirations of the newly united Britain to a prominent role in European politics were expressed in the *Entertainment* through a series of imperial Roman and ancient British tropes.[10] The oration delivered by the Dutch urged the new king to continue his predecessor's policy of supporting their fight against Spain.

Early modern England understood its political and social arrangements primarily in historical terms: above all, in terms of the history of medieval England and of ancient Rome. The utility of the recent past, especially the foreign past, was far less assured. Even so, in parliamentary speeches, sermons and elsewhere examples from contemporary English and continental history increasingly supplemented biblical, classical and medieval precedents. In the preface to *The Union of the Two Noble and Illustre Famelies of Lancastre & Yorke* (1548), an important source for Shakespeare and other playwrights, Edward Hall likened the Wars of the Roses, which in Elizabethan England would serve as the prime cautionary parable against civil dissension, to domestic broils in ancient Rome and in medieval and near-contemporary Europe:

> What mischief hath insurged in realms by intestine devision, what depopulacion hath ensued in countries by civil discencion, what detestable murder hath bene committed in cities by seperate faccions, and what calamitee hath ensued in famous regions by domesticall discord & unnatural controversy, Rome hath felt, Italy can testifie, Fraunce can bere witnes, Beame

[Bohemia] can tell, Scotlande may write, Denmarke can shewe, and especially thys noble realme of Englande can apparauntly declare and make demonstracion.[11]

Within half a century, not only the Lancaster–York conflict chronicled by Hall, but also virtually all of the continental disturbances that he cited, were re-enacted on the Elizabethan stage.

John Foxe's Protestant martyrology, *Actes and Monuments of these Latter and Perillous Dayes* (1563), which, like Hall's *Union*, was to provide source material for plays, mainly in the Jacobean era,[12] highlighted the importance of the recent past. Although his was a universal ecclesiastical history, Foxe's primary interest, flagged on the title-page, was '*speciallye in this Realme of England and Scotlande*'. He made a strong case for the utility of contemporary history – 'Now then if Martyrs are to be compared with martyrs, I see no cause why the martyrs of our time deserve any lesse commendation, than the other in the primitive Church.'[13] He updated his account for later editions, a process continued by others after his death. To the edition of 1583 Foxe attached an account of the St Bartholomew's Day Massacre; the seventh edition of 1632 'annexed certaine additions, unto the time of our Soveraigne Lord King Charles now raigning'.

Foxe affirmed the power of examples drawn from foreign history. He situated the sufferings of the Marian martyrs alongside those of their German, French, Spanish and Italian co-religionists. In recounting the fates of his compatriots, men, women and children, many of humble origins, Foxe adopted a local, even parochial perspective. But he also analysed the implications of the confessional differences he was describing for Europe and the world at large. His narrative of the Parisian massacre and its strategic placement at the end of the book 'implied that the fate of English Protestants was directly tied to that of continental Protestantism.'[14] Yet even as he chronicled the struggle of European Protestants against the Popish Antichrist and his emissaries, the Catholic kings and princes, he lamented the division of Christendom in the face of the threat posed by Islam and its standard-bearer, the Ottoman Empire.

In the preface to *The History of the World* (1614), Sir Walter Ralegh too juxtaposed English and continental pasts. Ralegh offered a scathing review of English kings and gave equally short shrift to French and Spanish rulers. The example of native and foreign royalty alike, he claimed, shows the suffering and misfortunes that those unfit to govern visit on themselves and their subjects:

> Oh by what plots, by what forswearings, betrayings, oppressions, imprisonments, tortures, poysonings, and under what reasons of State, and politique subteltie, have these forenamed Kings, both strangers, and of our owne Nation, pulled the vengeance of GOD upon them-selves, upon theirs, and upon their prudent ministers! … But what of all this? and to what end doe we lay before the eies of the living, the fal and fortunes of the dead: seeing the world is the same that it hath bin; and the children of the present time, wil stil obey theyr parents? It is in the present time, that all the wits of the world are exercised.[15]

The notion that we can understand the present by studying the past was a Renaissance commonplace. So was the assumption that human nature is always and everywhere the same. But Ralegh's comparison, ostensibly to the king's credit, of James I with this rogues' gallery of English and continental tyrants carried a *frisson* of danger. Alongside Ralegh's insistence on the condign punishment that divine providence has in store not only for tyrants but also for their offspring and heirs, this analogy seems to have led to the book's suppression by the government for 'beeing too sawcie in censuring princes.'[16]

Foreign history was not an appropriate blueprint for the conduct of political life at home. John Hayward characteristically insisted on the superior authority of national past as a guide to national politics. 'Because it is dangerous to frame rules of Policie out of Countreys differing from us, both in nature and custome of life, and forme of government', he argued, 'no Histories are so profitable as our owne'.[17] Thomas Nashe praised plays based on medieval English history for their capacity to incite patriotic feelings. Thomas Heywood echoed Nashe's views. But Heywood also stressed the didactic efficacy of foreign history plays that, under the guise of allegory, reflect on the situation at home.[18]

Writing about very recent past – about 'our time', to use Foxe's phrase – was subject to official constraints. The second, updated edition of Raphael Holinshed's *Chronicles of England, Scotland, and Ireland* (1587) had been temporarily withdrawn from sale, reviewed and reformed before being approved for circulation; Fulke Greville, who proposed to write a life of Elizabeth early in James's reign, was ordered to abandon the project.[19] There were corresponding restrictions on the reporting of domestic news. When the first newsbooks appeared, their editors were licensed to cover only foreign affairs.[20]

The market for European news expanded in the late sixteenth and early seventeenth century. Reports were avidly sought from the continental theatres of war, in particular those where Englishmen were present, and from the most powerful courts, notably French and Spanish, where diplomatic leagues were brokered. Current happenings across the Channel were swiftly reported by word of mouth.[21] There were also manuscript newsletters, extensive pamphlet literature, and, from the early 1620s onward, corantos and printed newsbooks.[22] Translations multiplied of books describing the history, laws, customs and government institutions of European states.[23] English travellers, scholars, public servants and pamphleteers published competing accounts.[24] The Crown's foreign policy was communicated to the nation in royal proclamations such as Elizabeth's 'Declaration of the Causes Mooving the Queene of England to Give aide to the Defence of the People afflicted and oppressed in the lowe Countries'.[25] The proclamations were read from the pulpit and printed versions of them were displayed in market towns and cities. Recurrent levies and collections made in parishes across the country to redeem captives and prisoners of war were a constant reminder of England's continental entanglements.[26]

The theatre enabled spectators to visualize recent events in which living and often familiar figures had been involved. It invited them to celebrate English triumphs or to contemplate foreign crises. Led by

Count Maurice of Nassau, the combined Anglo-Dutch troops defeated the Spaniards at Turnhout in the Netherlands on 24 January 1598. By late October 1599, the victorious battle was being re-enacted in London by an unnamed acting company; the native heroes – Sir Robert Sidney and Sir Francis Vere – were instantly recognizable through distinctive make-up and dress.

Given the vicissitudes of travel in the period, it is astonishing how quickly news from the continent reached London and how promptly and widely it was disseminated. No less impressive is the swiftness with which foreign events could be transferred to the stage. On 3 May 1619 Johan van Olden Barnevelt, leading Dutch statesman and politician, was executed for treason at The Hague. The news reached London three days later. On 17 May *The Picture of Barneveltes Execucon*, a pamphlet account of the event, was entered in the Stationers' Register. A broadside ballad hostile to Barnevelt was published around the same time. By mid-August, Philip Massinger and John Fletcher's *The Tragedy of Sir John Van Olden Barnavelt* was playing at the Globe.[27] The process of translation to the stage had taken approximately three months. During that time the script had been commissioned, composed and licensed (although not without incurring official objections that required a degree of rewriting); the promptbook had been prepared and parts copied for actors; costumes had been purchased and the play rehearsed. *Barnavelt*, one contemporary reported, 'hath had many spectators'.[28]

In the early seventeenth century newsmongering became the target of satire, much of it in plays. A character in John Fletcher's *The Fair Maid of the Inn* (1626) proposes to establish 'A new office for writing pragmaticall Curranto's'; another, in James Shirley's *The Schoole of Complement* (1631), accuses impoverished soldiers of manufacturing false military news: they 'will write you a battle in any part of *Europe* at an houres warning, and yet never set foot out of a Taverne'. The prologue to Thomas Heywood and Richard Brome's *The Late Lancashire Witches* (1634) jokingly excuses the play's homespun subject matter by blaming it on the lull in the continental war and the resulting lack of news: 'Corrantoes failing, and no foot post late / Possessing us with News of forraine State, / No accidents abroad worthy Relation /

Arriving here, we are forc'd from our owne Nation / To ground the Sceane that's now in agitation.'[29]

Ben Jonson anatomized the manufacture and dissemination of news in his comic *tour de force*, *The Staple of News* (1626). Again, news from the continent is the centre of attention. Among the targets of outrageously nonsensical reports are: the Pope, the Emperor (Ferdinand II of Bohemia and Hungary), the King of Spain (Philip III), Duke Maximilian I of Bavaria (founder of the Catholic League in the Thirty Years War), Count Tilly (general of the League), Marco Antonio de Dominis, Archbishop of Spalato (a turncoat priest, who, following his conversion to Protestantism, resided in England before reconverting to Catholicism and returning to Rome, only to die in a papal prison) and Diego Sarmiento, Count of Gondomar (a brilliant Spanish diplomat, loathed in England, where he served as ambassador). Thus we hear that 'the *King* of *Spaine* is chosen *Pope*' (3.2.21), that the Emperor 'has resign'd, / And trailes a pike now, under *Tilly*' (3.2.24) and that Gondomar has developed 'A second *Fistula*' for 'cleansing his *posterior's*' with 'the poore *English-play* [Thomas Middleton's *A Game at Chess*, 1624], was writ of him' (3.2.207–8). *The Staple of News* pinpoints the competition and interdependence between manuscript and print publication. According to one of the characters, 'when *Newes* is printed, / It leaves Sir to be *Newes*', to which another replies: 'See divers mens opinions! unto some, / The very printing of them, makes them *Newes*' (1.5.48–9, 51–2). In this brilliant satire, Jonson exposes the mechanics and economics of newsmongering and the credulity of the populace to whom the news is sold.

Jonson's attack on journalism and the news industry could be applied, with little adjustment, to playwriting and the theatre business. Jonson recognizes that the rapidly proliferating newsbooks have begun to replace the drama as a vehicle for disseminating and interpreting foreign affairs. Renaissance plays set in Europe routinely drew on oral reports, manuscript newsletters, pamphlet literature, travel writings and historiography. A sensationalist tragedy about the slaughter of the French Huguenots on St Bartholomew's Day in 1572, Marlowe's *The Massacre at Paris* closes with the assassination of Henri III which occurred in 1589, a mere three years before the play's first recorded performance. Based, at least in part, on the author's firsthand knowledge of French politics, *The Massacre* adapted, rewrote and conflated a number of continental pamphlets, some pro-, some anti-Catholic.[30] In the absence of daily (until the 1620s, even of weekly) newsbooks, and with literacy levels low, plays such as *The Massacre* and *Barnavelt* made available to the wider public the information retailed in scribal and printed sources to which access was limited by social and economic standing.

Dramatizations of contemporary European history were in demand. But they were liable to irritate the authorities. Elizabethan regulation of the stage forbade the handling of 'either matters of religion or of the governaunce of the estate of the common weale'.[31] The rules, however, did not preclude representation of recent events on the continent or living European monarchs. Marlowe's *Massacre*, a play dealing overtly with religious conflict and featuring three successive French kings – Charles IX, Henri III and Henri IV – attracted no official disapproval. Nor did Peele's *Battle of Alcazar* (1588–9), nor yet the anonymous *Captain Thomas Stukeley* (1596), both of which depicted England's arch-enemy Philip II of Spain. Philip Henslowe's commission of a series of plays about French Wars of Religion for the Admiral's Men in 1598–9 indicates that he sensed profit, not trouble with the censors.

There is some evidence in Elizabeth's reign that diplomatic relations between European rulers could be strained by the staging of sensitive recent episodes. In 1602 Italian players in Paris were prevented from performing *L'Histoire Angloise contre la Roine d'Angleterre* due to a protest from the English ambassador, Sir Ralph Winwood. In response to objections 'by some Standers by, that the Death of the Duke of Guise hath ben plaied at London', Winwood explained that that 'was never done in the life of the last King'.[32] Winwood did not deny that Guise's death had been the subject of an English play that included among its *dramatis personae* Henri III who had ordered the duke's assassination. Winwood's defence rested on a claim that the piece appeared only after Henri III himself had died whereas the Italians were planning to attack a regnant queen.

Shortly after the accession of James I constraints on theatrical representation of foreign affairs were tightened. The closer control was prompted by the brouhaha over Chapman's *The Conspiracy* and *The Tragedy of Charles Duke of Byron* (1607–8), a drama about the fall of Henri IV's favourite, Charles de Gontaut, Duc de Biron. The French ambassador in London, de la Boderie, reported that the silenced players would be allowed to resume acting only 'on condition that they should no longer perform any modern histories nor speak of contemporary affairs on pain of death'.[33] Thereafter some such prohibition – though not the threat of the death penalty in the event of its violation – seems to have been in force. 'What Pen dares be so bold in this strict age, / To bring him while he lives upon the Stage?': thus the prologue to Wentworth Smith's *The Hector of Germany; or, The Palsgrave, Prime Elector* (performed 1614–15).[34] Smith was anxious to deny that he portrayed Frederick V, Elector Palatine, who only the previous year had wed James's daughter Elizabeth. As Hans Werner has noted, however, Smith's play, which barely concealed current events under the guise of medieval history, was indeed a compliment to Frederick.[35] The furore over Middleton's *A Game at Chess* (1624), an allegorical treatment of Anglo-Spanish relations, furnishes another reference to the prohibition: 'His Majesty remembers well there was a commandment and restraint given against the representing of any modern Christian Kings in those stage-plays.'[36]

James I was famously jealous of his royal prerogative and mastery of foreign policy. 'Whether I shall send twenty thousand or ten thousand, whether by Sea or by Land, East or West', he told Parliament, 'you must leave that to the King.'[37] Given James's insistence on the *arcana imperii*, the Jacobean authorities' censorship or suppression of dramatic commentary on foreign affairs in *Barnavelt* or *A Game at Chess* can be seen as an attempt to forestall the theatre's interference with the government's diplomatic efforts. Even so, the injunction against depicting modern continental royalty was not rigorously enforced. The crux was not whether a play presented a living Christian prince but how it did so. Sir George Buc's reformations of *Barnavelt* reveal a concern that Prince Maurice of Orange be shown favourably. Only exasperation with what he perceived as disrespectful treatment of the prince led Buc to note: 'I like not this: neither do I think that the pr. was thus disgracefully used. besides he is to[o] much presented.'[38] The objection was still to the manner of Maurice's presentation and the scope of his role, not to his presence in the play. *A Game at Chess*, with its portrayal of Philip IV of Spain, King James, Prince Charles, the Duke of Buckingham, and others had been licensed by Sir Henry Herbert and banned by his superiors only after a sensational run of nine days in which the 'personation' of living figures had become apparent. Herbert clearly did not see depiction of modern European rulers in itself as wrong.[39] Nor, under Charles I, did Henry Glapthorne excite the intervention of the censor by including Emperor Ferdinand II in his *Albertus Wallenstein, late Duke of Fridland (c. 1635)*.[40]

The number of history plays set in contemporary Europe – over two dozen between 1588 and 1640 – attests to their commercial appeal and popularity with audiences. That there were not more may have been due, in part, to censorship restrictions that, as we have seen, were imposed and intermittently applied in the early Stuart era. Audiences were naturally avid for pungent accounts of continental goings-on: an anodyne depiction of Barnevelt's fall would hardly have been worth the investment. Yet the precarious political viability of history plays about contemporary affairs meant that the financial outlay could be lost if the play were banned prior to or during the first run – as was the case when the Privy Council ordered the suppression, on 22 June 1617, of an 'enterlude concerning the late Marquesse d'Ancre', the favourite of the French dowager queen who had been murdered less than two months earlier, on 24 April.[41] Censorship is a form of reception and the nervous reaction of the authorities to protests from foreign diplomats highlights the risks involved in staging the present or the recent past. In any case, the stage life of contemporary histories was short. In contrast to plays about ancient Rome or medieval England that, if successful, would enter the company repertory and continue to bring profit, documentary pieces stood to make money mainly during their first (and often last) run. Once their topical appeal disappeared, the market for revivals waned.

EUROPE AND EUROPEANS IN
MASQUE AND PAGEANT

In the highest seate a Person representing *Troynovant* or the City, inthroned, in rich Habilaments; beneath her, as admiring her peace and felicity, sit five eminent Cities, as *Antwerpe, Paris, Rome, Venice* and *Constantinople*.[42]

History plays set on the continent dealt with specific nations and states. But what was the idea of Europe that informed them? How was that idea expressed in emblematic genres such as masques and civic pageants? In the sixteenth century the concept of Europe competed with the older notion of Christendom that it eventually supplanted. The conception of the European continent as a geographical rather than a confessional entity was a sign that the unity of the Christian world was irrevocably broken. In the aftermath of the Reformation, denominational divisions pitted Catholics against Protestants within and across nations and to some extent also across state boundaries.[43]

Catholic and Protestant powers occasionally sought alliance with Islamic states. The notion of Christendom, however, continued to be invoked. There were repeated calls for Christians of all persuasions to join in a campaign to repulse the infidel. Foxe wondered whether 'the proud pope' or 'the barbarous Turke' were the greater enemy of Christ's church and the more palpable incarnation of the Antichrist.[44] Throughout her reign Elizabeth was urged to assume the leadership of European Protestants. More ambitiously and more controversially, she was also counselled to steer 'the IMPERIALL SHIP, of the most parte of Christendome'.[45] In 1589, Scotland's young Calvinist king, James VI, enthusiastically celebrated the Catholic victory over the Turks at Lepanto in 1571 with a versified encomium. After his accession to the English throne, the British Solomon's most cherished ambition was to effect, by peaceful means, 'the reunion of Christendom'.[46]

Confessional differences provided one context for the development of the idea of Europe. Another, broader frame was the product of voyages of discovery, colonial expansion and the race for empire. Not coincidentally, the adjective 'European' entered the English language in the late sixteenth century when England's naval power increased and when her adventurers, pirates and merchants belatedly joined the scramble for the benefits of overseas expansion and trade.[47] From this perspective, too, Europe could be seen as both unified and deeply divided.

Europe was routinely contrasted with Asia, Africa and America, her culture and civilization being seen as innately superior to those of the rest of the world. This European pre-eminence was epitomized by the iconography of some contemporary maps and emblematic forms of theatre.[48] In Thomas Campion's masque for the wedding of Robert Carr, Earl of Somerset, and Frances Howard in 1614, Europe is shown as empress among lesser royalty:

> *Europe* in the habit of an Empresse, with an Emperiall Crowne on her head.
> *Asia* in a Persian Ladies habit, with a Crowne on her head.
> *Africa* like a Queene of the Moores, with a crown.
> *America* in a skin coate of the colour of the juyce of Mulberies, on her head laye round brims of many coloured feathers, and in the midst of it a small Crowne.[49]

We encounter a similar emblematic portrayal of the four continents in one of the *tableaux vivants* devised by John Squire for his *Tes Irenes Trophoea*, a Lord Mayor's Show for the year 1620:

> the 4 parts of the *World, Asia, Africa, America*, and *Europa*, each of them inviting their trade unto their coasts. *Asia* was attired in an antique habit of peach coloured Sattin, and buskins of the same, a Coronet on her head, and a censor in her hand reaking with *Panchayian* spices: *Africa* a *blackmoore* in a naked *shape*, adorned with *beads*, and in her hand the branch of a *Nut-megg-tree*: *America* a tawny Moore, upon her head a crowne of *feathers*, and bases of the same; at her backe, a quiver of shafts, and in her hand a *Parthian bow*: *Europa* in a robe of *Crymson* taffaty, on her head an imperiall crowne conferred on her by the other three as *Empresse* of the *earth*, and holding in her hand a cluster of grapes, to signifie her full swolne plenty.[50]

The differences between Campion's and Squire's versions of the trope mark the distance between court and City values and interests. Mounted annually by London's Livery Companies, the Lord Mayor's Show celebrated the installation of the new mayor on 29 October.[51] Ever more opulent and visually arresting, in the early seventeenth century they rivalled the splendour and challenged the ideology of the court masque. The shows extolled commerce, industry and charity; they commemorated the establishment of London's elective government; and they paid tribute to the company from among whose ranks the new mayor had been chosen. They also offered the new incumbent advice under the cloak of praise. Occasionally, they alluded to domestic or foreign affairs. *Tes Irenes Trophoea* 'figur[ed] the traffique or trade of the ... company of the *Haberdashers*', of which the new mayor was a member. Squire's personified continents are welcoming towards the English traders. Asia is depicted with spices and Africa with nutmeg, both being products much coveted on European markets. The printed description of the pageant implies that Europe has been as it were elected to imperial dignity by the other three continents.

The assumption of European superiority towards the indigenous populations was difficult to sustain. For one thing, the distinction between the ostensibly civilized Europeans and the uncouth denizens of other climes was qualified by the contempt for the white barbarians of Europe: the Irish (less often the Scots), Lapps, Livonians and 'Goths'. For another, Europeans – French, English, Scottish, Irish – were no less concerned about when and how they themselves had become civilized.[52] Thus Camden's *Britannia* documented the island's past as a Roman province, while several Jacobean plays set in ancient Britain – Shakespeare's *Cymbeline* (1608–11), John Fletcher's *Bonduca* (1611–14) and R.A.'s *The Valiant Welshman* (1610–15) – used the Roman conquest to compare the values of the Romans and of the Britons, and assess the price of Rome's military triumph and its civilizing mission.[53]

Confessional divisions originating in the Old World were transferred to the New. In travel writings, historical narratives and imaginative literature, European Protestants were depicted as bringers of enlightenment and truth to the natives, Black Legend Spaniards as monsters of cruelty.[54] In Thomas Middleton's Lord Mayor's Show for 1613, *The Triumphs of Truth*, English traders are the agents of the Moors' conversion to Christianity. Here is the Moorish king's narrative of his and his people's experience:

> By the religious conversation
> Of English merchants, factors, travellers,
> Whose Truth did with our spirits hold commèrce
> As their affaires with us: following their path,
> We all were brought to the true Christian faith:
> Such benefit in good example dwells,
> It oft hath power to convert infidels.[55]

Implicit in the reference to 'the true Christian faith' is the contrast with popery. Were they to come into contact with the Spaniards, the outcome would be enforced conversion of the Moors to a false religion.

Records of the reception of Renaissance plays and pageants are sparse. But, as an eyewitness report on the production of another of Middleton's mayoral shows demonstrates, they could provoke unintended reactions. In *The Triumphs of Honour and Industry* (1617) Middleton apparently set out to glorify the beneficial influence of trade on international relations. His principal conceit was a 'Pageant of Several Nations' that 'move[d] with a kind of affectionate joy both at the honour of the day's triumph and the prosperity of Love, which by the virtue of traffic is likely ever to continue.' Among those represented were: 'An Englishman. A Frenchman. An Irishman. A Spaniard. A Turk. A Jew. A Dane. A Polander. A Barbarian. A Russian or Muscovian.' Characteristic attributes of clothing associated with those nationalities – such as the Russian's fur hat or the Englishman's beaver[56] – made them instantly recognizable to the audience. Two of the figures, the Frenchman and the Spaniard, had speaking roles: 'the zeal and love of the Frenchman and Spaniard ... who, not content with a silent joy, like the rest of the nations, have a thirst to utter their gladness, though understoood of a small number'.[57]

Lofty ideals of universal peace bred by commercial exchange were not what struck those assembled to watch *The Triumphs of Honour and*

Industry on 29 October 1617. We find a vivid account of the crowd's reaction in one of the dispatches of Orazio Busino, the Venetian envoy to England:

> Among the figures represented was a Spaniard, wonderfully true to life, who imitated the gestures of that nation perfectly. He wore small black moustachios and a hat and cape in the Spanish fashion with a ruff round his neck and others about his wrists, nine inches deep. He kept kissing his hands, right and left, but especially to the Spanish Ambassador, who was a short distance from us, in such wise as to elicit roars of laughter from the multitude.[58]

Whether this manner of delivery had been suggested to the actor by Middleton – devisers of pageants normally supervised and directed them – or whether it was a piece of fortuitous improvisation prompted by the presence of the Spanish ambassador is unclear. Whatever the case, the crowd's derisive response to the Spaniard's antics reflects the unpopularity of James's pro-Spanish policies and public antagonism towards the Spanish ambassador, Gondomar.[59] Middleton's pageant highlights a distinction between an essentially topical allusion to foreigners, often hostile or competitive, and a more historical allusion to a sometimes common past.

Masques and civic pageants created competing images of Europe and Europeans in order to explore Europe's position *vis-à-vis* the rest of the world and to comment on the relations among the various European nations. The perspective of the court masque was sometimes in conflict with the mercantilist outlook of the civic shows, although ideological differences between the two forms cannot be reduced to a simple dichotomy.[60] James's plan for the union of England and Scotland was endorsed both by civic pageantry – *The Magnificent Entertainment* (1604) for the royal entry by Dekker, Jonson and Middleton and *The Triumphes of Re-united Britania* (1605), a Lord Mayor's Show by Anthony Munday – and by court theatricals such as Jonson's *Hymenai* (1606) and Campion's *Lord Hay's Masque* (1607). Shortly thereafter the cancelled 'Masque of Truth' (1613) as well as the mayoral shows by

Dekker (1612), Middleton (1613, 1617, 1622) and Webster (1624) were urging the king to adopt a militant Protestant stance in foreign policy.[61]

The emblematic mode of masques and pageants, however, precluded accommodation of sustained narratives of European affairs. Those were, instead, evoked symbolically. Thomas Heywood's *Londini Status Pacatus; or, Londons Peaceable Estate* (1639), the last Lord Mayor's Show to pass through the streets of London before the English Civil War, is a case in point. Heywood had probably based the final pageant, 'the calamities of War, and the blessednesse of peace', on a recent pamphlet *The Lamentations of Germany* (see Figure 7). The pageant contrasted the ravages inflicted on Europe's peoples and landscape by the Thirty Years War with the benefits of peace that Stuart Britain still enjoyed, however precariously, and that it would forfeit, were it to descend into the kind of internecine strife that was tearing the continent apart. This application was elucidated by the Genius of the City:

> And such a time is *War*, and such the throwes
> Our *neighbour Nations* travell *now* in; woes
> Quite desperate of delivery: whilst *calme Peace*,
> *Prosperity*, and *Plenty*, with *increase*
> Of all concatinated *Blessings* smile
> With cheerefull face on this *sole-happy Isle*.

Heywood explained that 'the Company of Artillery men completely armed ... expresse[d] Warre: and the Livery and gown-men [were] the Embleme of peace'.[62] Given the generalized iconography of the pageant, the audience had to have the message spelled out: mere visual representation would not suffice.

If the dramatic form of court masques and civic shows imposed limitations on their presentation of European politics, the occasional character of the two genres – single performance was the norm for both – prevented masques and pageants from exerting the sort of impact that public plays, performed in London and on provincial tours, were able to achieve by dint of their social outreach and iterability.

FIGURE 7 Illustrations of atrocities during the Thirty Years War, from Philip Vincent, *The Lamentations of Germany: Wherein, as in a glasse, we may behold her miserable condition, and reade the woefull effects of sinne* (1638), pp. 9 (tortures) and 44 (cannibalism). The book was a source for Thomas Heywood's Lord Mayor's Show, *Londini Status Pacatus* (1639).

THEATRICAL TOPOGRAPHY AND
FOREIGN AFFAIRS

My Lord, no Court with England may compare,
Neither for state nor civill governement:
Lust dwelles in *France*, in *Italie*, and *Spaine*,
From the poore pesant to the Princes traine,
In *Germanie* and *Holland* riot serves,
And he that most can drinke, most he deserves:
England I praise not, for I here was borne,
But that she laugheth the others unto scorne.[63]

Political and religious preoccupations guided the dramatists' choice and treatment of contemporary settings. Chief among European ones were Italy, France, the Iberian peninsula, the Netherlands and Germany. French and Spanish history plays proliferated in England from the late 1580s until the 1620s. In the first two decades of the seventeenth century we find a cluster of Italian and Italianate plays. The outbreak of the Thirty Years War in 1618 turned attention towards the German states.[64]

Most plays set on the European continent had fictional or fabulous plots. A smaller proportion, mainly tragedies, provided factual, or ostensibly factual, accounts of events in continental Europe. Some concentrated on recent episodes (*The Massacre at Paris*, 1593; *Sir John Van Olden Barnavelt*, 1619; *Albertus Wallenstein*, c. 1635); others took up mythic or medieval history or pseudo-history (the anonymous *The Weakest Goeth to the Wall*, c. 1595–1600; the anonymous *Charlemagne or The Distracted Emperor*, c. 1604; William Heminge's Merovingian *The Fatal Contract, A French Tragedy*, c. 1639). Those set in an unspecific past often alluded teasingly to recent happenings. 'Names, events and places of recent Iberian history are suggestively implied in the play's dialogue', notes David Bevington in his edition of Thomas Kyd's *The Spanish Tragedy* (c. 1586–90),

but without much precision. Spain had defeated Portugal in the bloody battle of Alcantara in 1580; Portugal was ruled after 1582 by a viceroy; Terceira, in the Azores, fell to the Spanish in

> 1583. *The Spanish Tragedy* begins with the defeat of the
> Portuguese viceroy, and alludes to Terceira at I.iii.82.[65]

Concern about Spain's imperial ambitions, reflected in its recent
annexation of Portugal, explains the allusiveness of Kyd's play. *The
Spanish Tragedy* is not a history play, although, like many dramatizations
of contemporary history, it is resolutely topical.

Broadly speaking, history plays set in Catholic or predominantly
Catholic countries such as Italy, France, Spain and Portugal were
anti-Catholic in outlook. So were those dramatizing the fault-lines
of confessional conflicts such as the clash between Catholics and
Protestants in the Low Countries. But long-term changes in England's
relations with her continental neighbours such as the rapprochement
with France and war with Spain under Elizabeth or the pursuit of peace
with Spain under James as well as specific events, whether domestic
(Gunpowder Plot) or foreign (Henri IV's conversion to Catholicism),
influenced dramatic treatment of Catholic nations and states.

Given its division into several city-states, Italy posed less danger
than France or Spain. Its threat was perceived to be moral rather than
political. Commercial rivalry too played a part in shaping English
attitudes towards the Italians. In his contribution to Holinshed's
Chronicles, William Harrison warned of the hazards of travel to Italy.
'Italie', he wrote, 'is not to be seene without a guide, that is, without
speciall grace given from God, bicause of the licentious and corrupt
behaviour of the people.'[66] 'O Italie', apostrophized Thomas Nashe, 'the
academie of man-slaughter, the sporting place of murther, the
Apothecary-shop of poyson for all Nations: how many kind of weapons
hast thou invented for malice?'[67] Associated, as in Harrison and Nashe,
with religious, moral and political decay, Italy provided ready-made
settings for bloody tales of incest, betrayal and revenge: Middleton's *The
Revenger's Tragedy* (1606–7), set in an unidentified duchy of Italy, and
his *Women Beware Women* (*c.* 1620–4), set in Florence; Webster's
Italianate tragedies, *The White Devil* (1612), set in Rome and Padua,
and *The Duchess of Malfi* (1613–14), set in Amalfi (some scenes taking
place in Rome, Loreto, the vicinity of Ancona and Milan). All these

plays portray Italy as a site of popish superstition that rends the fabric of society and destroys ethical norms in political life. Yet these pieces do not exploit the historical implications of their plots even when those are based on fact. Rather, as Albert H. Tricomi has argued, the Italianate revenge tragedies and tragicomedies by Middleton, Marston and Webster deploy their deliberately vague settings to reflect on the evils of European courts as seats of favouritism, despotism and corruption.[68]

There was the Italy of the principalities and there was the Italy of papal Rome. The latter provided settings for plays in which both specific location and historical content were what mattered. Vilification of the papacy was a theme of such late Elizabethan plays as Marlowe's *Doctor Faustus* (1588–92), with its anti-popish antics, and no doubt the lost *Pope Joan* (*c.* 1580–92), which purveyed the scandalous story of a female Pope. In the immediate aftermath of the Gunpowder Plot of 1605, we find two history plays set partly in Rome that exploited and further fomented anti-Catholic sentiment: Barnabe Barnes's *The Devil's Charter* (1606) and Thomas Dekker's *The Whore of Babylon* (1606–7). The former is reminiscent of Marlowe's *Faustus* in its use of magic and the devils, while the latter reproduces recent history under a veil of Spenserian allegory.

A lurid melodrama of papal corruption, Barnes's *The Devil's Charter* recounts the downfall of Pope Alexander VI. The play dwells on the degeneration of Catholic clergy that manifests itself in their promiscuity and sexual deviancy (having fathered several illegitimate children, Barnes's Pope seduces a young man and later arranges for his lover's murder); political duplicity (the Pope and his son, the infamous Caesar Borgia, plot to gain political control over Italy – which involves them in a series of perjuries, betrayals and murders); and irreligion (in a quasi-Faustian deal, Barnes's Pope has sold his soul to the devil and is hauled off to hell amid thunder and lightening, '*with fearefull noise: the divells thrust him downe and goe [off] Triumphing*').[69] Through the sensationalism of his portrayal of the Borgias, which occasionally borders on the grotesque, and through his tragedy's providential ending, Barnes encourages the spectators' sense of moral superiority. The foreign in *The Devil's Charter* equals moral and sexual otherness and abnormality.

For all the supernatural machinery of magic and devils, Barnes insists on the factuality of his tragedy, which is based on an account by the Florentine historian and political thinker, Francesco Guicciardini. 'Francis Guicchiardine', as Barnes renders him, functions as a chorus, introducing and commenting on the action, bridging gaps in the narrative, summarizing events that occurred after the play's close such as Caesar Borgia's ignominious death, and pointing out the poetically just outcome of the story he has presented in 'this tragike myrrour'.[70]

The moral purpose of Dekker's *The Whore of Babylon* was similar to Barnes's: to expose the evil and treachery of the papacy. Yet it was also broader and more ambitious. The historical framing of Dekker's play, too, was more complex. Barnes's spectacular staging of the downfall of a late fifteenth-century Pope (Alexander VI died in 1503) was designed to discredit the Catholic Church and show that its corruption laid Rome at the mercy of foreign powers, France and Spain. But Barnes did not present the papacy as a political threat to England. Nor did he draw parallels between the past and the present. Dekker did both. *The Whore of Babylon* is an all-out assault on the forces of international Catholicism and their repeated attempts to subvert the English monarchy. Its action revolves around Catholic-inspired conspiracies against Queen Elizabeth (the Babington, Parry, Ridolfi and Lopez plots), the Northern Rebellion, and the launching of the Spanish Armada, as an apocalyptic struggle between true Christianity and the popish Antichrist. In the annals of that struggle the Gunpowder Plot is but the latest episode. Dekker adapts the allegorical frame of Spenser's *The Faerie Queene* and brings together national and biblical pasts: chronicles, pamphlets, tracts and the Book of Revelation. Pagan Rome merges seamlessly with papal Rome and biblical Babylon, Fairy Land with post-Reformation England and biblical Israel.

Dekker's prologue stressed the transparency of the historical allegory: 'the weakest eye, / Through those thin veils we hang between your sight / And this our piece, may reach the mystery'. Given the play's reliance on the emblematic mode of civic pageantry and on the conventions of historical costume drama, the audience would have had little difficulty in recognizing the principal actors – Elizabeth, Burleigh,

Leicester, Nottingham and their Babylonian opponents. In order to make the 'mystery' less mysterious for the reader of the printed quarto of 1607, Dekker supplied explanatory glosses in the list of dramatis personae ('Titania, the Fairie Queen, under whom is figured our late Queen Elizabeth', 'The Empress of Babylon, under whom is figured Rome') and marginal annotations identifying specific figures (kings of Spain, France and the Holy Roman Empire) and events (the arrival of Dutch envoys in England). In the preface, he defended himself against charges that his play was marred by lapses of chronology:

> And whereas I may, by some more curious in censure than sound in judgment, be critically taxed that I falsify the account of time, and set not down occurrents according to their true succession, let such that are so nice of stomach know that I write as a poet, not as an historian, and that these two do not live under one law.[71]

Dekker's apologia added fuel to the controversy over the veracity of historical drama that had been instigated by the publication of Ben Jonson's Roman tragedy *Sejanus His Fall*, in 1605. Jonson held that the first requirement for tragedy was 'truth of Argument'.[72] His adversaries dismissed as pedantic Jonson's extensive citation of classical sources; and they claimed poetic licence in the treatment of historical materials. 'I have not labored in this poeme, to tie my selfe to relate any thing as an historian', wrote John Marston in the preface to *The Wonder of Women; or, The Tragedie of Sophonisba* (1606), 'but to inlarge every thing as a Poet. To transcribe Authors, quote authorities, and translate Latin prose orations into English blank-verse, hath in this subject beene the least aime of my studies.'[73] Dekker clearly echoes Marston. Yet, whereas Jonson, Marston and others disagreed about the proprieties of dramatizing the classical past, Dekker was alone in justifying the manipulation of events that were fresh in the memory of his audience.

History plays set in papal Rome, whether allegorical such as *The Whore of Babylon* or mimetic such as *The Devil's Charter*, were firmly anti-Catholic. The anti-Catholic stance of plays with French, Spanish and Portuguese settings was more carefully calibrated. In the 1590s France was the subject of documentary drama chronicling its bloody and drawn-out religious wars: Marlowe's *The Massacre at Paris* (1593), Drayton and Dekker's *1–3 Civil Wars of France* (1598) and Dekker's *The First Introduction of the Civil Wars of France* (1599). With its massacres, battles, treasons and assassinations, recent French history was eminently stageable. Sensationalism aside, it served as a warning against the dangers of sectarian division and disputed succession at a time when England's prospects for domestic peace looked bleak.[74] In the early decades of the seventeenth century, we find a series of tragedies by Chapman set in the French court: *Bussy D'Ambois* (1604–5), *The Revenge of Bussy d'Ambois* (1610), *1–2 Byron* (1607–8) and *Chabot Admiral of France* (1611–13). Most describe the fall of the favourite or would-be favourite.[75] To the category of the favourite play may also have belonged several lost plays: the anonymous *Biron* (1602); *The Unfortunate General or the French History* (1603) by John Day, Richard Hathway and Wentworth Smith, which may have provided an alternative account of the Duc de Biron; the anonymous *Marquis D'Ancre* (1617), a topical piece prompted by the murder of Concino Concini, Maréchal d'Ancre, favourite of Marie de' Medici;[76] *Guise* (before 1623) by John Webster and *The Duke of Guise* by Henry Shirley (before 1627), both of which probably traced the rise and fall of the eponymous nobleman. (Guise's murder had already been staged in Marlowe's *Massacre*.)[77] Whether concerned with civil war or courtly intrigue, plays set in near-contemporary France are seldom unreservedly anti-Catholic or anti-French. Even Marlowe's *The Massacre at Paris*, which has been read as a relentless onslaught on Catholicism, takes care to distinguish not only Catholics from Huguenots but also nefarious and scheming Catholics such as Guise from the less obviously evil Henri III, who in due course becomes England's ally and dies at the hands of a Catholic fanatic.

The treatment of Spain differs from that of France in several important respects. First, French histories, whether mythic, medieval or contemporary, are more numerous. Although some pieces such as the anonymous *Philip of Spain* (1602) have been lost, the number of plays set in contemporary Spain comes nowhere near matching the number about contemporary France. Second, late Elizabethan historical drama is almost uniformly anti-Spanish. The anti-Spanish outlook, however, is not conveyed through chronicle-like dramatizations of Spain's history but rather through an emphasis on Spanish cruelty and treachery towards other nations and states, principally the Dutch, the Portuguese, the English and the conquered peoples of the New World. The anonymous *A Larum for London or the Siege of Antwerp* (1594–1600) furnishes a blood-soaked horror-show of Spanish atrocities committed during the capture of Antwerp in 1576 when over 6,000 citizens were slaughtered by the Duke of Alva's troops. Based on George Gascoigne's *The Spoil of Antwerp* (1576), a pamphlet published within months of the bloodbath,[78] *A Larum* outdoes even Marlowe's *Massacre* (which it imitates) in its unremitting stress on Catholic ruthlessness, brutality and covetousness. The young and the old, men and women, the Dutch and the English fall prey to the Spaniards. Infanticide, rapes and summary executions are the order of the day. In one of the scenes Spanish soldiers slay two small children, a boy and a girl, in the presence of their aged parents, one of whom is blind. The projected response to the staging of Spain's intervention in the Netherlands was uncomplicated: hatred of the Spaniards and outrage at their inhuman conduct. As its title makes clear (and as its prologue and epilogue further elaborate), the tragedy is a warning to the English: unless they arm and strengthen alliances with continental Protestants, they too will succumb to Spanish might.

If plays dealing with Spanish–Dutch relations wrung the viewers' emotions, those concerned with Spain's annexation of Portugal appealed to their sense of realpolitik. Peele's *The Battle of Alcazar* (1588–9) and the anonymous *Captain Thomas Stukeley* (1596), both of which offer cameo portraits of the Spanish court, denounce Philip II's Machiavellian statesmanship, especially his alleged betrayal of King Sebastian of Portugal. Sebastian's death at Alcazar, for which – contrary to the historical record – Peele holds Philip responsible, brought Portugal under Spanish rule. Spain's Iberian domination was widely seen as but a step towards its ultimate goal – universal monarchy.[79] Chettle and Dekker's lost *Sebastian, King of Portugal* (1601) presumably further demonized the Spanish king's role in bringing about Sebastian's fall and his country's enslavement.

Peele's *Battle of Alcazar* stands out as an ambitious attempt to analyse international relations. By delineating the competition of several states not only in Europe but also in North Africa, Peele accentuates the cross-cutting of political and religious interests. England's colonial endeavour in Ireland, Spain's designs on Portugal and the papacy's sponsorship of Stukeley's Irish mission are placed within the wider context of relations between Christianity and Islam. Catholic powers are shown in league with Islamic ones: for all his neo-medieval rhetoric proclaiming his venture to be a crusade against the infidel, Sebastian supports a Moorish usurper, Muly Mahamet. His adversary, Abdelmelec, is in turn allied with the Ottoman Turks, whose presentation is far from the stereotype identified in Renaissance drama by some modern critics.[80] Contending with Irish Catholics close to home, England is faced with external intervention in its affairs that has been underwritten by the Pope. Given Spain's ascendancy over the Iberian peninsula, England would do well, Peele implies, to support the Portuguese cause and, perhaps, to broach alliance with the Ottoman Turks.

The 'Presenter' stresses the factuality and currency of the history the spectators are about to see: 'Sit you and see this true and tragicke warre, / A modern matter full of bloud and ruth.'[81] Coming shortly after the defeat of the Armada, *The Battle of Alcazar* was designed to pump up patriotic feeling during preparations of England's mission in support of the Portuguese pretender Don Antonio in the summer of 1589. The play needs to be read alongside other works Peele composed immediately before and after that event. His 'A farewell entituled to the famous and fortunate Generalls of our English forces' (dedicated to Sir John Norris and Sir Francis Drake, who were accompanied by the Earl of Essex) alludes to recent stage offerings, his own *Battle of Alcazar* among them, and proposes a bold route of conquest for the Protestant English. As in *The Battle of Alcazar*, the enemy is the popish Antichrist rather than the Islamic infidel. Peele's assessment corresponds closely to the *status quo* in the 1580s when Elizabeth dallied with the Turkish sultan (to whom the English supplied arms) in order to weaken the Catholic forces on the European continent:[82]

> Bid Theaters and proude Tragaedians,
> Bid Mahomets Poo [*sic*], and mightie Tamburlaine,
> King Charlemaine, Tom Stukeley and the rest
> Adiewe: to Armes, to Armes, to glorious Armes,
> With noble Norris, and victorious Drake,
> Under the sanguine Crosse, brave Englands badge,
> To propagate religious pietie,
> And hewe a passage with your conquering swords ...
> Even to the Gulfe that leades to loftie Rome,
> There to deface the pryde of Antechrist,
> And pull his Paper walles and popery downe:
> A famous enterprise for Englands strength,
> To steele your swordes on Avarice triple crowne,
> And clense Augeus staules in Italie.
> To Armes my fellow Souldiers, Sea and land
> Lie open to the voyage you intende:
> And sea or land bold Brittons farre or neere,
> What ever course your matchless vertue shapes,
> Whether to Europes boundes or Asian plaines,
> To Affricks shore, or rich America ...
> You follow Drake by Sea, the scourge of Spayne ...
> You follow noble Norrice, whose renowne
> Wonne in the fertile fieldes of Belgia,
> Spreades by the gates of Europe, to the Courts
> Of Christian Kings and heathen Potentates.[83]

The Portuguese expedition proved 'a resounding failure'.[84] Peele's 'An Eclogue Gratulatory. Entitled: To the Right Honorable, and Renowned Shepherd of Albion's Arcadia: Robert Earl of Essex and Ewe', composed shortly after Essex's return to England on 4 July,[85] celebrated the earl's safe homecoming even as it mourned England's unsuccessful intervention on the continent. The anticlimactic pastoral mode replaced the hopeful militarism of the earlier 'Farewell'.

Following the accession of James I and the peace treaty with Spain, stage propaganda against Spain and the Spanish abated – although not for lack of effort on the part of the playwrights. We have noted the partisan reception of Middleton's mayoral show in 1617. The records of the Master of the Revels list several anti-Spanish plays that were either suppressed or censored. They came at two moments. The first coincided with James's pursuit of the Spanish match for Prince Charles and his stubborn refusal to engage in a continental war in support of his Protestant son-in-law Frederick V, Elector Palatine in the early 1620s. The second came in the aftermath of Charles I's disastrous war with Spain (1625–9), when Britain's aggressive policy towards the Habsburgs was in ruins. Exploiting widespread jubilation at the return from Madrid of Prince Charles and the Duke of Buckingham without the infanta in October 1623, Middleton's *A Game at Chess* drew protests from the Spanish ambassador, Don Carlos de Coloma. Although the script had been licensed by Herbert, its performance was stopped by order of the Privy Council.[86] Philip Massinger's *Believe as You List* (1631), written after the conclusion of the Treaty of Madrid (5 November 1630), which spelt Britain's effective withdrawal from the Thirty Years War, was refused a licence 'because itt did contain dangerous matter, as the deposing of Sebastian king of Portugal, by Philip the <Second,> and ther being peace sworen twixte the kings of England and Spayne'.[87] The play was approved for performance only after Massinger had transferred the action from recent times to classical antiquity, substituting Rome and Antioch for the objectionable Spain and Portugal. Herbert also took exception to the unlicensed production of the anonymous *The Spanish Viceroy* (1633) and exacted a letter of apology from the players.[88] Recording the king's objection to a passage in Massinger's *The King and the Subject* (1638), which Charles judged 'too insolent, and to bee changed', Herbert wrote: 'Note, that the poet makes it the speech of a king, Don Pedro king of Spayne, and spoken to his sujects [*sic*].'[89] Not only was the speech an unbridled manifesto of royal absolutism; it was attributed to the ruler of a state traditionally associated with despotism and abrogation of subjects' rights.

Only when Charles I was at war with Spain do we find a potentially anti-Spanish play, the anonymous *Dick of Devonshire* (1626), which may have had the government's blessing. The piece mixes a fabulous romantic plot with the story of Richard Peeke, an Englishman captured during the humiliatingly ineffectual naval attack on Cadiz in November 1625 and released by the Spaniards in recognition of his prowess. Upon his return home, Peeke was graciously received at court on 18 May 1626. He dedicated to the king the printed account of his adventure, *Three to One: Being, An English–Spanish Combat* (1626), on which the subsequent play was based.[90]

The contrast between late Elizabethan plays such as *The Battle of Alcazar* and the early Caroline *Dick of Devonshire* is startling. Whereas the former exudes confidence in England's power, the latter is shot through with diffidence and self-doubt. Dicke Pike, prisoner of the Spaniards, before whom he exhibits his martial skills, is far removed from the swashbuckling Stukeley, who negotiated as an equal with Iberian kings and the Pope. Although Stukeley's reputation had been sullied by his conversion to Catholicism, he none the less cut a heroic figure in both play and ballad.[91] By contrast, Devonshire Dicke, whose Protestant credentials are impeccable – he firmly resists attempts by two Irish friars to convert him (2.2.1469–1523) – never attains to heroic status. The sense of past glory that the present has failed to recapture is evoked by the play's nostalgia for Elizabethan heroes. Largely irrelevant in terms of plot development, a long exchange between two English merchants (1.2.93–231) juxtaposes the current Anglo-Spanish war and the clash between the two nations some four decades earlier. The merchants specifically cite Drake's audacious anti-Spanish privateering and the defeat of the Armada, both of which lived on in popular memory as shining examples of English warlike glory. Caroline England sadly lacked the military muscle to match them.

The tone of theatrical accounts of contemporary Spain changed from defiance and outrage in late Elizabethan drama to more muted and subtle condemnation of Spanish guile in Jacobean and Caroline plays. The topicality of Anglo-Spanish relations may explain the proliferation, in the 1620s and 1630s, of plays, not necessarily historical, with the word 'Spanish' in the title: Fletcher and Massinger's *The Spanish Curate* (1622), Dekker's *The Noble Spanish Soldier* (1622), Middleton and Rowley's *The Spanish Gypsy* (1623), Henry Shirley's *The Spanish Duke of*

Lerma (date unknown), three anonymous plays, *The Spanish Contract* (1624), *The Spanish Viceroy* (1624) and *Spanish Purchas* (1639), and Davenant's *The Spanish Lovers* (1639). There was also an amateur Oxford piece, *A Spanish Tragedy of Petrus Crudelis* (?1626–48).[92]

The expression of anti-Catholic sentiments too became less explicit, even if, during brief intervals such as the immediate aftermath of the Gunpowder Plot, the authorities momentarily condoned direct attacks on papistry. There are numerous instances of the Master of the Revels excising violently anti-Catholic passages.[93] The censor's watchfulness may explain why several Jacobean playwrights chose to translate the overt confrontation between Protestants and Catholics in contemporary Europe, which Elizabethan drama had staged without compunction, into ostensibly innocuous clashes between paganism and Christianity. Both Henry Shirley's *The Martyr'd Soldier* (*c.* 1619) and Massinger and Dekker's *The Virgin Martyr* (1620) offer timely reflections on the early stages of the Palatinate Crisis by disguising quasi-Foxean martyrology as a conflict between Vandals and Christians, and ancient Romans and early Christians, respectively.[94] Versions of Foxe's book itself make an appearance, except that in both cases their compilers are the persecutors rather than the persecuted. *The Martyr'd Soldier* opens with Genzerick, the King of the Vandals, on his deathbed calling on his attendants to 'unclaspe that booke, / Turne o're that Monument of Martyrdomes: / Read there how *Genzerick* has serv'd the gods / And made their Altars drunke with Christians blood'. When someone observes that ''Tis swelld to a faire Volume', the king wistfully rejoins: 'Would I liv'd to adde a second part too't.'[95] In *The Virgin Martyr* the villain Theophilus exults over 'My Muster-booke of Hel-hounds', which records acts of unspeakable cruelty towards the British and the Anglo-Saxons (*sic*) that he committed out of zeal to 'our Romane gods'.[96] The allusion to Roman Catholicism is nothing if not transparent. Buck's 'new reforming [of] the *Virgin-Martyr* for the Red Bull' on 6 October 1620 suggests that more pointed parallels may have been intended by the author and blocked by the censor.[97]

With the advent of Jacobean peace, Spain's military threat receded and Holland's commercial threat rose.[98] That process too was mirrored in the drama. In the 1590s the Dutch had been routinely shown as victims of Spanish oppression in need of English succour. Within thirty years, we find not only a complex analysis of Holland's domestic and religious politics in which Britain had a stake (*Sir John Van Olden Barnavelt*) but also blatantly anti-Dutch pieces prompted by the massacre of ten English merchants at Amboina in the Moluccas or Spice Islands in February 1623.[99] News of the carnage, which reached London in June 1624, delayed the signing of the Anglo-Dutch treaty that was part of a campaign towards war against Spain in the spring and summer of 1624.[100] Fearful of public opinion inflamed against the Dutch, the authorities suppressed a play about the Amboina massacre that had been commissioned by the East India Company in 1625.[101] Amboina remained a sensitive topic. In the following decade indignant references to it were deleted by the censor from *The Launching of the Mary* (1633), an otherwise turgid piece by a minor functionary of the East India Company, Walter Mountfort.[102] The growth of anti-Dutch feeling attests to the heightening of mercantile rivalry between England and the United Provinces that was beginning to jeopardize their alliance against Catholic Spain.

If the French Wars of Religion produced a cluster of French history plays, and the Armada a cluster of Spanish ones, the outbreak of the Thirty Years War stimulated interest in northern Europe, in particular Germany and Sweden. According to Werner, of the dramatic works mounted between 1620 and 1642, 'fifty-five plays, entertainments and masques contained allusions to the Thirty Years' War and ten were entirely devoted to it'.[103] Among the latter were: Dekker's *Gustavus, King of Sweden* (*c.* 1632), presumably prompted by the death of the great Protestant hero Gustavus Adolphus after the Battle of Lützen in Germany on 16 November 1632; Brome and Heywood's *The Life & Death of Sir Martin Skink with the Warres of the Low Countries*, which, Martin Butler suggests, 'exploit[ed] interest in the siege of the Spanish garrison at Schenck's Sconce in 1635–36'; and the *Play of the Netherlands* (date unknown) – none of which survives – as well as Henry Glapthorne's *Albertus Wallenstein*, which retailed the extraordinary career and assassination at Eger in Bohemia, on 24 February

1634, of imperial commander and Gustavus Adolphus's nemesis, Albrecht von Wallenstein, Duke of Friedland.[104]

While many Renaissance scripts concerned with continental affairs have been lost and are now known only through references in Henslowe's diary or Herbert's papers, enough survive to give us a fair idea of how the theatre responded to recent and not so recent events across the Channel. By contrast, the world of metropolitan and provincial fairs inhabited by itinerant showmen, with their wax figures, glassworks and puppets, has vanished almost without a trace. Yet they too helped disseminate images of Europe and its peoples. In 1633 one Thomas Gibson presented Norwich City Council with 'a licence under the hand and seale of the master of the Revelles ... to shewe the pictures in wax of the Kinge of Sweden & others'.[105] Gibson and his troupe were allowed to set up shop for four days. The shows, displays and puppetry during the week-long fair following the famous Oxford Act in 1634 highlight popular appetite for representations of biblical history, exotic climes and the Thirty Years War:

> the best thing to see
> Had been *Jerusalem* or *Nineveh*,
> Where, for true Exercise, none could surpass
> The Puppets, and *Great Britaines Looking Glass*.
> Nor are those names unusuall; *July* here
> Doth put forth all th' Inventions of the year:
> Rare Works, and rarer Beasts do meet; we see
> In the same street *Africk* and *Germany*.
> Trumpets 'gainst Trumpets blow, the Faction's much,
> These cry the Monster-Masters, Those the *Dutch*.[106]

The eclectic menu of the Oxford fair resembled the repertory of London playhouses.[107]

Elizabethan plays about contemporary Europe were formally and stylistically diverse. Whereas dramatic chronicles covered years or even decades in a country's past (*Massacre, 1–3 Civil Warres of France*), historical travelogues ranged over lands and climes (*Alcazar, Stukeley*). Narrower in scope, siege plays and battle plays alternated scenes of combat and political machination (*A Larum* and, probably, the lost *Turnholt*, *Stuhlweissenburg* and *The Siege of Dunkirk*). Some pieces avoided focus on dominant individuals; others featured a strong central figure – king, favourite, adventurer (for example, bio-dramas of Philip of Spain, Guise, Stukeley). Those generic traits were shared by history plays more distant in time or place. Thus dramatic chronicles of civil strife unfolded in Roman antiquity (Thomas Lodge's *The Wounds of Civil War*, 1588), in medieval England (Shakespeare's *1–2 Henry IV*, *c.* 1596–8) and in sixteenth-century Turkey (Robert Greene's *Selimus*, *c.* 1591–4). Marlowe's quasi-historical *1–2 Tamburlaine* (1587–8) traversed the better part of the known world. Favourites rose and fell in plays set in Plantagenet England and in ancient Rome (Marlowe's *Edward II*, 1592; Jonson's *Sejanus*, 1603).

The onset of the Stuart era transformed the forms and preoccupations of historical drama. If there is one overarching thematic and generic development that marks the transition from Elizabeth to James and that therefore shapes the presentation of contemporary Europe, it is the change in focus from civil war and disputed succession to courtly corruption and royal tyranny. That change, we shall now see, was motivated by concern about domestic, not foreign affairs.

TOPICAL APPLICATIONS

You can apply this.[108]

New scripts were commissioned and old ones updated and revived with an eye to their topical currency. That varied, depending on whether audiences were simply shown what went on elsewhere and steered towards an interpretation or whether they were also alerted to analogies between home and abroad. To display the courage of the Dutch in their struggle against Spain was one thing, to demonstrate how religious division and lack of an heir plunged France into a bloody civil war was another. The former bred sympathy and confirmed or argued the need for a broad Protestant alliance but offered no parallel with England's domestic politics. The latter, in addition to its news value, provided a timely reminder of what might await England should she too fail to work out a satisfactory religious settlement and determine who would succeed the last Tudor monarch. 'The afflictions of France', wrote one commentator, 'may be Englands looking glasse, and their neglect of peace our continued labour and studie how to preserve it.'[109]

Two issues were at the forefront of national politics during Elizabeth's reign: religion and the succession. The queen was repeatedly urged to implement strong measures against the recusants, to marry and produce an heir, and to name a successor.[110] This explains why so many Elizabethan plays chronicled the French Wars of Religion and why so few dealt with Spain's domestic affairs as opposed to its imperial plans. The shift from the Catholic Valois to the (initially) Protestant Henri Bourbon, and the internecine strife that accompanied it, seemed far more pertinent to England's troubles. The Spanish Habsburgs, after all, faced neither dynastic interruption nor religious dissension at home.

If the arrival of James I removed old concerns, it created new ones. People now worried about courtly corruption and the control of upstart favourites – Carr and later Buckingham – over the counsels of the king; and they raised the spectre of royal absolutism and tyranny. Hence the proliferation of plays set in early modern European courts, Webster's and Middleton's Italianate tragedies and Chapman's French ones prominent among them. As subject matter changes, so do means of dramatic expression. In Elizabethan dramatizations of continental affairs such as *The Massacre at Paris*, *A Larum* and, presumably, *1–3 Civil Wars of France*, armies march, swords clash, mobs gather. In Jacobean and Caroline drama – Chapman's French histories and the Italianate tragedies by Middleton, Webster and Ford – mass spectacle is less frequent. Conflict is conducted indoors within enclosed royal courts more often than outdoors in the public arena or on the battlefield. Its principal weapons are now words, not swords. Speech becomes less candid, more contrived and artificial. Momentum is carried more by ideas and verbal cut and thrust than by physical action. Rapid and fluid stage movement yields to more static and formal stage arrangements. Short scenes and swift changes of locale give way to greater unity of time and place.

Plays about contemporary Europe risked official disapproval or suppression if they were deemed to endanger foreign policy or when the trappings of foreign history concealed a controversial approach to domestic matters. In 1608 Chapman's *Byron* plays came under fire from the French ambassador, de la Boderie, who violently objected to what he saw as a demeaning – and untrue – image of the French court. He specifically cited the scene in which the queen is shown slapping the royal mistress, Madame de Verneuil. The Privy Council took heed of the complaint and suppressed the play. Chapman was forced temporarily to go into hiding and later had difficulty getting the play licensed for publication. Yet, as Richard Dutton has observed, the authorities' readiness to act on de la Boderie's intelligence may have had more to do with their realization that Chapman had touched on his own country's troubled past than with diplomatic *politesse*. For the scene in question furnished one more hint that the fall of Henri IV's marshal and favourite was meant to stir up memories of Elizabeth's general and favourite, the Earl of Essex, whose execution for treason preceded Biron's by a year.[111] Essex is named elsewhere in the play. 'The Queene of *England*', recalls Byron, 'Told me that if the wilfull Earle of *Essex*, / Had usd submission, and but askt her mercie, / She would have given it, past resumption.' Yet he hastily dismisses the value of this cautionary example – 'He yet was guiltie, I am innocent.'[112] Whereas the historical Marie de' Medici is not known to have struck her ladies-in-waiting, the historical Elizabeth assaulted hers when their affairs with the favourite came to light. Given the government's sensitivity to the Essex imbroglio and the difficulties experienced by Jonson over *Sejanus* and by Daniel over *Philotas*, Dutton's hypothesis appears eminently plausible.

Chapman's diptych suggested a specific parallel between Byron and Essex. But correspondences between home and abroad need not be so direct. One way of highlighting the relevance of topics broached in a continental setting was to devote part of the dialogue to a comparison with England. Another was to introduce flesh-and-blood Englishmen. Henri III in Chapman's *Bussy D'Ambois* praises the court of Elizabeth, for, 'as Courts should be th'abstracts of their kingdomes, / In all the

Beautie, State, and Worth they hold; / So is hers, amplie'. 'Our French Court', he says, 'Is a meere mirror of confusion to it.'[113] The *Revenge of Bussy D'Ambois* features Clermont's description of an encounter with 'a great and famous Earle / Of England ... the Earle of Oxford'.[114] Englishmen are the Dutchmen's brothers-in-arms in *Turnholt* and fellow sufferers in *A Larum*. Prince Maurice commends the loyalty of English troops in *Barnavelt*, a play that also hails an unnamed Englishwoman as a paragon of common sense and proper public and personal conduct, contrasting her with foolish Dutchwomen. An English envoy appears in the concluding scene of Marlowe's *The Massacre* and is entrusted with Henri III's valedictory message to Elizabeth.

Such devices could serve many functions. At their most innocuous they reminded the audience of the English presence and of English interests on the continent, or juxtaposed native bravery and frankness to foreign cowardice and guile. As victors (*Turnholt*) or victims (*Larum*), English characters could be effective in boosting national pride or cautioning against complacency and false security. Yet the motives behind their inclusion were seldom uncomplicatedly patriotic or didactic. Some such pointers encouraged the spectator to recognize similarities between home and abroad; others worked to distance the alien country or nation or religion. Naturally, many plays exploited the double perspective, tempting the viewer to note points of contact even as they emphasized differences – political, religious, ideological – between the continental setting and contemporary England. When the French king in Chapman's *Bussy* self-critically examines the vices of his court – 'The King and subject, Lord and everie slave / Dance a continuall Haie; Our Roomes of State, / Kept like our stables; No place more observ'd / Than a rude Market place' (1.2.26–9) – the comparison with the idealized image of Elizabeth's court redounds to the disadvantage of James I's. Although in a few cases the allegorical frame dominates, normally the audience is led to approach the foreign world on its own terms.

THE DRAMA AND POLITICAL THOUGHT

it is
No such strange crime to disobey a prince,
In things unjust.[115]

There was, then, a broad correspondence between the subject matter of historical drama and the political concerns of late Elizabethan and early Stuart England, both foreign and domestic. Yet the political dimension of the drama was not restricted to timely themes and tropes. Some history plays were unabashedly topical, others deliberately abstract and speculative. The former, like current pamphlets, poems, ballads and sermons, intervened in or commented on specific political crises – the Essex rebellion, the Gunpowder Plot, the Palatinate débâcle, the Spanish match. The latter, mostly closet pieces by Sir Fulke Greville (*Alaham* and *Mustapha*) and Sir William Alexander (*Monarchicke Tragedies*), were dramas of ideas rather than action, comparable to political tracts in prose and verse. Most commercial scripts brought together elements of both kinds of political engagement.

The theatre was a potent and accessible venue and historical drama an effective medium for articulating and disseminating political ideas. Topical applications that could be made of plays, whether based on fact or fiction, have been extensively studied. By contrast, the drama's contribution to political thought is less familiar territory. There have been, it is true, attempts to elucidate the role of Roman plays in transmitting republican ideas. By setting their tragedies against the backdrop of ancient Rome at various stages of its development – monarchy, consular republic, decemvirate, principate and empire – and by having their protagonists passionately debate the merits and evils of these forms of government, Jonson, Shakespeare, Massinger, Fletcher, Heywood, Webster and many other playwrights brought to life for thousands of spectators the accounts of classical historians and of their recent translators and commentators.

As historians have recognized at least since the early writings of J.G.A. Pocock, references to medieval England and ancient Rome were ubiquitous in politics and public argument.[116] Yet contemporary

Englishmen were not merely backward-looking. They were aware of, and sometimes strikingly receptive to, new political ideas originating on the continent. Original versions and translations of the writings of Guicciardini, Machiavelli, Calvin, Beza, du Plessis-Mornay, Languet, Bodin and others, as well as responses to and refutations of them, circulated in both manuscript and print.[117] Plots and ideas derived from them informed several plays set in contemporary Europe – *The Massacre*, *The Whore of Babylon*, *1–2 Byron*, *Barnavelt*, *Wallenstein*. Renaissance playwrights deployed recent European history to probe the merits of various forms of government and to comment on relations between rulers and subjects.

A problem that exercised the minds of early modern Englishmen was the transition from one form of government to another, and the risks and benefits it entails. The systemic shift most frequently presented on the Renaissance stage was the demise of the Roman republic and the emergence of the empire of the Caesars. Yet similar issues could be fielded in plays set closer in space and time. In the 1580s the rebellious provinces of the Spanish Netherlands constituted themselves as a republic. *Sir John Van Olden Barnavelt* traces the gradual erosion of the authority of the States of Holland and raises questions about the future constitution of the country. The tragedy is more than a contest between the once all-powerful magistrate Barnavelt and the States' military commander Maurice, Prince of Orange. It is a clash of political ideologies. 'Would you change the goverment, / make it a Monarchie?' (ll. 90–1) demands one of Barnavelt's allies in the opening scene. The first article of indictment for treason brought against him charges Barnavelt with seeking 'to renounce, and break, the generallity, and unitie of the State' (ll. 2196–7). He retaliates by accusing Prince Maurice of harbouring absolutist designs. In a speech that compares Maurice's campaign to that of the Roman Octavius when he angled for the principate, Barnavelt warns his compatriots: 'when too late you see this Goverment / changd [to a Monarchie] to another forme, you'll howle in vaine / and wish you had a *Barnavelt* againe' (ll. 2445–6). The play invites spectators to compare the conduct of political life under monarchical and republican regimes. On two separate occasions, first in a soliloquy and then in a public defence delivered during his arraignment, Barnavelt recalls his successful diplomatic transactions with various European monarchs, Elizabeth and James among them, on behalf of the republican United Provinces.

In Elizabethan and early Stuart England, debates about and imaginative re-creations of ancient republics were largely academic. For while commendations of antique Roman virtue abounded, and while certain Roman institutions such as elective government at municipal or local level were admired and emulated, no one advocated the abolition of monarchy.[118] By contrast, Calvinist resistance theory, which served to justify the Huguenot revolt against Catholic sovereigns and which, many feared, could be used to underwrite rebellion against legitimate authority, seemed immediately relevant. So did Catholic justifications of rebellion. Only slightly less influential were absolutist principles promoted by Bodin that French kings had begun to put in practice.[119] Charles I, as he fought an abortive war with Spain and then France, looked to the example of the Bourbons. His exasperation with Parliament and growing determination to rule without it were signalled in an exchange recorded in 1626 by the Venetian ambassador, in which Charles had 'spoken ... of the means used by the Kings of France to rid themselves of Parliament'.[120]

Catholic ideas of resistance mirrored Protestant ones. Sponsored by Spain, the French Holy League orchestrated ideological and military opposition to the Protestant Henri IV. The excommunication of Elizabeth by the Pope led her Catholic subjects to the conclusion that they no longer owed her allegiance, and that they were therefore within their rights to disobey her. In the next reign, the Catholic-inspired Gunpowder Plot provoked the imposition of an Oath of Allegiance and further fuelled the controversy over private conscience and public duty.

Whether and, if so, under what circumstances subjects had just cause to rise against their ruler was an uncomfortable question, given that successive English governments aided Protestant rebels on the continent. A sermon delivered in April 1622 by an Oxford man, John Knight, cited 'the writings of David Pareus and the example of James's assistance to the Huguenots to affirm that "subjects se defendendo in case of Religion might take up arms against their Sovereign'". Since James I was suspected of Catholic sympathies, even of intention to convert, Knight's argument, Thomas Cogswell has noted, cut close to the bone.[121]

As with French Huguenots, English sympathy for the plight of the Dutch derived from commonality of religion. Commitment to Protestantism overrode orthodox belief in the wrongfulness of rebellion. Possibly to avoid this ideological double-bind, *A Larum for London* reinterpreted Spain's attempt to suppress the Dutch revolt as an act of aggression. Marlowe used a similar ploy in *The Massacre*. By avoiding references to earlier Huguenot campaigns he created the impression of an unprovoked Catholic onslaught on the passive and loyal Protestants. This is not to say that Navarre and his followers are free from the opprobrium of insurgency. Navarre has recourse to standard arguments of the resister: that he is acting in self-defence, that he is fighting Guise, the Pope and Spain rather than his king, and that God, whose truth he upholds, is on his side. Although some of those claims are borne out by the action – Navarre's mother has been poisoned and he himself has barely escaped alive, Guise admits to being in the Spanish pay and to furthering his own monarchical ambitions, and King Henri III eventually joins forces with his 'brother' Navarre and his 'sister' the English Elizabeth – Navarre's specious rhetoric exposes his self-serving ends and Machiavellian posturing.

If the essence of drama is conflict, in the *Massacre at Paris* and other theatrical re-creations of contemporary Europe that conflict involved not only individuals, nations, states, religions and ethical systems but also theories of political behaviour. While the same was true of other kinds of drama, most obviously of Roman plays, the distinctiveness of depictions of contemporary events consisted in their lack of historical closure. For, when Marlowe's Protestant protagonists insisted on their right to resist their Catholic monarch, French Catholics and English recusants alike were making similar claims. Only the future would prove the outcome of real-life actions undertaken on either side of the Channel to back those claims.

Long disparaged as 'docudrama', news play or mere stage propaganda, Marlowe's *The Massacre at Paris* has only recently come under serious critical scrutiny. Topical plays and civic shows by less well-known figures have fared much worse. Unlike Shakespeare's allusive treatment of continental politics, the depictions of contemporary Europe by Marlowe, Peele, Dekker, Middleton, Massinger, Fletcher, Chapman and Glapthorne were flagrantly direct and often controversial. By bringing to the stage current crises in France, Holland or Germany, these writers were making pointed allusions to domestic affairs, foreign policy or sometimes both. Like the developing news industry and pamphleteering, the drama exploited and heightened public concern about England's role in European and global politics. 'Hee is acting his part in the eye of the whole world', Thomas Scott wrote of James I, 'he is working his Master-piece in the publique market, and trying his exact skill in *King-craft* with the greatest *States* and *Statists* in Christendome; that is, with *Rome, Spaine, Austria, Italy, Machiavel,* and the extracted strength and quintessence of all these, the *Jesuites.*'[122] Whereas Scott's pamphlet invoked a theatrical metaphor, plays about contemporary Europe literally re-enacted before metropolitan and provincial audiences the political manoeuvres of 'the greatest *States* and *Statists* in Christendome'.[123]

Chapter Six

SHAKESPEARE'S IMAGINARY GEOGRAPHY

François Laroque

Even though the canon is full of allusions to maps, to the lie of the land, to forests, seas, foreign countries and cities, to places and place-names, the word geography never appears in it. Shakespeare's plays repeatedly emphasize locality, seen both as real places and as dream-like backdrops ('the baseless fabric of this vision', *Tem* 4.1.151), mere stage settings, elements of dramatic décor. Now, geography, maps, places and telling details will be needed in drama so as to allow the spectators to 'suspend disbelief' and supply with their imagination what can only be suggested on the empty space of the public theatres' stages, as the Prologue of *Henry V* invites them to do:

> Can this cockpit hold
> The vasty fields of France? Or may we cram
> Within this wooden O the very casques
> That did affright the air at Agincourt?
> O pardon, since a crooked figure may
> Attest in little place a million,
> And let us, ciphers to this great account,
> On your imaginary forces work.
> Suppose within the girdle of these walls
> Are now confined two mighty monarchies ...
> Piece out our imperfections with your thoughts.

> Into a thousand parts divide one man
> And make imaginary puissance.
>
> (Prologue 11–25)

At the end of *A Midsummer Night's Dream*, the poet's pen becomes a means to scan space, to people the void as it were by inventing or representing *topoi*, places, contours, by providing an identity and a face to the blanks on the map:

> The poet's eye, in a fine frenzy rolling,
> Doth glance from heaven to earth, from earth to heaven;
> And as imagination bodies forth
> The forms of things unknown, the poet's pen
> Turns them to shapes, and gives to airy nothing
> A local habitation and a name.
>
> (*MND* 5.1.12–17)

Like the cartographer drawing a map with rivers, mountains and cities on it, the poet has the power to make the invisible visible by providing it with a local address and an identity, so that it may then be recognized and inventoried. And even if geography is used as a metaphor for poetic creation which, in Theseus' soliloquy, is combined with images drawn from the arts of gynaecology or obstetrics as the means to 'body forth' a world of its own, to give life and reality to the world of the imagination, this statement remains in itself a little general or even theoretical. It seems that the playwright naturally associates his characters with a certain type of space (the city or the court) which is then seen as opposed to another place which lies poles apart from it (a forest, a heath or a house), so that a number of imaginary or fictive elements are being superimposed on the real maps and real places (as in Figure 8).[1] The exact habitation is left rather vague, so that its name may become suggestive of multiple associations or connotations. Such names as Arden, India, Venice, Illyria, Egypt, Rome or Bermuda carry over with them a number of poetic echoes and symbolic correspondences. These complex signifiers are invested with a specific magic. They become incantations endowed with a strong evocative power or equivocations,

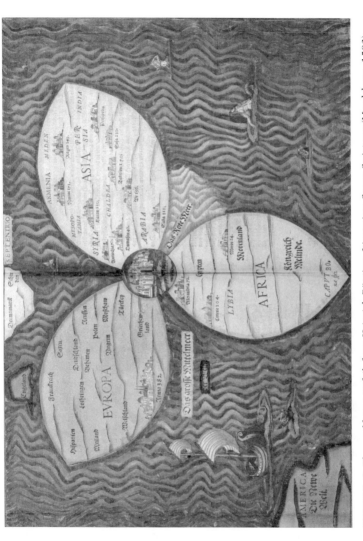

FIGURE 8 The world as a trefoil, from Heinrich Bünting, *Itinerarium Sacrae Scripturae* (Magdeburg, 1582).

which makes them ambiguous and evasive, so that meaning often fails
to be fixed or circumscribed. As Richard Wilson puts it,

> the fact remains that so many of these plays contain aporia, blind
> spots, or liminal places which give them meaning, and retain the
> potential for resistant readings to the extent that, though under
> the very eye of power, they are never in its sight: worlds within –
> rather off-stage.[2]

In his book on Renaissance geography, the French historian Numa Broc
makes the claim that the only Shakespearean play which reveals a true
geographic background is *The Tempest*, and that most of the places
mentioned by the playwright are merely dramatic scenery, even though
some of the details he sometimes gives tend to show that he had read
the most important travel books of his day (the narratives compiled by
Richard Eden and Hakluyt).[3]

It is true that Shakespeare seems to have inherited from classical
writers like Pliny and Herodotus as well as from medieval traditions of
marvellous and imaginary islands. The latter are remarkable for their
naïve endeavours to locate the particular situation of the legendary
kingdom of Prester John, for instance. So, when Shakespeare makes
Milan a harbour in *The Two Gentlemen of Verona* (*TGV* 1.1.71) or when
he provides landlocked Bohemia with deserts and a sea coast in *The
Winter's Tale* (*WT* 3.3),[4] he situates himself within this tradition of
impossible locations and imaginary geography. Contemporary maps
and atlases were also read then as fantastic books of illustrations with
images of the Amazons, the Blemmyes (described by Othello as 'men
whose heads / Do grow beneath their shoulders', *Oth* 1.3.145–6) and
other monsters painted in medieval illuminations.

Even though the histories and the tragedies are almost all situated
within the confines of Europe (the exception is *Antony and Cleopatra*
with its powerful Egyptian and eastern scenery), they also often allude
to worlds elsewhere – to India, Arabia and Africa.[5] Indeed, Europe was
often defined in opposition to the world of pagans and infidels which
was associated with barbarity, as in Lear's furious rejection of 'the
barbarous Scythian / Or he that makes his generation messes / To

gorge his appetite' (*KL* 115–17). So, real geography in Shakespeare often seems to be paired with a kind of imaginary twin or double place: the city of Verona and the forest in *The Two Gentlemen of Verona*, Athens and the wood in *A Midsummer Night's Dream*, the court and the forest of Arden in *As You Like It* or Venice and Belmont in *The Merchant of Venice*. This serves to add a sense of perspective, a look 'out there' in a blurred and distant background that opens up vistas and space for the spectators 'to make imaginary puissance' (*H5* Chorus 25). The function of this double space is to allow the presented topography to be seconded and prolonged (or contradicted) by another space that brings escape, exile or nostalgia. According to Richard Wilson, these localities were enclaves, or 'pockets of resistance', for Catholic dissidents and fugitives who were trying to evade the close surveillance of the Elizabethan police.[6] This movement is even more obvious in the comedies and in the creation of a magic green world with its sanctuaries for the refugees and rites of passage for the young, even in those that have been labelled as comedies of 'the closed world'[7] like *Love's Labour's Lost*, *Much Ado about Nothing* and *Twelfth Night*. It is interesting that these comedies, which represent almost half of the whole canon, all take place outside England, except for *The Merry Wives of Windsor*, which simply prolongs Falstaff's Saturnalian tricks and parasitic comedy in the Boar's Head tavern in Eastcheap, moving them from the field of carnival and politics to that of love intrigues and scheming.

Geography is thus associated with evasion, with detours and indirections, for those in quest of liberty because, for various reasons, they are obliged to live in a country or a city which, for some reason or other, like Denmark to Hamlet, has become a prison for them. Invested with the romance of travels, with the magic of faraway lands and exotic places, geography is also linked with desire, with seduction, with the specific fascination of foreign languages and strange idioms. It awakens curiosity and a sense of wonder, and is tied up with a need to discover the unknown. So, if there are undeniable echoes of classical antiquity and of the fabulous, enchanted worlds of medieval literature, the important place ascribed to geography, whether it is real or imaginary in Shakespeare's dramatic world, is also part and parcel of the

Renaissance taste for discovering, a taste which suddenly changed the world into a *Wunderkammer* or cabinet of curiosities.

BODILY MAPS: GEOGRAPHY AS AN ANATOMY OF THE WORLD

In *The Comedy of Errors*, the female body is connected with a number of foreign countries and exotic places in the bawdy jesting of the two Syracusans, Antipholus and his servant Dromio, when they come across Nell, the kitchen wench of Ephesus:

DROMIO S.   ... yet is she a wondrous fat marriage.

ANTIPHOLUS S.   How dost thou mean, a fat marriage?

DROMIO S.   Marry, sir, she's the kitchen wench, and all grease ... I warrant her rags and the tallow in them will burn a Poland winter ... she is spherical, like a globe; I could find out countries in her.

ANTIPHOLUS S.   In what part of her body stands Ireland?

DROMIO S.   Marry, sir, in her buttocks; I found it by the bogs.

ANTIPHOLUS S.   Where Scotland?

DROMIO S.   I found it by the barrenness, hard in the palm of the hand.

ANTIPHOLUS S.   Where France?

DROMIO S.   In her forehead ...

ANTIPHOLUS S.   Where England?

DROMIO S.   I looked for the chalky cliffs, but I could find no whiteness in them. But I guess it stood in her chin, by the salt rheum that ran between France and it.

ANTIPHOLUS S.   Where Spain?

DROMIO S.   Faith, I saw it not; but I felt it hot in her breath.

ANTIPHOLUS S.   Where America, the Indies?

DROMIO S.   O, sir, upon her nose, all o'er-embellished with rubies, carbuncles, sapphires, declining their rich aspect to the hot breath of Spain, who sent whole armadoes of carracks to be ballast at her nose.

ANTIPHOLUS S.   Where stood Belgia, the Netherlands?

DROMIO S.   O, sir, I did not look so low.

(CE 3.2.92–138)

This comic enumeration of female body parts according to their tentative resemblance to European countries works like some grotesque, Rabelaisian blazoning, like one of the counter-blazons which scoffed at the artificial conceits of the poetic genre in vogue with French Pléiade poets. This geographic 'blazon', obviously derived from the anatomic 'blazons' of Renaissance sonneteers, may be regarded as a burlesque anticipation of Hamlet's 'country matters' (*Ham* 3.2.115). Indeed the Prince's flippant and fairly misogynistic equation of female genitalia with rural or rustic topography sounds like a late and elliptic reminiscence of the comic itemization, in the early play, of a number of bawdy or satirical associations between geography and the female body. In the passage from *The Comedy of Errors*, the yoking of Ireland with the buttocks is noted by Michael Neill as a 'parodic version of the woman's body as map' after quoting a contemporary text indulging in what he calls an 'unashamed erotic blazoning of the map of Ireland'.[8] The blazon makes a number of links and punning echoes between the names and sites of the female body and those of various European and non-European countries. Its source may be traced back to the engraving chosen to illustrate 'Queen Europa' in Sebastian Münster's *Cosmographia* (1588), where Europe is represented as a strongly built woman holding a globe in her right hand and a sceptre in her left, with Africa on the top left-hand side, Asia underneath her feet, Scandia or Scandinavia at the level of her waist on the right-hand side of the picture (see Figure 9). Spain corresponds to her head and face, France to her upper chest, Germany to her breasts, while Greece and Tartary are roughly equated with the places of her feet underneath her long gown. What contributes to making the description both funny and fantastic in *The Comedy of Errors* is that Nell's body is mostly read or parsed in terms of European countries, even though she is supposed to reside in the city of Ephesus in Asia Minor. This Europe-centred geography is part of Shakespeare's use of a double space that combines closeness and distance, familiarity and strangeness. Such grotesque comedy turns the body into a *mappa mundi* where microcosm and macrocosm mirror each other and intersect in many ways. This is the most systematic and also the earliest example of Shakespeare's

FIGURE 9 'Queen Europe' from Sebastian Münster's *Cosmographia* (1588).

resorting to the technique of landscape anamorphosis in which body and landscape are made interchangeable,[9] but it is used in other plays as well. In *A Midsummer Night's Dream*, 'a brow of Egypt' (*MND* 5.1.11) denotes dark skin colour, the equivalent of 'Ethiop' (*MND* 3.2.257) or 'tawny Tartar' (*MND* 3.2.263), an image used by Helena to insult her former friend Hermia, who is a small brunette. In *The Merry Wives of Windsor*, Falstaff calls Mrs Page 'a region in Guiana' (*MW* 1.3.66) and the two wives he is courting, or 'trading', his 'East and West Indies' (*MW* 1.3.68).[10] In spite of the reputation of Guiana as an 'eroticized land',[11] it is quite clear that, right from the beginning, the possible seduction of the two Windsor wives is linked not so much to the satisfaction of lust as to Falstaff's greed. Indeed, both wives do look like a possible Eldorado to the dilapidated, out-at-elbow knight who has apparently always been a sponger at the expense of women. Titania describes her pregnant female friend gossiping with her 'in the spiced Indian air, by night' like a 'big-bellied' sail and a ship 'rich with merchandise' (*MND* 2.1.124–34). The geography of fairyland is here marked with a nostalgia for a past golden age as well as with a mercantile drive in which fertility is rendered in terms of the laws of economic, rhetorical and maternal exchange.[12] The changeling boy stands for the rules of trade, for substitution, or hypallage, and for surrogate motherhood. Femininity, sisterhood and fairy lore are all tightly interwoven in these hauntingly beautiful exotic associations that combine fantasy and sad reality (allusion to the death of the delivering mother). In *Twelfth Night*, the converted, cross-gartered Malvolio, who obeys every point of the letter he has found in the garden, smiles and smiles again in front of the Lady Olivia. Maria graphically describes this radical change of his in terms of geographic novelty: 'he does smile his face into more lines than is in the new map with the augmentation of the Indies' (*TN* 3.2.73–4). The image reveals the enormous changes and drastic revisions to which old maps were constantly submitted in the period, and it also indirectly suggests the particular blend of curiosity and anxiety in Europe's own representation of itself when confronted with the rest of the world constantly shifting its face.

In its meteorological variants, geography serves to describe humours like rage, anger and violent passion. In *The Taming of the Shrew*, Katharina is said to be as rough as 'the swelling Adriatic seas' (*TS* 1.2.69–73), while Othello, after swearing to Iago that his resolution to blow 'All my fond love … to heaven' (*Oth* 3.3.448) is now irreversible, resorts to topographical images borrowed from Turkish geography, i.e. to a liminal space situated at the border between Europe and Asia:

> Never, Iago. Like to the Pontic sea
> Whose icy current and compulsive course
> Ne'er keeps retiring ebb but keeps due on
> To the Propontic and the Hellespont:
> Even so my bloody thoughts with violent pace
> Shall ne'er look back, ne'er ebb to humble love
> Till that a capable and wide revenge
> Swallow them up.

> (*Oth* 3.3.456–63)

This famous passage is a metaphoric description of the Black Sea flowing into the sea of Marmora and then into the Dardanelles, according to Pliny's description which Shakespeare had read in Philemon Holland's translation.[13] This may be a way for Othello to associate himself with Turkish cruelty, since the Turks had a reputation for inhumanity in the Renaissance, and thus to put himself in a murdering mood, as he does in the end when he commits suicide by telling the story of a 'malignant and a turbanned Turk', the 'circumcised dog' whose throat he had cut in Aleppo for beating a Venetian and traducing the state (*Oth* 5.2.350–4).

But Shakespeare's imaginary topographies do not always stretch that far, as England is also described as an ideal, almost mythical country or as an eroticized body in the maps, especially when it is about to be divided or carved between rebels or inheritors. His use of geography for dramatic and poetic purposes is always a negotiation between the distant 'out there' and the very close, the familiar which is not seen or ignored because it is perceived as everyday or too obvious.

THE IMAGINATION OF SPACE:
MAPS AND GAPS

In *Richard II*, the dying John of Gaunt depicts a sort of patriotic last will and testament in the form of a topographic poem, whose function is to extol England's past to denounce the present misrule of King Richard:

> This royal throne of kings, this sceptred isle,
> This earth of majesty, this seat of Mars,
> This other Eden, demi-paradise ...
> This happy breed of men, this little world,
> This precious stone set in the silver sea,
> Which serves it in the office of a wall,
> Or as a moat defensive to a house,
> Against the envy of less happier lands;
> This blessed plot, this earth, this realm, this England,
> This nurse, this teeming womb of royal kings,
> Fear'd by their breed, and famous by their birth,
> Renowned for their deeds as far from home,
> For Christian service and true chivalry,
> As is the sepulchre in stubborn Jewry ...
> England, bound in with the triumphant sea,
> Whose rocky shore beats back the envious siege
> Of wat'ry Neptune, is now bound in with shame,
> With inky blots and rotten parchment bonds.

> (*R2* 2.1.40–2, 45–55, 61–4)

This patriotic piece, which Michael Neill has styled a piece of 'cartographic lyricism',[14] is particularly complex and labyrinthine, because it is essentially meant as a deathbed attack against Richard and thus serves the purposes of satire and polemics. It also provides a kind of syncretic vision in images that blend pagan and Christian elements: Mars and Neptune are found here almost side by side with Eden and 'Christian service'. The text further introduces a parallel between western fame ('deeds', 'chivalry') and eastern glory ('the sepulchre in stubborn Jewry'). At the end of the soliloquy, the written text is superimposed upon the geographic contours of the land. Here, the picture of the English 'rocky shore' 'bound in with the triumphant sea' slowly dissolves into the 'rotten parchment bonds' 'bound in with shame' and stained with 'inky blots'. The grand natural seascape that represents the island's specific spatial configuration is suddenly and literally reduced to the equivalent of Shakespeare's foul papers, even if, according to Ben Jonson, 'he never blotted out line'.[15]

This is paradigmatic of the division of the kingdom and of the reduction or shrinking that inevitably follows the successive rebellions and civil strife of the War of the Roses. In the first part of *Henry IV*, the rebels Mortimer, Glendower and Percy meet to share the kingdom on the map:

GLENDOWER

Come, here is the map. Shall we divide our right
According to our threefold order ta'en?

MORTIMER

The Archdeacon hath divided it
Into three limits very equally ...

HOTSPUR

I do not care. I'll give thrice so much land
To any well-deserving friend;
But, in the way of bargain, mark ye me,
I'll cavil on the ninth part of a hair.
Are the indentures drawn? Shall we be gone?

(1H4 3.1.68–71, 133–7)

The word 'indentures' refers both to the turning of the river Trent as well as to an apprentice's contract, which again suggests the equation of place and parchment. The English countryside and its varied geographic *topoi* and place-names are reduced to a drawing, to a handwritten text that may be changed or corrected in order to satisfy a bargain or some stubborn cavilling like Harry Percy's. Moreover, the landscape is sexualized and envisioned as a male body with allusions to 'a rich bottom' and to 'gelding'. This should be related to Westmorland's narrative of the horrible mutilation of Mortimer's 'butchered' soldiers after the defeat of his army in Wales. The 'beastly shameless transformation' (*1H4* 1.1.44) of the English dead at the hands of the Welshwomen certainly obliquely hints at castration and probable display of their bloody genitals. So the use of the verb 'geld' in the reconciliation scene is certainly not innocent in such context.

In *King Lear* another map is produced on stage as Lear is about to divide his kingdom between his three daughters in a proportion that will vary according to the love they declare they bear him. It is interesting that beyond England, France and Germany there are no geographical references in this tragedy, while the characters – Burgundy, Albany, France, Gloucester, etc. – are called by their titles and not by their Christian names. Frederick Flahiff establishes a parallel between Lear's division of the kingdom between his three daughters and Noah's ritual division of the world between his three sons Japheth, who receives Europe, Ham, who is given Africa, and Shem, who inherits Asia (compare Figure 8).[16] Lear's division is equated with a dismemberment and the geographic map with a cannibalistic mess where he 'gorges' his daughters' appetite. This is further shown in the king's use of digestive metaphors when he decides to deprive Cordelia of her inheritance: 'With my two daughters' dowers, digest this third' (*KL* 1.1.129). It is as if Lear, when he gives away his crown, were in fact feeding his dismembered body politic to those he will later call his 'pelican daughters' (*KL* 3.4.74). Such identification between land and body was characteristic of chorography, for instance in Richard Carew's *Survey of Cornwall*, where the anatomical metaphor is recurrent.[17] In this archaic world of proto- or pseudo-history, geography seems to be fading into the misty distance of legend and myth while maps become emblematic representations or woodcuts illustrating the various *topoi* of *mundus inversus*.

We find further examples of this technique in Shakespeare's representation of France. After describing this country as a kind of Eden ('this best garden of the world, / Our fertile France', *H5* 5.2.36–7) it soon becomes a *trompe l'œil* in which cities may be read as maids and vice versa:

KING ... you may ... thank love for my blindness, who cannot see
    many a fair French city for one fair French maid that stands in my
    way.
FRENCH KING Yes, my lord, you see them perspectively, the cities
    turned into a maid.

(H5 5.2.313–17)

As in the case of ancient Troy, which became identified with the figure
of Helen, the whole of France becomes encapsulated, incorporated
rather, in the person of Princess Katherine, whom the English king is
wooing. A similar situation lies behind the plot of *Love's Labour's Lost*,
which, according to Geoffrey Bullough, refers to the historical meeting
between Henri de Navarre and Marguerite de Valois in the city of Nérac
in 1578.[18] The French princess came there with her mother, Catherine
de' Medici, and her escort of pretty ladies-in-waiting. This provided the
occasion of brilliant court entertainment with amusements such as
hunting and tennis, as well as dancing and wooing ladies (a favourite
occupation of the French gallant). Meanwhile, serious negotiations
were being conducted for Marguerite's dowry which included the
province of Aquitaine. The French context of the comedy is completed
by the presence of many French names in the play, like Dumaine,
Longaville, Berowne (Biron), Boyet or Marcadé. Even Moth, a possible
anagram of Thom and topical allusion to Thomas Nashe, may refer to
the French *mot* ('word'). Indeed, Henry Woudhuysen wonders if
Shakespeare intended his audience to regard the name as French,
possibly referring to the treacherous governor of Gravelines in 1578
who was known in England as la Mothe or la Mote.[19] Finally, I would
suggest a quibble on Navarre, a country here synonymous with some
kind of 'neverland'. In *All's Well That Ends Well*, the French court is
evoked in Helen's healing of the king in Paris and in her being rewarded
with the choice of a husband among the French lords at the court. This
suddenly makes for a very heavy atmosphere leading to Lafeu's wry
remarks about 'These boys are boys of ice ... they are bastards to the
English; the French ne'er got 'em' (*AW* 2.3.94–6). Parolles, the
embodiment of French 'words', who uses some graphic swearing like

'*Mor du vinager*' (*AW* 2.3.45), finally decides that 'France is a dog-hole' (*AW* 2.3.273) and encourages Bertram to leave Paris in order to go to the wars. He is some parodic Hotspur who never means what he says and who, like Bertram in the end, will be confronted with the vacuity of his own words and be branded as an utter coward.

But, besides the mocking or bitter overtones of his romantic and satiric comedies, Shakespeare's theatre of the world often takes us back to old times and ancient worlds, thus creating a certain nostalgia for a past golden age, just as it also opens up some semantic and onomastic ambiguity, which allows two worlds, two periods, two different cultures to converge or coincide. At the end of *1 Henry VI*, Suffolk, after he has seduced Margaret and made her his mistress, manages to convince the king to marry her. In his final triumphant aside, he introduces a parallel between Greek myth and English history which recurs in the three parts:

> Thus Suffolk hath prevailed, and thus he goes,
> As did the youthful Paris once to Greece,
> With hope to find the like event in love –
> But prosper better than the Trojan did.
> Margaret shall now be queen, and rule the King:
> But I will rule both her, the King and realm.
>
> (5.4.103–8)

At the beginning of *2 Henry VI* Suffolk is back on stage to tell King Henry how he married his queen by proxy:

> in the famous ancient city Tours,
> In presence of the Kings of France and Sicil,
> The Dukes of Orleans, Calaber, Bretagne and Alençon,
> Seven earls, twelve barons and twenty reverend bishops,
> I have performed my task and was espoused.
>
> (1.1.5–9)

3 Henry VI completes the picture when Edward of York says to Margaret:

> Helen of Greece was fairer far than thou,
> Although thy husband may be Menelaus.
>
> (2.2.146–7)

It is becoming obvious at this point that the legendary city of Troy is indeed superimposed upon the modern city of Tours, and the phonetic echo between the two names may be the reason why Shakespeare changed the historical place of the marriage, which actually took place in Nancy, in Lorraine, in the east of France.[20] In this perspective or topological combination, Suffolk becomes identified with Paris, Margaret with Helen, and Henry with Menelaus, the betrayed husband. As in *Henry V*, maid and city become interchangeable. In a similar way, the Kentish gentleman, Alexander Iden, who disposes of the wild rebel Jack Cade when he finds him hungrily roaming for food inside his garden, bears a name that introduced possible associations with the biblical garden of Eden. By cutting off the rebel's head and bringing it to the king in London, he puts an end to the nightmare of popular riot and revolt and is knighted by Henry VI (*2H6* 5.1.78).

Similar toponymic echoes are often found in the comedies. In *The Merchant of Venice*, Gratiano's triumphant cry, 'We are the Jasons, we have won the fleece', is immediately followed by Salerio's anticlimactic 'I would you had won the fleece that he hath lost' (3.2.240–1). Gratiano hints at the myth of the Argonauts and the golden fleece, which is equated in the play with Portia's rich portion and fair hair, while Salerio alludes to Antonio's recent loss of his fleet via a pun on the words fleece/fleets. So the romantic plot and more realistic merchant world of enterprise and risk are here placed back to back. Another echo or pun in the same play is found in Launcelot's associations between the names 'Scylla' (referring to the Homeric name for the dangerous strait of Messina in the *Odyssey*) and Shylock when he says to Jessica: 'Truly then I fear you are damn'd both by father and mother: thus when I shun Scylla (your father), I fall into Charybdis (your mother)' (3.5.14–16). The modern geography of the comedy thus collapses Renaissance maritime routes upon the legendary sites of ancient myth.

In *As You Like It*, the forest of Arden stands for something like an Edenic world which is initially equated with the myth of the golden age by Charles the Wrestler:

OLIVER Where will the old Duke live?

CHARLES They say he is already in the Forest of Arden, and a many merry men with him; and there they live like the old Robin Hood of England. They say many young gentlemen flock to him every day, and fleet the time carelessly as they did in the golden world.

(1.1.110–15)

The medieval legend of Robin Hood, linked with the notion of popular justice and liberty, is here associated with the games and amusements of the morris dance in a place which seems to combine the biblical Garden of Eden with the name of the dramatist's mother, born Mary Arden. This may be why Shakespeare has chosen to move from the original Ardennes in eastern France, which was the location of Thomas Lodge's *Rosalynde*, the main source for the play, to the English forest of Arden, near the town of Warwick, even though, as Anne Barton reminds us,[21] most of it had probably been already hacked down in Shakespeare's days. In his recent British Academy lecture, Richard Wilson connects the golden world of the forest of Arden with that of Catholic resistance:

> There is … a plausible theory that the 'old religious uncle' who taught 'Ganymede' his oratory … is identifiable with Shakespeare's kinsman, Edward Arden, whose house at Park Hall in the Forest of Arden was a secret academy where the disaffected ex-Sheriff of Warwickshire indoctrinated a cadre of Catholic hotheads to detest Elizabeth … [this led] to his own execution and ruin for Mary Arden's family … But what is significant is how, in the fictional forest, such fanaticism is nullified … Rosalind had begun the play by fleeing 'To liberty, and not to banishment' in an Arden that Catholic critics locate – via Amiens who sings in praise of exile – in the Ardennes of the seminaries.[22]

Such topographic and onamastic links between Shakespeare's own kin, the significance of France and French names, and the secret religious line connecting Arden and Ardennes through Catholic affiliation is certainly important, since it helps clear up an intriguing aspect of the play that is not easily explained by most editors and critics.

This argument enhances the polar complementarity between 'worlds without' and 'worlds within' that politicizes the usual court–country opposition in pastoral drama and literature. New historicist criticism provides a political and ideological context which brings to light the generic divides and geographic contractions that differ from literary tradition or the so-called 'archetypal patterns' of the European imaginary. The opposition between Sicilia and Bohemia in *The Winter's Tale* reveals many anachronisms and inconsistencies, as critics have repeatedly pointed out. The time gap of sixteen years between Acts 3 and 4 is matched by a divide between a Greek, wintry Sicilia, normally regarded as pastoral territory, and a late spring Bohemia, with its sheep-shearing feast, a country whose geography seems more confused, since it is provided with a sea-coast. This apparent blunder, on the part of the playwright, has produced as much critical commentary as his description of the Mannerist Italian painter, Giulio Romano, as a 'sculptor'.[23] Shakespeare deliberately transposed the expected qualities or characteristics of the two countries north and south, inverting their respective tragic and idealized aspects. But, for Richard Wilson, 'even the Bohemian festival of *The Winter's Tale* is revealed to be "fully integrated into the international economy", with its exchange of wool for commodities like raisins, sugar, and spices'.[24] The feast is indeed presided over by the trickster and con-man pedlar, Autolycus, a complex comic character who is also a ballad-singer and entertainer, and who fleeces the shearers by stealing their purses at the feast. Imaginary as it may be, this world, in spite of its many unmistakable pastoral overtones, appears far from perfect. Actually, it is simply repeating in a minor key the sombre events of the first part in Sicilia. The contours of this European map thus remain rather blurred and altogether indistinct. Interestingly enough, on Münster's illustration for 'Queen Europe' (see Figure 9), Sicilia is identified with the globe held in the queen's right hand, while Bohemia is enclosed within a grove in the middle of her chest, facing Sicilia alongside a slightly oblique line. When we look at it, it becomes obvious that Sicilia and Bohemia are far apart and yet very much like complementary kingdoms on the map.

THE 'INFINITE VARIETY' OF
SHAKESPEARE'S GEOGRAPHY:
FROM *UTOPIA* TO *TERRA INCOGNITA*

In an English context, the question of exile makes geography and travel a negative experience unless it is linked to the return home, to the rediscovery of the native land. The motherland, like the patronym, is indeed the key to identity as well as to power, especially in the history plays. It is described as a womb, as a garden, a *hortus conclusus* protected behind natural walls. Against this, two of the great tragedies take place in the British Isles (England and Scotland), while all the comedies but one are situated in foreign European countries – Italy mostly, but also France and Austria, or never-never lands like Illyria or Arden.

Illyria, already mentioned in 2 *Henry VI*, where we find an allusion to 'Bargulus, the strong Illyrian pirate' (4.1.107), appears mainly in *Twelfth Night*. It is a name which Shakespeare found in Cicero's *Offices* and Ovid's *Metamorphoses*, and which roughly corresponded to the Adriatic coast of former Yugoslavia. Indeed, according to Harry Levin, 'This Illyrian seaport – it could well be Dubrovnick, formerly Ragusa in its more Italian days – seems to suit these Italian visitors who came from Messaline, wherever that may have been.'[25] But Illyria is also very much a country of the mind, or a nowhere place, whose name simultaneously suggests and combines the words illusion and lyrics, both very present in the comedy.[26] For Roger Warren and Stanley Wells, Illyria cannot be reduced to any precise geography, so that each director may choose his/her own interpretation of the place, an idea incidentally very present in the subtitle of the play, 'What you will': 'Each of these aspects of Illyria – the geographical or Mediterranean, the specifically English, the magical, and the sense of a country of the mind – can be illustrated by the prominence each has been given in notable stagings.'[27] This is also the point made by Leah Marcus, who, after noting that 'in Shakespeare, place is often left mysterious, or at least undefined, until well into the play', remarks that 'Illyria was scarcely familiar territory, more significant, perhaps, for its evocation of like-sounding exotica – Elysium, delirium – than for concrete geopolitical associations.'[28] Moreover, the vague, rather ambivalent space of the play is divided into Duke Orsino's palace and Olivia's house, as often happens in Shakespeare's Italian plays that are split into two different settings, like Venice and Belmont in *The Merchant of Venice* or Venice and Cyprus in *Othello*. Such double geography carefully avoids any precise localization and it evades possible topical references as well as most of the expected stereotypes about a particular well-known place or country. The Italian settings of his plays are rarely realistic or recognizable except for a few vague associations. According to Angela Locatelli:

> Shakespeare's geography seems ... to be very far from documentary, but can be even more 'convincing' than an actual journal. This happens because Shakespeare's geography unfolds along a double axis: it lingers between information and utopia, social criticism and idealisation, and above all between description and prescription.[29]

Such vagueness serves more than it actually defeats the purposes of the playwright, who uses the very indistinguishability of place to inscribe a set of latent or oblique allusions to England, to English places and English topics, while he is in fact describing Italy:

> Shakespeare's city settings are vague or specific geography. The Arno in Florence or the Adige in Verona ... are never mentioned. When the Rialto in Venice or St Gregory's Well near Milan is alluded to, it comes as a surprise ... One might conclude that this vagueness is purposeful ... More importantly Italy serves in part as metaphor for Shakespeare's England.[30]

In Shakespeare's Italian geography, there are some blatant errors: for example, the way between Milan and Mantua is described as mountainous (*TGV* 5.2.46–7); and Milan is depicted as a sea-port mainly connected by water to Verona, when Proteus says to Speed, who is looking for his master, 'But now he parted hence to embark for Milan' (*TGV* 1.1.71). Manfred Pfister sees the study of Shakespeare's Italian geography as an illustration of the 'law of diminishing returns', arguing that 'the more information scholars gather together concerning

Renaissance Italy and the Elizabethan awareness of Italy, the less this knowledge increase yields new insights into the plays of Shakespeare and his contemporaries'.[31] To him the important issue is not 'how Shakespeare's Venice and Shakespeare's Belmont relate to the topographical reality of the sixteenth century but how they relate to each other as two different English constructions of Italy'. Similarly, Pfister shows that imaginary places are being constructed out of bits and pieces drawn from European and transatlantic toponyms:

> the Americas, bearing an Italian name, intuited by Florentine cosmographers, and first 'discovered' by an Italian in Spanish services, were to English adventurers and colonists not only a place of encounter with savage aborigines, but also with Mediterranean Catholicism. Prospero's island is at one and the same time Mediterranean and Transatlantic, an island between Naples and Tripolis and one of the far Bermudas.[32]

Referring to what they call '*The Tempest*'s ambiguous geography', Virginia and Alden Vaughan conclude that the play multiplies its possible origins, so that 'Ireland meshed eclectically in the playwright's mind with colonial and other contextual concerns about Africa, America and Europe.'[33] At the crossroads between Europe and Africa, Europe and America, Shakespeare's late romance remains very much a kind of enigmatic geographic palimpsest which post-colonial studies have wanted to connect with the New World, then with Africa and more recently with Ireland.[34]

Another fairly ambiguous and mysterious place in this imaginary European geography is the Austrian city of Vienna. For Leah Marcus, the Vienna of *Measure for Measure* is to be identified with the London of James I, while it still retains strong suggestions of empire and Catholic domination through the allusions to the Habsburgs. What Marcus calls 'the play's strange doubling' may, when combined with the disparities or incongruities in the Folio text, 'map out a space of indefinition associated with the extent of empire'.[35] Contrary to this English reading of the problem play, Gary Taylor has recently argued in 'Shakespeare's Mediterranean *Measure for Measure*'[36] that most of the names in the play are Italian, that Italy was then frequently associated with fornication and prostitution, and that the city of Vienna, of no interest whatsoever to English audiences in 1604, was in fact meant to evoke the Italian town of Ferrara. Noting the presence of a disguised Duke of Ferrara in plays by Mason and Fletcher, Taylor makes the point that the text of *Measure for Measure*, as we have it, is not the one originally written by Shakespeare but the one probably adapted by Thomas Middleton in 1621. To a Calvinist like Middleton, Vienna indeed represented a religious and political threat because of the devious despotism associated with Habsburg rule. A similar situation is found in the play within the play in *Hamlet*, when the Prince presents the *Mousetrap* plot to Ophelia as 'the image of a murder done in Vienna – Gonzago is the Duke's name, his wife Baptista' (3.2.233–4), adding a little later that 'the story is extant, and written in very choice Italian' (256–7). To the 1982 Arden editor, Harold Jenkins, who glosses the passage in the Longer Notes at the end,

> *The Murder of Gonzago* ... is based on an actual murder, that of the Duke of Urbino in 1538. Gonzago, however, was not the name of the Duke, but of his alleged murderer, Luigi Gonzaga, a kinsman of the Duke's wife, Leonora Gonzaga.[37]

This Italian connection in *Hamlet* therefore just widens the scope of the play's already vast geography, since, besides Denmark and Elsinore, Norway, Poland, Paris and England, we find various allusions to Italy and Italian Machiavellianism.

Another set of embedded allusions in *Hamlet* are those that concern Poland. As Harold Jenkins points out, in the First Quarto Ophelia's father was called Corambis – a name that was subsequently changed to Polonius.[38] The moot 'sledded Polacks' image in 1.1.66, sometimes read as 'sleaded pollax', or 'pole-axe', should be included in that particular geographic context. But Jenkins finds the first gloss more relevant than the second, and he quotes a passage from Ortelius's *Epitome of the Theatre of the World* to illustrate his point: 'Ortelius ... tells how in the frozen fens of Lithuania, then "under the crown of

Polonia", men "pass over the ice with sleds drawn by horses".'[39] Later on in the play (*Ham* 4.4), Fortinbras and his army want to march over Denmark into Poland 'to gain a little patch of ground' (18), which seems to place Denmark between Norway and Poland. Jenkins then explains it as follows: 'The Elizabethan geography of those parts is often confused ... But it is not profitable to seek geographical precision for what Shakespeare is content to leave vague.'[40]

Shakespeare's geography, being confused between east and west or north and south, and then remarkable for its very vagueness, should probably be allowed to remain vague. Indeed, the playwright has more to gain by creating a complex network of associations and signifiers than in trying to pin down his localities and backgrounds with the utmost precision, with a scrupulous, quasi-scientific sense of observation and detail, which might then be thought of as restrictive. Moreover, this is what gives theatrical directors a free hand for the choice of locale and costume in their productions.

In *Othello*, the various characters are linked to various Italian cities, Venice of course, but also Florence (for characters like Michael Cassio), while Othello himself remains fairly mysterious as a 'Moor', as E.A.J. Honigmann reminds us:

> Be he a black or a north African Moor ... Othello's otherness remains. He is more than a stranger, he comes from a mysteriously 'other' world, a world that lies beyond our reach, hinted at rather than defined. Despite his identification with Venice and Christianity the Moor cannot shake off this mystery, a by-product of his dark skin and of the associations this had in European minds.[41]

The tragedy is remarkable for changing the location from Venice to Cyprus at the end of Act 1, a move that makes us pass from the world of sexual intrigue and comedy to that of a domestic tragedy fuelled by jealousy, passion and treachery. It is interesting that the name Venice is used by Iago to tease and torment the general by rubbing salt into his wounds and to make him feel even more of a 'stranger' in a city of which he had dreamt he could become a citizen:

> In Venice they do let God see the pranks
> They dare not show their husbands.
>
> (Oth 3.3.205–6)

Venus is here slyly associated with Venice, not only by way of a silent, subtextual paronomasia but because Cyprus (where he has arrived) was also known as the island of Venus; the goddess had indeed been born there and her cult was celebrated in her temple at Paphos. So when the action shifts from Venice to Cyprus the modest Venetian, Desdemona, is progressively demonized into a hot Venusian whore by Iago's insinuations. The geographic imaginary which was then part and parcel of the mythology of Venus becomes particularly important in this distant outpost of Europe which had just been reclaimed from the Turks by the Venetian fleet and the providential tempest (as happened when Philip of Spain launched his 'invincible Armada' against the English coast). Venus, who was married to the ugly, black-faced Vulcan (because of the smithy he was working in underground), enjoyed her amorous exploits with Mars in erotic scenes which inspired Venetian painters like Titian. This mythical episode, even though it is never directly mentioned, seems quite present in the subtext of *Othello*, and it combines geography, jealousy and imagination with inflamed or inflammatory fantasies. The effect of it all is to poison the mind of the Moor with Desdemona's 'liaison' with his 'lieutenant', Michael Cassio.[42] Exotic places situated beyond the limits of Europe often took on this inflammatory function and contributed to the mapping out of a space situated between desire and terror. In *Othello*, the mental cartography that transcends the enclosed world of the domestic tragedy is clearly to be found in the suburbs of hell (*Oth* 4.2.65, 93–4). Meanwhile the Moor himself describes the 'compulsive course' of his bloody thoughts in terms of a geographic projection he compares with the irreversible flow of the Pontic sea into the Propontic and the Hellespont (*Oth* 3.3.456–9).

Even though such faraway regions were generally thought of as being situated within the boundaries of early modern Europe, one should also take into account the geography of exile as Shakespeare represents it. In *As You Like It*, the forest of Arden, even though it works as a sanctuary for those banished from court by Duke Frederick, can alternately be regarded as a world within or a world elsewhere. But in Touchstone's punning reference to Ovid's exile among the Goths (*AYL* 3.3.7–8), we are reminded of the poet's banishment by Augustus and of the sad years he spent among the 'barbarous' Getae near the Pontic sea.[43] The jester's quip serves to establish a parallel between his own exile in the forest and the poet's expulsion to the remote borders of the civilized world, while it provides a wry negative image that serves to counter or subvert the suave pastoral clichés. In a truly Rabelaisian, grotesque conceit, the fool and the poet are here put back to back.

But the pains of exile are most forcefully rendered by Bolingbroke, who very bitterly responds to his father Gaunt's comforting words in *Richard II*:

> O, who can hold a fire in his hand
> By thinking on the frosty Caucasus?
> Or cloy the hungry edge of appetite
> By bare imagination of a feast?
> Or wallow naked in December snow
> By thinking on fantastic summer's heat?
>
> (*R2* 1.3.294–9)

Caucasus, the mountain range separating Europe from Asia, is seen as beyond the reach of civilization and the name is certainly used to suggest a long period of cold wintry life. It is thought of as another negative of England, a place situated poles apart from his current residence. It serves as a powerful geographic metaphor to render in graphic terms the sadness of distance and isolation from friends, kin and country. This set of imagery seems to be looking ahead to *The Winter's Tale* and its Russian associations in Hermione's trial scene, when the Sicilian queen publicly reminds her judges that her father was the Emperor of Russia (*WT* 3.1.119). The reference to Russia fits in with the word winter in the title but, when combined to the word 'emperor', it also offers a thumbnail description of an atmosphere of despotism and paranoia associated with the character and misrule of Ivan the Terrible in the Jacobean imaginary:

With its strange cartographic accretions and what Stephen Orgel has dubbed its 'incomprehensibility', *The Winter's Tale* makes sense in terms of this alien model ... The king [Leontes] inhabits a world of secrecy, suspicion, and spying that has no proper name until the playwright asks his audience to think on the emperor of Russia. The Sicilian king is trapped in a Muscovite bind, struggling to control his wife's talk in a precarious court while attempting to be hospitable.[44]

But all this may also be read as a distant echo of the atmosphere at the court of Richard II, a king who is presented as a capricious and unpredictable man and a vain and tyrannical ruler reversing his own decisions (like Leontes, who disbelieves the Delphic oracle, he refuses to take advantage of the divine ordeal of the tournament to make his choice between the two challengers Mowbray and Bolingbroke), while insistent rumours about the part he supposedly played in the murder of his uncle Gloucester maintain a heavy atmosphere of suspicion around him.

Shakespeare's European geography, although very present in most of his plays, reveals fairly vague contours that can only rarely be circumscribed or apprehended with real clarity or precision. More often than not, the topographic indications will consist of a name or set of names, in a scene or décor situated somewhere in England, Italy or France. His playtexts are filled with allusions to cities, nations, traditions, costumes and manners that seem to make them real and lifelike. But they work as a kind of *trompe l'œil*, since each particular landscape, generally coupled with its contrary or complement elsewhere (as in the Athens/wood, Venice/Belmont, Arden/court oppositions), may also serve to refer to another in a roundabout or allusive way, as in the analogies between Vienna and Jacobean London in *Measure for Measure* or between Sicilia and Russia in *The Winter's Tale*. This provides the spectator with a perspective effect, or anamorphosis, when the place changes or dissolves into another as in a masque.

Shakespeare's maps mix real and imaginary names but they also point to some underground routes whose traces have been erased and are kept only in men's memories:

> And the quaint mazes in the wanton green
> For lack of tread are undistinguishable.
>
> (*MND* 2.1.99–100)

The old Catholic ceremony of the Rogations, also known as Perambulations, which had been preserved in a simplified form by the Anglican church, was intended as a device for inscribing local topography in children's memories in the ritual, recurrent parish practice of 'the beating of the bounds'.[45] The existence of such mental maps (some of them due to clandestine protection as in the secret itineraries of the Jesuits and recusant priests) may be one of the reasons why the outlines of Shakespeare's Europe are left so vague or allusive. The written map was then used as a mnemotechnic code as well as like a real topographic representation. Another explanation may be found in the playwright's desire to suggest a number of possible or tentative connections and correlations between the various places he used as settings for his plays, so as to encourage circulation from the one to the other. This palimpsest-like geography, which superimposes stratum upon stratum, meaning upon meaning, with further associations provided by puns, echoes and correspondences, combines the classical, the medieval and the early modern in a constellation of routes leading to no particular place or centre. Few are those among Shakespeare's cross-dressed heroines, roamers, pilgrims, adventurers, rebels or exiles who are effectively guided by maps, since, more often than not, maps will appear as stage props or projections of fantasy as in *1 Henry IV* when the rebels want to divide the kingdom into three parts.

In this way, Shakespeare's European maps take us into the heartland of fantasy. They lead us to a number of vague territories or forests where fairies, witches, hungry bears, rich heiresses with a golden fleece or magic handkerchiefs are just so many signs that history is always interspersed with *fabula* and real topography with fantasy. They are all imaginary.

Chapter Seven

EUROPE'S MEDITERRANEAN
FRONTIER: THE MOOR

Nabil Matar and Rudolph Stoeckel

The safest generalization to make about Shakespeare's work is probably Robin Headlam Wells's observation: 'One of Shakespeare's most characteristic techniques is to present us with evidence whose apparently contradictory nature makes it seem impossible for us to make a rational judgement on the character or problem concerned.'[1] This is true whether the problem happens to be geography (where exactly does *The Tempest* take place?) or race (is Cleopatra to be imagined as a Macedonian queen, or as a tawny gypsy?). If it is difficult to determine Shakespeare's attitude toward such conflicting characters as Hal and Hotspur, or Antony and Brutus, the problem becomes even more perplexing when we are faced with the enigmatic characters who inhabit, or arrive from the region beyond Shakespeare's Mediterranean frontier. Although A.J. Hoenselaars calls it perhaps 'an unduly severe verdict', G.K. Hunter argues that 'geographical exactitude was no part of the literary tradition, and even those writers who "should have known better" show astonishing carelessness about place-names and modes of transport, using them for their associations, not for their reality'.[2] The same could be said for Shakespeare's treatment of race: Shakespeare's 'Moors' are an ill-defined group from the bottom third of 'the three-nooked world' (*AC* 4.6.6). Where is it that Aaron imagines he can 'cabin' with his son once he escapes the white world toward which he expresses such contempt? And what are we to make of Caliban, who seems to be a conflation of Moor, Amerindian, and subhuman beast?

In 1610, just as Shakespeare was reaching the end of his dramatic career, he reflected in *The Tempest* on Europe and its most adjacent and challenging frontier – Africa. Shipwrecked somewhere in the Mediterranean, Sebastian and Antonio discussed the separation between the two continents as if the distance were incalculable. Claribel, who had married the King of Tunis, was 'Ten leagues beyond man's life; she that from Naples / Can have no note, unless the sun were post – / The man i'th' moon's too slow' (2.1.247–9). Neither commonality nor proximity was conceivable between Europe and its African counterpart. Separating these two worlds was the 'Mediterranean', which Shakespeare had mentioned only once before (*LLL* 5.1.61). Beyond Europe's Mediterranean frontier, out into the Atlantic, Shakespeare had little familiarity and less insight – indeed, he never mentions the 'Atlantic' in any of his plays, although he does mention 'Bermoodas' and Mexico, Guinea, the 'Indies' and America 'on her nose' (*CE* 3.2.150). Despite the fascination, not a single New World character appears in his drama.

Meanwhile, Africa is 'glamorous and dangerous'[3] – the frontier in Englishmen's principal navigations and discoveries across the seas. Still, it is not clear how, from the borders of an England negotiating its relations with its Scottish and Irish neighbours, Shakespeare viewed 'Europe' and indeed the national identities within Europe (although Portia's summary of national characters may provide a glimpse, *MV* 1.2). At a time when England was shifting its allegiance from 'Europe to Britain', and Europe looked as though it were going to be 'out of the British Isles',[4] Shakespeare seemed unsure whether Europe was a geographic, religious or cultural entity. Neither was he sure about Africa, which appeared as a geographical composite consisting of exotic places such as Egypt, Tunis, Carthage, Algiers, Morocco and Mauritania, with peoples of differing complexions and religions – Moors and Turks, savages and anthropophagi.[5] Of these peoples, only the Moors appeared on Shakespeare's stage: with their black skin, woolly hair and thick lips, they were racially apart – which is how the London audience and the rest of the country saw them (*Titus Andronicus* was very popular in London as well as in the provinces).[6] To

Shakespeare and his Elizabethan and early Jacobean contemporaries, the Moors were the inhabitants of the Barbary coast of North Africa (Morocco, Algeria and Tunisia), had dark skin (varying between brown and black) which distinguished them from 'Turks',[7] and followed religions that ranged from paganism to 'Mahumetanism' to Christianity. They were the most prominent non-European protagonists on the English stage – reflecting the high profile that the Barbary coast enjoyed in early modern English diplomacy, commerce and military alliance. Theirs was by far a more challenging presence than any other outsider's: it was the Moor and not the Jew who was 'the crucial other to English identity'[8] in early modern English imagination – and in the drama of Shakespeare.

THE ELIZABETHAN PERIOD

During Shakespeare's lifetime, Europe had three frontiers that defined it. The first frontier was the Ottoman–Habsburg in central Europe, which flared up in the great Hungarian war of 1593–1606. Despite the support which England showed for that war – with the English ambassador in Istanbul, Edward Barton (1588–98), accompanying Sultan Mehemet III on the campaign of 1596 – Shakespeare (unlike Marlowe or Greene) did not allude to it in his plays. The two other fronts/frontiers were across the Mediterranean: the eastern Mediterranean frontier commonly known as the 'Levant' and the Barbary coast of North Africa. The battle of Lepanto in 1571, in which the Ottoman fleet was defeated by a Spanish–papal fleet under the command of Don Juan, half-brother of King Philip II of Spain, had resulted in the division of the Mediterranean into an eastern basin, under Ottoman hegemony, and a western basin from Tunisia westward. This basin constituted a theatre of rivalry between, on the one hand, Morocco and the Ottoman-controlled (but strongly autonomous) regencies of Algeria, Tunisia and Libya (Tripoli) and, on the other, Christian fleets from Spain, Italy and, later, France, England and Malta. These frontiers were porous, as trade went hand in hand with sea battles, piracy and captivity with ambassadorial representation, and religious conversion with commercial settlement. Furthermore, the frontiers often changed as European countries developed rivalries with each other that led to co-operation with particular Islamic countries; while Muslim potentates, in need of allies or of technological assistance, broke rank from Islamdom to establish co-operation with the monarchs of Christendom.

The Levant frontier opened for England with the arrival in Constantinople (October 1578) of William Harborne, dressed in Turkish clothes, and riding in the company of the returning Turkish ambassador from Poland. Although, as Hakluyt showed, there had been earlier English trade into the Levant (1511 is the first of Hakluyt's records), it was Harborne who negotiated in 1580 a commercial treaty, the 'Capitulations', with the 'Musulmanlike highnesse' Sultan Murad III.[9] Three years later, and upon being appointed 'Orator, Messenger, Deputie and Agent' for the Levant Company, Harborne kissed the sultan's hand and presented a gift of English goods: 'a most beautiful watch set with jewels and pearls, ten pairs of shoes, two pretty lap dogs, twelve lengths of Royal cloth, two lengths of white linen and thirteen pieces of silver gilt'[10] – an eager advertisement of English-made products that he hoped the sultan would encourage his subjects to buy. Henceforth, English ships sailed the Mediterranean selling their national products, while distributing Turkish goods not only within the empire but also in the rest of Asia and Africa. So successful was Harborne in advancing the cause of English commerce and shipping that by the time he left Constantinople in 1588 'England was supreme among foreigners in the councils of the Sultan.'[11]

This commercial venture led to an intellectual venture too in the form of Hakluyt's *Principal Navigations*, which appeared just a year after Harborne's return. The impact of the Levant was felt now in narratives that became available to English readers for the first time in a convenient tome. The Levant was also encountered in the arrival of Barbary horses into royal stables, along with spices, indigo, silk, drugs, cotton wool and cloth, currants, dyes, white soap, carpets, quilts, goatskins, galls and other commodities – many of which items were noted by Shakespeare. As Lisa Jardine and Jerry Brotton have shown, the impact of the Levant and North Africa had already been felt in

European households and palaces since the beginning of the sixteenth century;[12] by its end, England was prospering from the Mediterranean trade. The new charter granted to the Levant/Turkey Company in January 1592 extended the routings of the 'worshipful companie of the English Marchants for the Levant' from Venice to Tripoli, Cairo, Tunis, Aleppo and Arabia – all of which places informed Shakespeare's dramatic imagery.

As well as providing transportation for Moors and Turks travelling from Morocco to Egypt and from Tunis to Constantinople, English ships also carried English (and Scottish) freebooters, travellers, entrepreneurs and adventurers who inaugurated the 'discoveries' of the Islamic world: by 1596, there was already a small community of Britons living in Aleppo (as there were other European enclaves in North Africa and Istanbul). The larger edition of Hakluyt in 1599–1600 included a whole volume on the Levant, North Africa, sub-Saharan Africa and Asia. Such interest in the culture, religion and history of the Ottoman dominions not only translated into plays on the London stage, but led to the first study by an English writer on the Islamic world: Richard Knolles's *History of the Turkes* (1603), which went into numerous printings during Shakespeare's lifetime (and which may have been one of the sources for *Othello*).[13] The Turk/Ottoman had become part of English imagination, fear and envy – as English dramatists such as Greene, Kyd, Mason, Heywood and others showed.[14]

It was the Barbary frontier, however, which captured Shakespeare's dramatic imagination. For it was, after all, the first region in the Islamic world to elicit a royal corporation from the queen in 1585 (the Levant Company was incorporated in 1588 and the East India Company in 1600). The frontier had opened in the early days of Queen Elizabeth's reign when hundreds of Englishmen travelled to Morocco to work, trade, convert to Islam or turn pirate in port cities such as Tripoli, Algiers, Tunis, Tetuan, Al-Araish and many others.[15] As a frontier, it was not completely distinguished in English imagination from the Levant: in the second volume of *Navigations*, describing regions 'within the Streight of Gibraltar', Hakluyt mixed his material about the Ottoman Empire with material about Morocco. Even to a learned world

observer like him, the political, linguistic and ethnic divisions of the
Mediterranean were not too clear. Hakluyt also joined 'the Canarian
Ilands, to the kingdoms of Barbarie, to the mightie rivers of Senega and
Gambra'.[16] The merging of the North African with the sub-Saharan –
the latter a region that had attracted English investors in slavery – also
confused English writers about the religious and racial differences
between the Moors of North Africa, who arrived in London as royal
ambassadors and delegates, and those south of the Sahara who, from
the 1570s on, arrived as slaves and worked as servants, prostitutes and
entertainers in London.[17]

In January 1589 the first official delegation from Morocco, led by a
Moorish ambassador, arrived in London to negotiate the possibility of
Anglo-Moroccan co-operation against Spain. It was in response to this
negotiation that Peele composed his play, *The Battle of Alcazar*, which
presented the first Moors on the English stage.[18] Peele's play dramatized
the 1578 victory of the Moroccans over the Christian armies led by the
Portuguese king, Sebastian, and which included a group of English
soldiers who had fought and died under Thomas Stuckley. Just over a
decade after that victory, the Moroccans of the king who had defeated
the Christians arrived in the court of Elizabeth. Their presence in
London awakened playwrights' fear of the non-Christians who were
about to co-opt the queen into a dangerous political strategy. The
queen, after all, was known for her close correspondence with the
Moroccan king, Mulay Ahmad al-Mansur. In 1589 it was (falsely)
reported from Brussels that '30,000 Moors' and 'ten to twelve
thousand Englishmen' were going to join forces against Spain's Holy
League.[19] For the groundlings in the pit, who would be pressed into
such a battle, and for the playwrights who entertained them, such
Anglo-Moroccan amity was threatening.

Some time later, Shakespeare and Peele composed *Titus Andronicus* –
which included Aaron, the stereotype that dominated many later
representations of the Moor in English drama. He is a Moor who has
entered the European polis, is in sexual control of the Gothic queen and
is plotting against the Roman state. We can only imagine how Aaron
comports himself in Act 1 as he silently watches Roman society wilfully

self-destructing. The underlying moral pattern of the play is its trajectory from the familial and political chaos of the first act to Lucius' vow 'to govern so, / To heal Rome's harms, and wipe away her woe' (5.3.147–8), although we are not confident about the Rome that will consist of Lucius, Goth allies and a fractious senate and *plebs*. Rome's harms include the eponymous hero killing his own son and sacrificing Tamora's son, and the newly proclaimed emperor Saturninus unexpectedly choosing to marry the queen of the Goths twenty lines after having promised that 'Lavinia will I make my empress' (1.1.244). As untidy and confusing as the first act is, it introduces two themes which will be important in understanding the threat that Shakespeare's Mediterranean Others present to the Europe which he confronts: marriage and coherent polity, the two institutions which for Shakespeare are often inseparable, and which provide the possibility of living a civilized life – if no Moor is there to violate them.

Not only Roman society but *Titus* itself is in danger of descending into chaos until Aaron appears at the beginning of the second act to give the play a much-needed dramatic focus. Derek Traversi has noted that Aaron's soliloquy (2.1.1–25) 'brings a new sense of life to the play',[20] and it is easy to agree with Harold Bloom that 'without Aaron, *Titus Andronicus* would be unendurable'.[21] Aaron is one of the characters like Falstaff or Shylock who seem to have picked up dramatic momentum as the play goes on, and who take over the work whether Shakespeare intended it or not. Curiously, in Act 5, Shakespeare has Aaron appear in a totally irrelevant little postscript of malevolence in which he confirms the indelibility of his evil, observing:

> I am no baby, I, that with base prayers
> I should repent the evils I have done.
>
> (5.3.184–5)

It is pointless to look too hard for a motive for Aaron's murderous exuberance. He is an 'irreligious Moor' and 'Chief architect and plotter of these woes' (5.3.120–1), but his purpose seems to be nothing more complicated than a desire to 'wanton' with Tamora (1.1.520), cuckold the insipid Saturninus ('better than he have worn Vulcan's badge', 589) and cause 'his shipwrack and his commonweal's' (523). Although Aaron 'proves to be quite at ease in Graeco-Roman culture',[22] his main concern seems to be to destroy it. The only time Aaron describes himself as being vengeful there is no suggestion that his rancour is directed toward any specific person or cause; it is just part of his Saturnine humour:

> No, madam, these are no venereal signs;
> Vengeance is in my heart, death in my hand,
> Blood and revenge are hammering in my head.
>
> (2.2.38–40)

Having shown Aaron as total evil, Shakespeare directly relates that evil to blackness: 'my cloudy melancholy, / My fleece of woolly hair that now uncurls / Even as an adder when she doth unroll' (2.3.33–5). Such an emphasis on blackness had not appeared in *The History of Titus Andronicus*, which Shakespeare may have known, but so haunted is Shakespeare by the blackness of the Moor that he racializes him and bluntly associates his evil with his skin colour. Indeed, up until the middle of Act 3, only the audience knows how evil Aaron is, not his Roman victims. In the forest episode, his only action is to locate the bag of gold; nobody suspects that he is implicated in the murder. In 3.1, Titus still thinks him 'gentle Aaron' (158). All of a sudden, and without any apparent reason, Marcus and Titus begin vilifying him for being 'a black ill-favoured fly' and 'a coal-black Moor' (3.2.67, 79). After Aaron cuts off Titus' left hand, Shakespeare makes him exult in his evil/blackness:

> O, how this villainy
> Doth fat me with the very thoughts of it.
> Let fools do good and fair men call for grace,
> Aaron will have his soul black like his face.
>
> (3.1.203–6)

Whatever else Peacham's sketch of *Titus* tells us, it is that Aaron was unambiguously black, while the illustration at the front of the chapbook, *The History of Titus Andronicus*, shows his Negroid representation on the stage (Figure 10).[23]

FIGURE 10 From *The History of Titus Andronicus* (n.d.), an eighteenth-century chapbook giving a prose version of the story.

   The most noticeable way that Aaron differs from the Romans, and especially Titus, is that he is 'As true a dog as ever fought at head' (5.1.102), and his language is consistent with his propensity to sudden violence. Probably the most gruesome example of this is when he stabs the nurse to prevent her from identifying the black child as Tamora's and his. As she screams in pain, he mocks her by squealing '"Wheak, wheak!"– so cries a pig prepared to the spit' (4.2.148). While Titus, Lucius and Marcus spend much of their time delivering long speeches, Aaron in vigorous concise language gets to the brutal point as quickly as a dagger stroke.

CHIRON   Thou hast undone our mother.
AARON   Villain, I have done thy mother.

                                                                            (4.2.77–8)

His invective is invigorating and gruesomely comic. He stands in vivid contrast to the cultural and ethical values invoked by the Roman allusions to the foundational myths of Dido and Aeneas, Tarquin and Lucrece and Junius Brutus – all of which mean exactly nothing to

Aaron. He is satisfied with keeping Tamora 'fettered in amorous chains' (1.1.514) and savaging the Romans, who are bound by quaint notions of justice, piety, conscience, and other foolish 'popish tricks and ceremonies' (5.1.76). He is the destroyer of states, the violator of queens, and the master of deception and rapine.

Whether Shakespeare really thought Aaron's son could have been found next to a 'ruinous monastery' or whether Roman virtue was somehow akin to 'popish tricks', the conflation of Roman and Christian suggests the complex of values which stand in opposition to this alluring but destructive force, this 'misbelieving Moor' (5.3.143). Aaron's son is the only thing towards which he shows any affection. But he knows that if the two of them were to achieve any sort of bearable existence it would have to be far from Rome. If Aaron had been able to escape, to 'cabin' with his child in a cave, and 'feed on berries and on roots' (4.2.179), he might have found himself in a world of nature, perhaps like Caliban's isle, more appropriate to his savage hatred of a society whose boundary he had penetrated. For he knows full well that he is not of the polis nor does he belong to it. In a final irony, Shakespeare buries him within the walls of Rome, the 'commonweal' whose destruction he sought, while Tamora, the empress, will be denied burial in Roman soil and thrown forth 'to beasts and birds of prey' (5.3.197), though earlier she had ironically claimed to be 'Incorporate in Rome' (1.1.467). But their son, Aaron's 'beauteous blossom' (4.2.74), escapes unscathed the general slaughter of Act 5. This 'thick-lipp'd slave' will survive and in one guise or another appear in Shakespeare's later works – to remind us of the link between the blackness of the Moor, his devilish violation of the white woman and his danger to civil society and the state. In this respect, Aaron, this 'excellent piece of villainy', anticipates the last 'Moor' on Shakespeare's stage, Caliban, 'got by the devil himself' (1.2.320), who dreams of raping Miranda and peopling the isle with Calibans. Both Aaron and Caliban belong to a 'vile race' from beyond Shakespeare's frontier of the Mediterranean (1.2.359).

Aaron is 'unquestionably the heir of Muly Mahamet' in Peele's play, *The Battle of Alcazar*.[24] Like Aaron, Muly Mahamet wields a scimitar, and in his penultimate soliloquy he imagines the destruction of Sebastian and the 'Portugals' who have come to help him, in the same way that in his opening soliloquy, Aaron reflects on the destruction of Rome. Upon his defeat, and like Aaron too, Muly thinks of a place in which he can hide, 'some unfrequented place, / Some uncouth walke where I may curse my fill' (5.1.1268–9).[25] Both Peele and Shakespeare created the image of the African/black Moor that informs later English imagination, but it was Shakespeare who introduced the Moor in the context of sexual encounter with the white/European woman. Neither Muly Mahamet nor any of the other Moors in *The Battle of Alcazar* poses a sexual threat to the Christian society of Sebastian, nor indeed had any of the Moors in the 1589 delegation. But, as soon as Shakespeare introduced his Moor, he sexualized him and set him before the white woman. Until the last Moor in his plays, Shakespeare will always view the Moor in the context of relationships with, and lust for, the European woman.

In 1595 another Moroccan delegation arrived in London, consisting of an ambassador, Ahmad bin Adel, two alcaydes, and a retinue 'of twentye five or thirtye persones'.[26] This delegation may have inspired Shakespeare to include the noble Morochus among Portia's suitors in *The Merchant of Venice*. As Barthelemy has noted, the Prince of Morocco is the first 'non-villainous' Moor in English drama.[27] One reason for the non-villainous Moor and the dramatic change from Aaron to the Prince lies in the growth of Anglo-Moroccan relations: Elizabeth and Mulay al-Mansur co-operated closely in their military and diplomatic strategies, especially after Morocco was transformed into a nearby Eldorado with legends about its gold that drew on both classical sources and contemporary reports. In 1591 al-Mansur had sent his troops into the sub-Saharan region of modern-day Niger, defeated the Songhay king, and seized his gold-mines. As part of the capitulation, the sub-Saharan king started sending an annual tribute of gold which arrived in such vast quantities that in August 1594 a letter sent from Marrakesh to London mentioned 'mules laden with gold', which had reached the Moroccan city from the conquered Sudan.[28]

Eager to tap into al-Mansur's wealth, Queen Elizabeth repeatedly asked for help in order to build up a strong front against Spain. She also appealed to al-Mansur to support the reinstalment of Don Antonio, the claimant to the Portuguese throne, who had sought shelter in England after Philip II had seized the Portuguese crown in 1580. On this particular visit, the ambassador was to negotiate with the queen the request that she had passed on to al-Mansur via the Ottoman sultan for her ships to use the Atlantic port of Santa Cruz and for permission to build a fort in order to sail against the Spanish gold fleet. It is not surprising, in light of the close diplomatic and commercial co-operation between England and Morocco, that Shakespeare's Prince of Morocco was a Moor familiar with Europe, even as far north as England. For the first (and last) time on the Elizabethan stage, a playwright showed a Moor who referred to England: 'They have in England / A coin that bears the figure of an angel / Stamp'd in gold' (*MV* 2.7.55–7). The Moor represented the new gold and the 'new money' that was changing the Mediterranean basin. Fully aware of the golden riches of the Moors (the Moroccan ruler, al-Mansur, came to be known as 'the golden', *al-dhahabi*), Shakespeare made Morocco open the golden casket and find a moralization against gold ('All that glisters is not gold', *MV* 2.7.65) – a moralization that Shakespeare's queen, with her dire need for Moroccan gold, could not but have found depressing.

Morocco is a splendid and colourful character, even if slightly comic by sophisticated Venetian (or perhaps Belmont) standards. His migration to Belmont is 'half medieval pilgrimage, half barbarian invasion'.[29] Shakespeare does not allow us to forget that his blackness is threatening and devilish: still, so that this invasion is not to be taken too seriously, we have only to imagine the consequences if it had been Aaron who had appeared. We know Morocco has little chance of winning Portia's hand, and when he introduces himself with a reference to his colour we wonder if he already suspects that it presents an insuperable barrier between himself and marriage to any fair 'creature northward born' (2.1.4). His first words are 'Mislike me not for my complexion', and he departs to a casual, if racist, joke from Portia: 'Let all of his complexion choose me so' (2.7.79). He is no Aaron, but there is at least a subtle echo of the combination of sexual attractiveness and warrior-like ferocity that often characterizes Shakespeare's Moors:

> this aspect of mine
> Hath fear'd the valiant, – by my love I swear,
> The best-regarded virgins of our clime
> Have lov'd it too.

(MV 2.1.8–11)

Though he may have some affinity to the *miles gloriosus*, Morocco has fought against 'the Sophy and a Persian prince / That won three fields of Sultan Solyman' (2.1.25–6). He may not qualify as a candidate for Portia's hand, but he would be taken seriously as a Venetian *condottiere*.

Unlike Aaron, Morocco suggests that he would change his 'hue' in order to marry Portia. But, of course, a Moor cannot change his hue; Jessica can, however, change her religion. Shakespeare seems to have considered religion a more malleable category than race. When Morocco offers to make an incision to compare his blood with a European's, 'northward born, / Where Phoebus' fire scarce thaws the icicles' (2.1.4–5), Portia tells him that 'I am not solely led / By nice direction of a maiden's eyes' (2.1.13–14), an uncanny foreboding of the situation in *Othello*. By following her father's will, her 'destiny / Bars me the right of voluntary choosing' (2.1.15–16). It is impossible not to wonder whether Shakespeare might have had the *Othello* premise in mind when he presented another Venetian woman with the option of either voluntarily choosing a Moor or following her father's will. In *The Merchant of Venice* we never imagine Morocco, brandishing his scimitar, living happily with Portia in Belmont. At the end of the play, Morocco, who had a retinue of Moors with him, just like the London delegation, disappears and the Venetians pair off together. Miscegenation is prevented, social order is preserved, and Venice/Belmont will not have to contend with an outsider inside the marital institution – nor inside the polis. The mistake that was made in admitting Aaron into the Roman centre stage will not be repeated in Venice or Belmont. The Moor stays apart and away.

After the departure of the delegation, and for the next few years, rumours of an Anglo-Moroccan alliance between Elizabeth and

EUROPE'S MEDITERRANEAN FRONTIER: THE MOOR   233

al-Mansur continued to spread across Europe, with the Fugger scribe in Brussels reporting on 26 July 1597 that the English fleet was headed to 'Africa and Barbary to stir up the Moors ... and descend upon Spain'.[30] The Moroccans, rich in gold, were eager to join England, strong in naval power, to attack the Spaniards.[31] So eager were the English and the Moroccan monarchs to co-ordinate strategy and plot against Spain that in 1599 al-Mansur sent another ambassador to discuss a possible alliance with Elizabeth. We know from the English translation of the letter which the ambassador carried with him, dated 27 February 1601,[32] that al-Mansur sought an alliance against the Spanish-held possessions in North Africa and America. He was also eager to join in an attack on Spain itself in order to fulfil his age-old dream of liberating the Andalus. Finally, he proposed a joint alliance against the Turks in Algeria – his nemesis and constant enemies – showing how much realpolitik was more important for him than religious commonality.

During the ambassador's visit, a secret development occurred. Unfortunately, whatever transpired in the meetings between Queen Elizabeth and Ambassador Abd al-Wahid al-Annuri was never put down in writing. But what has survived is a letter in Arabic by Mulay al-Mansur (23 Shaaban 1009/1 May 1601) responding to the queen after al-Annuri's return from England. Through this letter, it is possible to reconstruct what had happened during the negotiations. Evidently the wily queen refused to commit herself to an alliance and thought to outmanoeuvre the Moroccan king. She was not going to support hardened Muslims in taking over Spain or the American possessions of Spain; nor in entering a war against the Turks the benefits of which would be more Moroccan than English. So she tried to win over the ambassador as a representative of the most well-organized military force in Morocco – the Moriscos. Through the ambassador, she told al-Mansur – and the Arabic original records his refusal – that she would be willing to reach an agreement on military co-operation only if he would send her the Morisco contingent in his army. That contingent would travel to England and come under the English fleet command: the soldiers would be given all the weapons they needed (for which al-Mansur had been willing to pay) along with all the naval facilities needed for military action. And then they would be led to war against Spain. England would thus fight the Spaniards with Moroccan soldiers. The ambassador promised to relay the request to his ruler, but other Moriscos in the delegation seemed to have decided to act on their own. The situation grew dangerous to the ambassador, who had a possible revolt on his hands. What happened later is not clear, but a rumour circulated in London that the ambassador and his advisers 'poisoned their interpreter, being borne a Granado ... [and also] their revernd aged pilgrime'.[33] Perhaps those Moriscos/Granadans grew too supportive of the queen, whom they praised for her 'estate and bountie', and became eager to join her enterprise without even consulting with al-Mansur.

It is not surprising that al-Mansur rejected Elizabeth's offer. He suspected that the queen was trying to collude with the Moriscos behind his back:

> So-and-so, the Andalusian [the Arabic term for Morisco], came before our high porte and relayed to us all your intentions and plans which you had discussed with him and conveyed to him. We listened with attentive ears until we understood them all, and became alert to all that you had planned.

We shall not send them over, he continued, 'because we fear that they may be swayed [against us] by the enemy. The enemy will find occasion and then they will be exposed to danger. We do not want to put them in danger, because they are not alone in this matter.'[34] Indeed, al-Mansur informed her that his forces had captured an Englishman who had been spying, a merchant 'who had been nosy and acted in a manner different from other [English] merchants. He had been found inquiring about matters that did not concern him. We now inform you about his status.' Al-Mansur was anxious about what the queen seemed to be plotting with the Moriscos, whom he knew were eager to leave Africa for Europe, Islamdom for Christendom. But he also wanted to keep open the possibility of co-operation with the queen and thus concluded that he was willing to send the whole Moroccan army against Spain, 'one hundred thousand gunmen and cavalry', but not the Moriscan contingent on its own.

Did Elizabeth's attempted collusion with the Morisco ambassador influence the making of the figure of Othello? There are some important similarities between al-Annuri and Othello, although they do not extend to skin colour. Shakespeare firmly distinguished in *Othello* between the Moor and the Turk – whether 'Turk' meant Muslim ('Are we turned Turks?', 2.3.166) or Ottoman, invading Cyprus or getting killed in Aleppo. Such a distinction correctly corresponds to the Morisco, indeed, general Moroccan, hostility to Ottomans. This distinction was emphasized by Shakespeare, for no similar emphasis on the Turk had been present in *Hecatommithi*; it was Shakespeare who introduced the Moor–Turk collision, replicating thereby the rivalry between the Ottomans and the Moroccans that had prevailed throughout the 1580s and 1590s. The confrontation between al-Mansur and both Murad III and Mehemed III was widely known in Europe, since, in his eagerness to keep the Ottomans out of Morocco, al-Mansur had been co-operating with England, France and Holland, exchanging his gold, sugar and saltpetre for weapons and munitions. The Ottomans repeatedly voiced their displeasure to al-Mansur about his pro-Christian policies – which helped consolidate the image of the Moors in English (and European) writings as enemies of the Turks.[35] Hakluyt included an account by Laurence Aldersey, who had seen in 1586 'a prince of the Moors prisoner ... [who was to be presented] to the Turk',[36] while John Pory, in his 1600 translation of Leo Africanus's *History*, described the Turks 'abas[ing] and bring[ing] to extreme miserie the Christians and Moores their subjects'.[37] The 'and' may have suggested to English readers not only the solidarity of the two groups against the Muslim Turks but a possible commonality in religion too. Othello, therefore, may have been inspired by the Morisco ambassador – in his role as a Morisco defender of Christendom.[38]

But, as with the earlier Moors, Shakespeare remained apprehensive about their admission to Europe, whether to Venice or London, and their participation in Christian affairs. In the first act of *Othello*, Shakespeare makes it clear that Othello is essentially above Venetian law because of his value as a mercenary. He is in the Christian polis but not of it. Even greater than Brabantio's error in judging his daughter's affections was his naïve belief that the Duke would put Brabantio's 'particular grief' above 'the general care' (*Oth* 1.3.55–6). Both Iago and Othello knew better. But Othello was correct in his assessment of the outcome of any conflict between the 'law' and the impending crisis posed by the Turkish fleet. The Duke promises Brabantio that he will call down 'the bloody book of law' (68) to punish whomever was responsible for the 'foul proceeding' of bewitching his daughter. That resolve dissipates when he discovers that the accused is 'this Moor, whom now, it seems, / Your special mandate for the state affairs / Hath hither brought' (72–4). The state will accommodate him, despite his being a Moor who has seduced a Venetian: fighting the Turks is Venice's priority, and Venice is colour-blind and will permit a Moor into the nuptial bed – if that is the way to keep him on Venice's side.

In Act 2, not only does the scene move away from the civilizing world of Venice, but the threat that validated Othello's value to the state is dissipated in a sudden and providential storm. Robin Headlam Wells has noted that 'the fatal ease with which man is capable of transforming himself into a "brute beast" is an explicitly stated theme in *Othello*'.[39] It is surely significant that the chaos that descends upon the Venetians in Cyprus is on the occasion of the nuptial celebrations of Othello's marriage. Now that the storm has 'bang'd the Turks', the only enemy is the absence of any restraints that existed in Venice. In Cyprus, the characters will be subject to 'the very elements of this warlike isle' (2.3.54). As Alvin Kernan has noted, on Cyprus 'passions are more explosive and closer to the surface than in Venice, and here, instead of the ancient order and established government of *the City*, there is only one man to control violence and defend civilization – the Moor Othello, himself of savage origins and a converted Christian'.[40] Othello, on the other hand, was always an outsider from some wasteland of caves, deserts and cannibals – a world that sounds surprisingly like Caliban's and like that to which Aaron and Muly Mahamet sought to go.

Except for the remark that he is going to return to Mauritania, where Desdemona would be as lost to the world as Claribel in Tunis, we really have little knowledge of Othello's origins.[41] This is consistent with Shakespeare's treatment of the 'extravagant' and 'rootless' strangers that his North Africans seem to be; also the wandering magician. In one of the more interesting adjustments to his source, Shakespeare alters the pattern of the handkerchief that plays so crucial a role in *Othello*. In Cinthio the handkerchief is 'embroidered in the Moorish fashion', but Shakespeare gives it a mysterious Egyptian lineage: 'there's magic in the web of it'.[42] It was woven by a sibyl out of silk bred of 'hallowed' worms and 'dyed in mummy, which the skilful / Conserved of maidens' hearts' (3.4.76–7). The handkerchief has powers of enchantment:

> She told her, while she kept it,
> 'Twould make her amiable, and subdue my father
> Entirely to her love.

(3.4.60–2)

And one begins to wonder if Shakespeare were not suggesting that there might have been something to Brabantio's claim that Desdemona had been bound 'in chains of magic' (1.2.65).[43]

The Moor is once again associated with 'amorous chains' of the sort that held Tamora prisoner to Aaron, and the 'strong Egyptian fetters' that Antony feels holding him from his Roman duty. Shakespeare is never so crude as to set up a strictly binary scheme with good Europe on one side, and evil transgressors on the other. As in *Titus Andronicus*, where the Romans are not entirely admirable, so in *Othello*, where the Duke and his law seem more driven by self-interest than by an objective examination of the arguments. (And in *Antony and Cleopatra* the evidence on either the Roman or the Egyptian side makes a judgement almost impossible.) Perhaps it is Iago who had it right when he warned that without reason to cool our 'carnal stings, our unbitted lusts' we shall arrive at the kind of 'preposterous conclusions' that accompany the intrusion of such black-skinned Moors (*Oth* 1.3.330–2). If the play begins with a heroic warrior fighting for Christians against the Turks, it ends with that warrior destroyed after he has broken through the Christian barriers of race and colour. While Shakespeare recognizes a role for the Moor in the Moor–Christian alliance against the Turks, he is apprehensive about the presence of the Moor in the European home. A line needs to be drawn for the Moor: he must remain outside the polis

– to fight for it. But he must not be brought inside it into social and marital life. Even Shylock had realized that the Venetians would never permit a 'bond-slave' (as Brabantio described Othello, 1.2.99) to marry one of their own. But Othello defied the Venetians and fulfilled what Shylock had taunted them with.

In this respect Othello poses a greater threat than Aaron, for whom any marriage within the Roman state is never presented as a possibility. Othello is closer to the centre of the polis than Aaron could ever get, since his position as outsider is mitigated by his marriage to Desdemona, and that marriage's ratification by the Duke. So long as that marriage survives, Othello will be incorporated in the state and becomes the only one of Shakespeare's Moors whose role in the European city will have to be negotiated. It may be for this reason that Shakespeare neither allows, as Cinthio had, for a lengthy stay together in Venice for Othello and Desdemona, nor even, it would seem, for the consummation of that marriage in the city. It will be in Cyprus that the 'celebration of his nuptial' will take place (2.2.7), and, instead of centring on the much anticipated battle with the Turk, the focus shifts from fleets and stratagems to Othello and Desdemona's bed. In the first act Othello's bed had been 'the flinty and steel couch of war' (1.3.231). Once he is in Cyprus, it is not long before his marriage bed becomes tainted by Iago's pornographic insinuations: 'Naked in bed Iago, and not mean harm?' (4.1.5). Desdemona asks Emilia to 'Lay on my bed my wedding sheets' (4.2.106) and in their next scene together Othello informs Desdemona that 'Thou art on thy death-bed' (5.2.51). This is the 'preposterous conclusion' of their marriage in which wedding sheets become winding sheets. As Othello stabs himself and falls across her body, the tableau presents a fitting monument to the one marriage that Shakespeare depicted between a European and a Moor from beyond the frontier.

The Mediterranean Ottoman Empire was a major force in the forging of early modern English/British identity; and in *Othello* as well as numerous other Elizabethan and Jacobean plays the danger of the Turks is emphasized. But, in the only play where Shakespeare addressed the military threat of the Turks, he showed it lurking at the frontiers of the Christian world – and then defeated. Indeed, throughout the Elizabethan period, he had shown no interest in the Turkish scourge of Christendom and had focused on Moors. That Shakespeare reflected in his plays the London mood in regard to these Moors and their dealings with the English queen is important; for toward the end of the reign of Elizabeth – that same queen who had had dangerous dealings with Moors – he created the most detailed and heroic portrait of any Moor in Elizabethan and Jacobean drama. And it was a Moor who was an enemy of the Turks.

THE JACOBEAN PERIOD

The accession of James I to the throne in 1603 completely changed Britain's Mediterranean strategy and scuttled the pro-Moroccan policy. In 1604, when *Othello* was first performed before the king, James signed a peace treaty with Spain, thereby identifying England's enemy as the 'Mahometan', not the Catholic. Actually, James initiated an attack on the Ottoman Turks: in December 1604 it was reported by the Fugger scribe that 'the King of England will take steps against the Turks'.[44] It is not surprising, therefore, that the play was presented before him: only by displaying a Moor fighting against the Turks could Shakespeare appeal to his king who had written a poem against the 'circumcised Turband Turkes', *Lepanto* (1603).[45] As Othello strutted the stage, he represented to the London audience the tragic potential of the Moors: able warriors, Christian fanatics, serviceable if they remained at the frontiers against the Turks, but dangerous and disruptive if brought into Christendom.

The last two 'Moors' in Shakespeare's plays are not Moors in the sense that Othello or Aaron are: although their colour does not determine their character, the 'tawny' Cleopatra and the darksome Caliban are presented as African outsiders who are intent on destroying the characteristically European institutions of marriage and political society. With the earlier Moors, they share in being excluded from the ordered and hierarchical society of Rome or Naples. *Antony and Cleopatra* enlists the contrast between the stabilizing element of marriage in the

Roman/European settings, and its absence in the region beyond the Mediterranean frontier. The colour motif is now eliminated, although the themes of marriage (or the impossibility of marriage) and the protection of the polity dominate the relationship between the Roman and the Egyptian, the European and the North African.

It is the Romans who are identified with marriage in *Antony and Cleopatra*, and these political arrangements masquerade as high Roman virtue.[46] This is especially true of Antony's marriage to Octavia. This marriage's 'political and personal bankruptcy serves to legitimize for the play's audience Antony's return to a union with Cleopatra that exists outside of the institutions of marriage, family, and the state'.[47] Antony himself makes the point succinctly: 'I will to Egypt: / And though I make this marriage for my peace, / I' th' East my pleasure lies' (*AC* 2.3.37–9). The play shows Antony and Cleopatra regressing from being types of Mars and Isis to becoming an 'old ruffian' (4.1.4) and a 'right gipsy' (4.12.28). There is never any possibility that the last of the conquerors, Octavian, will become another Aeneas bewitched by this 'great fairy'. To him she is not a dish, but a trophy: 'her life in Rome / Would be eternal in our triumph' (5.1.65–6). Knowing perfectly well that, for all Octavian's assurances, 'he words me girls', Cleopatra becomes at the end 'a dish for the gods' (5.2.273) because, whatever else she may be, she will never be a wife, and 'Antony and Cleopatra's symbolic marriage ... does not reconcile them to the social order.'[48]

Throughout, Cleopatra mocks Antony's contradictory status as Roman conqueror bound by Roman marriage. 'What, says the married woman you may go?' (1.3.21). At every stage of the play she demonstrates her continuing obsession with Antony's wife, whether Fulvia or Octavia. As Antony lies dying, she triumphantly claims:

> I am safe.
> Your wife Octavia, with her modest eyes
> And still conclusion, shall acquire no honour
> Demuring upon me.

(4.15.27–30)

And as she herself is about to die, she finds satisfaction in knowing that

I
Will not wait pinioned at your master's court,
Nor once be chastised with the sober eye
Of dull Octavia.

(5.2.52–5)

Although Cleopatra seems to express contempt for these dull and sober Roman wives, Shakespeare clearly distinguishes between the Romans who submit to authority, and the Egyptians who transgress all moral and conventional limits. When sarcastically Cleopatra asks, 'Can Fulvia die?' (1.3.59), we realize that in so far as she represents the world of Roman probity and civil law – however imperfect that world appears – then Fulvia cannot die. It is this knowledge that adds such irony and pathos to Cleopatra's vision of Antony as her husband when he realizes that he will only 'be / A bridegroom in my death' (4.14.100–1).

Shakespeare's play offers no villain, no figure of inexplicable evil like Aaron or Iago. The tragedy consists largely in the impossibility of consolidating two entirely different worlds: the alluring but apolitical (alluring perhaps *because* apolitical) world of Egypt into the totally politicized (and somewhat sterile) world of Rome. The metaphor of the marriage suggests, as it does elsewhere in Shakespeare, the force of a fundamental 'European' civilizing institution. This by no means clarifies the impossibly complicated set of alternative values with which we are presented in this richest of Shakespeare's confrontations between Mediterranean civilizations. It does, however, illustrate Shakespeare's continuing fascination with, and wariness of, the alluring world beyond Europe. And if the tawny Cleopatra is to be seen as 'black' then Shakespeare sustains the anxiety in regard to the Mediterranean Other.[49]

The European–African interaction dominated the relationship between Antony and Cleopatra – as it had Aeneas and Dido in Marlowe's play about two decades earlier (where Dido's army is that of 'Moors', 4.4.62). Shakespeare focused on the attractiveness of a feminine Africa to the male European – but also on the fetters which chained the Europeans to the allure of Africa. By the time Shakespeare wrote *The Tempest*, however, a few years after *Antony and Cleopatra*, these fetters had become quite real. For the Mediterranean was now dominated by 'little wars' (Braudel's phrase) between Europeans and Africans, Christians and Muslims, renegades and captors and captives. Both Europeans and North Africans seized men, women and children, chained and humiliated them, bargained for them, bought and sold them, thereby producing an image of the Mediterranean as a locus of multi-religious, multinational and multi-ethnic piracy, privateering and abduction. Captivity and kidnapping ruled the waves – activities in which both Moors and Englishmen, Italians and Tunisians all took part in slave markets ranging from Genoa to Tunis, Cadiz to Salé, and Istanbul to Alexandria. The presence of captured Moors on Christian soil, and the presence of Christian captives on Islamic soil, inspired numerous writers to examine the impact of intercultural encounters on readers and audiences. From Spain to England, Cervantes and Lope de Vega, Heywood and Massinger depicted numerous captivity scenes in their work – and the tensions of religious conversion, miscegenation and cultural transformation.

Shakespeare situated the events of *The Tempest* within the literature of North African captivity, which had become quite popular in England.[50] With Prospero's capture of the travellers in *The Tempest*, the island became like an 'Algerine' captivity compound, run, however, not by a North African but by a European tyrant who domineered over a shipload of European Christians, a half-Moor and a spirit. Indeed, if Shakespeare recalled some of his countrymen who were living as pirates in the North African regions, capturing fellow countrymen and enslaving them – and the most notorious examples were Francis Verney and John Ward, who were celebrated in English song and ballad for their wealth and adventure – then *The Tempest* could well fit into the captivity literature that described the Barbary coast with its multi-religious and multinational corsairs as well as the mixed nationalities of captives.[51] Indeed, Ferdinand and Miranda repeat the theme in Cervantes' 'The captive's tale' in *Don Quixote* – of a captive falling in love with his captor's daughter. Shakespeare shows Ferdinand being put to hard labour by his captor, Prospero, in the manner that European captives were forced to work; how love blossomed between captive and captor's daughter (although, in this case, approved and supervised by the father), and finally how the two were able to return to Europe and to a happily consummated love.

Prospero seems a rather harsh autocrat, but he will not make the same mistake as Alonso (or the Duke in *Othello*) and allow his daughter to couple with a thing of darkness. Caliban's ancestry is at least half Moorish, and Miranda's choice (were she free to make one) would have to be between Caliban and Ferdinand. Her choice is not so much between 'loathness and obedience' (*Tem* 2.1.131) as it is between North Africa and Naples, and in *The Tempest* there is none of the fatal attraction offered by Cleopatra or Othello. Like his first Moor, Aaron, Shakespeare's last Moor is beyond redemption, a savage who combines with his Moorishness American and Irish racialization, and therefore cannot be changed.[52] It offends some critics that Miranda chooses obedience, but the play, while granting it its mystery, seems to argue that the imperfect but hierarchically structured world of Prospero is preferable to Gonzalo's pretty but unrealistic utopia, or to Caliban's anarchic notion of 'freedom'.[53] The shock expressed by the nurse and Tamora's sons at Aaron and Tamora's 'joyless, dismal, black and sorrowful issue' (4.2.78) may suggest the revulsion that Shakespeare's audience would have felt for Caliban's desire to rape Miranda and people the isle with Calibans. If Cleopatra is 'fire and air' (*AC* 5.2.288), Caliban is 'earth' (*Tem* 1.2.314). Before Prospero arrived he existed in a natural Cyclopean world, but then, like Cyclops, he turned out to be a 'drunken monster' (2.2.175).

Prospero's famously ambiguous admission that 'this thing of darkness I / Acknowledge mine' (5.1.275–6) could mean that there is a potentially subversive element in all of us, and Shakespeare's plays clearly show that his England and Italy do not lack an abundance of scoundrels and thugs. Antonio and Sebastian are good examples of this. As Thomas Starkey observes in the *Dialogue* (1534), reasonable order in the commonwealth 'hangeth upon one pin'.

The pin that I speak of is this: to have a good prince to govern and rule. This is the ground of all felicity in the civil life. This is the foundation of all good policy in such a kind of state as is in our country.[54]

Shakespeare seems to suggest in his 'frontier' works that one of the major threats to 'civil life' is the presence of 'things of darkness'. At the end, the civilized Europeans will leave the island to return to civilization, while Caliban, the savage Moor, will remain, sole master of a barren isle beyond the seas.[55] For Caliban is without community, having lived in a totally natural state. Once he was incorporated into the little world of Prospero and Miranda, he rebelled. For the modern sensibility it is hard to blame Caliban, but Shakespeare seems to have imagined Caliban as a potentially murderous 'thing of darkness' – savage, poisonous and abhorred.[56] Caliban would seem to be the logical inhabitant of Gonzalo's ideal, primitivist, golden-age plantation where there is 'no marrying 'mong his subjects' (2.1.166). There is not only no marriage, but 'No occupation, all men idle, all' (155). *The Tempest* seems to argue the opposite: a healthy society is based upon a willing submission to authority, symbolized by baseness 'nobly undergone' and marriage, the fundamental institution of an ordered civilization.

RELIGION OR RACE: WHO IS THE EUROPEAN AND WHO THE MOOR?

Unlike his Spanish contemporaries with their numerous plays about Christians in North African regions, Shakespeare did not write a single play about an English man or woman (such as Heywood's Bess in *The Fair Maid of the West*) travelling or living in the Mediterranean basin. Instead, Shakespeare was interested in the Moor in Europe, although no Moor is depicted on English soil; the furthest the Moor can get from Africa is Italy, at the front line of the frontier. There were Moors, or rather Moriscos, in Spain (until the expulsion of 1609), and it is quite possible, as Eric Griffin has shown, that Shakespeare conceived of Iago and Roderigo as Spaniards in Italy, thereby explaining their murderous hatred of the Moor of Venice.[57] Moors dominated the frontier – a frontier that was markedly un-urban: not a single Moor on the Shakespearean stage hails from a city or is able to live in any city, or survive it.[58] In the one case where a 'negro'/'Moor' woman is in the city (*MV* 3.5.35–6) she is there as a whore – and therefore not part of the city. Shakespeare's Moors are from the frontier of civilization and humanity, representing racial Otherness that was impossibly problematic – much more so than religious Otherness.

It is not insignificant that when Shakespeare chose to treat religious Otherness he presented it in the context of conversion – an Otherness that had been, at least nominally, defeated. He showed the conversion of Shylock, a Jew, and of Othello, a heathen or pagan, to Christianity – thereby proclaiming Christianity's victory over the religions most widely encountered by early modern Europeans on the Mediterranean frontiers. Yet it was not religion but blackness and the images of race that haunted Shakespeare,[59] since he did not depict or explore in any of his plays the religious world of the non-Christian (except in Shylock, and there by commonly known references to Judaism). In *The Merchant*, Shakespeare associated Morochus with Shylock – the only time when the two ethno-religious outsiders appeared together on the Shakespearean stage (although they do not meet).[60] At the beginning of the play (*MV* 1.3), Shylock entered, a Jew into a Christian world. He was immediately identifiable to the audience as different by his 'Jewish gabardine' (1.3.107);[61] he could have also been distinguished by his foreign appearance[62] – if Shakespeare was basing him on the Portuguese, Dr Lopez.[63] Despite these differences, Shylock could still be changed into a 'European' if he changed his religion and dress; there was nothing permanent about his 'Jewishness' (which is why Portia could not distinguish between the Jew and the merchant). Although Shakespeare complicated the figure of Shylock (unlike his precursors, Marlowe, Wilson and Greene, who gave stereotypically negative characterizations of Jews), he still treated Shylock from a traditionally Pauline perspective, and integrated him, by force, into Christian Europe. The Jew was an 'alien' (4.1.345) in Europe but the prejudice against him was 'theological rather than racial':[64] by converting, he would become a citizen of Venice. After all, he already shared with the Christians a common Scripture, as the biblical discussion with Antonio and the allusions to the prophet Daniel show (1.3). Furthermore, Shylock's daughter, who from the opening of the play was intent on converting, and therefore never presented herself as 'Jewish' in either speech or scriptural allusion, would marry a Christian and be completely accepted (she was unhesitatingly given charge of Portia's household). That is why, once Shylock gave up his Jewishness, he disappeared from the play and the romance then continued.

Soon after Shylock exited the stage, the Moor entered (at the beginning of Act 2), a black man into a white world.[65] While Shylock lived in Venice, among the Christians (and not in a ghetto), the Moroccan prince could not become part of the city – indeed, he appeared and disappeared as a solitary type, without having a 'tribe' and a 'nation' to support him. For there was clear unease about the possibility of his marrying Portia. The reference to Launcelot later in the play doing something to the 'Negro' woman/harlot that need be answered to the commonwealth suggests (however lightheartedly) that in the world of the *Merchant* miscegenation is not something to be condoned by the state. Lorenzo implies that his marriage to a Jew is less offensive than Launcelot's impregnating a 'Negro'. The difference is in Jessica's having been absorbed into the (Christian) Venetian community through marriage. Jessica's marriage is a completely different type of assimilation from Shylock's forced conversion. Although it is difficult for a modern audience to accept Shylock's humiliation and exclusion, the play is a comedy and so we have to assume that Shakespeare's audience found the spectacle of his final integration satisfying and funny although 'profoundly anti-Semitic'.[66]

Shakespeare introduced his Moorish figures in the framework of racial difference while leaving their religions unclear and more dependent on dramatic convention than theological identity.[67] Still critics have maintained that in *Othello*, and presumably in other representations of the Elizabethan and Jacobean Moor, 'religious difference [was] more powerfully felt than racial difference';[68] and Islam and not blackness was the spectre that haunted early modern

Europe.[69] No evidence has been presented to demonstrate Othello's 'Islam': one critic has claimed that Othello can be shown to be Muslim because he swore by God the 'merciful and cruel', which recalled God the 'merciful and compassionate' of the Qur'an. Despite the contradiction in the quotations and the absence of an English translation of the Qur'an in England in the early seventeenth century, Othello could not but have been quoting 'Allah'.[70] Other critics have confirmed Othello's Islam by reference to the cultural history of the period, and the overall encounter between Christendom and Islam: the blackness of Muslims, and thus Othello, wrote Ania Loomba, can be 'traced' back to Parzival[71] – as if what applied in medieval Germany remained unchanged in Renaissance England. For Loomba, Othello was a 'Muslim soldier' and also 'a Christian soldier'.[72]

Nothing in *Othello* shows that the Moor was 'Muslim' (despite Thomas Rymer's angry insistence that he was a 'Turk'):[73] nor, for that matter, had any of the Moors on the English stage uttered anything remotely 'Islamic' in theology or Scripture. Peele's Moors in the *Battle of Alcazar* swore by classical deities; the Prince of Morocco went to an unidentifiable (pagan?) 'temple' to pray (contrast him with Shylock, who went to a synagogue, and with Bassanio, who went to a church);[74] Eleazar in *Lust's Dominion* did not say anything Islamic either (he was, after all, a convert to Christianity), while, as Naseeb Shaheen has pointed out, in Act 5 Othello made thirteen allusions to biblical and liturgical sources.[75] Nor did Shakespeare distinguish the Moor Othello by anything supposedly 'Islamic': the reference to the 'turban' and the circumcision characterize the enemy 'Turk' – and therefore are not the Moor's. Indeed, the reference to circumcision calls into question the claim that Othello had been a Muslim at all, as Samuel Chew noted long ago.[76] As for the turban, although it is not known how Othello was dressed on stage, he could not have worn a turban,[77] and in all the great theatrical representations of Othello he has not worn one.[78] For the turban was the most obvious and decisive signifier of a Muslim in early modern England; converts to Islam were summarily denounced as having 'donned the turban'.[79] The Moor of Venice who was defending Christendom against the turbaned Turks would not have worn one.

Along with Aaron (whose Peacham drawing shows him without a turban) and Morochus, Othello was as non-Islamic as was the Soldan of Egypt in Greene's *Orlando Furioso* (*c.* mid-1590s).

What Shakespeare knew about 'Islam' and what he showed of his knowledge of Islam *in his plays* is very limited. He mentioned 'Mahomet' only once in his whole work (*1H6* 1.2.240) and 'Alcoran' never (contrast him, for instance, with Marlowe in *Tamburlaine* 1 and 2, where there are thirty-five references to Muhammad and four to 'Alcaron'). Shakespeare knew about Islam as an alien empire with its peculiar political and social culture.[80] He was aware of the dangerous Turkish/Ottoman Empire: he referred to 'Sultan Solyman' (who had died in 1566) fighting the Persians (*MV* 2.1.26) – although much closer to his time, Sultan Murad III had fought against them, too; to eunuchs serving among the Turks; to the lust of the Turk and the 'tributes' he collected (but the very popular word 'seraglio' did not appear); to the despotic court in Constantinople over which the Turk presided; and to the enmity which the Turk had for the Christian and his cross (*AYL* 4.3.33).[81] There is little doubt that Shakespeare was not as well informed about Islam or Muslims as, for instance, his contemporary playwright Cervantes, who described Moors after having lived among them in Algiers as a captive for five years (and on whose plays English dramatists drew for their Moorish plots). In the plays he set in North Africa, Cervantes accurately depicted Islamic cultural norms, nomenclature, religious customs, military and political leaders, and inter-African rivalries. He exhibited his intimate familiarity with events and personalities so much that critics have been able to identify the historical figures behind his dramatis personae. Plays such as *Los Baños de Argel* and *El Trato de Argel* demonstrate Cervantes' knowledge of the Moors of North African Islam – in a manner that no English playwright even came close to.[82] Neither Shakespeare nor any of his English contemporaries described North African Islam from anything close to Cervantes' personal experience and historical knowledge. All their plays, after all, depended for their 'Moorish' plots on European sources; none concocted his own plots in the manner of Cervantes.

As far as Shakespeare was concerned, the threat that Othello posed lay not in religion, but in the coal-black colour of his skin. The same danger had been presented in Aaron – who despite swearing once by the wounds of Christ (*Tit* 4.2.73) was associated because of his black skin with the devil. Indeed, as Shakespeare showed, Aaron is 'valorous' but 'irreligious', 'misbelieving' and 'unhallowed'. It is precisely this combination of ferocity without any moral direction whatever that makes him so frightening and memorable. It is not that he has a *different* religion, but that he has no religion at all, with blackness set against the whiteness of the Romans:

> What, what, ye sanguine, shallow-hearted boys,
> Ye white-limed walls, ye alehouse painted signs!
> Coal-black is better than another hue
> In that it scorns to bear another hue;
> For all the water in the ocean
> Can never turn the swan's black legs to white.
>
> (4.2.99–104)

A similar emphasis on the association between blackness and danger appears in Shakespeare's depiction of Othello. Significantly, Cinthio had not elaborated on the physically differentiating features of the 'Moro, molto valoroso'; Shakespeare, however, did, thereby distinguishing the Moor from the European.[83] As Michael Neill has observed, Purchas had united the Europeans through a common whiteness, while all other colours were associated in 'a common non-Europeanness'.[84] Further-more, when Shakespeare portrayed Moors, he racialized and blackened them in such a way that they looked completely different from the Moors who had been visiting England for decades. The Moors who came to London during Shakespeare's lifetime were North African, with Mediterranean features – the kind of features which Coleridge insisted on when he described Othello as 'a high and chivalrous Moorish chief'.[85] There were Moors who, when Europeans dressed like them, could well have evoked the question: which is the Moor and which is the European? In Jules Chifflet's *Les Marques d'honneur de la maison de Tassis* (1645), it is very difficult to distinguish, in two paintings by the

FIGURE 11 (a) Mulay Hasan, Hafsid Bey of Tunis; (b) Johann Baptista of Tassis, dressed in the fashion of the court of Mulay Hasan; both from Jules Chifflet, *Les Marques d'honneur de la maison de Tassis* (1645).

pupils of Rubens, between the exiled Mulay Hasan, the Hafsid Bey of Tunis, and Johann Baptista, both in their hunting clothes outside Brussels (see Figure 11). A North African 'Moor' could well pass for a 'European'.

Shakespeare's descriptions in the plays leave no doubt that the Moors he created were sub-Saharan and could never be confused with Europeans.[86] None of the ambassadors who visited England in 1589, 1595 and 1600 had sub-Saharan features because they were all Moriscos – which is why al-Mansur fixed on them for the journeys. But, ever since Bernard Harris published a reproduction of the portrait of al-Annuri,[87] critics have suggested that that ambassador to London had inspired Othello. 'Did Shakespeare', asked Loomba, 'picture Othello like the slightly menacing turbaned and aristocratic figure shown in a contemporary picture?'[88] But al-Annuri was not Negroid, as his 'picture' clearly shows (especially when seen in colour).[89] He was a Morisco with features not too different from the Italian Iago with the Spanish-sounding name. It is not possible to extrapolate from the painting the Othello with the thick lips, black visage and Negroid features.[90] Furthermore, English accounts about the visit of the Moroccan delegation to London did not mention anything about the racial characteristics of the visitors – not in the way that Eleazer and Othello were racially profiled in the plays. One account written from Morocco by John Waring to Robert Cecil in June 1600 described the political stature and personality of all the leading members of the delegation.[91] Richard Tomson, also writing from Morocco in July 1600, provided important information about the ambassador: he was from Fez, not from Marrakesh (the region to which Mulay al-Mansur belonged), and was accompanied by a number of other Moroccans, including a translator who used Italian in his negotiations with the queen.[92] Nothing was mentioned by either writer about the guests' racial peculiarity and the (im)moral implications thereof. The other account, written after the Moroccans' departure in January 1601, told how the delegation members visited Hampton Court and street markets in London, went to Whitehall to attend Queen Elizabeth's coronation day, looked and observed, asked questions (al-Annuri was proficient in Spanish), and were so inquisitive that they roused suspicion and subsequent anger/anxiety.[93] Again, what is striking about this account is that, much as it shows the Moors in an antipathetic light, it does not vilify them for their colour or race.[94]

In the diplomatic discourse of Elizabethan England, be it in letters, memoranda and even public announcements (as in the 1596 banishment order), there was no outburst of racial antipathy against the Moors. Shakespeare and his fellow playwrights, however, were anxious about the blackness rather than the religion of the Moors, perhaps because they saw the dramatic potential of a black man on stage and, even more, of a black man with a white European woman. They thus presented 'sooty', thick-lipped and Negroid black men whom they demonized for their skin colour and other qualities associated with Africans. It was these Moors, sub-Saharan in their features and physiognomy, who appeared on the Shakespearean stage. Like other Londoners, Shakespeare knew about the visits of Moroccans, and modelled some of his characters on them; but the text of his plays reveals that he deliberately racialized them, seeking to emphasize the danger of a coal-black man in the context of European sexual and political life. Not one Moor in his or his contemporaries' plays remains in, or survives the encounter with, Europe.

Whatever Shakespeare wrote about the Moor, ranging from expressions of revulsion to ambiguous admiration to racial anxiety, he recognized the Moor as the most destabilizing figure in the European encounter with the world beyond its white/Christian frontiers. A contemporary of Shakespeare's, in perhaps the first gloss on *Titus Andronicus*, summarized the antipathy to the Moor:

> See iustice done on Aron that damn'd Moore,
> By whom our heauie haps had their beginning:
> Then afterwards to order well the state,
> That like euents may nere it ruinate.[95]

NOTES

INTRODUCTION: SHAKESPEARE AND RENAISSANCE EUROPE

1. Edward Chaney, *The Evolution of the Grand Tour: Anglo-Italian Cultural Relations since the Renaissance* (London and Portland, Oreg., 1998); John Stoye, *English Travellers Abroad, 1604–1667*, rev. edn (New Haven and London, 1989).
2. Thomas Nashe, *The Unfortunate Traveller and Other Works*, ed. J.B. Steane (Harmondsworth, 1972), p. 341.
3. It was argued that learning languages was of great benefit to one's nation: see Warren Boutcher, '"A French Dexterity, & an Italian Confidence": new documents on John Florio, learned strangers and Protestant humanist study of modern languages in Renaissance England from *c*. 1547 to *c*. 1625', *Reformation*, 2 (1997), 39–109.
4. Nashe, *Unfortunate Traveller*, p. 343.
5. Stuart Gillespie, *Shakespeare's Books: A Dictionary of Shakespeare Sources* (London, 2001), pp. 384–9; William Shakespeare, *Love's Labour's Lost*, ed. H.R. Woudhuysen (Walton-on-Thames, 1998), pp. 70–1, *passim*.
6. See, for example, Angela Locatelli, 'The fictional world of *Romeo and Juliet*: cultural connotations of an Italian setting', in Michele Marrapodi, A.J. Hoenselaars, Marcello Cappuzzo and L. Falzon Santucci, eds, *Shakespeare's Italy: Functions of Italian Locations in Renaissance Drama* (Manchester, 1993), pp. 69–84, at pp. 79–80.
7. See Katherine Duncan-Jones, *Ungentle Shakespeare: Scenes from his Life* (London, 2001), pp. 25–6.
8. John Gillies, *Shakespeare and the Geography of Difference* (Cambridge, 1994). See also Geraldo U. de Sousa, *Shakespeare's Cross-Cultural Encounters* (Basingstoke, 1999). The history of geography is analysed in Robert J. Mayhew, *Enlightenment Geography: The Political Languages of British Geography, 1650–1850* (Basingstoke, 2000) and 'Geography, print culture and the Renaissance: "The road less travelled by"', *History of European Ideas*, 27 (2001), 349–69.
9. See David McPherson, *Shakespeare, Jonson and the Myth of Venice* (Newark, NJ, 1990).

10. See Virginia Mason Vaughan, *Othello: A Contextual History* (Cambridge, 1994), pp. 22–3 and part 1, *passim*.

11. See McPherson, *Shakespeare, Jonson and the Myth of Venice*; J.R. Mulryne, 'History and myth in *The Merchant of Venice*', in Marrapodi *et al.*, eds, *Shakespeare's Italy*, pp. 87–99.

12. For further comment, see Andrew Hadfield, *Literature, Travel, and Colonial Writing in the English Renaissance, 1545–1625* (Oxford, 1998), pp. 217–42; Andrew Hadfield, ed., *A Routledge Literary Sourcebook on William Shakespeare's 'Othello'* (London, 2002), *passim*.

13. See Barbara Everett, '"Spanish" Othello: the making of Shakespeare's Moor', in Catherine M.S. Alexander and Stanley Wells, eds, *Shakespeare and Race* (Cambridge, 2000), pp. 64–81; Hadfield, *Literature, Travel, and Colonial Writing*, ch. 4.

14. For details, see David Loades, *The Reign of Mary Tudor: Politics, Government and Religion in England, 1553–58*, 2nd edn (London, 1991), ch. 5.

15. For details, see John Guy, *Tudor England* (Oxford, 1988), ch. 12; Antonia Fraser, *Mary Queen of Scots* (London, 1969), pt 3.

16. See R.B. Wernham, *After the Armada: Elizabethan England and the Struggle for Western Europe, 1588–1595* (Oxford, 1984); Guy, *Tudor England*, ch. 12.

17. Most vigorously argued by the exiled English Jesuit, Robert Parsons, whose writings reached a wide audience in England: see *A Conference about the Next Succession to the Crowne of Ingland* (1594). See also Conrad Russell, *The Crisis of Parliaments: English History, 1509–1660* (Oxford, 1971), p. 256; and, more generally, John Guy, ed., *The Reign of Elizabeth I: Court and Culture in the Last Decade* (Cambridge, 1995).

18. Thomas Kyd, *The Spanish Tragedy*, ed. Philip Edwards (Manchester, 1959).

19. See Andrew Hadfield, 'Rethinking the Black Legend: sixteenth-century English identity and the Spanish colonial Antichrist', *Reformation*, 3 (1998), 303–22.

20. See William S. Maltby, *The Black Legend in England: The Development of Anti-Spanish Sentiment, 1558–1660* (Durham, NC, 1971); Charles Williams, *Queen Elizabeth and the Revolt of the Netherlands* (London, 1970).

21. For convenient overviews, see R.S. White, ed., *The Tempest: Contemporary Critical Essays* (Basingstoke, 1999); Peter Hulme and William H. Sherman, eds, *'The Tempest' and its Travels* (Philadelphia, 2000).

22. On the Ottoman Empire in Shakespeare's time, see Nabil Matar, *Turks, Moors and Englishmen in the Age of Discovery* (New York, 1999) and *Islam in Britain, 1558–1685* (Cambridge, 1998). On Shakespeare's reading Spenser, see Gillespie, ed., *Shakespeare's Books*, pp. 469–70; *Cymbeline*, ed. J.M. Nosworthy (London, 1955), pp. xvii–xx.

23. See James I, *His Maiesties Lepanto, or Heroicall Song* (1603). The victory actually did little to stem the challenge to Europe from the Ottoman Empire: see Matar, *Islam in Britain*, pp. 4–5.

24. On Mercator's influence, see E.G.R. Taylor, *Tudor Geography, 1485–1583* (London, 1930), pp. 84–8.

25. Gerardus Mercator, *Historia Mundi, or, Mercator's Atlas containing his cosmographicall description of the fabricke and figure of the world: lately rectified in divers places, as also beautified and enlarged with new mappes and tables / by the studious industry of Iudocus Hondy; Englished by W.S. . . .* (London, 1635). Europa was the daughter of the Phoenician king, Agenor, who was raped by Zeus in the form of a white bull. Her connection to the continent that bears her name is vague, as authorities such as Mercator and Ortelius acknowledge.

26. See John N. King, *Spenser's Poetry and the Reformation Tradition* (Princeton, NJ, 1990), pp. 71–5.

27. Mercator, *Historia Mundi*, p. 10.

28. Abraham Ortelius, *Theatrum Orbis Terrarum Abrahami Ortell Antuerp. geographi regii. The theatre of the whole world: set forth by that excellent geographer Abraham Ortelius* (London, 1608), fo. 3. On the influence of Ortelius, see Taylor, *Tudor Geography,* pp. 29–35, *passim*; Taylor, *Late Tudor and Early Stuart Geography, 1583–1650* (London, 1934), *passim*. For English descriptions of North Africans and Tartars in the sixteenth and seventeenth centuries, see Andrew Hadfield, ed., *Amazons, Savages & Machiavels: Travel and Colonial Writing in English, 1550–1630* (Oxford, 2001), pp. 127–35, 139–51.

29. Mercator, *Historia Mundi*, pp. 10–11.

30. Mercator, *Historia Mundi*, p. 12.

31. See Robert S. Miola, *Shakespeare's Reading* (Oxford, 2000); Kevin Sharpe, *Reading Revolutions: The Politics of Reading in Early Modern England* (New Haven, 2000); Ann Moss, *Printed Commonplace Books and the Structuring of Renaissance Thought* (Oxford, 1996). See also Walter J. Ong, *Ramus, Method and the Decay of Dialogue: From the Art of Discourse to the Art of Reason* (Cambridge, Mass., 1958).

32. See David Lindley, *The Trials of Frances Howard: Fact and Fiction at the Court of King James* (London, 1993), pp. 163–7.

33. On the Jews, see James Shapiro, *Shakespeare and the Jews* (New York, 1996).

34. For an analysis of these lines and their significance, see Andrew Hadfield, 'Shakespeare, John Derricke and Ireland: *The Comedy of Errors*, III.ii.105–6', *Notes and Queries*, 242 (March 1997), 53–4.

35. See Marcel Le Glay, Jean-Louis Voisin and Yann Le Bohec, *A History of Rome*, trans. Antonia Nevill, 2nd edn (Oxford, 2001), *passim*.

36. *Love's Labour's Lost* also alludes to France's fractious and violent recent history: see Robert White, 'The cultural impact of the Massacre of St Bartholomew's Day', in Jennifer Richards, ed., *Early Modern Civil Discourses* (Basingstoke, 2003), pp. 183–99, at pp. 192–4.

37. Robert M. Kingdon, *Myths about the St Bartholomew's Day Massacres 1572–1576* (Cambridge, Mass., 1988).

38. See Richard Dutton, *Licensing, Censorship and Authorship in Early Modern England: Buggeswords* (Basingstoke, 2000), ch. 7.

39. See Park Honan, *Shakespeare: A Life* (Oxford, 1998); Andrew Gurr, *The Shakespearian Playing Companies* (Oxford, 1996); Andrew Hadfield, *Shakespeare and Renaissance Politics* (London, 2004), ch. 1.

40. Howard Erskine-Hill, *Poetry and the Realm of Politics: Shakespeare to Dryden* (Oxford, 1996), pt 1; Hadfield, *Shakespeare and Renaissance Politics*, ch. 2. On the revenge play, see John Kerrigan, *Revenge Tragedy: Aeschylus to Armageddon* (Oxford, 1996).

41. For two opposed readings of the evidence, see E.A.J. Honigmann, *Shakespeare: The 'Lost Years'*, 2nd edn (Manchester, 1998); David Daniell, 'Shakespeare and the Protestant mind', *Shakespeare Survey* 54 (2001), 1–12. See also Huston Diehl, 'Religion and Shakespearean tragedy', in Claire McEachern, ed., *The Cambridge Companion to Shakespearean Tragedy* (Cambridge, 2002), pp. 86–102.

42. See Thomas Healy, 'Selves, states, and sectarianism in early modern England', *English*, 44 (1995), 193–213.

43. For details, see *Macbeth*, ed. Kenneth Muir (London, 1951), introduction, pp. xxv–xxxii; Antonia Fraser, *The Gunpowder Plot: Terror and Faith in 1605* (London, 1996), pt 5.

44. For discussion, see Willy Maley, 'The Irish text and subtext of Shakespeare's English histories', in Richard Dutton and Jean E. Howard, eds, *A Companion to Shakespeare's Works*, vol. 2: *The Histories* (Oxford, 2003), pp. 94–124. On the Nine Years War, see Hiram Morgan, *Tyrone's Rebellion: The Outbreak of the Nine Years War in Tudor Ireland* (Woodbridge, 1993).

45. For discussion, see Andrew Hadfield, *Shakespeare, Spenser and the Matter of Britain* (Basingstoke, 2003), ch. 10; more generally, see W.B. Patterson, *King James VI and I and the Reunion of Christendom* (Cambridge, 1997).

46. On the development of the news book, see David Zaret, *Origins of Democratic Culture: Printing, Petitions, and the Public Sphere in Early Modern England* (Princeton, NJ, 2000); Joad Raymond, *Pamphlets and Pamphleteering in Early Modern Britain* (Cambridge, 2003).

47. See Adrian Proctor and Robert Taylor, *The A to Z of Elizabethan London* (London, 1979).

48. For details, see Norman Cohn, *The Pursuit of the Millennium: Revolutionary Millenarians and Mystical Anarchists of the Middle Ages* (London, 1957),

chs 12–13. See also Kristen Poole, *Radical Religion from Shakespeare to Milton: Figures of Nonconformity in Early Modern England* (Cambridge, 2000).

49. See *Love's Labour's Lost*, ed. Woudhuysen, introduction, pp. 61–74.

50. Hadfield, *Literature, Travel, and Colonial Writing*, pp. 46–58, 232, 235.

51. For details, see Gillespie, *Shakespeare's Books*, *passim*, and the introductions to the relevant Arden editions.

52. Extracts are included in Hadfield, ed., *Amazons, Savages & Machiavels*.

53. See the discussion in Raymond Williams, *Keywords: A Vocabulary of Culture and Society* (London, 1976), pp. 183–8.

54. See also Paulina Kewes, 'The Elizabethan history play: a true genre?', in Dutton and Howard, eds, *A Companion to Shakespeare's Works*, vol. 2: *The Histories*, pp. 170–93.

1: THE POLITICS OF RENAISSANCE EUROPE

1. *STC* 9188. Printed in Matthias A. Schaaber, *Some Forerunners of the Newspaper in England 1476–1622* (Philadelphia, 1929), p. 41.

2. H.S. Bennett, *English Books and Readers 1558–1603: Being a Study in the Book Trade in the Reign of Elizabeth* (Cambridge, 1965), pp. 56–8.

3. These particular publications were intended for foreign as well as domestic consumption: Schaaber, *Forerunners of the Newspaper*, pp. 41, 45.

4. Denis B. Woodfield, *Surreptitious Printing in England 1550–1640* (New York, 1973), pp. 26–33.

5. *STC* 174503.

6. *A Transcript of the Register of the Company of Stationers of London 1554–1640 AD*, ed. Edward Arber, vol. 3 (London, 1875). See, as other examples, the play or device of Robert Greene, *The Spanish Masquerado* (London, 1589) (*STC* 12310), and the discourse translated from the French, *The Present State of Spaine* (London, 1594) (*STC* 22996).

7. Lisa Ferraro Parmelee, *Good Newes from Fraunce: French Anti-League Propaganda in Late Elizabethan England* (Rochester, NY, 1996), pp. 31–2.

8. P. Handover, *Printing in London: from 1476 to Modern Times* (Cambridge, Mass., 1960), pp. 103–9; Fritz Levy, 'The decorum of news', in Joad Raymond, ed., *News, Newspapers, and Society in Early Modern Britain* (London, 1999), pp. 23–5; Bennett, *English Books and Readers*, pp. 104, 245–6; Woodfield, *Surreptitious Printing*, pp. 5–18.

9. *STC* 13119, 13120, 18456.

10. A.G. Dickens, 'The Elizabethans and St Bartholomew', in *Reformation Studies* (London, 1982), p. 475.

11. *STC* 22241–3, 5590.

12. For Henri's victories, see *STC* 13126, 13128, 13129, 13133 and 13146. See also note 51. For Rhineberg, see *STC* 17673; for Turnhout, *STC* 17678 and 22993; for Nieupoort, *STC* 17679, 17671 and 11029; for Bercke, *STC* 17680; for Grave, *STC* 12197, 18471, 4317 and 12196; for the siege of Ostend, *STC* 18893, 18894, 24651a, 18891, 18892, 17675 and 18895.

13. *STC* 6910.4.

14. Pamphlets relating to the assassination of Henri IV include *STC* 11275, 13136, 13137, 13140, 13142, 13147.5, 17661. For 'The reporte of a bloudie and terrible massacre' in Moscow, see *STC* 21461. For the expulsion of the Moriscos, see *Stationers' Register*, vol. 3, p. 213, and *STC* 22992.7.

15. *Stationers' Register*, vol. 3, pp. 220b, 224b; *STC* 177660.

16. Levy, 'The decorum of news', pp. 27–9.

17. *Newes out of France for the Gentlemen of England* (London, 1591) (*STC* 1030.7), sig. C2; Joad Raymond, *Pamphlets and Pamphleteering in Early Modern Britain* (Cambridge, 2003), p. 146.

18. Roger Hacket, *A Sermon Needfull for Theese Times* (Oxford, 1591) (*STC* 12589), especially sig. C3.

19. John Stow, *The Annales of England* (London, 1601), p. 1259; Millar MacLure, *Register of Sermons Preached at Paul's Cross* (Toronto, 1989), pp. 66, 72.

20. E. Lodge, *Illustrations of British History*, vol. 2 (London, 1838), pp. 370, 379; *The Letters of John Chamberlain*, ed. Norman Egbert McClure (Philadelphia, 1939), pp. 8, 83 (see also HMC [Historical Manuscripts Commission] *Salisbury*, IX, pp. 282–30); *The Diary of John Manningham*, ed. Robert Parker Sorlien (Hanover, NH, 1976), p. 154.

21. Henry Roberts, *The Most Royall and Honourable Entertainment of the Famous and Renowned King, Christian the Fourth* (London, 1606), sig. B2.

22. Adam Fox, *Oral and Literate Culture in England 1500–1700* (Oxford, 2000), pp. 354–82.

23. *Tudor Royal Proclamations*, ed. Paul L. Hughes and James F. Larkin, vol. 2 (New Haven and London, 1969), pp. 469–71. A similar proclamation against 'sundry lewd and seditious bruits' was issued in February 1587 (pp. 534–5).

24. *True Intelligence Sent from a Gentleman of Account* (1591) (*STC* 24620).

25. *STC* 17259. Mansell also pointed out that a pamphlet had been published which made no mention of his role or that of the English ships.

26. *STC* 24268.

27. For a discussion of some clues that can indicate the type of readership, see Paul J. Voss, *Elizabethan News Pamphlets: Shakespeare, Spenser, Marlowe and the Birth of Journalism* (Pittsburgh, Pa, 2001), pp. 78–82.

28. *STC* 17671 and 17671a. Walter Bigges, *A Summarie and True Discourse of Sir Francis Drake's West Indian Voyage* (London, 1589) (*STC* 3056, 3056.5, 3057).

29. *Diary of John Manningham*, p. 45; *STC* 24651a.

30. Paul H. Kocher, 'Contemporary pamphlet backgrounds for Marlowe's *The Massacre at Paris*', *Modern Languages Quarterly*, 8 (1947), pp. 151–73, 309–18; Voss, *Elizabethan News Pamphlets*, pp. 113–15.

31. D.C. Collins, *A Handlist of News Pamphlets 1590–1610* (London, 1943), p. 35.

32. *STC* 5042, 16849.3, 16850. Later histories of the civil wars also devoted space to these years; see notes 11 and 35.

33. *The Destruction and Sacke Cruelly Committed by the Duke of Guyse and his Company, in the Towne of Vassy* (London, 1562) (*STC* 11312).

34. *An History Briefly Contayninge that which hath Happened sens the departure of the House of Guise* (London, 1562), sig. A4 (*STC* 11277).

35. The best general accounts in English of the civil wars can be found in: R.J. Knecht, *The Rise and Fall of Renaissance France 1483–1610*, 2nd edn (Oxford, 2001); J.H.M. Salmon, *Society in Crisis: France in the Sixteenth Century* (Cambridge, 1980); Mack P. Holt, *The French Wars of Religion 1562–1629* (Cambridge, 1995).

36. *The Fyrst Parte of Commentaries, concerning the State of Religion, and the Common Wealthe of Fraunce, under the Reignes of Henri the Second, Frauncis the Second, and Charles the Ninth. Translated out of Latine into Englishe, by Thomas Tymme* (London, 1573) (*STC* 22241), sig. B3.

37. See, for example, *A Short Discourse of the Meanes that the Cardinal of Loraine Useth, to Hinder the Stablishing of Peace, & to Move New Troubles in Fraunce* (London, 1568) (*STC* 5011).

38. *CSP Foreign 1560–61*, p. 567.

39. Andrew Pettegree, *Foreign Protestant Communities in Sixteenth-Century London* (Oxford, 1986), pp. 210–12, 271–2.

40. François Hotman, *A True and Plaine Report of the Furious Outrages in France* (London, 1573) (*STC* 13847); Jean de Serres, *The Lyfe of the Most Godly, Valeant and Noble Capteine and Maintener of the Trew Christian Religion in Fraunce, Iasper Colignie* (London, 1576) (*STC* 22248). Other works on the massacre were available in French: Q. Skinner, *The Foundations of Modern Political Thought*, vol. 2 (Cambridge, 1978), pp. 304–5.

41. *CSP Foreign 1572–1574*, p. 185. Catherine was also blamed for the massacre in *A Mervaylous Discourse vpon the Lyfe, Deedes, and Behaviours of Katherine de Medicis* (Heidelberg, 1575) (*STC* 10550), p. 101.

42. In accounts of the 1580s and 1590s, however, Guise was seen as a main instigator of the massacre, described in one account, for example, as 'that bloudthirstie Butcher, and unnaturall Murtherer of Christians': *The Miserable Estate of the Citie of Paris* (1590) (*STC* 19197), sig. A2.

43. Alan Stewart, *Philip Sidney: A Double Life* (London, 2000), pp. 88–9.

44. Anne Dowriche, *The French Historie, that is, A Lamentable Discourse of Three of the Chiefe, and Most Famous Bloodie Broiles that have Happened in France* (London, 1589) (*STC* 7159.3), fos 24ᵛ–33; *The Mutable and Wavering Estate of France from the Yeare of our Lord 1460 until the Year 1595* (London, 1597) (*STC* 11279), pp. 52, 90.

45. Dickens, 'The Elizabethans and St Bartholomew', p. 474.

46. Parmelee, *Good Newes from Fraunce*, pp. 76–90.

47. Susan Doran, *Monarchy and Matrimony: The Courtships of Elizabeth I* (London, 1996), pp. 164–72.

48. A justification of the Catholic position was published in *A Declaration of the Causes that have Moved the Cardinal of Bourbon … to Oppose Themselves to those, which by all Meanes do Seeke to Subvert the Catholike Religion* (London, 1585) (*STC* 13092), esp. pp. 2–7.

49. François Hotman, *The Brutish Thunderbolt: or rather Feeble Fier-Flash of Pope Sixtus the Fift, against Henrie the most Excellent King of Nauarre*, trans. Christopher Fetherstone (London, 1586) (*STC* 13843.5).

50. For English foreign policy after 1588, see Wallace T. MacCaffrey, *Elizabeth I: War and Politics 1588–1603* (Princeton, NJ, 1992); R.B. Wernham, *After the Armada: Elizabethan England and the Struggle for Western Europe 1588–1595* (Oxford, 1984) and *The Return of the Armadas: The Last Years of the Elizabethan War against Spain 1595–1603* (Oxford, 1994).

51. *A Briefe Discourse of the Merveylous Victorie Gotten by the King of Navarre, against those of the Holy League, on the Twentieth of October 1587* (London, 1587) (*STC* 13129).

52. *A Declaration of the King's Pleasure Published after his Departure from Paris* (London, 1588) (*STC* 13093), p. 10.

53. Antony Colynet, *The True History of the Ciuill Warres of France, betweene the French King Henry the 4. and the Leaguers from 1585 untill October 1591* (1591), pp. 305, 334.

54. English translations are *STC* 13096, 13098 and 13098.2.

55. Lodge, *Illustrations*, vol. 2, p. 373.

56. *The Whole and True Discourse of the Enterprises and Secrete Conspiracies that have bene made against the Person of Henri de Valois* (London, 1589) (*STC* 13103).

57. Handover, *Printing in London*, pp. 103–9; Levy, 'The decorum of news', pp. 23–5; Bennett, *English Books and Readers*, pp. 104, 245–6; Schaaber, *Forerunners of the Newspapers*, pp. 169–72; Parmelee, *Good Newes from Fraunce*, pp. 30–1.

58. Luke Wealsh, *A True Discourse of the Most Happy Victories Obtayned by the French King* (London, 1589) (*STC* 13143), sig. B3.

59. *An Excellent Ditty vpon Ashwednesday being the Fourth Day of March Last Past* (1590) (*STC* 13135) and *A Discourse and True Recitall of Euerie Particular of*

the *Victorie Obtained by the French King* (1590) (*STC* 13131). See also *The Copie of a Letter* (London, 1590) (*STC* 10411) and *The True Discourse of the Wonderfull Victorie* (London, 1590) (*STC* 13145); and D.C. Collins, *A Handlist of News Pamphlets 1590–1610* (London, 1943), p. 5.

60. *The Miserable Estate of the Citie of Paris at this Present* (London, 1590), pp. 3–4 (*STC* 19197).

61. *True Newes, concerning the Winning of the Towne of Corbeyll* (London, 1590) (*STC* 13146), sig. A2.

62. *The True Reporte of the Service in Britanie* ... (London, 1591) (*STC* 18655), sig. A2.

63. *A Journall, or Briefe Report of the Late Service in Britaigne* (London, 1591) (*STC* 13156), sig. B2; Colynet, *The True History,* pp. 533–4. The Welshman Williams, who has been seen as the model for Fluellen in *Henry V,* was given a magnificent military funeral at St Paul's in 1595.

64. *Aduertisements from Britany, and from the Low Countries* (London, 1591) (*STC* 13156), sigs C2–3; *Aduertisements from Britany, and from the Low Countries. In September and October* (London, 1591) (*STC* 3802.5), sigs B4–C2.

65. Sir Thomas Coningsby, 'Journal of the siege of Rouen 1591', ed. John Gough Nichols, *Camden Miscellany,* vol. 1 (1847), pp. 38–9; *A Discourse of that which is Past* (London, 1592) (*STC* 11270), p. 6.

66. Michael Wolfe, *The Conversion of Henri IV: Politics, Power and Religious Belief in Early Modern France* (Cambridge, Mass., 1993), p. 30.

67. *CSP Domestic 1591–4,* pp. 353, 368.

68. *The Oration and Declaration of the French King, Henrie the Fourth* (London, 1590) (*STC* 13114), sig. A3.

69. For contemporary newsletters, see *STC* 13117, 13138. For a later history which ignored his conversion, see Edmond Skory, *An Extract out of the Historie of the Last French King Henri the Fourth* (London, 1610) (*STC* 22629). The conversion is discussed with approval in Pierre Matthieu, *The Heroyk Life and Deplorable Death of the Most Christian King Henri the Fourth* (London, 1612) (*STC* 17661), pp. 32–3. It was criticized in *The Mutable and Wavering Estate of France,* p. 140.

70. Wealsh, *A True Discourse,* sig. A3.

71. *STC* 13119, 73535.

72. *Newes From Brest* (London, 1594) (*STC* 18654); *The Fugger News-Letters 1568–1605,* ed. Victor von Klarwill (London, 1926), p. 262. For a modern account, see John S. Nolan, *Sir John Norreys and the Elizabethan Military World* (Exeter, 1997), pp. 204–17.

73. *Acts of the Privy Council of England,* ed. J.R. Dasent *et al.,* new series, 46 vols (London, 1890–1964) (hereafter *APC*) *1595–6,* p. 340; *CSP Domestic 1595–7,* p. 203.

74. Jean du Nesme, *The Miracle of the Peace in Fraunce* ... (London, 1599) (*STC* 7353.5).

75. *A Lamentable Discourse* (London, 1610) (*STC* 19565); *A True Report of the Most Execrable Murder* (*STC* 13147.5). Pierre Matthieu, *The Heroyk Life and Deplorable Death: The Sighes of Fraunce for the Death of their Late King, Henri the Fourth* (London, 1610) (*STC* 13140), contains a drawing of the assassination and describes the funeral and coronation. Henri's death is also described in Skory, *An Extract*, and Claude Morillon, *The Funerall Pompe and Obsequies of the Most Mighty and Puissant Henri the Fourth* (London, 1610) (*STC* 13136). See Jean Loiseau de Tourval, *Three Precious Teares of Blood* (London, 1611) (*STC* 13142), p. 5, for the elegiac verse. Philippe de Mornay, *A Discourse to the Lords of the Parliament* (London, 1611) (*STC* 13134), touches on the murder. Henri's death was also discussed in Jean Loiseau de Tourval, *The French Herald* (London, 1611) (*STC* 11374).

76. *The Terrible and Deserved Death of Francis Ravilliack* (Edinburgh, 1610) (*STC* 20755.5).

77. *Stationers' Register*, vol. 3, pp. 220b, 224b; *STC* 17818.

78. *The French Kinges Declaration and Confirmation of the Proclamation of Nantes* (London, 1613) (*STC* 16831.5); *A True Relation of the Conferences and Proceedings concerning the Peace and Mutuall Agreements betweene the King of France, and Prince of Conde* (London, 1616) (*STC* 16833).

79. The best work in English on the revolt is still Geoffrey Parker, *The Dutch Revolt* (London, 1977).

80. The number of refugees who arrived in England cannot be accurately calculated. A government survey of March 1568 counted 9,302 aliens in the City and Westminster of whom 77 per cent were reported as Dutch, but not all these had left their homes for reason of religion. See Laura Hunt Yungblut, *Strangers Settled Here Amongst Us* (London, 1996), p. 21.

81. *A Declaration and Publication of the Most Worthy Prince of Orange, contaynyng the Cause of his Necessary Defence against the Duke of Alba by William I, Prince of Orange, 1533–1584* (London, 1568) (*STC* 25708), sigs A3–4, B2. For those who read Latin, see *Libellus supplex imperatoriae maiestati caeterisq[ue]* (London, 1571) (*STC* 18440). See also *An Answer and True Discourse to a Certain Letter Lately Sent by the Duke of Alba (in Maner of a Pardon) to those of Amsterdam* (London, 1573) (*STC* 540) and *A Supplication to the Kings Maiestie of Spayne* ... *By which is Declared the Originall Beginning of al the Commotions [and] Troubles happened in the sayd Low Countrie* (London, 1573) (*STC* 25710).

82. *Stationers' Register*, vol. 2, pp. 308, 313, 341.

83. George Gascoigne, *The Spoyle of Antwerpe* (London, 1576) (*STC* 11644); George Gascoigne, *A Larum for London, or The Siedge of Antwerpe* (London, 1602) (*STC* 16754).

84. Ralph Norris, *A Warning to London by the Fall of Antwerp* (London, 1577) (*STC* 18656). Other ballads were also licensed for sale but have not survived.

85. Barnabe Riche, *Allarme to England* (London, 1578) (*STC* 20979), sigs **3–4.

86. *Somers Tract*, vol. 1, p. 410; *A Most Necessary and Godly Prayer, for the Preservation of the Right Honourable the Earle of Leicester* (London, 1585) (*STC* 7289).

87. Thomas Churchyard, *The Epitaph of Sir Phillip Sidney* (London, 1586) (*STC* 5228); John Phillips, *The Life and Death of Sir Phillip Sidney* (London, 1587) (*STC* 19871); Angel Day, *Upon the Life and Death of the Most Worthy, and Thrise Renowned Knight, Sir Phillip Sidney* (London, 1586) (*STC* 6409); George Whetstone, *Sir Phillip Sidney, his Honorable Life, his Valiant Death, and True Vertues* (London, 1587) (*STC* 25349).

88. Gerard Prouninck, *A Shorte Admonition or Warning, upon the Detestable Treason wherewith Sir William Stanley and Rowland Yorke haue Betraied and Deliuered for Monie unto the Spaniards, the Towne of Deuenter, and the Sconce of Zutphen* (London, 1587) (*STC* 23228.7).

89. Thomas Greepe, *The True and Perfecte Newes of the Woorthy and Valiaunt Exploytes, performed and doone by that Valiant Knight Syr Frauncis Drake* (London, 1587) (*STC* 12343); George Peele, *A Farewell* (London, 1589) (*STC* 19537); Henri Haslop, *Newes out of the Coast of Spaine* (London, 1587) (*STC* 12926); Walter Bigges, *A Summarie and True Discourse of Sir Francis Drake's West Indian Voyage* (London, 1589) (*STC* 3056, 3056.5, 3057, 3171.6). According to the latter's preface in two of the editions, the book was intended to be published earlier but was postponed because of the coming of the Spanish Armada. Captain Bigges had died on the voyage and his work was completed by others.

90. De Lemar Jensen, 'The Spanish Armada: the worst kept secret in Europe', *Sixteenth Century Journal*, 19 (1988), pp. 621–47; *A True Discourse of the Armie which the King of Spaine Caused to bee Assembled in the Haven of Lisbon* (London, 1588) (*STC* 22999).

91. Alexandra Walsham, *Providence in Early Modern England* (Oxford, 1999), pp. 245–66; *Armada 1588–1988: The Official Catalogue* (London, 1988), pp. 274–84.

92. *The Politique Takinge of Zutphen Skonce, the Winning of the Towne, and Beleagering of Deuenter* (London, 1591) (*STC* 26134.5); *True Newes from one of Sir Fraunces Vere's Companie* (London, 1591) (*STC* 24652).

93. See note 14. The history is Jan Janszn Orlers, *The Triumphs of Nassau* (London, 1613) (*STC* 17676 and 17677).

94. *Chamberlain's Letters*, p. 153.

95. *A True Discourse of the Ouerthrowe giuen to the Common Enemy at Turnhaut* (London, 1597) (*STC* 17678), especially sigs A1–2. See also *STC* 22993, a

translation from the French, where Sidney and Vere are given less prominence but also praised.

96. *Chamberlain's Letters*, pp. 103–4.

97. A facsimile version of the ballad is in D.C. Collins, *Battle of Nieuport 1600*, Shakespeare Association Facsimiles, 9 (Oxford, 1935).

98. *Chamberlain's Letters*, p. 161.

99. *Chamberlain's Letters*, pp. 139, 143, 146; *APC 1601–1604*, pp. 37, 73, 145, 487.

100. Stow, *Annales*, p. 1283.

101. *A Publike Declaration made by the United Protestant Princes Electors and other Princes ... of the Holie Empire* (London, 1610) (*STC* 11795); *The Wars in Germany* (London, 1614) (*STC* 11796); Charles Demetrius, *Newes from Gulick and Cleue* (London, 1615) (*STC* 14838); *A Relation of all Matters Passed* (London, 1614) (*STC* 20862).

102. *Newes out of Germanie* (London, 1612) (*STC* 11794), sig. A2.

2: ENGLISH CONTACT WITH EUROPE

1. These sentiments are echoed by Lucentio and Petruchio (*TS* 1.1.1–24 and 1.2.49–57).

2. See Luigi da Porto, *Historia novellamente ritrovata di due nobili amanti* (Venice, 1530). Shakespeare may even have focused on the Mountacutes/Montagues not through any Italianate interest but primarily as a means of paying tribute to the family of the Earl of Southampton's mother, the (English) Montagus. See *Romeo and Juliet*, ed. Brian Gibbons (London, 1980), p. 31.

3. Roger Ascham, *The Schoolmaster* (1570), ed. Lawrence V. Ryan (Ithaca, NY, 1967), p. 66. For the myth of Circe, in which a group of Odysseus' men are transformed into pigs while retaining their human minds, see Homer's *Odyssey*, book 10.

4. Virginia F. Stern, *Sir Stephen Powle of Court and Country* (London and Toronto, 1992), p. 39.

5. A.J. Hoenselaars, *Images of Englishmen and Foreigners in the Drama of Shakespeare and His Contemporaries: A Study of Stage Characters and National Identity in English Renaissance Drama, 1558–1642* (London and Toronto, 1992), pp. 18–19; *'The Passions of the Minde in Generall' by Thomas Wright: A Reprint Based on the 1604 Edition*, ed. Thomas O. Sloan (Urbana, Ill., 1971), Preface, pp. lxii–lxiii.

6. Park Honan, *Shakespeare: A Life* (Oxford, 1998), pp. 325–8. Shakespeare's landlord, a wig-maker called Christopher Mountjoy, had been a resident of Crécy but fled France in the wake of the St Bartholomew's Day Massacre of 1572.

7. E.A.J. Honigmann, *Shakespeare: The 'Lost Years'*, 2nd edn (1985; repr. Manchester and New York, 1998), p. 1, emphasizes that, even though these years are usually dated as running from 1585 (when Shakespeare disappears from the Stratford records) until 1592, with respect to documenting his movements, the 'lost years' could well begin much earlier, since, apart from three specific dates between 1582 and 1585, no hard information is known about Shakespeare's personal whereabouts.

8. S. Schoenbaum, *Shakespeare's Lives* (Oxford and New York, 1970), pp. 258–9, 393, 720.

9. Honan, *Shakespeare*, pp. 106–7.

10. *Much Ado* also reflects this popular conjunction of the two cities through the interaction of Claudio (a Florentine) and Benedick (a Paduan).

11. Edward Chaney, *The Evolution of the Grand Tour: Anglo-Italian Cultural Relations since the Renaissance* (London and Portland, Oreg., 1998), pp. 70–8, 95.

12. William Thomas, *Principal Rules of the Italian Grammar, with a Dictionary* (1550). Thomas also resided at Naples and Rome during 1547–8 before returning to England in 1549.

13. William Thomas, *The History of Italy* (London, 1549, 1561), ed. George B. Parks (Ithaca, NY, 1963), p. 83.

14. Thomas, *History of Italy*, pp. 105, 108.

15. See Andrew Hadfield, *Literature, Travel, and Colonial Writing in the English Renaissance 1545–1625* (Oxford, 1998), pp. 24–32.

16. As late as 1596, Queen Elizabeth was still attempting to negotiate with King Henri IV of France for the return of Calais. See Michael G. Brennan, Margaret P. Hannay and Noel J. Kinnamon, 'Robert Sidney, the Dudleys, and Queen Elizabeth', in C. Levin, J. Eldridge Carney and D. Barrett-Graves, eds, *Elizabeth I: Always Her Own Free Woman* (Brookfield, Vt, 2003), pp. 20–42, 36.

17. Thomas Hoby's account while at Venice of the obscure hatred between 'two great families, whiche of long time have bine deadlie ennemies th'on to th'other, Della Turre and Soveragnani', offers an interesting precursor to Shakespeare's Montagues and Capulets.

18. Thomas Hoby, 'A Booke of the Travaile and Lief of Me, Thomas Hoby, with Diverse Things Woorth the Notinge' (BL Egerton MS 2148), ed. E. Powell, in *Camden Miscellany*, 10 (1902); Chaney, *Evolution of the Grand Tour*, pp. 6–7, 64–5, 97.

19. Thomas Wilson, *The Art of Rhetoric* (1560), ed. Peter E. Medine (Pennsylvania, 1994), pp. 5–6, 71, 169, 177, 188; Hoenselaars, *Images of Englishmen and Foreigners*, p. 20.

20. See Jonathan Woolfson, *Padua and the Tudors* (Toronto and Buffalo, 1998).

21. A.H.S. Yeames, 'The Grand Tour of an Elizabethan', *Papers of the British School at Rome*, 7 (1914), 92–113.

22. Ascham, *The Schoolmaster*, pp. 61, 60.

23. Lawrence V. Ryan, *Roger Ascham* (Stanford, Calif. and London, 1963), pp. 2–3, 7, 49, 116, 119–92, 258–9; Ascham, *The Schoolmaster*, pp. 60–75; Chaney, *Evolution of the Grand Tour*, 76.

24. Lincoln's party were also treated to another Italian entertainment at the Château de Madrid. Such performances were an established part of diplomacy. In March 1571, for example, Lord Buckhurst had gone to France to congratulate Charles IX on his wedding and his party was entertained by the renowned Compagnia de' Gelosi 'with a comedy of Italians': E.K. Chambers, *The Elizabethan Stage*, 4 vols (Oxford, 1923), vol. 2, p. 261.

25. James M. Osborn, *Young Philip Sidney, 1572–1577* (New Haven, 1972), p. 117.

26. For more detailed accounts of Philip Sidney's continental travels, see Osborn, *Young Philip Sidney*; Katherine Duncan-Jones, *Sir Philip Sidney: Courtier Poet* (London, 1991), pp. 63–85; and Alan Stewart, *Philip Sidney: A Double Life* (London, 2000), pp. 68–138.

27. Edward Webbe's *Rare and Most Wonderful Things* (1590) describes Oxford's participation in challenges at tilt at Palermo in Sicily. On his return to England, Oxford believed that his wife had cuckolded him; and this may have inspired Greene's *Pandosto* (itself a source for *The Winter's Tale*), in which the daughter of a falsely accused queen is brought up by shepherds in Sicily. See Chaney, *Evolution of the Grand Tour*, pp. 10–12.

28. A jotting in Stephen Powle's notebook, *c.* 1580: Stern, *Sir Stephen Powle*, p. 87, quoting Bodley MS Tanner 309, fo. 205^{r}.

29. Bodl. Addit. MS, C 173; John Stoye, *English Travellers Abroad 1604–1667*, rev. edn (New Haven and London, 1989), p. 138.

30. Stern, *Sir Stephen Powle*, p. 83; Chaney, *Evolution of the Grand Tour*, p. 66.

31. A.L. Rowse, *Ralegh and the Throckmortons* (London, 1962), pp. 80–94.

32. HMC [Historical Manuscripts Commission] De Lisle and Dudley, II.95–6.

33. Honan, *Shakespeare*, pp. 51–2, 64; Honigmann, *'Lost Years'*, pp. 5, 116–17.

34. Honigmann, *'Lost Years'*, pp. 8–11, citing *Acts of the Privy Council*, XIII.149.

35. Margaret Mary Littlehales, *Mary Ward: Pilgrim and Mystic 1585–1645* (Tunbridge Wells, 1998).

36. Thomas Frank, 'An edition of "A Discourse of HP his Travelles" (MS Rawlinson D 83)', unpublished University of Oxford B.Litt. thesis (1954).

37. HMC Salisbury, VII.10.

38. Jonathan Bate, 'The Elizabethans in Italy', in Jean-Pierre Maquerlot and Michèle Willems, eds, *Travel and Drama in Shakespeare's Time* (Cambridge, 1996), pp. 56–8.

39. Stewart, *Philip Sidney*, pp. 285, 296. For the Sidneys and Tacitus, see also Germaine Warkentin, 'The world and the book at Penshurst: the Second

Earl of Leicester (1595–1677) and his library', *The Library*, 6th series, 20 (1998), 325–46, 341. For Robert Sidney's annotated copy of Justus Lipsius's 1585 edition of Tacitus, see BL MS C 142e.13.

40. Hadfield, *Literature, Travel, and Colonial Writing*, pp. 34–44. See also Sir Thomas Palmer, *An Essay of … Travels into Foreign Countries* (1606), dedicated to Prince Henry.

41. R.C. Bald, *John Donne: A Life* (Oxford, 1970), pp. 45, 50–2; John Carey, *John Donne: Life, Mind and Art* (London, 1981); Chaney, *Evolution of the Grand Tour*, pp. 77, 201, n. 60.

42. David Riggs, *Ben Jonson: A Life* (Cambridge, Mass. and London, 1989), p. 18.

43. R.B. Wernham, 'Christopher Marlowe at Flushing in 1592', *English Historical Review*, 91 (1976), 344–5; Charles Nicholl, '"Faithful dealing": Marlowe and the Elizabethan intelligence service', in Paul Whitfield White, ed., *Marlowe, History, and Sexuality* (New York, 1998), pp. 1–14.

44. Willem Schrickx, 'Anthony Munday in the Netherlands in October 1595', *Notes and Queries*, 242 (1997), 454–5.

45. *Oxford Dictionary of National Biography* article.

46. Antonia Fraser, *Mary Queen of Scots* (1969; repr. London, 1971), pp. 285–6, 298–9.

47. Mark Eccles, 'Samuel Daniel in France and Italy', *Studies in Philology*, 34 (1937), 148–67; Joan Rees, *Samuel Daniel: A Critical and Biographical Study* (Liverpool, 1964), pp. 5–8.

48. *The Works of Thomas Nashe*, ed. R.B. McKerrow and F.P. Wilson, 5 vols (Oxford, 1966), vol. 2, p. 301; vol. 3, p. 324; vol. 5, pp. 13–15.

49. Diana Poulton, *John Dowland* (1972; repr. London, 1982), pp. 35–41. Other English-born musicians, such as Antonio Ferrabosco (who provided the score for several of Jonson's masques), were of Italian parentage.

50. Thomas Coryat, *Coryat's Crudities Hastily Gobled Up in Five Moneths Travells* (1611), 2 vols (Glasgow, 1905), vol. 1, p. 386; Chambers, *Elizabethan Stage*, vol. 2, pp. 89–91, 262–5, 271–94; Andrew Gurr, *The Shakespearean Stage, 1574–1642*, 2nd edn (Cambridge, 1980), pp. 34, 86–7; Jerzy Limon, *Gentlemen of a Company: English Players in Central and Eastern Europe, 1590–1660* (Cambridge, 1985); Willem Schrickx, *Foreign Envoys and Travelling Players in the Age of Shakespeare and Jonson* (Gent, 1986).

51. Honan, *Shakespeare*, p. 99; G.K. Hunter, 'Elizabethans and foreigners', *Shakespeare Survey*, 17 (1964), repr. in Catherine M.S. Alexander and Stanley Wells, eds, *Shakespeare and Race* (Cambridge, 2000), pp. 37–63, quoting from *Huguenot Society Publications*, vol. 10, pt 1 (1900), p. 365; E.A.J. Honigmann, 'Shakespeare and London's immigrant community circa 1600', in J.P. Vander Motten, ed., *Elizabethan and Modern Studies* (Gent, 1985), pp. 143–53.

52. Informative accounts of similar experiences were compiled by (possibly) Sir Thomas Berkeley (who travelled in 1610 through Flanders, Germany, Switzerland and Italy); Thomas Wentworth, later First Earl of Strafford (who had married Clifford's sister, Anne, and was in France in 1612); and Sir Thomas Puckering (who reached Venice in 1614). See Stoye, *English Travellers Abroad*, pp. 23–62; HMC Salisbury, XXI.104–13, 137–49; PRO SP 94/17; BL Sloane MS 682; Sheffield Public Library, Wentworth Woodhouse MSS; BL Harl. MS 7021.

53. HMC De L'Isle and Dudley, III.372.

54. University of Leeds, Brotherton MS Trv.q.3, ed. M.G. Brennan (Leeds, 1993), fos 53, 208.

55. Sir Roy Strong, *Henry Prince of Wales and England's Lost Renaissance* (London, 1986), pp. 27–9.

56. Coryat, *Crudities*, dedication.

57. *CSP Domestic 1610*, p. 581; BL MS Harleian 7007, fos 255, 266; Strong, *Henry Prince of Wales*, pp. 72–3 and plates 18–20; Stoye, *English Travellers Abroad*, pp. 51, 125; Thomas Birch, *The Life of Henry Prince of Wales* (London, 1760), appendix.

58. Graham Parry, *The Golden Age Restor'd: The Culture of the Stuart Court, 1603–1642* (Manchester, 1981), pp. 80–1; Strong, *Henry Prince of Wales*, p. 108; *CSP Domestic 1610*, pp. 122–3.

59. Parry, *The Golden Age Restor'd*, pp. 95–136.

60. Dudley Carleton, *Dudley Carleton to John Chamberlain 1603–1624: Jacobean Letters*, ed. Maurice Lee, Jr (New Brunswick, NJ, 1972), pp. 53–6, 67–8.

61. Fynes Moryson, *An Itinerary* (1617), 4 vols (Glasgow, 1907–8), vol. 3, pp. 431–2.

62. See Brian Parker, 'Jonson's Venice', in J.R. Mulryne and Margaret Shewring, eds, *Theatre of the English and Italian Renaissance* (Basingstoke, 1991), pp. 95–112.

63. Cf. the advice in Jonson's *Epigram I*, which could well be applied to travel guidebooks: 'Pray thee take care, that tak'st my book in hand, / To read it well; that is, to understand.'

3: SHAKESPEARE'S READING OF MODERN EUROPEAN LITERATURE

1. See, for example, Ben Jonson, *The Silent Woman*, 1.2: 'He must have Seneca read to him, and Plutarch, and the Ancients; the moderns are not for this disease.'

2. One further deliberate restriction is that this chapter does not touch on the traditions of Italian comedy treated by Richard Andrews in chapter 4.

3. For a summary of the case for Buchanan's influence on Shakespeare, and of secondary literature on the subject, see Stuart Gillespie, *Shakespeare's Books: A Dictionary of Shakespeare Sources* (London, 2001), pp. 71–4. A major recent study is David Norbrook's '*Macbeth* and the politics of historiography', in Kevin Sharpe and Steven N. Zwicker, eds, *Politics of Discourse: The Literature and History of Seventeenth-Century England* (Berkeley, 1987), pp. 78–116.

4. For a standard study of the intertwinings of these novelists' work, see Yvonne Rodax, *The Real and the Ideal in the Novella of Italy, France and England* (Chapel Hill, NC, 1968).

5. T.W. Baldwin, *William Shakspere's Small Latine and Lesse Greeke*, 2 vols (Urbana, Ill., 1944), developed an elaborate case for Shakespeare's latinity. Though its details are frequently open to challenge, its general conclusions have tended to gain broad acceptance.

6. See, in particular, J.W. Lever, 'Shakespeare's French fruits', *Shakespeare Survey*, 6 (1953), 79–90.

7. One of the strongest instances consists of some unusual vocabulary in *Othello*. See E.A.J. Honigmann, '*Othello*, Chappuys, and Cinthio', *Notes and Queries*, 211 (1966), 136–7.

8. For a recent review of such evidence, see Naseeb Shaheen, 'Shakespeare's knowledge of Italian', *Shakespeare Studies*, 47 (1994), 161–9. Shaheen also discusses the evidence as to Shakespeare's use of Florio's manuals.

9. There are signs of second-hand knowledge of it, as is to be expected. See, for example, William J. Kennedy, '"Sweet Theefe": Shakespeare reading Petrarch', *Annals of Scholarship: An International Quarterly*, 6 (1989), 75–91.

10. A useful recent discussion of the idiosyncrasies of English Renaissance translations, and the reasons for them, is Warren Boutcher's essay 'The Renaissance', in Peter France, ed., *The Oxford Guide to Literature in English Translation* (Oxford, 2000), pp. 45–55.

11. Judith Lee, 'The English Ariosto: the Elizabethan poet and the marvelous', *Studies in Philology*, 80 (1983), 27–99. This essay investigates the qualities of Harington's translation at large.

12. It has been noted that John Eliot's French-language manuals contained some quotations from Rabelais. For Rabelais's impact in England, including remarks on Shakespearean connections, see Anne Lake Prescott, *Imagining Rabelais in Renaissance England* (New Haven, 1998).

13. Most of the evidence on this point is rehearsed by Clifford Leech in his Arden (series 2) edition of *The Two Gentlemen of Verona* (London, 1969).

14. Treatments of Yong/Montemayor's presence in these plays include *The Two Gentlemen of Verona*, ed. Leech, and similarly Harold F. Brooks's Arden

edition of *A Midsummer Night's Dream* (London, 1979). In the case of *As You Like It* the relationship may run through Lodge's *Rosalynde*.

15. *A Critical Edition of Yong's Translation of George of Montemayor's Diana and Gil Polo's Enamoured Diana*, ed. Judith M. Kennedy (Oxford, 1968), p. lii.

16. Geoffrey Bullough puts this somewhat more reservedly or prosaically: 'Montemayor's *Diana* became [Shakespeare's] text-book of amorous entanglements and sentiment': Geoffrey Bullough, ed., *Narrative and Dramatic Sources of Shakespeare*, 8 vols (London, 1957–75), vol. 1, p. 211.

17. Mario Praz, 'Ariosto in England', in *The Flaming Heart: Essays* (New York, 1958), pp. 287–307 (p. 305); the following quotation is from p. 301.

18. Barbara Reynolds, introduction to her translation, *Orlando Furioso*, 2 vols (Harmondsworth, 1975), vol. 1, p. 25.

19. It is usually accepted that Shakespeare knew both these versions of the story directly (whether in the Italian or in the translations of Harington and/or Belleforest), but the principal point here would be unaffected even if he did not, because all the non-dramatic handlings available derived either from Bandello or Ariosto. These primary sources and others are assembled in Bullough, ed., *Narrative and Dramatic Sources*, vol. 2.

20. *Much Ado about Nothing*, ed. A.R. Humphreys (London, 1981), p. 13. Humphreys's detailed analysis of the elements taken respectively from Ariosto and Bandello appears on pp. 6–13.

21. A helpful recent account of the work of the *novellieri* for students of English literature is Robin Kirkpatrick, *English and Italian Literature from Dante to Shakespeare* (London, 1995), pp. 229–39.

22. Rodax, *The Real and the Ideal in the Novella*, p. 83.

23. Kirkpatrick, *English and Italian Literature*, p. 284. Leo Salingar, *Shakespeare and the Traditions of Comedy* (Cambridge, 1974), pp. 302–3, also has a discussion of these points, with general consideration of Shakespeare's debt to the novella, pp. 303–4.

24. Three differently oriented scholarly treatments of this area are Robert K. Presson, *Shakespeare's 'Troilus and Cressida' and the Legends of Troy* (Madison, Wis., 1953); W.B. Drayton Henderson, 'Shakespeare's *Troilus and Cressida*: yet deeper in its tradition', in Hardin Craig, ed., *Essays in Dramatic Literature: The Parrot Presentation Volume* (1935; repr. New York, 1967), pp. 127–56; and more recently Heather James, *Shakespeare's Troy: Drama, Politics, and the Translation of Empire* (Cambridge 1997).

25. The editor quoted is J.M. Nosworthy, *Measure for Measure* (Harmondsworth, 1969), p. 16.

26. It is necessary to add that Shakespeare would have known the tale in Painter's accurate *Palace of Pleasure* rendering, perhaps in Boccaccio's original Italian, and just possibly in Antoine Le Maçon's attractive French

version. On the last possibility, see Herbert G. Wright, *Boccaccio in England from Chaucer to Tennyson* (London, 1957).

27. Leah Scragg, *Shakespeare's Alternative Tales* (London, 1996), p. 117. Scragg's is the fullest recent account of the play's relation to the novel story.

28. For a summary of the connections and further bibliography, see Gillespie, *Shakespeare's Books*, pp. 407–10.

29. For a recent fuller treatment of Silvayn and Shakespeare, see Neil Rhodes, 'The controversial plot: declamation and the concept of the "problem play"', *Modern Language Review*, 95 (2001), 609–22.

30. Alice Harmon, 'How great was Shakespeare's debt to Montaigne?', *Publications of the Modern Language Association of America*, 57 (1942), 988–1008, rightly points out that a large number of local correspondences between their work could be attributed to their common use of some of the many collections of (mainly classical) precepts and *loci communes* – neither Shakespeare nor the humanists need have read Seneca, Cicero or Plutarch in 'primary' form but only in digests.

31. A recent discussion of the relationship, outlining a case for the *Institutio* as a source for quite specific aspects of the play, is Marcella Quadri, 'Erasmus' prince and Shakespeare's king: the case of *Henry V*', in Claudia Corti, ed., *Silenos: Erasmus in Elizabethan Literature* (Pisa, 1998), pp. 67–85.

32. A general study of Shakespeare and the *Moriae Encomium* is Walter Kaiser, *Praisers of Folly: Erasmus, Rabelais, Shakespeare* (London, 1964). For *Lear*, see recently Claudia Corti, 'Erasmus' folly and Shakespeare's fools', in *Silenos*, pp. 13–40. A detailed, though not entirely persuasive, treatment of *Hamlet* in this connection, with a few suggested echoes of Chaloner, is Frank McCombie, '*Hamlet* and the *Moriae Encomium*', *Shakespeare Survey*, 27 (1974), 59–69.

33. This is to say nothing of his modes of expression; for suggestions about the influence of Erasmus's *De Copia* on Shakespeare's way of writing in general, see Marion Trousdale, *Shakespeare and the Rhetoricians* (London, 1982).

34. Although verbal parallels do not support the connection, John X. Evans has recently argued for some parallels of imagery in 'Erasmian folly and Shakespeare's *King Lear*: a study in humanist intertextuality', *Moreana: Bulletin Thomas More*, 103 (series 27) (1990), 3–23.

35. Emrys Jones, *The Origins of Shakespeare* (Oxford, 1977), pp. 10, 13.

36. *Proverbs or Adages by Desiderius Erasmus ... Englished (1569) by Richard Taverner*, ed. DeWitt T. Starnes (Delmar, NY, 1956), fo. 23^{r-v}.

37. The Erasmian passage is at 1.408 of the *Adagia* (Basle, 1574). For this Shakespeare–Horace connection via the *Adages*, see T.W. Baldwin, *On the Literary Genetics of Shakspere's Poems and Sonnets* (Urbana, Ill., 1950),

pp. 134–6, and, for further refinements, Kenneth Muir, 'Shakespeare and Erasmus', *Notes and Queries*, 201 (1956), 424–5. A recent treatment of the *Adagia* and Shakespeare, with many further references, is Rita Severi, 'Tracks. The Erasmian legacy and Shakespeare: examples from the *Enchiridion* and the *Adagia*', in Corti, ed., *Silenos*, pp. 87–113.

38. My translation, from *Machiavelli and his Friends: Their Personal Correspondence*, ed. James B. Atkinson and David Sices (DeKalb, Ill., 1996), B1111: 'entro nelle antique corti degli antiqui huomini, dove . . . mi pasco di quel cibo, che solum è mio, a ch'io nacqui per lui'.

39. John Roe, *Shakespeare and Machiavelli* (Cambridge, 2002), p. xiii.

40. For the possible effect of Gentillet's work on English drama involving Machiavellian reference, see Roe, *Shakespeare and Machiavelli*, pp. 6ff.

41. The classic study of the 'Machiavel' at large is Mario Praz, *Machiavelli and the Elizabethans* (London, 1928), repr. in Praz, *The Flaming Heart*.

42. *The Prince*, trans. Robert M. Adams (New York, 1992), pp. 42–3.

43. For a treatment of Bolingbroke in this connection, see Irving Ribner, 'Bolingbroke: a true Machiavellian', *Modern Language Quarterly*, 9 (1948), 177–84.

44. Barbara Riebling, 'Virtue's sacrifice: a Machiavellian reading of *Macbeth*', *Studies in English Literature*, 31 (1991), 273–86.

45. Perhaps the standard work of the period, now very seriously dated, is George Coffin Taylor, *Shakespeare's Debt to Montaigne* (Oxford, 1925). A presentation of all parallels reported by commentators up to the 1980s is found in William Flygare, *Montaigne-Shakspere-Studies* (Kyoto, 1983).

46. Fresh evidence on two smaller-scale passages has been presented by Eleanor Prosser, 'Shakespeare, Montaigne, and "the rarer action"', *Shakespeare Studies*, 1 (1965), 261–4, and Gail Kern Paster, 'Montaigne, Dido, and *The Tempest*: "How came that widow in?"', *Shakespeare Quarterly*, 35 (1984), 91–4.

47. Two sophisticated recent studies along these lines are Geoffrey Miles, *Shakespeare and the Constant Romans* (Oxford, 1996), on how Montaigne's presentation of certain classical ideas, especially constancy as a form of Stoicism, affected Shakespeare; and Hugh Grady, *Shakespeare, Machiavelli, and Montaigne: Power and Subjectivity from 'Richard II' to 'Hamlet'* (Oxford, 2002), concentrating on Montaigne's presentation of subjectivity. One more specific area that may merit further investigation is *King Lear*. Kenneth Muir thought Montaigne's influence on the play 'substantial': Muir, *The Sources of Shakespeare's Plays* (London, 1977), p. 239.

48. Michel de Montaigne, *The Essayes or Morall, Politike and Millitarie Discourses . . . done into English by . . . John Florio* (London, 1603), p. 102. Though it was not published until 1603, it is often accepted that Florio's translation would have

been available to Shakespeare for some years before this date through manuscript copies known to have been in circulation.

49. My understanding of this point as concerns both *The Tempest* and other Shakespearean *loci* is indebted to Fred Parker, 'Shakespeare's argument with Montaigne', *Cambridge Quarterly*, 28 (1999), 1–18. For earlier observations on the gaps between Shakespeare and Montaigne in the Gonzalo passage, with the suggestion that they may reflect Shakespeare's use of a further range of sources, see Margaret Hodgen, 'Montaigne and Shakespeare again', *Huntington Library Quarterly*, 16 (1952), 23–42 (esp. 39–42).

50. Parker, 'Shakespeare's argument', pp. 4–5.

51. Parker, 'Shakespeare's argument', p. 12.

52. For these echoes, see Madeleine Doran, *Endeavors of Art: A Study of Form in Elizabethan Drama* (Madison, Wis., 1954), pp. 387–9, and Shaheen, 'Shakespeare's knowledge of Italian', pp. 167–9. It is possible they are accidental, and Shakespeare did not know Cinthio's acting text at all.

53. For a summary account, see Gillespie, *Shakespeare's Books*, pp. 181–4.

4: SHAKESPEARE AND ITALIAN COMEDY

1. 'Italian stories on the stage' is the title of Louise George Clubb's contribution to Alexander Leggatt, ed., *The Cambridge Companion to Shakespearean Comedy* (Cambridge, 2002), pp. 32–46.

2. Leo Salingar, *Shakespeare and the Traditions of Comedy* (Cambridge, 1974), p. 188; ch. 5, 'Shakespeare and Italian comedy', is still an essential contribution to the topic.

3. Ariosto's *La cassaria* and *I suppositi* were printed (admittedly without the author's permission) *c.* 1510, not long after their first performances. In 1521, the publication of Bibbiena's *Calandra* (perf. 1513) and Machiavelli's *Mandragola* (perf. *c.* 1518) clearly indicated the new status which drama was acquiring. The first retrospective anthology of Italian playtexts (by the Florentine Giovan Maria Cecchi) appeared in 1550.

4. For a detailed account of the rise and development of Italian comedy, see Richard Andrews, *Scripts and Scenarios: The Performance of Comedy in Renaissance Italy* (Cambridge, 1993). See also Richard Andrews, 'Cinquecento theatre', in C.P. Brand and L. Pertile, eds, *The Cambridge History of Italian Literature* (Cambridge, 1996), pp. 277–98.

5. This was the year of the production of Giraldi's 'satyr play' *Egle*. In the event many of *Egle*'s characteristics were not followed up, and the 'regular' pastoral genre was launched more recognizably, still in Ferrara, by Beccari's *Il sacrificio* of 1554–5. See Andrews, 'Cinquecento theatre', pp. 292–8.

6. For a detailed account of how Italian discussions of pastoral tragicomedy affected Shakespeare and English drama, see Robert Henke, *Pastoral Transformations: Italian Tragicomedy and Shakespeare's Late Plays* (Newark, NJ, 1997).

7. Anglophone readers should not allow themselves to form a view of the phenomenon without first reading two essays in particular: Louise George Clubb, 'The law of writ and the liberty: Italian professional theater', which is the epilogue to her *Italian Drama in Shakespeare's Time* (New Haven and London, 1989), pp. 249–80; and Michael Anderson, 'The law of writ and the liberty', *Theatre Research International*, 20, 3 (1995), pp. 189–99. See also Robert Henke, *Performance and Literature in the Commedia dell'Arte* (Cambridge, 2002); Kenneth and Laura Richards, *The Commedia dell'Arte: A Documentary History* (Oxford, 1990).

8. Shakespeare, *The Tempest*, ed. Frank Kermode (London and New York, 1954; repr. 1980), introduction, p. lxviii.

9. For some overdue exploration of this point, see Tim Fitzpatrick, *The Relationship of Oral and Literate Performance Processes in the Commedia dell'Arte: Beyond the Improvisation/Memorisation Divide* (Lewiston, Queenstown and Lampeter, 1995); Henke, *Performance and Literature*.

10. For an account of all these tendencies, see Clubb, *Italian Drama, passim.*

11. Frances Barasch surveys the careers of Italian actresses contemporary with Shakespeare in 'Italian actresses in Shakespeare's world: Flaminia and Vincenza', *Shakespeare Bulletin*, 18, 4 (2000), 17–21, and 'Italian actresses in Shakespeare's world: Vittoria and Isabella', *Shakespeare Bulletin*, 19, 3 (2001), 5–9. Pamela Allen Brown investigates whether negative images of the actress/whore are actually reflected in Shakespeare's texts, in 'The Counterfeit *Innamorata*, or, The Diva Vanishes', *Shakespeare Yearbook*, 10 (1999), 402–26.

12. Clubb, *Italian Drama*, p. 256.

13. The concept is explained in Clubb, *Italian Drama*, Prologue, pp. 1–26.

14. Translated from the dedicatory letter in Alessandro Piccolomini, *La sfera del mondo* (Venice, 1561); the original is quoted in Daniele Seragnoli, *Il teatro a Siena nel Cinquecento* (Rome, 1980), p. 99. For a longer translated extract, see Andrews, *Scripts and Scenarios*, pp. 105–6.

15. This has been fully noted by Salingar, *Shakespeare and the Traditions*, pp. 190 and 228–38, though it is less often recognized by individual editions and studies of the play.

16. *Tempest*, ed. Kermode, pp. lxvi–lxx.

17. Ferdinando Neri, *Scenari delle Maschere in Arcadia* (Città di Castello, 1913); Kathleen Lea, *Italian Popular Comedy* (Oxford, 1934), vol. 1, pp. 201–3, and vol. 2, pp. 444 and 509.

18. I have examined the phenomenon of the 'elastic gag' in Andrews, 'Scripted theatre and the *commedia dell'arte*', in J.R. Mulryne and M. Shewring, eds, *Theatre of the English and Italian Renaissance* (Basingstoke, 1991), pp. 21–54; and in Andrews, *Scripts and Scenarios*, pp. 175–85.

19. For more on this sequence, see Andrews, 'Shakespeare, Molière et la commedia dell'arte', in Irène Mamczarcz, ed., *La Commedia dell'arte, le théâtre forain, et les spectacles de plein air en Europe, XVIe–XVIIIe siècles* (Paris, 1998), pp. 15–27.

20. This body of material, already recognized in 1934 as relevant by Lea, *Italian Popular Comedy,* vol. 2, pp. 464–71, has been arbitrarily designated '*commedia ridicolosa*' by Italian critics. For an account of these plays, with some full texts, see Luciano Mariti, *Commedia ridicolosa . . ., storia e testi* (Rome, 1978).

21. See Andrews, '*Arte* dialogue structures in the comedies of Molière', in C. Cairns, ed., *The Commedia dell'Arte from the Renaissance to Dario Fo* (Lampeter and Newiston, NY, 1985), pp. 141–76; and Andrews, 'Shakespeare, Molière'.

22. Clubb, *Italian Drama*, draws attention more than once to these tragic subversions of comic formulae: for example, on pp. 9–12, 18, 23–5.

23. The subject is fully explored by Louise George Clubb in her joint edition with Robert Black of the early play *Parthenio* (1520): see their *Romance and Aretine Humanism in Sienese Comedy* (Florence and Siena, 1993).

24. '1531, Sienese style', in that their years started and ended in March; this explains the date often given in older editions and studies.

25. See Richard Andrews, 'Anti-feminism in *commedia erudita*', in J. Clare and R. Eriksen, eds, *Contexts of Renaissance Comedy* (Oslo, 1997), pp. 11–31.

26. For a full analysis of the contrast between these two plays, see Salingar, *Shakespeare and the Traditions*, pp. 211–18 and 239–42. See also Robert C. Melzi, 'From Lelia to Viola', *Renaissance Drama*, 9 (1966), 67–81.

27. See Clubb, *Italian Drama*, pp. 55–63, and the whole of her ch. 3, 'Woman as wonder', pp. 65–89.

28. See, for example, Guido Ruggiero, *The Boundaries of Eros: Sex Crime and Sexuality in Renaissance Venice* (Oxford, 1985).

29. Although the Pedant in Italian written comedy and the Dottore in the *commedia dell'arte* are obviously related, it is possible to make some distinction between them. The Dottor Graziano mask spoke Bolognese dialect, and quickly settled into a pattern of speaking reams of nonsense based on distorted malapropisms. Pedants were more obviously pedantic, and larded their speeches with Latin. Both of them were inclined to be long-winded, and to find endless lists of synonyms for simple words.

30. G.P. Krapp in 1916, as quoted by G.K. Hunter in his Arden Shakespeare edition of *All's Well* (London, 1959), p. xlvii. The parasite figure, borrowed

from Roman comedy, was very common in the earliest Italian plays that based themselves on classical models, though he fades out later in the century.

31. The omission of the name Arlecchino here is deliberate. Harlequin was a French demon figure, imported into Italian *commedia dell'arte* by the aggressive genius of a single actor, Tristano Martinelli (1557–1630). By the eighteenth century, the mask had been 'naturalized' in Italian theatre as an equivalent of the Bergamask peasant Zani, speaking the same dialect; but this process took longer than some historians have acknowledged. Harlequin's dominance in European images of 'Italian comedy' was really forged by a succession of performers in the Comédie Italienne in Paris between about 1650 and 1750.

32. This lineage seems obvious to Italianists, but it has only been fully identified by Henke, in *Pastoral Transformations*, ch. 5, pp. 107–19.

33. Both these one-act entertainments are edited by Giorgio Padoan in Ruzante, *I dialoghi ... etc.* (Padua, 1981). For Ruzante in general, see Ronnie Ferguson, *The Theatre of Angelo Beolco (Ruzante): Text, Context and Performance* (Ravenna, 2000).

34. Martin Banham, '*The Merchant of Venice* and the implicit stage direction', *Critical Survey*, 3, 3 (1991), 269–74. The specific gag of a character failing (or pretending to fail) to find someone whom the audience can plainly see can in fact be found in some Italian scripts: cf. Andrews, 'Shakespeare, Molière', p. 18.

35. See *Measure for Measure*, ed. J.W. Lever (London, 1965), pp. xx–xxii.

36. This was the view, among others, of H.D. Gray, as outlined and discussed in Kermode's introduction to *Tempest*, pp. xx–xxi.

37. This was shown by more than one contributor to a conference on 'Harlequin versus Hamlet' at the University of Westminster, London, December 2002. The proceedings will eventually be published by Edwin Mellen Press.

38. Anthony Sher, *The Year of the King* (London, 1985), p. 46.

5: CONTEMPORARY EUROPE IN ELIZABETHAN AND EARLY STUART DRAMA

1. A.J. Hoenselaars, *Images of Englishmen and Foreigners in the Drama of Shakespeare and His Contemporaries: A Study of Stage Characters and National Identity in English Renaissance Drama, 1558–1642* (London and Toronto, 1992), p. 154.

2. *Henslowe's Diary*, ed. R.A. Foakes and R.T. Rickert (Cambridge, 1964), pp. 98–103.

3. Ivo Kamps, *Historiography and Ideology in Stuart Drama* (Cambridge, 1996), p. 145.

4. J.R. Mulryne, 'Transformations: European history in the plays of Shakespeare's contemporaries', in M.T. Jones-Davies, ed., *L'Histoire au temps de la Renaissance* (Paris, 1995), pp. 59–70, at pp. 59–60; Hoenselaars, 'Shakespeare and the early modern history play', in Michael Hattaway, ed., *The Cambridge Companion to Shakespeare's History Plays* (Cambridge, 2002), pp. 25–40, at p. 32.

5. Alfred Harbage, *Annals of English Drama 975–1700*, rev. S. Schoenbaum, 3rd edn, rev. Sylvia Stoler Wagonheim (London and New York, 1989), pp. 146ff. *The Rebellion of Naples, or The Tragedy of Massenello. Commonly so called: But Rightly Tomaso Aniello di Malfa Generall of the Neopolitans. Written by a Gentleman who was an eye-witnes where this was really Acted upon that bloudy Stage, the streets of Naples. Anno Domini MDCXLVII* (London, 1649) drew a parallel between the upstart Neapolitan fisherman and Oliver Cromwell. On late seventeenth-century dramatizations of history, see Paulina Kewes, 'Otway, Lee and the Restoration history play', in Susan J. Owen, ed., *A Companion to Restoration Drama* (Oxford, 2001), pp. 355–77.

6. Rowland White to Sir Robert Sidney, 26 October 1599, *Sydney Papers: Consisting of a Journal of the Earl of Leicester, and Original Letters of Algernon Sydney*, ed. R.W. Blencowe (London, 1825), vol. 2, p. 136, cited in E.K. Chambers, *The Elizabethan Stage*, 4 vols (Oxford, 1923; repr. 1945), vol. 1, p. 322, n. 2. I have silently modernized the usage of 'i/j' and 'u/v' in this and subsequent quotations.

7. *Proceedings in the Parliaments of Elizabeth I*, ed. T.E. Hartley, 3 vols (London and New York, 1981–95), vol. 1, p. 37.

8. *The Passage of our most drad Soveraigne Lady Quene ELYZABETH through the Citie of LONDON to WESTMINSTER, the daye before her Coronation, Anno 1558–9*, in John Nichols, ed., *The Progresses and Public Processions of Queen Elizabeth*, 3 vols (London, 1823), vol. 1, pp. 42, 53, 58. On Elizabethan foreign policy, see Simon L. Adams, 'Britain, Europe, and the world', in Patrick Collinson, ed., *The Sixteenth Century, 1485–1603* (Oxford, 2002), pp. 189–215; Susan Doran, *England and Europe, 1485–1603* (London and New York, 1986; 2nd edn 1996).

9. *The Magnificent Entertainment: Given to King James, Queene Anne his Wife, and Henry Frederick the Prince, upon the Day of His Majesties Tryumphant Passage (from the Tower) through His Honourable Citie (and Chamber) of London, being the 15. of March. 1603. As well by the English as by the Strangers: With the speeches and Songes, delivered in the Severall Pageants*, in John Nichols, ed., *The Progresses, Processions, and Magnificent Festivities of King James the First*, 4 vols (London, 1828), vol. 1, p. 344.

10. Graham Parry, 'The iconography of James I', in *The Golden Age Restor'd: The Culture of the Stuart Court, 1603–42* (Manchester, 1981), pp. 1–39, and 'Ancient Britons and early Stuarts', in Robin Headlam Wells, Glenn Burgess and Rowland Wymer, eds, *Neo-Historicism: Studies in Renaissance Literature, History and Politics* (Cambridge, 2000), pp. 153–78.

11. Edward Hall, *The Union of the Two Noble and Illustre Famelies of Lancastre & Yorke*, 2nd edn (London, 1550), sig. A1^r.

12. Judith Doolin Spikes, 'The Jacobean history play and the myth of the elect nation', *Renaissance Drama*, n.s., 8 (1977), 117–49.

13. John Foxe, *Acts and Monuments of Matters Most Most Speciall and Memorable, hapening in the Church, with an Universall Historie of the Same*, 7th edn, 3 vols (London, 1632), sig. 3B3^r. Two editions in Latin preceded the English one of 1563. See Tom Betteridge, *Tudor Histories of the English Reformations, 1530–83* (Aldershot, 1999), p. 175, n. 39.

14. Betteridge, *Tudor Histories*, p. 211.

15. Sir Walter Ralegh, *The History of the World* (London, 1614), sig. C2^r. On Ralegh's conception of the past, see Daniel R. Woolf, *The Idea of History in Early Stuart England: Erudition, Ideology, and 'The Light of Truth' from the Accession of James I to the Civil War* (Toronto, 1990), pp. 45–55.

16. John Chamberlain's letter to Dudley Carleton of 22 December 1614, cited in Cyndia Susan Clegg, *Press Censorship in Jacobean England* (Cambridge, 2001), p. 96. For the circumstances of the book's suppression, see pp. 96–102.

17. Hayward's claim was in part self-serving: it appeared in the dedication to Prince Charles of an English history that he had undertaken at the behest of Prince Henry (*The Lives of the III. Normans, Kings of England: William the First. William the Second. Henrie the First* (London, 1613), sig. A4^r).

18. Thomas Nashe, *Pierce Penilesse His Supplication to the Divell* (1592), in *The Works of Thomas Nashe*, ed. R.B. McKerrow, rev. F.P. Wilson, 5 vols (London, 1904; repr. Oxford, 1958), vol. 1, pp. 212–13; Thomas Heywood, *An Apology for Actors* (London, 1612), sig. F3^v.

19. Cyndia Susan Clegg, *Press Censorship in Elizabethan England* (Cambridge, 1997), pp. 138–69; Woolf, *The Idea of History*, p. 123.

20. Joseph Frank, *The Beginnings of the English Newspaper* (Cambridge, Mass., 1961).

21. Adam Fox, *Oral and Literate Culture in England, 1500–1700* (Oxford, 2000), esp. ch. 7, 'Rumour and news', pp. 335–405.

22. Frank, *Beginnings of the English Newspaper*; F.J. Levy, 'Staging the news', in Arthur F. Marotti and Michael D. Bristol, eds, *Print, Manuscript, and Performance: The Changing Relations of the Media in Early Modern England* (Columbus, 2000), pp. 252–78.

23. Markku Peltonen, *Classical Humanism and Republicanism in English Political Thought, 1570–1640* (Cambridge, 1995), pp. 102ff.; Daniel R. Woolf, *Reading History in Early Modern England* (Cambridge, 2000).

24. See Michael G. Brennan's chapter 2 in this volume, pp. 53–97.

25. *Tudor Royal Proclamations*, ed. Paul L. Hughes and James F. Larkin, 3 vols (New Haven and London, 1964–9), vol. 1, pp. xxi–xliii. See esp. the proclamation of 27 September 1579, ordering suppression of John Stubbes's *The Discoverie of a Gaping Gulf*, a book that attacked the queen's projected Anjou match (vol. 2, pp. 445–9); the proclamation of 14 April 1591, 'Prohibiting traffic with rebels of French King' (vol. 3, pp. 77–9); and the proclamation of 16 September 1591, 'Prohibiting trade with Spain' (vol. 3, pp. 83–6).

26. Roslyn L. Knutson, 'Elizabethan documents, captivity narratives, and the market for foreign history plays', *English Literary Renaissance*, 26 (1996), 75–110. See also G.A. Starr, 'Escape from Barbary: a seventeenth-century genre', *Huntington Library Quarterly*, 29 (1965–6), 35–52; Nabil I. Matar, 'The renegade in English seventeenth-century imagination', *Studies in English Literature*, 33 (1993), 489–505; Matar, 'Turning Turk: conversion to Islam in English Renaissance thought', *Durham University Journal*, 86 (1994), 33–41; Matar, introduction to Daniel J. Vitkus, ed., *Piracy, Slavery, and Redemption: Barbary Captivity Narratives from Early Modern England* (New York, 2001); Daniel J. Vitkus, 'Turning Turk in *Othello*: the conversion and damnation of the Moor', *Shakespeare Quarterly*, 48 (1997), 145–76.

27. Levy, 'Staging the news', p. 258.

28. T.H. Howard-Hill, 'Buc and the censorship of *Sir John Van Olden Barnavelt* in 1619', *Review of English Studies*, n.s., 39 (1988), 39–63, and '"Crane's promptbook" of *Barnavelt* and theatrical processes', *Modern Philology*, 86 (1988–9), 146–70.

29. Cited in *Ben Jonson*, ed. C.H. Herford and Percy and Evelyn Simpson, 11 vols (Oxford, 1925–52), vol. 10, p. 256; Thomas Heywood and Richard Brome, *The Late Lancashire Witches*, ed. Laird H. Barber (New York and London, 1979), p. 137.

30. P.H. Kocher, 'Contemporary pamphlet background for Marlowe's *The Massacre at Paris*', *Modern Language Quarterly*, 8 (1947), 151–73, 309–18; Julia Briggs, 'Marlowe's *Massacre at Paris*: a reconsideration', *Review of English Studies*, 34 (1983), 257–78.

31. The proclamation of 16 May 1559, printed in Chambers, *Elizabethan Stage*, vol. 4, pp. 263–4, at p. 263. For discussion, see Richard Dutton, *Mastering the Revels: The Regulation and Censorship of English Renaissance Drama* (Iowa City, 1991).

32. Sir Ralph Winwood to Sir William Cecil, 7 July 1602, in Winwood, *Memorials of Affairs of State in the Reigns of Elizabeth and James*, 1.425, cited in Chambers, *Elizabethan Stage*, vol. 1, p. 323, n. 1. We do not know how Winwood countered further criticism that 'the Massacre of St Bartholomews hath ben publickly acted, and this King [Henri IV] represented upon the stage'.

33. De la Boderie to the Marquis de Sillery, 8 April 1608, cited in Dutton, *Mastering the Revels*, p. 183. For the transcript of the original letter, see Chambers, *Elizabethan Stage*, vol. 3, pp. 257–8.

34. Wentworth Smith, *The Hector of Germany; or, The Palsgrave, Prime Elector* (London, 1615), sig. A2ᵛ.

35. Hans Werner, '*The Hector of Germanie, or The Palsgrave, Prime Elector* and Anglo-German relations of early Stuart England: the view from the popular stage', in R. Malcolm Smuts, ed., *The Stuart Court and Europe: Essays in Politics and Political Culture* (Cambridge, 1996), pp. 113–32.

36. Sir Edward Conway to the Privy Council, 12 August 1624, cited in Chambers, *Elizabethan Stage*, vol. 1, p. 327.

37. *Lords Journals*, 3.282–3, cited in Thomas Cogswell, 'The politics of propaganda: Charles I and the people in the 1620s', *Journal of British Studies*, 29 (1990), 187–215, at p. 192. See also Thomas Cogswell, *The Blessed Revolution: English Politics and the Coming of War, 1621–1624* (Cambridge, 1989), ch. 5.

38. Sir George Buc, *Sir John van Olden Barnavelt* (Oxford, 1979 [1980]), p. 13.

39. Richard Dutton, *Licensing, Censorship and Authorship in Early Modern England* (Basingstoke, 2000), pp. 132–61.

40. The licence is printed in *The Control and Censorship of Caroline Drama: The Records of Sir Henry Herbert, Master of the Revels 1623–73*, ed. N.W. Bawcutt (Oxford, 1996), p. 205.

41. Letter from the Privy Council to Sir George Buc, Master of the Revels, cited in G.E. Bentley, *The Jacobean and Caroline Stage*, 7 vols (Oxford, 1941–68), vol. 5, p. 1371.

42. John Webster, *Monuments of Honor* (1624), in *The Complete Works of John Webster*, ed. F.L. Lucas, 4 vols (London, 1927; repr. New York, 1966), vol. 3, ll. 95–8.

43. Denys Hay, *Europe: The Emergence of an Idea* (Edinburgh, 1957, repr. 1968); John Hale, *The Civilization of Europe in the Renaissance* (New York, 1994).

44. Foxe, *Acts and Monuments*, vol. 1, p. 989.

45. This claim was made on the title-page woodcut of John Dee's *General and Rare Memorials Pertayning to the Perfect Arte of Navigation* (London, 1577), which showed Elizabeth at the helm of the ship labelled Europa (reproduced on the cover of the present volume). See Frances A. Yates, *Astraea: The Imperial Theme in the Sixteenth Century* (London, 1975; repr. 1993),

pp. 49–50; Lesley B. Cormack, 'Britannia rules the waves?: images of empire in Elizabethan England', in Andrew Gordon and Bernhard Klein, eds, *Literature, Mapping, and the Politics of Space in Early Modern Britain* (Cambridge, 2001), pp. 45–68, at pp. 47–51.

46. Franklin L. Baumer, 'England, the Turk, and the common corps of Christendom', *American Historical Review*, 50 (1944), 26–48; William Brown Patterson, *King James VI and I and the Reunion of Christendom* (Cambridge, 1997).

47. Hay, *Europe*, p. 107; Nicholas Canny, ed., *The Origins of Empire: British Overseas Enterprise to the Close of the Seventeenth Century*, vol. 1 of *The Oxford History of the British Empire* (Oxford, 1998); David Armitage, *The Ideological Origins of the British Empire* (Cambridge, 2000).

48. On the cartographic origins of this allegorical conceit, see Hay, *Europe*, pp. 104ff.

49. Thomas Campion, *The Description of a Maske . . . At the Mariage of . . . the Earle of Somerset . . . and the Lady Frances Howard* (1614), in *Campion's Works*, ed. Percival Vivian (Oxford, 1909), p. 152. Cf. the presentation of Europe, Asia and Africa in 'The Masque of Truth' (1613). A contemporary description of this lost and unperformed masque is reproduced in David Norbrook, '"The Masque of Truth": court entertainments and international Protestant politics in the early Stuart period', *The Seventeenth Century*, 1 (1986), 81–110, at pp. 101–5.

50. John Squire, *Tes Irenes Trophoea; or, The Tryumphs of Peace* (London, 1620), sig. A3^v.

51. David Bergeron, *English Civic Pageantry, 1558–1642* (London, 1971), pp. 123–241; Lawrence Manley, *Literature and Culture in Early Modern London* (Cambridge, 1995), pp. 212–93; James Knowles, 'The spectacle of the realm: civic consciousness, rhetoric and ritual in early modern London', in J.R. Mulryne and Margaret Shewring, eds, *Theatre and Government* (Cambridge, 1993), pp. 157–89.

52. Arthur H. Williamson, 'Scots, Indians and empire: the Scottish politics of civilization, 1519–1609', *Past and Present*, 150 (1996), 46–83, esp. pp. 47–56; Nicholas P. Canny, 'The ideology of English colonization: from Ireland to America', in David Armitage, ed., *Theories of Empire, 1450–1800* (Aldershot, 1998), pp. 179–202.

53. Tristan Marshall, *Theatre and Empire: Great Britain on the London Stages under James VI and I* (Manchester, 2000); Jodi Mikalachki, *The Legacy of Boadicea: Gender and Nation in Early Modern England* (London, 1998).

54. Cf. Richard Eden's translation of Peter Martyr's *The Decades of the Newe Worlde or West India* (London, 1555), which was published under Philip and Mary: 'the Spaniardes as the ministers of grace and libertie, browght unto

these newe gentyles the victorie of Chrystes death wherby they beinge subdued with the worldely sworde, are nowe made free from the bondage of Sathans tyrannie' (sig. aii^v).

55. Thomas Middleton, *The Triumphs of Truth* (1613), in *The Works of Thomas Middleton*, ed. A.H. Bullen, 8 vols (New York, 1964), vol. 7, p. 248.

56. For a jocular list of such sartorial attributes, see a song in Thomas Heywood's Roman tragedy, *The Rape of Lucrece* (London, 1608): 'The *Spaniard* loves his ancient slop; / The *Lumbard*, his Venetian, / And some, like breech-lesse women goe: / The *Russe, Turke, Jew*, and *Grecian* ... The *Turke* in Linnen wraps his head, / The *Persean* his in Lawne too, / The *Russe* with sables furres his Cap, / And change, will not be drawne too' (sig. F4^{r–v}). On the costuming of foreigners, see Jean MacIntyre and Garrett P.J. Epp, '"Cloathes worth all the rest": costumes and properties', in David Scott Kastan and John D. Cox, eds, *A New History of Early English Drama* (New York, 1997), pp. 269–85, at p. 278.

57. Thomas Middleton, *The Triumphs of Honour and Industry* (1617), in *Works*, vol. 7, pp. 299, 301–2, 300.

58. *CSP Venetian*, vol. XV, p. 62. Earlier in his report Busino describes another anti-Spanish incident he witnessed on that day (p. 61).

59. R. Malcolm Smuts, 'Public ceremony and royal charisma: the English royal entry in London, 1485–1642', in Lee Beier, David Cannadine and James Rosenheim, eds, *The First Modern Society: Essays in English History in Honour of Lawrence Stone* (Cambridge, 1989), pp. 65–93, at p. 75.

60. Nancy E. Wright, '"Rival traditions": civic and courtly ceremonies in Jacobean London', in David Bevington and Peter Houlbrook, eds, *The Politics of the Stuart Court Masque* (Cambridge, 1998), pp. 197–217.

61. Norbrook, '"The Masque of Truth"'.

62. *Londini Status Pacatus; or, Londons Peaceable Estate* (1639), in Thomas Heywood, *Pageants: A Critical Edition*, ed. David M. Bergeron (New York and London, 1986), ll. 424–5, 507–12, 459–61; Hans Werner, 'The Lamentations of Germany*: a probable source for Heywood's *Londini Status*', *Notes and Queries*, 41 (1994), 524–9.

63. *The True Chronicle Historie of the Whole Life and Death of Thomas Lord Cromwell* (c. 1599–1602), in *The Shakespeare Apocrypha, Being a Collection of Fourteen Plays which have been Ascribed to Shakespeare*, ed. C.F. Tucker Brooke (Oxford, 1908), 3.3.78–85.

64. The range of foreign nationalities and locations can be traced through Thomas L. Berger, William C. Bradford and Sidney L. Sondergard, eds, *An Index of Characters in Early Modern English Drama: Printed Plays, 1500–1660*, rev. edn (Cambridge, 1998), and Edward H. Sugden, *A Topographical Dictionary to the Works of Shakespeare and his Fellow Dramatists* (Manchester, 1925).

65. Thomas Kyd, *The Spanish Tragedy*, ed. David Bevington (Manchester, 1996), p. 2. See also J.R. Mulryne, 'Nationality and language in Thomas Kyd's "The Spanish Tragedy"', in Jean-Pierre Maquerlot and Michèle Willems, eds, *Travel and Drama in Shakespeare's Time* (Cambridge, 1996), pp. 87–105.

66. Raphael Holinshed, *Chronicles of England, Scotland and Ireland*, 6 vols (London, 1807), vol. 1, p. 253.

67. Thomas Nashe, *Pierce Penilesse*, in *Works*, ed. McKerrow, vol. 1, p. 186.

68. Albert H. Tricomi, *Anti-Court Drama in England, 1603–1642* (Charlottesville, Va, 1989), pp. 95–130. See also Ann Rosalind Jones, 'Italians and others: *The White Devil* (1612)', in David Scott Kastan and Peter Stallybrass, eds, *Staging the Renaissance: Reinterpretations of Elizabethan and Jacobean Drama* (New York and London, 1991), pp. 251–62.

69. Barnabe Barnes, *The Devil's Charter*, ed. Jim C. Pogue (New York and London, 1980), ll. 3575–7.

70. Barnes, *Devil's Charter*, l. 3606. For the play's sources, see Barnes, *Devil's Charter*, introduction, pp. 6–22.

71. Thomas Dekker, *The Whore of Babylon*, ed. Marianne Gateson Riely (New York and London, 1980), p. 106, ll. 5–7; p. 96; pp. 131–3; p. 162; pp. 102–4, ll. 1–28.

72. Ben Jonson, 'To the readers', in *Ben Jonson*, vol. 4, p. 350, ll. 18–19.

73. John Marston, *The Wonder of Women; or, The Tragedie of Sophonisba*, ed. William Kemp (New York and London, 1979), p. 72.

74. On dramatizations of French history, see Richard Hillman, *Shakespeare, Marlowe and the Politics of France* (Basingstoke, 2002); Andrew M. Kirk, *The Mirror of Confusion: The Representation of French History in English Renaissance Drama* (New York, 1996). On the public perception of French crises in Renaissance England, see J.H.M. Salmon, *The French Religious Wars in English Political Thought* (Oxford, 1959); Lisa Ferraro Parmelee, *Good Newes from Fraunce: French Anti-League Propaganda in Late Elizabethan England* (Rochester, 1996); Robert M. Kingdon, *Myths about the St Bartholomew's Day Massacres 1572–1576* (Cambridge, Mass., 1988).

75. Blair Worden, 'Favourites on the English stage', in J.H. Elliott and L.W.B. Brockliss, eds, *The World of the Favourite* (New Haven and London, 1999), pp. 159–83.

76. On d'Ancre, see J.-F. Dubost, 'Between *Mignons* and principal ministers: Concini, 1610–1617', in Elliott and Brockliss, eds, *The World of the Favourite*, pp. 71–8.

77. Another play on a French theme was Thomas Dekker and John Day's *A French Tragedy of the Bellman of Paris* (1623). See Bentley, *Jacobean and Caroline Stage*, vol. 3, p. 246.

78. *A Larum for London* (Oxford, 1913), p. v.

79. Franz Bosbach, 'The European debate on universal monarchy', in Armitage, ed., *Theories of Empire*, pp. 81–98, esp. pp. 90–2.

80. Samuel Chew, *The Crescent and the Rose: Islam and England during the Renaissance* (New York, 1937), pp. 469–540. For recent reassessments, see Nabil Matar, *Turks, Moors and Englishmen in the Age of Discovery* (New York, 1999); Jonathan Burton, 'Anglo-Ottoman relations and the image of the Turk in *Tamburlaine*', *Journal of Medieval and Early Modern Studies*, 30 (2000), 125–57; Daniel Vitkus, introduction to his edition of *Three Turk Plays from Early Modern England: Selimus, Emperor of the Turks; A Christian Turned Turk; and The Renegado* (New York, 2000).

81. *The Life and Works of George Peele*, ed. Charles Tyler Prouty *et al.*, 3 vols (New Haven, 1952–70), vol. 2, ll. 49–50.

82. See Burton, 'Anglo-Ottoman relations', on attempts to find confessional commonalities between Protestantism and Islam, notably the anti-idolatrous bent of the two religions that are thus opposed to Roman Catholicism.

83. *Life and Works of George Peele*, vol. 1, ll. 20–7, 34–45, 58, 62–5.

84. Wallace T. MacCaffrey, *Elizabeth I: War and Politics 1588–1603* (Princeton, NJ, 1992), p. 248.

85. The entry in the Stationers' Register was made on 1 August 1589. See *Life and Works of George Peele*, vol. 1, p. 80.

86. Dutton, *Licensing*, pp. 132–61.

87. Bawcutt, ed., *Control and Censorship*, pp. 171–2.

88. Bawcutt, ed., *Control and Censorship*, pp. 158, 183; Dutton, *Mastering the Revels*, pp. 236–7.

89. Bawcutt, ed., *Control and Censorship*, pp. 203–4.

90. *Dick of Devonshire* (Oxford, 1955), pp. viii–ix.

91. Claire Jowitt, *Voyage Drama and Gender Politics 1589–1642: Real and Imagined Worlds* (Manchester, 2003), pp. 65ff.

92. Bentley, *Jacobean and Caroline Stage*, vol. 3, pp. 417–21, 257–60, 458–9; vol. 5, pp. 1455, 1412–13, 1410, 1411–12; Bawcutt, ed., *Control and Censorship*, pp. 138, 205, 206.

93. For a particularly revealing example, see Bawcutt's account of Herbert's censorship of Walter Mountfort's *The Launching of the Mary*, in *Control and Censorship*, pp. 52–7, at p. 56.

94. Bawcutt, ed., *Control and Censorship*, p. 135.

95. Henry Shirley, *The Martyr'd Souldier* (London, 1638), sig. B1^v.

96. Philip Massinger and Thomas Dekker, *The Virgin Martyr*, in *The Dramatic Works of Thomas Dekker*, ed. Fredson Bowers, 4 vols (Cambridge, 1953–61), 5.1.13, 19.

97. Bawcutt, ed., *Control and Censorship*, p. 135.

98. On the dispute over trade and navigation, see Armitage, *Ideological Origins*, pp. 108ff.

99. Licensed on 15 September 1624, that is, approximately two months after news of the Amboina massacre had reached London, the anonymous (and since lost) *A Tragedy called the Faire Star of Antwerp* may have reverted to the earlier model of representing Spanish–Dutch (and English–Dutch) relations. If so, it would have made Dutch ingratitude all the more glaring. See Bentley, *Jacobean and Caroline Stage*, vol. 5, pp. 1327–8.

100. Cogswell, *Blessed Revolution*, p. 274.

101. Dutch ministers resident in London alerted the Privy Council to the company's sponsorship of the play (and painting) to prevent potential anti-Dutch riots. See Bawcutt, ed., *Control and Censorship*, pp. 54–5.

102. For example, 'the unmatcht vile, miserable, torture, / Those dutch inflicted on some English men / at that Amboyna', Walter Mountfort, *The Launching of the Mary* (Oxford, 1933), ll. 118–20; Bawcutt, ed., *Control and Censorship*, pp. 53ff., 70.

103. Werner, *'The Hector of Germanie'*, p. 113. On the ideological significance of the Thirty Years War, see Marvin A. Breslow, *A Mirror of England: English Puritan Views of Foreign Nations, 1618–1640* (Cambridge, Mass., 1977).

104. Bentley, *Jacobean and Caroline Stage*, vol. 3, pp. 76, 250–1; vol. 5, p. 1382; vol. 4, pp. 477–8; Bawcutt, ed., *Control and Censorship*, p. 204; Martin Butler, *Theatre and Crisis, 1632–42* (Cambridge, 1984), p. 235, and 'Entertaining the Palatine Prince: plays on foreign affairs, 1635–1637', *English Literary Renaissance*, 12 (1983), 319–44.

105. Bawcutt, ed., *Control and Censorship*, p. 181.

106. William Cartwright's poem, dedicated to Brian Duppa, *'immediately after the Publick Act at Oxon. 1634'*, *The Poems and Plays of William Cartwright*, ed. G. Blakemore Evans (Madison, Wis., 1951), p. 455, cited in Bawcutt, ed., *Control and Censorship*, p. 77.

107. Roslyn L. Knutson, *The Repertory of Shakespeare's Company, 1594–1613* (Fayetteville, Ark., 1991), and 'Elizabethan documents, captivity narratives, and the market for foreign history plays'.

108. Fletcher and Massinger, *Sir John Van Olden Barnavelt* (1619), l. 2440.

109. Preface to *The Mutable and Wavering Estate of France ... with an Ample Declaration of the Seditious and Trecherous Practises of that Viperous Brood of Hispaniolized Leaguers* (1597), cited in Salmon, *French Religious Wars*, p. 38.

110. Susan Doran, *Monarchy and Matrimony: The Courtships of Elizabeth I* (London, 1996).

111. Dutton, *Mastering the Revels*, pp. 182–7. The scene was omitted from the published text. For a discussion of an application by an early reader of the *Byron* play to both Elizabethan court politics and the Thirty Years War, see

Albert H. Tricomi, 'Philip, Earl of Pembroke, and the analogical way of reading political tragedy', *Journal of English and Germanic Philology*, 85 (1986), 332–45.

112. George Chapman, *The Tragedie of Charles Duke of Byron*, ed. John B. Gabel, in *The Plays of George Chapman: The Tragedies with Sir Gyles Goosecappe*, ed. Allan Holaday, G. Blakemore Evans and Thomas L. Berger (Cambridge, 1987), 5.3.139–42, 146. All further references will be to this edition.

113. Quarto 1 of George Chapman, *Bussy D'Ambois: A Tragedie*, ed. John H. Smith, in *Plays*, 1.2.19–21, 24–5.

114. George Chapman, *The Revenge of Bussy D'Ambois*, ed. Robert J. Lordi, in *Plays*, 3.4.85–6, 95.

115. Henry Glapthorne, *Albertus Wallenstein* (c. 1635), in *The Old English Drama: A Selection of Plays from the Old English Dramatists* (London, 1825), vol. 2, pp. 7–8.

116. J.G.A. Pocock, *The Ancient Constitution and the Feudal Law: A Study of English Historical Thought in the Seventeenth Century* (Cambridge, 1957; repr. 1987), *The Machiavellian Moment: Florentine Political Thought and the Atlantic Republican Tradition* (Princeton, NJ, 1975) and 'The sense of history in Renaissance England', in John F. Andrews, ed., *William Shakespeare: His World, His Work, His Influence*, 3 vols (New York, 1985), vol. 1, pp. 143–57.

117. Peltonen, *Classical Humanism and Republicanism*; Felix Raab, *The English Face of Machiavelli: A Changing Interpretation, 1500–1700* (London, 1964); Salmon, *French Religious Wars*, pp. 28ff. and Appendix A, 'A list of French works published in England 1560–98', pp. 171–80; George Garnett, introduction to his edition of Stephanus Junius Brutus, the Celt, *Vindiciae, Contra Tyrannos; or, Concerning the Legitimate Power of a Prince over the People, and of the People over a Prince* (Cambridge, 1994).

118. Blair Worden, 'Shakespeare and politics', *Shakespeare Survey*, 44 (1992), 1–15, and 'Republicanism, regicide and republic: the English experience', in Martin van Gelderen and Quentin Skinner, eds, *Republicanism: A Shared European Heritage*, 2 vols (Cambridge, 2002), vol. 1, pp. 307–27; Patrick Collinson, 'The monarchical republic of Queen Elizabeth I', in *Elizabethan Essays* (London, 1994), pp. 31–56; Mark Goldie, 'The unacknowledged republic: officeholding in early modern England', in Tim Harris, ed., *The Politics of the Excluded, c. 1500–1850* (Basingstoke, 2001), pp. 153–94.

119. See the chapters by Robert M. Kingdon on Calvinist resistance theory, J.H.M. Salmon on Catholic resistance theory and J.P. Sommerville on absolutism, in J.H. Burns and Mark Goldie, eds, *The Cambridge History of Political Thought, 1450–1700* (Cambridge, 1991); Salmon, *French Religious Wars*, pp. 15–38; Parmelee, *Good Newes from Fraunce*, pp. 75–117.

120. *CSP Venetian 1625–6*, pp. 462, 508, cited in Richard Cust, *The Forced Loan and English Politics 1626–28* (Oxford, 1987), p. 40.
121. Cogswell, *Blessed Revolution*, p. 31.
122. Thomas Scott, *Belgicke Pismire* (London, 1622), sig. A4^v.
123. This essay was written during my tenure of the Benjamin N. Duke Fellowship at the National Humanities Center in North Carolina in 2002–3. I am grateful to the NHC for its generous support and to its library staff for their unfailing efficiency, courtesy and helpfulness. I also wish to thank Rob Hume, Bernard Wasserstein, Arthur Williamson, Blair Worden, the participants in the NHC's Medieval/Early Modern Writing Group, and the editors of this volume for their trenchant comments on earlier versions.

6: SHAKESPEARE'S IMAGINARY GEOGRAPHY

1. This is of course poles apart from Sir Francis Bacon's view, 'God forbid that we should give out a dream of our own imagination for a pattern of the world', quoted by Garrett A. Sullivan, Jr, *The Drama of Landscape: Land, Property, and Social Relations on the Early Modern Stage* (Stanford, Calif., 1998), p. 101.
2. Richard Wilson, 'A world elsewhere: Shakespeare's sense of an exit', *Proceedings of the British Academy*, 117 (London, 2002), pp. 165–99, at p. 173.
3. Numa Broc, *La Géographie de la Renaissance* (Paris, 1986), p. 225.
4. For Stephen Orgel, this corresponds to what he calls one of the 'two touchstones of theatrical perversity', then arguing that 'the Bohemian sea-coast ... is not an error, but one of the elements stamping the play as a moral fable like the title itself, it removes the action from the world of literal geographical space as it is removed from historical time': Shakespeare, *The Winter's Tale*, ed. Stephen Orgel (Oxford, 1996), p. 37.
5. J.D. Rogers's views on this are indeed both inaccurate and outdated: 'Although the frontiers of Europe shift from time to time and are not the same in the ancient and modern world, Shakespeare's plants, so to speak, are always rooted in European soil: their environment is invariably European ... Beyond these European limits lay the unknown, or hardly known, wonderland and discovery and romance, where monsters dwelt and miracles were common, and which Shakespeare regarded much as every instinctive geographer regards what lies half within and half without his intellectual horizon.' J.D. Rogers, 'Voyages and explorations: geography: maps', in *Shakespeare's England: An Account of the Life and Manners of his Age*,

2 vols (Oxford, 1932), vol. 1, pp. 170–2. John Gillies, *Shakespeare and the Geography of Difference* (Cambridge, 1994), was written in response to this view, which is no longer held 'respectable' (see p. 1).

6. Wilson, 'A world elsewhere', p. 170.

7. The concept is used as complementing the 'green world' idea introduced by Northrop Frye in Sherman Hawkins, 'The two worlds of Shakespearean comedy', *Shakespeare Studies*, 3 (1967), 63–80.

8. Michael Neill, 'Broken English and broken Irish: nation, language, and the optic of power in Shakespeare's histories', *Shakespeare Quarterly*, 45 (Spring 1994), 23–4.

9. In this connection, see our analysis pp. 204–5.

10. Shakespeare, *The Merry Wives of Windsor*, ed. Giorgio Melchiori (London, 2000).

11. Kim Hall, *Things of Darkness: Economies of Race and Gender in Early Modern England* (Ithaca, NY, 1995), p. 187.

12. Margo Hendricks, '"Obscured by dreams": race, empire, and Shakespeare's *A Midsummer Night's Dream*', *Shakespeare Quarterly*, 47 (Spring 1996), 37–60, underlines the similitude between Athens and India as both real and imaginary places in the play: 'Like Athens, India is an actual geographic place and, like fairyland, it is still figured as a place of the imagination' (p. 52).

13. Pliny, *Historie of the World*, trans. Philemon Holland (1601). See *Othello*, ed. E.A.J. Honigmann (Walton-on-Thames, 1997), p. 5.

14. Neill, 'Broken English and broken Irish', p. 14.

15. Ben Jonson, *Discoveries* (1630).

16. Frederick Flahiff, 'Lear's map', *Cahiers Élisabéthains*, 30 (October 1986), 25–6.

17. Richard Helgerson, 'The land speaks: cartography, chorography, and subversion in Renaissance England', in Stephen Greenblatt, ed., *Representing the English Renaissance* (Berkeley and London, 1988), p. 349.

18. Geoffrey Bullough, ed., *Narrative and Dramatic Sources of Shakespeare*, 8 vols (London, 1957–75), vol. 1, pp. 427–8.

19. *Love's Labour's Lost*, ed. H.R. Woudhuysen (Walton-on-Thames, 1998), pp. 344–5.

20. On this, see Michael Hattaway, ed., *The Second Part of King Henry VI*, New Cambridge Shakespeare (Cambridge, 1991), p. 80.

21. Anne Barton, 'Parks and Ardens', in *Essays Mainly Shakespearean* (Cambridge, 1994), p. 356.

22. Wilson, 'A world elsewhere', p. 179.

23. See, for instance, Harry Levin, 'Shakespeare's Italians', in Michele Marrapodi, A.J. Hoenselaars, Marcello Cappuzzo and L. Falzon Santucci,

eds, *Shakespeare's Italy: Functions of Italian Locations in Renaissance Drama*, rev. edn (Manchester and New York, 1997), p. 24. See also A.P. Riemer, *Antic Fables: Patterns of Evasion in Shakespeare's Comedies* (Manchester, 1980), p. 85: 'The Bohemian countryside is a world of radical improbabilities.'

24. Wilson, 'A world elsewhere', p. 171.

25. Levin, 'Shakespeare's Italians', p. 22.

26. According to A.P. Riemer, *Antic Fables*, pp. 97–8, 'Illyria is preposterous not because it cannot be found on a map or in a history-book, or because it is impossible to conceive of a society seemingly so substantial yet possessing no recognizable structure or solidity, but because the characters, their problems and their conflicts become increasingly more remote from the emotional lives and responses of ordinary mankind.'

27. Shakespeare, *Twelfth Night, or What you Will*, ed. Roger Warren and Stanley Wells (Oxford, 1995), p. 9.

28. Leah S. Marcus, *Puzzling Shakespeare: Local Reading and Its Discontents* (Berkeley, 1988), pp. 160, 161.

29. Angela Locatelli, 'The fictional world of *Romeo and Juliet:* cultural connotation of an Italian setting', in Marrapodi *et al.*, eds, *Shakespeare's Italy,* p. 72.

30. Murray J. Levith, *Shakespeare's Italian Settings and Plays* (London, 1989), p. 11. See also A.P. Riemer, *Antic Fables*, p. 65, where the landscapes of Shakespeare's comedies are analysed as 'ideal landscapes': 'The distortions and the rearrangement of everyday reality in most of the comedies represent artistic necessity the discovery of an ideal landscape in which playfully ambivalent concerns find a proper and comfortable environment.'

31. Manfred Pfister, 'Shakespeare and Italy, or, the law of diminishing returns', in Marrapodi *et al.*, eds, *Shakespeare's Italy,* p. 296.

32. Pfister, 'Shakespeare and Italy', p. 301.

33. Shakespeare, *The Tempest*, ed. Virginia Mason Vaughan and Alden T. Vaughan (Walton-on-Thames, 1999), pp. 44, 54.

34. Dympna Callaghan, 'Irish memories in *The Tempest*', in *Shakespeare Without Women: Representing Gender and Race on the Renaissance Stage* (London, 2000), pp. 97–138.

35. Marcus, *Puzzling Shakespeare*, pp. 200, 202.

36. Gary Taylor, paper given at the International Shakespeare Conference at Valencia, Spain, in April 1999. Forthcoming in the proceedings volume. I am grateful to Gary Taylor for allowing me to read his typescript.

37. Shakespeare, *Hamlet*, ed. Harold Jenkins (London, 1982), p. 507.

38. 'Polonius ... connects its bearer with Polonia (Poland)': *Hamlet*, ed. Jenkins, p. 421.

39. *Hamlet*, ed. Jenkins, p. 426.

40. *Hamlet*, ed. Jenkins, p. 527.

41. Shakespeare, *Othello*, ed. Honigmann, p. 27.

42. On this, see Philippa Berry, *Shakespeare's Feminine Endings: Disfiguring Death in the Tragedies* (London, 1999), pp. 96–7.

43. Shakespeare, *As You Like It*, ed. Agnes Latham (London, 1975), p. 79, n. 6.

44. Deryl W. Parker, 'Jacobean Muscovites: winter, tyranny, and knowledge in *The Winter's Tale*', *Shakespeare Quarterly*, 46 (Fall 1995), 335.

45. On this, see François Laroque, *Shakespeare's Festive World: Elizabethan Seasonal Entertainment and the Professional Stage* (Cambridge, 1991), p. 13; Richard Marienstras, 'La Fête des Rogations et l'importance des limites à l'époque élisabéthaine', in *L'Europe de la Renaissance: Cultures et civilisations, Mélanges offerts à Marie-Thérèse Jones-Davies* (Paris, 1988), pp. 109–26.

7: EUROPE'S MEDITERRANEAN FRONTIER: THE MOOR

1. Robin Headlam Wells, *Shakespeare Politics and the State* (London, 1986), p. 9.

2. A.J. Hoenselaars, 'Mapping Shakespeare's Europe', in A.J. Hoenselaars, ed., *Reclamations of Shakespeare* (Amsterdam, 1994), p. 238.

3. G. Wilson Knight, *The Crown of Life* (1947; New York, 1966), p. 215.

4. Willy Maley, '"This sceptred isle": Shakespeare and the British problem', in John J. Joughin, ed., *Shakespeare and National Culture* (Manchester and New York, 1997), p. 97.

5. In 'The construction of barbarism in *Titus Andronicus*' Virginia Mason Vaughan showed how the figure of Aaron the Moor derived from the repercussions of England's discovery of 'alien and "barbaric" peoples ... in Africa and the New World', in Joyce Green Macdonald, ed., *Race, Ethnicity, and Power in the Renaissance* (Cranbury, NJ, 1997), p. 169.

6. Gustav Ungerer, 'An unrecorded Elizabethan performance of *Titus Andronicus*', *Shakespeare Survey*, 14 (1961), 105.

7. As Anthony Gerard Barthelemy correctly points out, 'the single greatest difference between Turk and Moor seems to be the recognition of the ethnic difference and the Eurasian origin of the former group', *Black Face, Maligned Race: The Representation of Blacks in English Drama from Shakespeare to Southerne* (Baton Rouge, 1987), p. 183.

8. Martin Coyle, ed., *The Merchant of Venice* (New York, 1998), p. 11, commenting on James Shapiro, *Shakespeare and the Jews* (New York, 1996).

9. Richard Hakluyt, *The Principal Navigations, Voyages, Traffiques & Discoveries of the English Nation* (1600), 12 vols (Glasgow, 1904), vol. 5, p. 168.

10. *CSP Venetian*, entry no. 131.

11. Albert Lindsay Rowland, *England and Turkey: The Rise of Diplomatic and Commercial Relations* (New York, 1968), p. 65.

12. See Lisa Jardine, *Worldly Goods: A New History of the Renaissance* (London, 1996); and Lisa Jardine and Jerry Brotton, *Global Interests: Renaissance Art between East and West* (Ithaca, NY, 2000); and Jerry Brotton, *The Renaissance Bazaar* (Oxford, 2002).

13. F.N. Lee, 'Othello's name', *Notes and Queries*, n.s., 8 (1961), 139–41.

14. For still the most comprehensive study of the figure of the Turk and Moor in Renaissance drama and literature, see Samuel Chew, *The Crescent and the Rose: Islam and England during the Renaissance* (Oxford, 1937). See also Nabil Matar, *Turks, Moors and Englishmen in the Age of Discovery* (New York, 1999), ch. 2.

15. For surveys of the frontier, see Andrew Hess, *The Forgotten Frontier: A History of the Sixteenth Century Ibero-African Frontier* (Chicago and London, 1978); see also Palmira Brummett, *Ottoman Seapower and Levantine Diplomacy in the Age of Discovery* (New York, 1994), esp. ch. 7.

16. Quoted in Jack D'Amico, *The Moor in English Renaissance Drama* (Tampa, Fla, 1991), p. 9.

17. Peter Fryer, *Staying Power: The History of Black People in Britain* (London, 1984), ch. 1.

18. See the discussion of this play in relation to Anglo-Moroccan politics in Nabil Matar, *Britain and Barbary, 1589–1689* (forthcoming, 2004), ch. 1.

19. *The Fugger News-Letters, Second Series*, ed. Victor von Klarwill, trans. L.S.R. Byrne (London, 1926), p. 188.

20. D.A. Traversi, *An Approach to Shakespeare*, 3rd edn (New York, 1969), vol. 1, p. 49. This supports the prevailing view that Peele wrote Act 1 (and also 4.1). See Brian Vickers, *Shakespeare Co-Author* (Oxford and New York, 2002), pp. 166–7.

21. Harold Bloom, *Shakespeare and the Invention of the Modern* (New York, 1998), p. 82.

22. Niall Rudd, '*Titus Andronicus*: the classical presence', *Shakespeare Survey*, 55 (2002), 202.

23. As Brian Vickers states, it is likely that the illustration by Peacham is not of Shakespeare's play but of a German *Tito Andronico*. The fact remains that Peacham, whatever play he was illustrating, saw the Moor as a 'swart Cimmerian' (2.2.72): Vickers, *Shakespeare Co-Author*, p. 150.

24. Barthelemy, *Black Face, Maligned Race*, p. 96.

25. *The Dramatic Works of George Peele*, ed. John Yoklavich (New Haven and London, 1961).

26. Henry de Castries, *Les Sources inédites de l'histoire du Maroc par le Comte Henry de Castries, Première Série – Dynastie Saadienne, Archives et Bibliothèques d'Angleterre*, 3 vols (Paris, 1918–35), vol. 2 (1925), pp. 89–90.

27. Barthelemy, *Black Face, Maligned Race*, p. 147.

28. De Castries, *Sources inédites*, vol. 2, p. 84.

29. John Gillies, *Shakespeare and the Geography of Difference* (Cambridge, 1994), p. 67.

30. *The Fugger News-Letters, Second Series*, p. 295.

31. For a detailed discussion of the relations between Queen Elizabeth and Mulay Ahmad al-Mansur, see Nabil Matar, *Europe through Arab–Islamic Eyes, 1578–1727* (forthcoming), ch. 1.

32. De Castries, *Sources inédites*, vol. 2, p. 209.

33. De Castries, *Sources inédites*, vol. 2, p. 203.

34. *Rasail Saadiya*, National Library of Rabat, MS Kaf 278, fos 195–8.

35. For Morocco's middle position between Catholic Christendom and the Ottoman Empire, see Andrew C. Hess, 'The battle of Lepanto and its place in Mediterranean history', *Past and Present*, 57 (1972), 70.

36. Richard Hakluyt, *The Second Voyage of Master Laurence Aldersey, to the Cities of Alexandria and Cairo in Egypt, Anno 1586*, in *Hakluyt's Voyages*, ed. Richard David (Boston, Mass., 1981), p. 183.

37. Leo Africanus, *De Totius Africae Descriptione*, trans. John Pory, *A History and Description of Africa* (1600), 3 vols (London, 1896), vol. 1, p. 387.

38. Anthony Hecht has already argued for Othello as a Morisco: 'Othello', in *Obbligati: Essays in Criticism* (New York, 1986), p. 63.

39. Wells, *Shakespeare Politics and the State*, p. 20.

40. Alvin Kernan, '*Othello*: an introduction', in *Shakespeare: The Tragedies*, ed. Alfred Harbage (Englewood Cliffs, NJ, 1964), p. 78.

41. See the comment by Philip Butcher, 'Othello's racial identity', *Shakespeare Quarterly*, 3 (1952), 245.

42. *Othello*, ed. Alvin Kernan (Harmondsworth, 1963), p. 177.

43. For magic in the play, see David Kaula, 'Othello possessed: notes on Shakespeare's use of magic and witchcraft', *Shakespeare Studies*, 2 (1966), 112–32. For a discussion of the meaning of the handkerchief as an 'emblem of female, not male sexual power', see Carol Thomas Neeley, *Broken Nuptials in Shakespeare's Plays* (New Haven, 1985), pp. 128–31 and p. 238, n. 33.

44. *The Fugger News-Letters, Second Series*, p. 346.

45. *The Poems of James VI of Scotland*, ed. James Craigie (Edinburgh and London, 1955), vol. 1, p. 202.

46. Nicholas Brooke has similarly observed that in *Titus* 'the dignity of Roman nobility is founded on barbarous bestiality': '*Titus Andronicus* and *Romeo and Juliet*', in *Shakespeare: The Tragedies*, ed. Clifford Leech (Chicago, 1965), p. 256.

47. Neeley, *Broken Nuptials*, pp. 44–145.

48. Neeley, *Broken Nuptials*, pp. 137–8.

49. Kenneth Parker, however, strongly argues against a black Cleopatra, in *Antony and Cleopatra* (Plymouth, 2000). Still, in 1988, the African-American Francelle Dorn played Cleopatra in Washington DC's Shakespeare Theatre.

50. Richard Wilson, 'Voyage to Tunis: new history and the old world of *The Tempest*', *English Literary History*, 64 (1997), 333–57, has shown the background to the play to be pervasively Mediterranean; while Jerry Brotton blamed the post-colonialists for downplaying its Mediterranean setting, in 'Carthage and Tunis, *The Tempest* and tapestries', in Peter Hulme and William H. Sherman, eds, *The Tempest and its Travels* (Philadelphia, 2000), pp. 132–7.

51. See the discussion of English captivity literature in the introduction by Nabil Matar to the edition of captivity narratives, *Piracy, Slavery and Redemption*, ed. Daniel Vitkus (New York, 2001). See also Nabil Matar, 'English captivity accounts in North Africa and the Middle East, 1577–1625', *Renaissance Quarterly*, 54 (2001), 553–73.

52. Ronald Takaki, '*The Tempest* in the wilderness: the racialization of savagery', *The Journal of American History*, 79 (1992), 892–912.

53. For a valuable survey of the limitless adaptability of *The Tempest*, see *The Tempest*, ed. Virginia Mason Vaughan and Alden T. Vaughan (Walton-on-Thames, 1999), pp. 73–110.

54. Thomas Starkey, *Dialogue between Reginald Pole and Thomas Lupset* (c. 1534), quoted in Wells, *Shakespeare Politics and the State*, p. 33.

55. The conclusion of the play problematizes the colonial interpretation: see Barbara Fuchs, 'Conquering islands: contextualizing *The Tempest*', *Shakespeare Quarterly*, 48 (1997), 17–45.

56. For a discussion of the play in post-colonial theory, see Alden T. Vaughan and Virginia Mason Vaughan, *Shakespeare's Caliban: A Cultural History* (Cambridge, 1991), pp. 144–72.

57. Eric Griffin, 'Un-sainting James: or, Othello and the "Spanish Spirits" of Shakespeare's Globe', in Stephen Orgel and Sean Keilen, eds, *Shakespeare the Critical Complex* (New York and London, 1999), pp. 278–319; see also the earlier study by Barbara Everett, '"Spanish" Othello: the making of Shakespeare', in *Shakespeare Survey*, 35 (1982), 101–12.

58. Hence the representation of Othello as wild and bare-footed by Laurence Olivier, in a production that in the 1960s was hailed as most realistic and accurate.

59. See Emily C. Bartels, 'Making more of the Moor: Aaron, Othello, and Renaissance refashionings of race', *Shakespeare Quarterly*, 41 (1990), 433–52.

60. Earlier, in *Titus Andronicus*, Leslie A. Fiedler noted, 'Aaron's very name, of course, connects him with Jewish tradition: and like the tribe of Shylock, but unlike Othello and the Prince of Morocco, he is even described as "misbelieving" and "irreligious", an enemy of the true God': *The Stranger in Shakespeare* (New York, 1972), p. 178.

61. Jews were also distinguished on stage by their red hair/wig; it is significant that Shakespeare made no reference to this alleged physical feature: Russell Jackson, ed., *The Cambridge Companion to Shakespeare on Film* (Cambridge, 2000), p. 267.

62. Edmund Valentine Campos, 'Jews, Spaniards, and Portingales: ambiguous identities of Portuguese Marranos in Elizabethan England', *English Literary History,* 69 (2002), 599–616.

63. Sidney Lee, 'The original of Shylock', *Gentleman's Magazine* (1880), 185–220.

64. Michael J.C. Echeruo, 'Shylock and the "conditioned imagination": a reinterpretation', *Shakespere Quarterly,* 22 (1971), 5.

65. Alan Rosen, 'The rhetoric of exclusion: Jew, Moor, and the boundaries of discourse in *The Merchant of Venice*', in Joyce Green MacDonald, ed., *Race, Ethnicity, and Power in the Renaissance* (London, 1997), p. 74.

66. Bloom, *Shakespeare*, p. 171.

67. 'It is their [the Moors'] physical difference in association with cultural differences (a combination that is the primary basis for the category "race") that provokes their exclusion not just their religion': Kim F. Hall, 'Guess who's coming to dinner? Colonization and miscegenation in *The Merchant of Venice*', in Martin Coyle, ed., *The Merchant of Venice*, pp. 96–7.

68. Julia Reinhard Lupton, 'Othello circumcised: Shakespeare and the Pauline discourse of nations', *Representations*, 57 (1997), 73–89.

69. '"Delicious traffick": racial and religious difference on early modern stages', in Catherine M.S. Alexander and Stanley Wells, eds, *Shakespeare and Race* (Cambridge, 2000), p. 205. Other critics, however, have urged a Christian or a Christianized Othello who subscribed to Puritan marriage values: Stephen Greenblatt, *Renaissance Self-Fashioning: From More to Shakespeare* (Chicago, 1980), p. 242; cited in Walter S.H. Lim, *The Arts of Empire* (Delaware, 1998), pp. 117–18.

70. Daniel J. Vitkus, 'Turning Turk in *Othello*: the conversion and damnation of the Moor', *Shakespeare Quarterly,* 48 (1997), 171.

71. 'In order to trace the relationship between blackness and Islam, let us turn to a text written 300 years before Othello': Ania Loomba, *Shakespeare, Race, and Colonialism* (Oxford, 2002), p. 47.

72. Loomba, *Shakespeare, Race, and Colonialism*, pp. 95, 97.

73. Brian Vickers, ed., *Shakespeare: The Critical Heritage* (London and Boston, Mass., 1976), vol. 2, p. 29.

74. According to Michael Ferber, however, the Prince of Morocco was a Christian! 'The ideology of the *Merchant of Venice*', *English Literary Renaissance*, 20 (1990), 448. No evidence is provided, however.

75. Naseeb Shaheen, *Biblical References in Shakespeare's Tragedies* (Newark, Del., 1987), p. 126.

76. Samuel Chew, *The Crescent and the Rose: Islam and England during the Renaissance* (New York, 1937), p. 521, n. 2.

77. 'Some actors of Othello have worn a turban – an error, I think, since he is so proudly Christian': *Othello*, ed. E.A.J. Honigmann (Walton-on-Thames, 1997), p. 17.

78. From Edmund Kean and Ira Aldridge to Paul Robeson, Orson Welles, Godfrey Tearle, John Gielgud, James McCracken and Laurence Olivier.

79. See Nabil Matar, 'Renaissance England and the turban', in David Blanks, ed., *Images of the Other*, Cairo Papers in Social Science, 19 (1996), pp. 39–55.

80. See Nabil Matar, *Islam in Britain, 1558–1685* (Cambridge, 1998), for an examination of English familiarity with Islam.

81. For an early survey of 'Shakespeare and the Turk', before the topic became ideologically loaded, see John W. Draper, *Orientalia and Shakespeareana* (New York, 1977), study 9.

82. See the excellent study of Cervantes' familiarity with Algeria by Jaime Oliver-Asin, 'La hija de Agi Morato en la obra de Cervantes', *Boletain de la Real Academia Espanola*, 27 (1948), 245–339; Ottmar Hegyi, *Cervantes and the Turks* (Newark, Del., 1992).

83. As G.K. Hunter correctly observes, Shakespeare not only took over the Moor from Cinthio but was 'intensely aware of it [blackness] as one of the primary factors in his play': 'Othello and colour prejudice', *Proceedings of the British Academy*, 53 (1968), 139.

84. Michael Neill, '"Mulattos", "Blacks", and "Indian Moors": Othello and early modern constructions of human difference', *Shakespeare Quarterly*, 49 (1998), 369.

85. 'Table Talk', 22 December 1822, *Coleridge's Literary Criticism*, ed. J.W. Mackail (London, 1948), p. 244.

86. For the difference in Shakespeare's knowledge between black Moors and tawny Moors, what Eldred D. Jones describes as Africans and white Africans, see his discussion in *Othello's Countrymen: The African in English Renaissance Drama* (London, 1965), pp. 86–7.

87. Bernard Harris, 'A portrait of a Moor', *Shakespeare Survey*, 11 (1958), 89–97.

88. Loomba, *Shakespeare, Race, and Colonialism*, p. 92.

89. See the colour reproduction on the cover of Nabil Matar, *Turks, Moors and Englishmen in the Age of Discovery* (New York, 1999).

90. It is surprising to find E.A.J. Honigmann reproducing the picture and then stating that the ambassador's face 'seems to [be] right for Othello': *Othello*, p. 3.

91. De Castries, *Sources inédites*, vol. 2, pp. 161–3.

92. De Castries, *Sources inédites*, vol. 2, pp. 164–7. Rather curiously, however, the memorandum he presented to the queen was written in Spanish: vol. 2, pp. 177–9.

93. John Nichols, *The Progresses and Public Processions of Queen Elizabeth* (London, 1823), vol. 3, p. 516.

94. See the documents in de Castries, *Sources inédites*, vol. 2, pp. 184–5, 189, 190–2.

95. These lines, not included in the First Quarto, were first printed in the Second Quarto and then in the Folio edition of *Titus Andronicus*. 'Since Q2 was printed from a defective copy of Q1, it appears that someone composed this passage in an effort to reconstruct the unreadable original': *Titus Andronicus*, ed. Russ McDonald, Penguin Shakespeare (Harmondsworth, 2000), p. 106.

SELECT BIBLIOGRAPHY

This bibliography selects some principal primary and secondary books, but does not include articles. More detailed guidance for further reading is provided in the notes to individual chapters.

PRIMARY SOURCES

Ascham, Roger, *The Schoolmaster* (1570), ed. Lawrence V. Ryan (Ithaca, NY, 1967)

Bullough, Geoffrey, ed., *Narrative and Dramatic Sources of Shakespeare*, 8 vols (London, 1957–75)

Coryat, Thomas, *Coryat's Crudities Hastily Gobled Up in Five Moneths Travells* (1611), 2 vols (Glasgow, 1905)

Dallington, Robert, *A Method for Travell: Shewed by Taking the View of France* (London, 1605)

Hadfield, Andrew, ed., *Amazons, Savages & Machiavels: Travel and Colonial Writing in English, 1550–1630* (Oxford, 2001)

Hakluyt, Richard, *The Principal Navigations, Voyages, Traffiques & Discoveries of the English Nation* (1600), 12 vols (Glasgow, 1904)

Leo Africanus, *A History and Description of Africa*, trans. John Pory (1600), 3 vols (London, 1896)

Moryson, Fynes, *An Itinerary* (1617), 4 vols (Glasgow, 1907–8)

Ortelius, Abraham, *Theatrum Orbis Terrarum Abrahami Ortelii Antuerp. geographi regii. The theatre of the whole world: set forth by that excellent geographer Abraham Ortelius* (London, 1608)

Parr, Anthony, ed., *Three Renaissance Travel Plays* (Manchester, 1995)

Thomas, William, *The History of Italy* (London, 1549; repr. 1561), ed. George B. Parks (Ithaca, NY, 1963)

Vitkus, Daniel, ed., *Three Turk Plays from Early Modern England* (New York, 2000)

SECONDARY SOURCES

Alexander, Catherine M.S. and Wells, Stanley, eds, *Shakespeare and Race* (Cambridge, 2000)

Andrews, Richard, *Scripts and Scenarios: The Performance of Comedy in Renaissance Italy* (Cambridge, 1993)

Braudel, Fernand, *The Mediterranean and the Mediterranean World in the Age of Philip II*, 2 vols (London, 1966)

Chaney, Edward, *The Evolution of the Grand Tour: Anglo-Italian Cultural Relations since the Renaissance* (London and Portland, Oreg., 1998)

Chew, Samuel, *The Crescent and the Rose: Islam and England during the Renaissance* (New York, 1937)

Clubb, Louise George, *Italian Drama in Shakespeare's Time* (New Haven and London, 1989)

D'Amico, Jack, *The Moor in English Renaissance Drama* (Tampa, Fla, 1991)

Doran, Susan, *England and Europe, 1485–1603*, 2nd edn (London and New York, 1996)

—— *Monarchy and Matrimony: The Courtships of Elizabeth I* (London, 1996)

Gillespie, Stuart, *Shakespeare's Books: A Dictionary of Shakespeare Sources* (London, 2001)

Gillies, John, *Shakespeare and the Geography of Difference* (Cambridge, 1994)

Hadfield, Andrew, *Literature, Travel, and Colonial Writing in the English Renaissance, 1545–1625* (Oxford, 1998)

Hale, John, *The Civilization of Europe in the Renaissance* (New York, 1994)

Henke, Robert, *Pastoral Transformations: Italian Tragicomedy and Shakespeare's Late Plays* (Newark, NJ, 1997)

Hillman, Richard, *Shakespeare, Marlowe and the Politics of France* (Basingstoke, 2002)

Hoenselaars, A.J., *Images of Englishmen and Foreigners in the Drama of Shakespeare and His Contemporaries: A Study of Stage Characters and National Identity in English Renaissance Drama, 1558–1642* (London and Toronto, 1992)

Hulme, Peter and Sherman, William H., eds, *'The Tempest' and its Travels* (Philadelphia, 2000)

Jardine, Lisa, *Wordly Goods: A New History of the Renaissance* (London, 1996)

—— and Brotton, Jerry, *Global Interests: Renaissance Art between East and West* (Ithaca, NY, 2000)

Jones, Emrys, *The Origins of Shakespeare* (Oxford, 1977)

Kingdon, Robert M., *Myths about the St Bartholomew's Day Massacres 1572–1576* (Cambridge, Mass., 1988)

Kirkpatrick, Robin, *English and Italian Literature from Dante to Shakespeare* (London, 1995)

Knecht, R.J., *The Rise and Fall of Renaissance France 1483–1610*, 2nd edn (Oxford, 2001)

Limon, Jerzy, *Gentlemen of a Company: English Players in Central and Eastern Europe, 1590–1660* (Cambridge, 1985)

MacCaffrey, Wallace T., *Elizabeth I: War and Politics 1588–1603* (Princeton, NJ, 1992)

Maquerlot, Jean-Pierre and Willems, Michèle, eds, *Travel and Drama in Shakespeare's Time* (Cambridge, 1996)

Marrapodi, Michele, Hoenselaars, A.J., Capuzzo, Marcello and Santucci, L. Falzon, eds, *Shakespeare's Italy: Functions of Italian Locations in Renaissance Drama*, rev. edn (Manchester and New York, 1997)

Matar, Nabil, *Turks, Moors and Englishmen in the Age of Discovery* (New York, 1999)

Mattingly, Garrett, *The Defeat of the Spanish Armada* (London, 1959)

McPherson, David, *Shakespeare, Jonson and the Myth of Venice* (Newark, NJ, 1990)

Miola, Robert S., *Shakespeare's Reading* (Oxford, 2000)

Mulryne, J.R. and Shewring, Margaret, eds, *Theatre of the English and Italian Renaissance* (Basingstoke, 1991)

Pettegree, Andrew, *Foreign Protestant Communities in Sixteenth-Century London* (Oxford, 1986)

Raab, Felix, *The English Face of Machiavelli: A Changing Interpretation, 1500–1700* (London, 1964)

Roe, John, *Shakespeare and Machiavelli* (Cambridge, 2002)

Salingar, Leo, *Shakespeare and the Traditions of Comedy* (Cambridge, 1974)

Salmon, J.H.M., *The French Religious Wars in English Political Thought* (Oxford, 1959)

Schrickx, Willem, *Foreign Envoys and Travelling Players in the Age of Shakespeare and Jonson* (Gent, 1986)

Shapiro, James, *Shakespeare and the Jews* (New York, 1996)

Stoye, John, *English Travellers Abroad, 1604–1667*, rev. edn (New Haven and London, 1989)

Taylor, E.G.R., *Tudor Geography, 1485–1583* (London, 1930)

—— *Late Tudor and Early Stuart Geography, 1583–1650* (London, 1934)

Voss, Paul J., *Elizabethan News Pamphlets: Shakespeare, Spenser, Marlowe and the Birth of Journalism* (Pittsburgh, Pa, 2001)

Wedgwood, C.V., *The Thirty Years War* (London, 1938)

Wernham, R.B., *The Return of the Armadas: The Last Years of the Elizabethan War against Spain 1595–1603* (Oxford, 1994)

INDEX

This index covers only the main text, not the chronology or the endnotes. Nobles are indexed under their titles rather than their surnames.